Midnight Marquee Actors Series

PETER LORRE

Vanity Fair Portrait c. 1935

Midnight Marquee Actors Series

PETER LORRE

edited by
Gary J. Svehla
and
Susan Svehla

Luminary Press
Baltimore, Maryland

Interior and Cover Design: Susan Svehla

ISBN 1-887664-30-0Library of Congress Catalog Card Number 99-091382
Manufactured in the United States of America
Printed by Odyssey Press
First Printing by Midnight Marquee Press, Inc., December, 1997
Second Printing by Luminary Press an imprint of Midnight Marquee Press, Inc., March 2005

Acknowledgments: John Antosiewicz Photo Archives, Leonard Maltin, Photofest, Joe Treppe, Linda J. Walter, Buddy Weiss

Peter Lorre held a magnetic attraction for me as a young film buff that has never lessened over the years. He can often brighten a dull or mediocre film, and when given the chance—as in *M* or *Mad Love*, *The Maltese Falcon* or *Casablanca*, he can be brilliant. There has never been anyone else quite like him, an actor who carved his own highly individual niche on screen.—Leonard Maltin

TABLE OF CONTENTS

Lorre, around 1938.

INTRODUCTION

After covering the obvious horror film icons—Bela Lugosi, Boris Karloff, Lon Chaney, Jr. and Vincent Price—we at Midnight Marquee Press wanted to go in a slightly different direction for our fifth edition of the Midnight Marquee Actors Series, by highlighting quasi-"horror man," Peter Lorre.

While the other entries in the series were predominantly horror film actors (or recognized as such), Peter Lorre made many horror film appearances, but he was never actually considered a horror film star (although, near the end of his career, he worked with Karloff, Price and Rathbone). Instead, it was Lorre's persona, that of a quirky, deviant little man, sometimes charming, sometimes boiling over with venom in childlike temper tantrums, that made him a perfect match for horror films. However, this was the man who played opposite such mainstream stars as Clark Gable, Humphrey Bogart, Sydney Greenstreet, Kirk Douglas, Mickey Rooney and Bob Hope as well. Lorre felt just as comfortable enacting supporting roles in A films as he did starring in the Bs.

And what is most surprising is the lack of information published about Peter Lorre's private life. Even though Vincent Price was a very private person, he did grant tons of interviews and met his fans after theatrical tours across the United States. Lon Chaney, Jr. was also another enigma, but enough of his life was revealed through interviews and common anecdotes that some of that mystique has burned away. Peter Lorre remains the most elusive of all the stars thus far profiled in this series, and perhaps Lorre biographer Stephen Youngkin, who told us that Lorre lived a "double life," might be able to shed some light when his new book on Lorre becomes available sometime soon.

Thus, Lorre's body of work must tell the story. Whether he was doing comedy such as *Arsenic and Old Lace* or *The Raven*, playing the psychopathic fiend in *M* or *The Beast With Five Fingers,* or becoming the agent of espionage of *The Man Who Knew Too Much*,

An early portrait of the intense young actor.

Confidential Agent or *All Through the Night*, Peter Lorre connected with his audience in a mesmeric, sparkling manner. Behind all the dread and menace was always the human being, flawed as he may be, always becoming strangely sympathetic by nature of a kind side or humorous manner or an air of politeness. Even when his soul was black as pitch, something about Lorre made him forgivable, perhaps redeemable and worth saving or at least worthy of shedding a tear over. Lorre was an odd man, whether thin or obese, but the intensity of his performances always commanded audience attention. The way he utilized his voice and body—those bulging hard-boiled eyes, his obsessive stare, his clipped speech patterns, his whining cries of cowardliness, his juvenile over-excitement, his air of grandeur even when everything about him was falling apart—made Lorre a character actor with star visibility. And after becoming a cherished cinema caricature with a well-recognized persona, he even graduated to recognized menace in Warner Bros. cartoons.

Whether frustrating veteran screen bogey-man Boris Karloff because of his on screen ad-libs, cracking jokes with comic ace Bob Hope, terrifying the screen with his portrayal of menace in films such as *Mad Love* or *M,* or commanding warmth and compassion in films such as *The Verdict*, Peter Lorre was a versatile, exceptional screen presence. Sometimes the sad sack, other times the obsessed madman, but always the consummate professional who created a body of cinematic work that will live forever.

Gary J. Svehla
October 1999

Peter Lorre

M
1931
by Cindy Ruth Collins

On the afternoon of April 2, 1929 a Berlin paper proclaimed a new talent on the Berlin stage. The reviewer, Kurt Pinthus, had just seen a new, and frightful, face in a production of *Pioniere in Ingolstadt* (*Engineers in Ingolstadt*).

The face resembled that of a "hysterical philistine, whose goggle-eyes and bloated, yellowish head swelled out of the costume." The frightening figure "reel[ed] between dull apathy and hysterical outbursts" in a way that the reviewer had never seen before, and in a way which showed that the actor clearly had the potential to establish himself as a "player of the first-class"... if he could show himself capable of playing a wider range of roles.

"This fellow," noted Pinthus, "is called Peter Lorre."

Pioniere in Ingolstadt proved a breakthrough for Lorre, who had run away from home at 17 to pursue the life of an actor. Through this vehicle, he got a part in *Frühlings Erwachen* (*Spring's Awakening*): the role which so impressed Fritz Lang that the director approached Lorre on the spot and notified him that he would be cast in Lang's first sound picture. Lorre reportedly thought little of the offer, but two years later he nevertheless found himself in his first film, playing Hans Beckert—the pathological child-killer—in Fritz Lang's *M.*

In one of the film's first reviews, Leo Hirsch provides a brief sketch of the action:

> Eight children murdered. Berlin seeks the murderer. We see the newest crime...: the killer, the child, the abduction. The city is nervous. It seeks—it even raises the price on the killer's head—but it fails to find him. Raids. Nervousness. Every man on the street is suspected... The united underworld intervenes when the police fail. The beggars search. A blind man finds the murderer, who is then imprisoned in an office building. He is judged by a... committee, but is taken possession of by the police. (*Berliner Tageblatt*, 12 May 1931)

This sketchy synopsis, curiously, omits the parallel search by the police, their success in identifying the killer at precisely the same moment that the underworld does, and Lang's intercutting between these two searches to draw out the parallels. Though the beggars do locate Beckert on the street, chalk an "M" (*Mörder*: murderer) on his jacket

No children are safe when the killer's shadow looms over them in *M*.

to keep him easily in view and finally get their criminal allies to abduct him from the office building into which he retreats, the police investigation also pays off: Homicide detectives wait in Beckert's rooms even as the beggars chase the killer.

The most significant omission from Hirsch's synopsis, though, is its lack of commentary on the object of the search: Hans Beckert, *der Mörder*, himself.

Lorre won rave reviews for his portrayal of Beckert in Fritz Lang's *M.*

Even when Lorre is not on screen, his character is the center around which Lang's film revolves. In the opening sequence, his unseen shadow looms over the city. In a block of tenements, children sing of the killer who will chop them up, as a mother comments to her appalled friend that, despite the song's morbidity, the children are safe so long as they can be heard. Far from her mother's voice, the woman's daughter bounces a ball on her way home from school, stopping to throw it against a pole... on which a poster proclaims a reward of 10,000 marks, and asks the salient question: "Who is the Murderer?"

Thus far, we have only seen hints of the fear gripping the city, but as that question appears on-screen, the unseen shadow becomes visible. It crosses the poster in silhouette, and in a flat, emotionless voice, its possessor compliments the little girl on her ball. Her name, she tells him, is Elsie Beckmann. Hours later, a mob of city residents reads aloud of the new crime committed by "*der unbekannten Mörder*" ("the unknown murderer"): a little girl killed in the same method as all the others, a little girl named Elsie Beckmann.

It is one of the most gripping opening sequences in early sound cinema, raising audience tension by intercutting between the girl's neighborhood and her fatal walk home; between the mother's growing alarm and her daughter's death (which Lang implies by showing her ball roll away from some bushes and her new balloon fly up and catch on some wires).

During this opening sequence, too, we first hear the killer's signature, whistled by Lang himself. As the predator buys a balloon for Elsie, he whistles "In the Hall of the Mountain King"—the tune which will eventually give him away to the blind balloon vendor. At this point, the tune seems to have little significance, but later on we find that he whistles it whenever the urge to kill overtakes him.

Dramatic poster art for Lorre's film debut.

The tune he chooses—or which perhaps chooses him—possesses thematic significance for this film. In *Peer Gynt*, from which the tune comes, Peer Gynt leaves home when the parents of the girl he loves reject him. In one of his many adventures, he finds himself in the Hall of the Mountain King, where the King of the Trolls wants Peer to marry his daughter. Unfortunately, in order to marry her, Peer Gynt must himself become a Troll: he must grow a tail, slit his left eye so that he can see the world as a Troll sees it, and never again see the light of day.

Not surprisingly, Peer Gynt rejects the offer, and the Trolls vanish as a church bell rings in the distance. But the killer in *M* seems to have accepted the offer, or been compelled to accept it by internal forces beyond his control. He is the Peer Gynt who has become the Troll, who may have wanted love at one time, but who now simply preys on human beings. He has rejected human society, or been rejected by it, and his madness cuts him off from others. The crucial question in the film, asked explicitly at the end, is whether he has made this choice, or whether insanity has made it for him; whether he is acting out of malice or under compulsion.

Beckert uses a trip to the toy store to further entice a potential victim.

When we make our first intimate contact with Beckert, malice seems the answer. In typical Jack-the-Ripper fashion, he writes a letter to the press, taunting the police with the knowledge that he is the child killer, and has not yet finished his spree. Later, though, when we make even more intimate contact with him (in the sequence where we first see his face), the answer becomes less clear. As he stares at a shop window display of sharp scissors and knives, he sees the reflection of a little girl and clearly tries to fight off the impulse to kill her. Peter Lorre uses his body alone to convey the killer's angst: His eyes grow wide; his whole face and his shoulders drop in resignation; he wobbles like a drunken man, steadies himself, and then shuts his eyes… as if something is overtaking him. When he opens his eyes again, the object of his lust—his lust for blood and God knows what else—has stepped out of the frame, but he turns in her direction and steels himself to do the evil deed. His face changes from bland to determined. Then he tilts his body forward and strides toward her, whistling "In the Hall of the Mountain King." Despite his resistance, the Troll in him wins.

Thankfully, his attempt is thwarted by the appearance of the girl's mother. But Beckert must now find another victim, or fight the urge to try. His side-trip to a small café across the street shows the futility of his struggle. In his order ("Coffee… No. Vermouth, No! Cognac!"), he becomes increasingly hysterical as he twice changes orders to find what he hopes will most effectively drown out the "the Troll" in him that wants to kill and destroy and maim—ultimately to no avail. Once the blood-lust comes upon him, he has no power to stop it. Soon, he is again whistling his signature tune, and searching for another little girl.

One element worth noting at this point is that, though most of the film is extraordinarily chatty, Lang uses a good amount of silent technique in these scenes with Beckert.

Beckert seeks the madman in the mirror.

In the letter-writing sequence, he photographs Lorre from the back so that we can read the letter over his shoulder. Using letters and other forms of text (rather than intertitles) to convey information had been a staple of the German silent film industry, at least since Murnau had attempted to create "pure cinema" in films like *Nosferatu* (1922) and *The Last Laugh* (1924).

Taken alone, this scene would not indicate a continuation of silent technique. However, the scene where Beckert spots the little girl is almost entirely silent, even when the girl starts conversing with her mother. Lorre's part here, as mentioned above, is acted out solely by body language (though with a subtlety of understatement often missing from silent cinema). What Lang allows us to hear, though—footsteps and whistle—reveal the director's intent. Footsteps hint at pursuit, and will later be heard in a similarly silent sequence as the beggars literally pursue *der Mörder*. The whistle, though, overwhelms this scene, even drowning out the little girl's "Hello, mummy" (which is "heard" only in the subtitles). These particular sounds have the effect of placing us close to the killer's mind, of showing us that the whole world gets blotted out when he reverts to Troll.

This sound/silence structure to the film is somewhat curious. The search for the killer may be talk-talk-talk, but the object of that search is silence-silence-silence. In one talky sequence, we hear all about the killer's presumed *modus operandi*. In one of the silent sequences, we simply see it. We have already seen how he identifies a victim and approaches her. Now, though, we see him buy her a balloon, some confections and prepare to buy her a toy—all with the purpose of luring her into some bushes and slaughtering her, presumably with scissors or a knife. In fact, he draws out a sharp knife and cuts some fruit for his prospective victim (a knife which will later serve as a tool for his attempted escape from the office building attic). Throughout this sequence, the killer shows his frightening amiability, made all the more terrifying when the little girl innocently hands him the knife he dropped, the knife meant for her destruction. His charm has so seduced her that she even calls him "Uncle." Curiously the serial killer on which Beckert was loosely based had much of this same destructive charm.

In creating this killer and the search for him, Fritz Lang has drawn on real-life sources, most notably the Dusseldorf Ripper. In 1929 and 1930, Dusseldorf was plagued with a series of brutal crimes. A maniac was running loose, injuring and killing men, women and girls—mostly women and girls. He dispatched his victims through several different techniques: sometimes strangling them, sometimes stabbing their temples with scissors or knives, sometimes bashing their skulls with his hammer. The killer, who did write a letter to the police, eluded his pursuers for months; and according to some print sources from the time, even the criminal underworld joined in the search (*Films of Fritz Lang*, 155). Finally, Peter Kürten, the Dusseldorf killer, confessed to his wife, who turned him in the next day.

With this sensational series of killings coming to a close only a year earlier, the Kürten case made a natural subject for film. According to one famous anecdote, the working title for the film—*Mörder unter Uns* (*Murderer among Us*)—got Lang in trouble when the studio head refused him entry to start production. When Lang asked why he couldn't make a film about Peter Kürten, the exec relaxed and gave Lang the keys to the studio. Apparently the man, a member of the Nazi party, had thought by the title that Lang's film took aim at the Nazis (*Films of Peter Lorre*, 63).

When the film came out, certainly everybody assumed that it was based on the Kürten case. Reviews in *The New York Times*, *Variety* and *The Times of London* all mentioned the Dusseldorf killings in their headlines. On the day the film opened at the Cambridge Theater in London, in fact, *The Times of London* also reviewed Margaret Seaton Wagner's book *The Monster of Dusseldorf.*

Though (as Leo Hirsch pointed out) it would have been tasteless to present all the particulars of the Kürten case on film, Beckert does indeed resemble Kürten in several points: He charms victims into following him to remote places, he uses a knife (and clearly considers using scissors) on his victims, he writes a letter to police, and he eludes capture long enough to terrorize the entire city.

Given all this evidence, it is rather remarkable that Lang later denied that the film was based on Kürten. Beckert, though, does depart from Kürten in several important ways. While Beckert kills only one type of victim and has a single *modus operandi*, Kürten was a much more versatile killer. While Beckert clearly wishes to control his murderous impulses, Kürten allowed his free reign and spent a good bit of his time fantasizing about murder and mayhem. While Beckert approaches his victims on first sight, Kürten sometimes stalked victims for days prior to approaching them. While Beckert claims to remember nothing once the urge to kill possesses him, Kürten remembered most details of his crimes.

The difference here comes not simply from an attempt to clean up the Kürten case and make the killer watchable for viewers. The difference actually comes from Lang's underlying motive in creating the character. The *Berliner Tageblatt* reported, rather wryly I hope, that "The producers of Fritz Lang's film *M* communicate to us that it was

Lorre gives a tour-de-force performance as the serial killer.

not their intent to shoot a film in behalf of capital punishment." No it was not indeed! It was Lang's intent, in fact, to shoot a film in opposition to capital punishment, which he regarded as barbarous, state-supported murder (*Films of Fritz Lang*, 156). In order to make his point, he could not give his character Kürten's most monstrous qualities. He had to make his killer a pathetic little man, incapable of controlling himself and ultimately not responsible for his actions.

The kangaroo court sequence, Lorre's acting tour-de-force, embodies these different views in underworld boss Schraenker and Beckert. Beckert initially pleads his innocence, but when confronted by the blind balloon vendor his eyes get wide, and he backs up panic-stricken toward his accusers, as he repeats Elsie's name and screams "No!" Schraenker, ignoring Beckert's obvious horror at his own crimes, calls him at various times a "dog," a "filthy swine" and a "beast." When Beckert's defense demands that "This man be handed over to the police," Schraenker (un-subtitled) cries out "That is no man!" Schraenker, guilty of three murders himself, believes that the only course is to *render* Beckert "harmless" by killing him… rather than send him to an institution and have him *released* as "harmless," as has happened to this killer once before.

Schraenker—ironically the voice of social outrage toward the child murderer—has no remorse for his calculated crimes, while Beckert possesses tremendous remorse for his uncalculated ones. Beckert is a haunted man: haunted by the voices of his victims which pursue him down endless streets and which he can silence (only temporarily) by killing again. (One sad footnote to this scene: Some 10 years later, this dialogue

Fritz Lang took advantage of Lorre's remarkable acting ability in *M*.

was incorporated into the notorious Nazi "documentary" *Der Ewige Jude* (*The Eternal Jew.*) Though Lang's intent had been to plead for compassion for the criminally insane, the Nazis used it instead to demonstrate that Jews could not control their impulses and were "therefore unfit to live in a 'moral society.'" By that time, Lang and Lorre lived among Hollywood's refugees from Nazi Germany. Lang's wife, Thea von Harbou—who wrote that very piece of dialogue—had stayed behind, as a member of the Nazi party (*Films of Peter Lorre*, 64).

In its review of the subtitled version which played briefly in New York, *Variety* describes Lorre's tremendous acting feat in this scene, and throughout the film:

Beckert is trapped by members of the criminal underworld.

> It was no simple matter to establish a degenerate child murderer as the principal character, treat him as a despicable pathological freak of nature for over an hour, and then in the final ten minutes suddenly turn audience hate into sympathy. In less capable studio hands this fiend who murders golden haired little girls would call for hateful reaction all the way. But through the acting of Peter Loore [sic] and the direction of Fritz Lang the child killer becomes a pitiful figure, warranting pity rather than hate. (1933)

Reviews for this film, not surprisingly, were mixed. Many reviewers—like Leo Hirsch for the *Berliner Tageblatt*, Sydney W. Carroll for *The Times of London* and Mordaunt Hall for *The New York Times*—found the subject matter too repellant for cinematic entertainment. But reviews for Lorre's performance proved strikingly consistent.

Hirsch called the acting "splendid" all around. *Variety*, in its 1931 review (perhaps the first English-language review written on this film), noted that "Peter Lorre does unusually well as the murderer, changing from human despair to bestial lust." Britain's *The Spectator* claimed that "the acting of Peter Lorre as murderer is a remarkable study of a

degenerate seized periodically by a perverted sexual passion." *Time* held that "Peter Lorre distinguishes himself in a magnificent cast by his haunting performance as the murderer." And, in a review heralding the film as a modern example of "classical tragedy," (a.k.a. Sophocles, Shakespeare, et al.), *The Nation* stated that the credit for this film's rising to such heights comes ultimately from "the flawless acting of Peter Lorre."

One year after *M*'s opening, Lorre was a significant enough star that prominent film critic Herbert Ihering could write a sketch of him for the *Berliner Boersen-Courier*. Lorre, Ihering noted, is at his best in "ironical, ambiguous, charming-yet-infamous dichotomous" roles:

> In wicked harmlessness, diabolical kindness, cynical gentleness, crafty innocence, ironical smugness. It is here that his acting is correctly formulated, here that what he can do and who he is come together. Here, Lorre is first-class. Here, he is a modern play-actor.

From the early 1930s on, the truth was out there, and geniuses like Fritz Lang and Alfred Hitchcock took advantage of it: Lorre, quite simply, could electrify the screen, if given the chance. The trick was in the casting.

CREDITS: Producer: Seymour Nebenzal; Director: Fritz Lang; Writers: Fritz Lang, Thea von Harbou, Paul Falkenberg, Adolf Jansen, Karl Vash (Based on an Article by Egon Jacobson); Cinematographers: Fritz Arno Wagner, Gustav Rathje; Music: Edvard Grieg (from *Peer Gynt*); Editor: Paul Falkenberg; Art Directors: Emil Hasler, Karl Vollbrecht; Sound: Adolf Jansen; Set Designer: Edgar G. Ulmer (uncredited)

CAST: Peter Lorre (Hans Beckert); Otto Wernicke (Inspector Karl Lohmann); Gustaf Gründgens (Schraenker); Theo Lingen (Bauernfaenger); Theodor Loos (Police Commissioner Groeber); Georg John (Blind Peddler); Ellen Widmann (Mme. Becker); Inge

Landgut (Elsie); Ernst Stahl-Nachbaur (Police Chief); Paul Kemp (Pickpocket); Franz Stein (Minister); Rudolf Blümner (Defense Attorney); Karl Platen (Watchman); Gerhard Bienert (Police Secretary); Rosa Valetti (Landlady); Hertha von Walther (Prostitute); Fritz Odemar (The Cheater); Fritz Gnaß (Burglar)

Sources: Review of *Pioniere in Ingolstadt* by Kurt Pinthus, from *Berliner-8-Uhr-Abendblatt*, qtd. in "Peter Lorre" in *Streifzüge durch die Berliner Film-und Kinosgeschichte* (www.mwe.de/kino/personen/lorre-pe.htm); "Fritz Lang 'M'" by Leo Hirsch, *Berliner Tageblatt (Abends)*, 12 May 1931; "M" by "Magnus," in *Variety*, 2 June 1931: 15; "Poisoning the Public: Gangsters and Gold Diggers, The Dusseldorf Murders" by Sydney W. Carroll, in *The Times of London*, 19 June 1932: 6; "Peter Lorre" by Herbert Ihering, in *Berliner Boersen-Courier*, 24 June 1932, rpt. in *Von Reinhardt Bis Brecht*, Rowohlt, 1967: 19-20; "The Dusseldorf Murders" by Mordaunt Hall, in *The New York Times*, 3 April 1933: 3; "'M'" by "Bige." in *Variety*, 4 April 1933: 15; "The New Pictures: 'M'" in *Time*, 10 April 1933: 27; "Films: Tragedy and the Screen" by William Troy, in *The Nation*, 19 April 1933: 454-5; "The Cinema: 'M' at the Academy Cinema" by Charles Davy, in *The Spectator*, 20 October 1933: 522; *Peer Gynt* by Henrik Ibsen, Penguin, 1972; The *Films of Fritz Lang* by Frederick W. Ott, Citadel, 1979; *The Films of Peter Lorre* by Stephen D. Youngkin, James Bigwood and Raymond G. Cabana, Jr, Citadel, 1982; "The Dusseldorf Ripper" in *Jack the Ripper: The Complete Casebook* by Donald Rumbelow, Contemporary, 1988: 258-73.

F.P.1 ANTWORTET NICHT
1932
by David H. Smith

On rare occasions, revolutions transpire in a flash. A pair of self-taught engineers working in a bicycle shop, the Wright brothers made their first successful flight at Kitty Hawk, North Carolina, in 1903—two years after Wilbur Wright told his brother, Orville, that humans wouldn't fly for 50 years. "Ever since," he said later, "I have distrusted myself and avoided all predictions." Kurt Siodmak might have heeded his advice.

Born in Dresden, Germany, in 1902, Siodmak had a major success in 1931 with his science-fiction novel *F.P.1 antwortet nicht* (*F.P.1 Is Not Answering*). It told the quaintly passé story of sabotage and mutiny on the artificial island F.P. 1 (*Flugplattform 1*) in the Atlantic Ocean, where planes could refuel and pilots could rest. In the end, the platform is saved through the intervention of the pilot hero, dressed in the rugged height of '30s fashion with jodhpurs, leather aviator jacket and billowing silk scarf, amid as much froth in the soap-opera trimmings as there was in the briny breakers.

The idea for such a platform was based on the proposals of a German engineer, A.B. Henninger, whose plans were actively considered at the time both in the United States and in Germany. However, as transoceanic flight became more commonplace in the 1930s, and as the aircraft carrier replaced the battleship as the major unit in a modern fleet during World War II, his (and Siodmak's) idea rapidly became outmoded.

No matter such naïve anachronisms, Siodmak had 18 best-selling novels published in Germany before emigrating to the U.S.; this book, published in 1933 as *F.P.1 Does Not Reply* in America and as *F.P.1 Fails to Reply* in the UK, is the only one of those translated (by H.W. Farrel) into English.

Movie rights to the book were purchased by Universum Film Aktien Gesellscaft (UFA), the film production combine then recently saved from bankruptcy by a trust headed by Alfred Hugenberg (1865-1951), a wealthy press magnate (he owned 53 newspapers) who had become head of the German Nationalists in 1928.

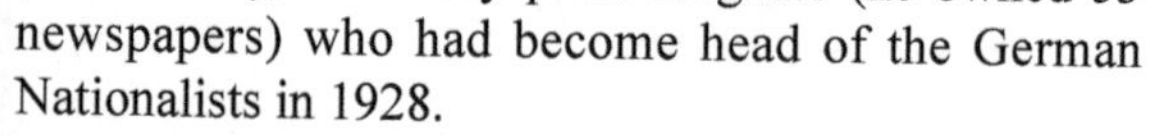

The economic might of UFA had created the first mass audience for film; the number of movie theaters in Germany grew from roughly 2,000 in 1918 to 5,000 at the beginning of the 1930s, and Hugenberg was eager to exploit his new media domain.

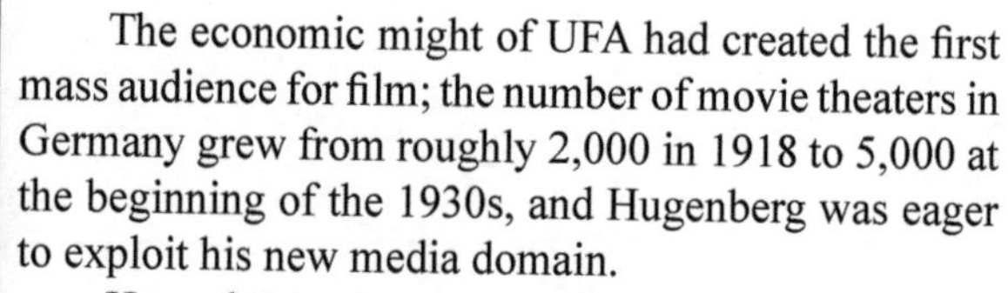

Hugenberg was a Nazi sympathizer devoted to Hitler even before the National Socialist German Workers' party came to power. Whereas UFA had once been a progressive film company trying consciously to raise film's aesthetic standards, Hugenberg, as UFA's board chairman, relegated experimentation to the margins (documentary, animation) and began producing a steady stream of politically inspired tales of heroism, heavy on nationalist propaganda.

And, as an example of this new-fledged Teutonic hubris, *F.P.1 antwortet nicht* fit the bill quite nicely, *danke schön.*

F.P.1 antwortet nicht was filmed in the final full year of the postwar Weimar Republic (1919-1933), in its throes from the inflation of the 1920s and the world depression of the early 1930s, coupled with social unrest stemming from the Draconian conditions of the Versailles Treaty. No matter the financial outlay demanded, UFA saw in *F.P.1 antwortet nicht* the chance to repeat the international commercial success of *Metropolis* (1927), even though that film's bloated 16-month shooting schedule and estimated seven million Deutsche-mark production cost had almost bankrupted the company.

Up till then, UFA's international hits had been musicals and comedies, usually shot in multi-language versions (German, French and English), such as *Der KongreB tanzt* (1931), *Die Drei von der Tankstelle* (1930), *Bomben auf Monte Carlo* (1931) and *Ich bei Tag und du bei Nacht* (1932). Fast-paced and witty, they carried across the world an image of Germany as youthful, sporty and vital.

Anticipating similar worldwide interest in their science fiction story, UFA entered into a co-production agreement with the Fox Film Corporation (later 20th Century-Fox) in the U.S. and with Gaumont, a Parisian production company, to again shoot three versions simultaneously with different casts in German, English (*Secrets of F.P.1* in the U.S. and just *F.P.1* in England) and French (*I.F. 1 ne répond plus*). There is the rumor of a Spanish version too, but its co-existence and -production with the other three seem unlikely.

Dubbing of foreign-language films was very difficult from a technical standpoint at this early stage of the "talkies" game, and few films were seen as universally in demand enough to make similarly complex international productions routine. But there was more to *F.P.1 antwortet nicht* than simply supplying the three principal casts with identical scripts.

Though he would sit in the director's chair for all three versions, Vienna-born Karl Hartl (1898-1978) retooled each to comply with each nation's sensibilities (finding himself Gallicized as "Charles Hartl" in the opening credits of the French one); and though the thrust of the story never changed, each version was as different as mustard and custard in terms of acting and editing.

As it concerns the German version starring Peter Lorre, UFA was naturally high-minded and cast only Germany's finest actors (conveniently all under exclusive contract). In the lead part as the romantic hero, macho Hans Albers had played on the Berlin stage and in silent German films, fast becoming the nation's number one screen favorite, akin to Clark Gable in the States. He was Mack the Knife in UFA's *Die Dreigroschenoper/The Threepenny Opera* (1931), the adventurer at *Die WeiBe Hölle vom Piz Palü/The White Hell of Pitz Palu* (1929) and

F.P. 1's floating platform

Hans Albers and a blond Peter Lorre as the photographer Johnny.

appeared in the classic *Der blaue Engel/The Blue Angel* (1930). Theorist Siegfried Kracauer (1889-1966), in his influential psychological study of the German film *From Caligari To Hitler: A Psychological History of the German Film* (1947), referred to Albers's screen characters as "human dynamo[s] with the heart of gold [personifying] what everybody wished to be in life."

Lantern-jawed heroine Sybille Schmitz had acted alongside Albers in Max Reinhardt's prestigious Deutsches Theater in Berlin, and had recently been signed to a five-year contract by UFA. Though only 22, she had already played in Metzner's *Überfall* (1928) and Pabst's *Das Tagebuch einer Verlorenen/Diary of a Lost Girl* (1929); she became most famous for her role as Léone in Swedish director Carl-Theodor Dreyer's dreamlike *Vampyr—Der Traum des Allan Grey/Vampyr* (where she was the only professional actress), shot as a silent film in France with exaggerated lip movements over a year before, and then taken to Berlin for post-synchronization (in English, French and German!).

But, most important was real star: the "floating platform" itself. Miniatures would inevitably have to be utilized, but the story begged for more believable effects than what international audiences had seen in recent years, i.e., cubist Martian architecture (*Aelita*), gold-filled lunar caves (*Die Frau im Mond/Woman in the Moon*) and airplane taxis ignoring aerodynamics by lazily turning without banking (*Metropolis*) amid 200-story art deco skyscrapers with rocket-powered elevators (*Just Imagine*).

The "actual" *Flugzeug Platform 1* was constructed on Griefswaldt Oie (home of the last wild Shetland ponies in Germany), an island about 35 miles out from Straislund in the strait between the Isle of Rügen and the German mainland. For scenes with the actors aboard the craft, a floating dry-dock 1,500 feet long and 400 feet wide was used; matched with aerial shots of a miniature version standing alone on a wrinkled sea, the entire concept seemed all the more plausible. Principal photographer Günther Rittau had worked similar optical magic for director Fritz Lang (1890-1976) in the aforementioned *Metropolis*.

For all its technical niceties, some critics remained unimpressed. Gene Wright, in *The Science Fiction Image*, thought the model "lack[ed] convincing detail." In an essay published in *Focus on the Science Fiction Film*, William Johnson criticized that the "effects [were] limited in scope." With the benefit of hindsight, *Science Fiction Cinema*'s Denis Gifford found the whole idea of a mid-ocean airdrome "rapidly obsolete" in light of the long-range aircraft developed soon after the movie's production.

But these are the views of writers who focused on the technicalities rather than the humanity of *F.P.1 antwortet nicht*. First and foremost, the movie is a human interest drama. In a nutshell, a two-fisted, love-'em-and-leave-'em pilot (Hans Albers) convinces shipbuilders to construct a floating airport in the middle of the ocean. A family business, the construction company is headed up by two brothers and their sister (Sybille Schmitz), who naturally begins to fall in love with the dashing aviator.

But he will have none of it, winging himself away to circumnavigate the globe non-stop in a new plane (a feat not accomplished in the real world until 1986). Of course, no one bothers to figure out that if he is successful, future mid-ocean pit stops will be all the more moot. Left in the lurch and to his own devices is Johnny, his itinerant biographer (Peter Lorre), a mousy little man hamstrung by a severe case of hero worship (inadvertently espousing the fast-growing Nazi sentiments of anti-Semitism and homophobia in the process), who bides his time until his idol's return by acting as the project's unofficial documentarian.

Despite the usual hardships and setbacks, the F.P. 1 is built and set in place, balanced on tanks of compressed air. The heartbroken sister has found a new, unrequited love in the platform's designer and commander (Paul Hartmann).

Saboteurs attack, however, even before the platform's "grand opening." They gas the crew and, to sink the craft, damage the ballast controls as the platform takes on water to stabilize itself before an oncoming squall (a crisis the climax never resolves).

The heroine sets her wounded pride aside and begs the vagabond pilot to fly her out to the F.P. 1 when, after gunshots are heard over the radio, communication is lost (hence the title). They land and revive the crew, who panic at their predicament and abandon the sinking platform. The pilot comes to realize he is the odd man out in the triangle now, but he is shamed into getting help by the idolatrous Johnny. All is made right at the end, and with a tip of his ailerons, the pilot buzzes off into perennial bachelorhood and perhaps other, unfilmed adventures.

Despite its title presence, the focus of the movie is never the platform itself, but rather the drama that surrounds its construction and deployment. No matter his prominent appearance in the credits (billed fourth), Peter Lorre's part is a small one, but it's 180 degrees away from what audiences might have expected of the diminutive actor after his role of the murderous pedophile in *M* the year before.

With a handful of cameos in interim films, *F.P.1 antwortet nicht* was his highest billing since that auspicious début, though his part here was not substantially larger than those sophomore efforts. And Lorre, all sleepily bug-eyed and sporting uncharacteristic bleached-blond hair, makes the most of it.

In the German version (only), there is a long scene set in a Hamburg hotel suite with the photographer and the pilot. Numbed by rejection, the Hungarian nebbish sits as the Hanseatic hero struts about the rooms, doting on him like a pet, urging him to share in his *joie de vivre* and boasting of his grand plans for the future after the platform is built. Johnny ignores his hero's entreaties, clutching his camera like it is the only friend he has in a world that technology is making smaller by the day. Though he strives to keep his face expressionless, Lorre's melancholy is clearly evident by his deflated-balloon posture and misty eyes. His emotional frailty is palpable.

The smallness of his part notwithstanding, Lorre was still singled out, for better or worse, in several reviews. "Magnus," in the January 17, 1933 edition of *Variety*, noted only that Lorre had a tendency to "exaggerate." Robin Cross, in *Science Fiction Films*, thought the actor provided just "a small touch in a human scale."

Conversely, Phil Hardy thought Lorre was "excellent" in *The Encyclopedia of Science Fiction Movies*. Furthering such sanction, co-authors James Robert Parrish and Michael R. Pitts proclaimed *F.P.1 antwortet nicht* to be "one of the best European sci-fi films of the 1930s" in *The Great Spy Pictures II*, making note of Lorre's "small but important assignment."

F.P.1 antwortet nicht was a popular hit in Germany, as were the international versions prepared in concert. The English version, starring Leslie Fenton, German expatriate Conrad Veidt (who had fled Hollywood two years earlier with the advent of "talkies" for fear his limited English would ruin his career!) and Jill (Mrs. Laurence Olivier) Esmond in the lovers' triangle, with British character actor Donald Calthorp (1888-1940) in the "Johnny" part (re-christened "Sunshine"). While presumptive, one can only picture Lorre and Veidt, united on the sets of *All Through the Night* and *Casablanca* 10 years later, reminiscing about their nonexistent co-starring roles aboard the F.P. 1 and, as all three troupes of actors reconvened at the end of each shooting day, wiling away their leisure hours playing Ping-Pong on the nearby island of Rügen.

With dialogue translated by Robert Stevenson and Peter McFarland (and Kurt Siodmak carelessly credited as "Slodmak"), the role of the hero-worshipping toady in the English version was far less poignant. "Sunshine" comes across only as hard-bitten and hard-boiled, an exemplar of the screen's ideal of the impassive newsman in a snap-brim hat with a dog-eared "PRESS" card tucked in the headband. For what it is worth, the English version was more than a half-hour shorter than the German one, punchier, yet losing little if anything but soapsuds in the telling.

(It has been reported that, in the original novel—unavailable for this retrospective—the photographer's character was a minor one, and the part was fleshed out at the suggestion of screenwriter Walter Reisch to take advantage of Lorre's growing screen popularity.)

The aftermath of *F.P.1 antwortet nicht* and some of its participants is the stuff of Hollywood legend; for others, it was "Hollywood Babylon." Hans Albers switched to character parts after his romantic leading days were gone, passing away in 1960. Paul Hartmann was equally successful in his later years, carving out a substantial film career in Germany (and even appearing in another Siodmak-based science-fiction thriller, *Der Tunnel*, in 1933). Toward the end of his days, he appeared in *The Longest Day* (1962), arguably the best of the seldom compelling all-star WWII dramas, and even in a 1966 episode of U.S. television's *Family Affair*! He died in 1977.

Sybille Schmitz's rising star soon plummeted earthward because, in the opinion of Joseph Goebbels, the Nazi Minister of Culture and Propaganda, she didn't look pure Aryan. She still managed to eke out a career on the German screen in the lean years which followed, but sadly took her own life in 1955 with an overdose of sleeping pills.

F.P.1 antwortet nicht's production team went on to make the plodding but atmospheric *Gold* in 1934, also starring Albers, under a similar deal for foreign film versions (though only a French version, *L'Or*, was finally produced). It dealt with the atomic transmutation of lead into bullion with special effects so convincing that, after World War II, the U.S. government screened it for scientists to see whether it showed the Germans capable of producing nuclear power with the supposed cyclotron. Rarely seen nowadays outside of film archives, *Gold* was decidedly more spectacular and reportedly even more nationalistic than *F.P.1 antwortet nicht*. The movie's lab sequences, laden with all manner of dazzling electrical effects, were later re-used by American producers for the talky and unusual *The Magnetic Monster* (1953).

Coincidentally, the latter film was scripted by "Curt" Siodmak, who had, after 18 movie credits in Europe, come to America in 1937 and would manage to amass 35 more in his long career. He wrote or co-wrote *The Wolf Man* (1941), *House of Frankenstein* (1944), *The Beast With Five Fingers* and many others.

After only a couple more, minor film roles, Lorre would go into exile from Germany, carrying with him no luggage but the stigma of a début that almost stereotyped his career as soon as it began. *F.P.1 antwortet nicht* is a movie that, while not aging well in terms of prophecy, shows an actor whose range was only beginning to be explored.

CREDITS: Producers: Eberhard Klagemann and Erich Pommer; Director: Karl Hartl; Adaptation: Walter Reisch "After Kurt Siodmak's Story"; Music: Hans-Otto Borgmann and Allan Grey; "Fleiger gruess mir die Sonne" by Allan Grey and Walter Reisch, sung by Hans Albers; Recorded on Tobis-Klangfilm; Photography: Günther Rittau, Konstantin Irmin-Tachert and Otto Becker; Sound: Fritz Thiery; Production Design: Erich Kettelhut; Technical Collaborator: A.B. Henninger; Editor: Willy Zeyn, Jr.; Special Effects: Theo Nischwitz and Konstantin Tschetwerikoff; a UFA picture; released on December 22, 1932; 109 minutes

CAST: Hans Albers (Major Ellisen); Sybille Schmitz (Claire Lennartz); Paul Hartmann (Captain B. E. Droste); Peter Lorre (Johnny, a reporter); Hermann Speelmans (Damsky); Paul Westermeier (Ship builder); Arthur Peiser (Man with toothache); Gustav Püttjer (Man with high voice); Georg August Koch (First officer); Hans Schneider (Second officer); Werner Schott (Matthias Lennartz); Erik Ode (Konrad Lennartz); Philipp Manning (Doctor); Georg John (Machinist); Rudolf Platte (Radio operator); Friedrich Gnas (Radio operator at Lennartzwerk shipyard)

ENGLISH VERSION CAST: Conrad Veidt; Leslie Fenton; Jill Esmond; George Merritt; Donald Calthorp; Francis L. Sullivan; Alexander Field

FRENCH VERSION CAST: Charles Boyer; Danielle Parola; Jean Murat; Pierre Brasseur; Marcell Vallé; Pierre Piérade; Ernest Ferny

THE MAN WHO KNEW TOO MUCH
1934
by Cindy Ruth Collins

> PUBLIC ENEMY OF ALL THE WORLD! Holding in the Hollow of His Hand the Fate of International Peace and Diplomacy. A RACKET THAT DWARFS ALL OTHERS! Gracious Murderer... Suave Sadist... Exploiting Women and Nations for Lust! YOU WILL BE LOST IN ITS SHOCKING STORY! (Text next to Lorre's image in the *Chicago Tribune* ad for *The Man Who Knew Too Much*)

When Peter Lorre first arrived in Britain, he knew only one English word: "yes"—or so he told a *New York Times* reporter some 10 years later.

He claimed to have gotten the role in *The Man Who Knew Too Much* shortly after his arrival by watching gestures and listening to tone of voice during a supper with Alfred Hitchcock. These observations enabled him to anticipate the director's jokes and laugh in the appropriate places at the punch lines. Thus he fooled Hitchcock into thinking that he knew English... and thus he got the part.

It is a typical actor's story, one in which the actor won the role by paying attention to character—the character of his director. Hitchcock's less dramatic version is more typically a director's story. In a 1968 interview with François Truffaut, Hitchcock claims simply that he insisted on getting Lorre for the part (*Hitchcock*, 61).

Whether Hitchcock's insistence came before or after the supper with Lorre, both men clearly benefited from having this actor play the villain in this film. Peter Lorre was the first world-class actor employed by Alfred Hitchcock. Not surprisingly, their collaboration revived Hitchcock's languishing career in the British cinema, and simultaneously established Lorre's on the English-speaking screen. Within five years, both men would be in Hollywood, where separately they would make some of the finest films in American film history.

Peter Lorre had fled to Austria and then France more than a year before this film's release, making him one of the first expatriate actors from Nazi Germany. As a vocal, and satirical, critic of the Nazi regime, he had put himself directly at odds with the Nazis. It could hardly have been a surprise when Sam Spiegel, the director on Lorre's latest picture, received warning that he, his cast and crew were in danger and should flee the country. They did, landing in Vienna to shoot *Unsichtbare Gegner* (*Invisible Opponent*)—Peter Lorre's last German-language feature before a brief return to Germany in the post-war era (*Films of Peter Lorre*, 33).

Peter Lorre as the murderous Abbott and Cicely Oats as Nurse Agnes. (Photofest)

Thankfully, Lorre's performance in *M* made an impression outside of Germany, and his abilities as a screen heavy placed him quickly in demand. Though Hitchcock was the first to cast him, Lorre soon had work lined up in Hollywood as well. He boarded ship for America, in fact, immediately after finishing Hitchcock's film.

Despite the ease with which he found work even early in his exile, the Peter Lorre of *The Man Who Knew Too Much* is a man in transition—a refugee, a recently escaped target in a mad manipulator's political game. These personal circumstances make it somewhat ironic that Hitchcock cast him as a political manipulator, moving people like pawns to suit his own ideological ends, whatever those are.

In *The Man Who Knew Too Much*, an English couple vacationing with their daughter in Switzerland inadvertently uncover an assassination plot against a statesman when their friend—a French secret agent working for the British government—is murdered. The assassins kidnap the daughter to silence the couple, but see their plot go awry as the husband tracks the assassins to their hideaway in Wapping and gets word to his wife to prevent the plotted assassination at the Albert Hall. Her scream at the appropriate moment sufficiently distracts the hitman so that he only wounds his target, and her pointing out the getaway car to the police allows them to track the shooter to the gang's hideaway.

In the climax, the police shoot it out with the assassins, killing them all except for the hitman, whom the wife shoots off the roof when he tries to use her daughter as a shield. The gang's mastermind (Abbott, played by Peter Lorre) is the final assassin killed. When the police enter the room where the gang members lie dead, they hear Abbott's watch ding several times from behind the door, then aim their weapons simultaneously, and fire in unison. When the police pull back the door, the fatally wounded ringleader falls limply to the floor, like a discarded rag doll.

Lorre's Abbott, not surprisingly, proves a multifaceted, internally contradictory character. It's hard to tell just how much of that complexity comes courtesy of the writers and how much from Lorre, but it's Lorre who brings Abbott to life and plays his many facets for all they're worth. During its first run, critics and audiences alike seemed astounded by this "new type of villain"—a villain who (as critic Otis Ferguson pointed out) shows "wickedness personified and made terrible by... contrast [with his] benign, jolly exterior."

That "jolly exterior" becomes apparent in the film's opening scene. When we first meet Abbott, Louis Bernard—the French secret agent—has accidentally knocked him down on a ski run. Abbott giggles as he brushes the snow off himself, and even jokes a bit with Mr. Lawrence, his future antagonist and father of the soon-to-be-kidnapped girl. When Lawrence asks "Are you all right sir?," Abbott laughingly replies: "Better ask my nurse. My English is not good enough for me to know."

This line about Abbott's English might possibly have been written into the film by Hitchcock himself, as a dig at (or tribute to) Lorre's own ignorance of the tongue. Hitchcock always loved a good laugh at the expense of his actors and found in Peter Lorre a kindred spirit who could hold his own against the director's legendary leg-pulls. The joke certainly fit. Unlike Bela Lugosi, who had played Dracula on stage long before translating the character to screen, Peter Lorre had almost no time to learn his lines in this unfamiliar language. He took lessons each night to learn his lines for the next day—learning what they meant and how to pronounce them, and then creating some acting business to go along with them. He had, of course, less than 24 hours to accomplish this feat before appearing in front of the camera. These constraints make Lorre's performance in this movie all the more remarkable. But it certainly didn't hurt that he and Hitchcock could both speak German.

While the joke about Abbott's command of English may hint at Lorre's linguistic handicap, it also reveals quite a bit about his character's personality. In this, his first line of the film, Abbott simultaneously shows his good-natured exterior and his duplicitous interior. This villain, unlike Lorre, is anything but ignorant of English, the language in which he conducts the business of his gang. Later, in fact, when he psychologically torments Lawrence with insinuations that he will kill both father and daughter, he even betrays his *fluency* in the language by quoting Shakespeare from memory, adding as an afterthought: "Great poet."

Abbott obviously enjoys using a jovial exterior to give cover for his unscrupulous ends. In a shooting contest between Jill Lawrence and Abbott's hitman Ramon, Abbott shows Jill's daughter Betty his "dinging" watch... immediately before her mother prepares to shoot. Betty, offended at being treated like a "baby," protests loudly enough to distract her mother; and Jill, naturally, misses the shot. Though Abbott appears on the surface to take a somewhat amused interest in the girl, he seems most interested in helping Ramon win the match, masking his cheating very cleverly. This scene, then, provides a nice symmetry with the one in Albert Hall, where Jill herself distracts Ramon from getting a kill shot on the statesman.

Whatever Abbott's motivation, he does use his "jolly exterior" to cover for a dangerous and villainous interior. During our last sight of him at the Swiss resort, he sits in the ballroom with a very attractive young woman, chortling at a practical joke that Lawrence has played on Louis Bernard. The ill-fated Bernard will shortly be dead, shot (we later learn) by Ramon—on orders from this innocuous, jovial man whom we would never think to suspect.

Throughout the Switzerland sequences, Hitchcock makes certain that the audience sees Abbott as the Lawrences do: as a light-hearted, harmless little man. He photographs him up close and in the light, but with a hat on (or from the left) to hide the hideous scar over the villain's right brow. Only once in Switzerland do we get a hint at what lurks beneath Abbott's smile. When Bernard has his skiing accident on the slopes and apologizes to Abbott for knocking him down, Abbott at first brushes off the incident, then notices who addresses him. He stops in mid-word, his eyelids droop, a look of menace plays briefly over his features, and then he recovers himself enough to finish excusing the accident.

In the London sequences, where his character becomes more overtly sinister, Lorre more frequently and extensively summons that dark and menacing look. But Hitchcock initially uses the camera alone to create the aura of menace. When Abbott first appears in dark and gritty East London, Hitchcock pulls the camera so far back that we see only a shadowy figure in a long overcoat and hat, a figure with indistinguishable features. The distinctive sounds of his voice and watch give him away, of course; but only when Ramon enters do we get our first clear look into Abbott's face. When he removes his hat (and Hitchcock moves the camera in), we note that a white streak, reminiscent of a skunk's, runs through the middle of his dark hair, while a long and nasty scar becomes visible over his brow. Abbott, finally unveiled, looks every bit the sort who could have international villainies up his sleeve, villainies meant to incite violence on the scale of WWI.

He only briefly calls up that menacing look when Ramon tells him that he will no longer allow himself to be "smuggled into this country for [Abbott] or anybody else," but the look appears more frequently once Lawrence infiltrates the gang's hideout and upsets the gang's plans. At least with Ramon, Abbott *can* assert control and remind him of the "price" of the marksman's "genius": to be smuggled anytime and anywhere that Abbott chooses. Lawrence, though, proves more clever and harder to cow than Ramon, and thus more frustrating and threatening to Abbott's designs.

As long as Abbott feels in control, he can appear light-hearted. He can laugh, joke, even tell Lawrence that he should "control his fatherly feelings" and not let emotions for his daughter give him away. But when Lawrence outsmarts Abbott by getting a matronly gang member to admit that his daughter is at the hideout, Abbott becomes intensely angry. Earlier, we've seen only slight hints at his anger, but now he tosses aside a chair and summons a very grim look to his face. Later, when Lawrence helps his pal Clive escape (so that he can warn the police and get Jill to leave for the Albert Hall), Hitchcock provides the first lengthy close-up of Abbott, focusing for several seconds just on that face, with its drooping eyelids, menacing scar, dangling cigarette and look of hate. Abbott even loses control of his emotions, of his external show of geniality, and shoves Lawrence's face back. Though he immediately reasserts his self-control, asking Lawrence's forgiveness, his cordiality clearly takes second place to his focus on the task at hand. He *will* not be swerved aside from his—or Ramon's—aim.

This pattern, in which Abbott moves from good humor when he feels in control to anger and frustration when his well-laid plans go bad, persists throughout the film. When Clive brings the police, immediately after Abbott finds that Jill has left for the Albert Hall, our villain rolls his eyes in frustration and tells his henchmen that if Lawrence runs to "shoot him," to "give him a bad leg," since the padding on the door

Lorre uses body language and facial expressions to convey his character's dual nature. (Photofest)

(which Lorre pats to emphasize his character's point) insures that "no one will hear." Just as Abbott hides his villainies behind a jovial exterior, he literally hides his gang's headquarters inside a pagan "church." In fact by posing as a sort of clergyman, he gets

Clive arrested—for "disorderly behavior in a sacred edifice." After regaining control in his handling of the police, Abbott returns in great humor. Such great humor that he can indulge in one of his favorite forms of comic relief: sadistically tormenting another human being.

Earlier, when the matronly gang member wanted to go home rather than get caught up in any "nasty business," Abbott laughed at her humiliation after one of his henchmen compelled her to remain by taking her clothes and putting her in Bermuda shorts. Now, Abbott feels so secure that he suggests bringing in Betty for the sake of his own amusement. He wants to see a "touching scene." Nothing, after all, could be more touching than "a father saying goodbye to his child—yes goodbye for the last time." Lawrence provides the appropriate response: just staring at his foe as if the man were a cockroach. Abbott, though, cannot comprehend that response. He apparently fails to grasp that he's a sick and evil man. That he is, in fact, a sadistic monster who finds humor in another man's torment.

Meyer Levin, the critic for *Esquire*, noted in 1933 that Abbott's character conformed to a pattern typical of some other contemporary villains and monsters: while "*Bride of Frankenstein* and *The Werewolf of London* present lonesome, sad monsters, who would be good, and human, if they but could," Abbott similarly "projects the dreadful beauty of a soul suffering under the compulsion to do wrong." In some ways, this statement rings quite true. Abbott has mixed feelings about what to do with Betty. He considers her "one of the sweetest children," yet in front of Lawrence he threatens to kill her. It's in front of his gang alone that he can claim he will release her if his plans go well. Abbott seemingly has no real desire to harm Betty, but he certainly relishes playing with her father's emotions, and causing Lawrence to suffer.

Lorre uses body language and facial expressions throughout the film to convey this dual nature. Abbott's body language, in fact, helps him get the upper hand when Clive arrives with the police: He rolls his eyes, fiddles with his jacket and even smirks to show disgust with Clive. Shortly after, when Abbott reappears to his gang and a nervous henchman has a gun pointed at the door, he walks into the room with an amused look on his face, puts his hands up as if under arrest and then lightly pushes the gun away. These bits of acting business are clearly Lorre's own creation, and they help make his character the "new" villain that so fascinated viewers in 1934 and '35.

The culmination of the actor's performance, though, comes once nearly all is lost for his character. On the radio broadcast from the Albert Hall, Abbott has heard Jill's scream… one second before Ramon's shot should have been fired. Consequently, he becomes horribly agitated. He paces back and forth before Ramon's arrival, then looks intently at the radio when he hears that "an attempt" has been made to assassinate the distinguished diplomat. In this scene, where Abbott discovers that his plan has not come off, Lorre provides Abbott with remarkable facial expressions. When he turns to Ramon, his whole body tenses up. He looks at his hitman with a combination of fear, hatred, loathing and anger. Yet when Ramon dismisses his latest failure, indicating that he missed the kill because of "that damned woman screaming," Lorre turns back toward the camera, Abbott's murderous rage transformed now into profound sadness. His plans have failed, and in his sorrow, he appears ready to cry. At this moment, he indeed "appears sad and pensive, like a musician whose inspiration has been destroyed by some accidental irrelevant force" (Sennwald).

And then there's Abbott's death. When the police pull back the door after shooting into it, Abbott still holds the gun perpendicular to the floor and still has the cigarette dangling from his mouth. But when he relaxes at the moment of death, the cigarette and gun fall to the floor, he collapses to his left, hits a table, bounces off and rolls 180 degrees onto the floor where his head rolls back before settling. It's a very convincing, fluid and graceful performance, with nothing stiff about it. Lorre completely gives himself into it.

While fate may not have dealt kindly with Abbott, Lorre and Hitchcock apparently had a lot of fun shooting this film. Both were young (Hitchcock nearly 35, and Lorre barely 30), and both loved practical jokes. In *The Dark Side of Genius*, Hitchcock biographer Donald Spoto notes that "When Lorre one day complained loudly that a suit he owned had been ruined in the studio, Hitchcock admonished that he was behaving childishly; within the week, Lorre received an identical, brand-new suit at his home, tailored by an expensive shop—but the suit was cut in infant-size" (142). And at some time after the shoot, when Lorre again came to England, the actor retaliated for another of Hitchcock's jokes by sending 300 singing canaries to the director's flat at three o'clock in the morning, a stunt which Hitchcock termed "one of the classic leg-pulls in British film land."

Perhaps the most entertaining story that Hitchcock tells about Lorre, though, appears in an article titled "My Life Among the Stars." While shooting *The Man Who Knew Too Much*:

> ...Peter Lorre got married. He was leaving for America immediately after we had finished shooting and for one reason or another we were a little behind schedule.
>
> Peter had to get married before he left because he was taking the future Mrs. Lorre with him, and the regulations on Ellis Island are so strict that two engaged people cannot travel together to America on the same boat without risk of unjustified scandal and delays with the immigration authorities and, occasionally, charges of "moral turpitude."
>
> So I gave Peter two hours off in the middle of a scene. He was getting married at Caxton Hall. He jumped into a car just as he was—makeup on, and a frightful scar painted on his forehead with collodion, an astringent that puckered the skin.

He had no time to take it off. If he had taken it off he would have had no time to put it on again! So you might have seen the scar bobbing on and off his brow during the picture, for we do not make a picture as you see it: The scenes are shot in any order that is most convenient or most economical.

Picture Peter, rushing from the studio to Caxton Hall and worried to death he might be held outside for coming in from a "brawl" where he had got scarred! He had to brush his hair forward to conceal it, go through the ceremony, and rush back and go on working. (43-44)

With bride in tow, Peter Lorre could brave the trip to America, where a strong performance in his first English-language feature quickly established him as a critical darling. When *The Man Who Knew Too Much* opened at New York's Mayfair in March of 1935, *Times* critic Andre Sennwald was so impressed that he wrote both a review for the film, and a *Sunday Times* feature on Lorre. Sennwald's critique sets the stage for what Lorre would later become—an icon of screen villainy, against his own desire. Although Lorre, according to Sennwald, "lacks the opportunity" in this film "to be the one-man chamber of horrors" that he was in *M*, he nevertheless makes Abbott "as malignant a flower of evil as the screen has produced."

Certainly this jovially sinister villain provided Peter Lorre with another of those dichotomous roles at which the actor so excelled. But Andre Sennwald dug out an even deeper truth. Lorre can play duality like his own best element because he is, at core, a "Poet of the Damned."

CREDITS: Producer: Michael Balcon; Associate Producer: Ivor Montagu; Director: Alfred Hitchcock; Writers: A.R. Rawlinson, Charles Bennett, D.B. Wyndham-Lewis, Emlyn Williams, Edwin Greenwood (Based on a Story by Bennett, Wyndham-Lewis); Cinematographer: Curt Courant; Music: Arthur Benjamin; Editor: H. St. C. Stewart; Musical Director: Louis Levy; Art Director & Set Director: Alfred Junge, Peter Proud; Unit Production Manager: Richard Beville; Sound: F. McNally

CAST: Leslie Banks (Bob Lawrence); Edna Best (Jill Lawrence); Peter Lorre (Abbott); Frank Vosper (Ramon); Hugh Wakefield (Clive); Nova Pilbeam (Betty Lawrence); Pierre Fresnay (Louis Bernard); Cicely Oates (Nurse Agnes); D.A. Clarke Smith (Binstead); George Curzon (Gibson); Henry Oscar (Dentist)

Sources: "Poet of the Damned" by Andre Sennwald, in *New York Sunday Times* (31 March 1935), Section 11, 3; "Mostly Clinical" by Otis Ferguson, in *New Republic* (1 May 1935): 341; "Candid Cameraman: Remarks on the Rise of the Villain as Hero and a Note on the Decline of Mae West" by Meyer Levin, in *Esquire* (July 1935): 152, 164; "Life among the Stars" by Alfred Hitchcock (1937), rpt. in *Hitchcock on Hitchcock*, ed. Sidney Gottlieb, Berkeley UP, 1995; *Dark Side of Genius: The Life of Alfred Hitchcock* by Donald Spoto, Little, Brown, 1983; *Hitchcock* by François Truffaut, Simon and Schuster, 1967; *The Films of Peter Lorre* by Stephen D. Youngkin, James Bigwood and Raymond G. Cabana, Jr, Citadel, 1982

CRIME AND PUNISHMENT
1935
by Don G. Smith

The ads for Columbia's *Crime and Punishment* (1935) announced that "A GREAT MASTERPIECE BECOMES A GREATER PICTURE." Well, by any defensible standards, the advertising ballyhoo greatly overstates. Actually, a great masterpiece became a *good* picture. Perhaps the running time of 88 minutes is simply too little time to adequately adapt a novel of such complexity. Missing from the film, for example, are the vivid character studies of Svidrigailov and Marmeladov, and the harrowing dream of a tortured and killed horse. Still, even given two or three hours, it is hard to see how any film could top the book. This is to take nothing away from the Columbia Pictures crew, from director Josef von Sternberg or from the stars: Peter Lorre, Edward Arnold and Marian Marsh.

Posters for the film featured the sinister face of Peter Lorre and the determined countenance of Edward Arnold. Between them, Marian Marsh leans seductively against a lamp post. These images capture perfectly the two most important factors in the film's success: conflict and atmosphere. While cinematographer Lucien Ballard and director von Sternberg are largely responsible for the atmosphere, the conflict relies on flawless acting by Peter Lorre and Edward Arnold.

Briefly stated, the plot is as follows. Raskolnikov (Lorre), a student of great promise, graduates from the university with highest honors and publishes a brilliant paper on criminology. Despite his ability, he still lives in poverty. To raise some money, Raskolnikov patronizes an old pawnbroker, outside whose door he meets Sonya, a young woman forced into prostitution in order to feed her young brother and sister. Convinced that his own intellectual superiority elevates him beyond good and evil, and outraged at the injustice he sees around him, Raskolnikov kills the old pawnbroker and steals her money. Impressed with Raskolnikov's reputation, Inspector Porfiry invites the initially rattled young man to aid in the investigation of the crime. Raskolnikov's self-confidence soon causes him to enter into a cat and mouse game with Porfiry, who becomes convinced of Raskolnikov's guilt but must find a way to make him confess. As Raskolnikov and Porfiry match wits, the former becomes increasingly guilt-plagued, and with Sonya's loving support, he finally agrees to turn himself in to Porfiry as the killer.

Without a doubt, Lorre gives one of the greatest performances of his career in *Crime and Punishment.*

As the film opens, the audience is informed that "The time of our story is any time, the place anyplace where human hearts respond to love and hate, pity and terror." To Lorre's credit, he successfully exhibits all four emotions as Raskolnikov. As he steps

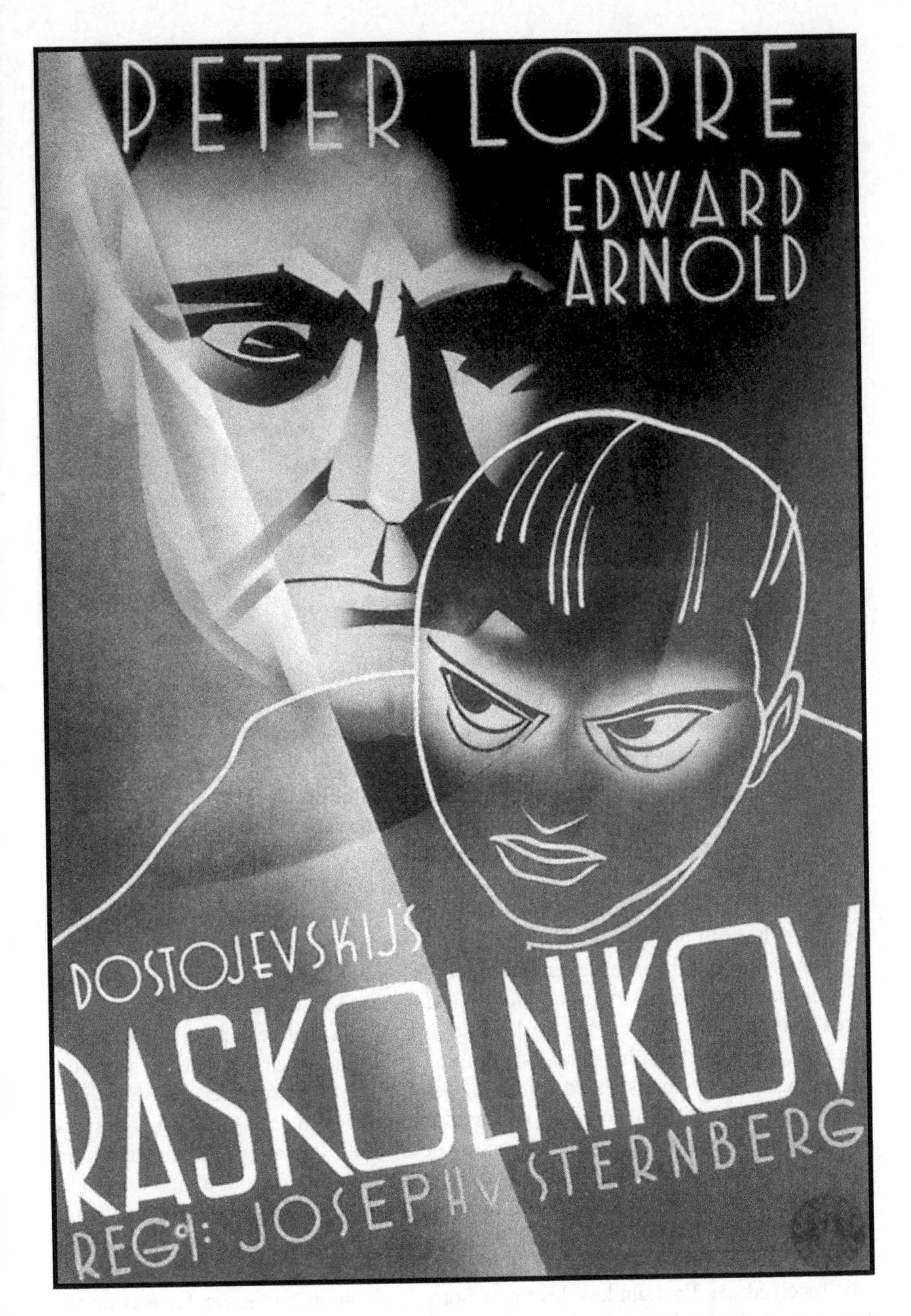

forward out of the shadows at the graduation ceremony, his face is both intense and troubled. We soon discover why. Raskolnikov is proud and self-confident. He feels that his intellectual superiority entitles him to a better life. Yet, in his room, he uses pieces

Peter Lorre as the doomed Raskolnikov and Marian Marsh as Sonya. (Photofest)

of newspaper to cover the holes in his shoes while admiring the portraits of Napoleon (power) and Beethoven (genius) that hang on his wall. There just isn't any justice in the world! Napoleon was a superior man untroubled by conventional morality, and he acted accordingly in taking what he needed and wanted. That was justice! Lorre's diminutive physical stature makes him a perfect Raskolnikov—the little man who wants to be big, considers himself big, and thinks that the world should conform to that reality.

Though Lorre is an excellent Nietzschean Superman, he also exhibits pity and love for his financially struggling mother and sister, the latter of whom was unjustly fired from her job. So great are Raskolnikov's concerns that he selflessly sends them the money earned from his heralded criminology paper. When pride keeps him from accepting a loan from his friend Dmitri, he goes to an old pawnbroker and offers her a watch given to him by his recently deceased father. Though he asks for 50 rubles, she callously insists on paying only 10—take it or leave it. Retaining a calm exterior, the indignant Raskolnikov answers, "Give me the 10 and let me get out of here before..."

Outside the pawnbroker's door, Raskolnikov meets Sonya, who is also visiting the pawnbroker. Raskolnikov feels pity and love for her, just as he does for his own impoverished family. He even slips one of Sonya's siblings some of the money he has just received. As Raskolnikov learns of Sonya's situation, his anger focuses on the pawnbroker. "Somebody should push her straight through into the next world," he growls. "What use is that money to her? It could save a hundred lives like yours and mine. It is plain old arithmetic, you know... She ought to be stamped out! Black beetle squatting up there on her money box. It would be a service to humanity."

Lorre's deadly musings demonstrate that though Raskolnikov feels pity for the poor, his respect for human life itself does not extend much past expediency. Lorre stares with penetrating eyes while contemplating the injustice of the world and the emerging conviction that he, as a superior being, has the right to kill in order to bring justice as he sees it.

Lorre exhibits all the elements of conflict that make Raskolnikov a complex character. After leaving Sonya, he experiences yet another insult when shoved by a cop who mistakes him for a bum. Upon arriving home, he writes in his journal that for the first time in his life he is contemplating committing a crime. Perhaps just one more slight or case of injustice will push him over the edge.

That push comes when Raskolnikov's sister, Antonya, agrees to marry the wealthy but arrogant Mr. Lucien. When Antonya, her mother and Mr. Lucien come to Raskolnikov's shabby room to announce the engagement, Raskolnikov immediately sees that Lucien will keep Antonya cruelly under his thumb and use the marriage to manipulate the behavior of their mother as well. "Money! Money!" Raskolnikov screams and furiously pushes items off his desk to the floor. The push is symbolic of the final push that makes Raskolnikov a murderer, and Lorre brings all of Raskolnikov's indignant anger to the surface in these scenes. Yes, he imagines voices of conscience warning him not to commit the murder, but his resolve is strong. He will not heed the pleadings of his better nature.

Employing a poker (rather than Dostoyevsky's more grisly hatchet), Raskolnikov kills the pawnbroker (in the novel he also kills the pawnbroker's sister for being in the wrong place at the wrong time) and immediately panics when two men knock at the door. Perspiring with a pounding heart, he makes his clumsy escape.

When the police go to Raskolnikov's room next day and ask him to report to the police station, he again becomes undone. His nerves are taut, he is pale and perspires. How, he wonders, have they discovered that he is the murderer? He becomes manic when discovering that he has been called in to account for his lack of rent payments. In a fine scene, when police drag in a poor painter accused of the murder, Raskolnikov passes out at the mention of the word "murder," after which Chief Inspector Porfiry solicits his expertise in solving the case. So credible is Lorre's performance that we can almost identify with his fear, a sign that perhaps we side with him on some level, that we identify with his pain. Perhaps Lorre is portraying a man who has done what many of us would do if only we lacked the moral scruples and possessed the courage.

"Fear is the key to catching criminals," Porfiry tells Raskolnikov, and suddenly the game is afoot. Raskolnikov calmly explains to Porfiry that ordinary men must obey the law because they are ordinary, but extraordinary men have a right to break the law because they are extraordinary. Such superior men should not be judged by normal standards. For instance, Napoleon caused the deaths of millions, yet he built an empire and is today considered a great man.

Porfiry is unimpressed. And he begins to wonder about Raskolnikov, especially when the latter pronounces the suspect not guilty on the basis of appearance. This judgment is, of course, way off the mark, but Lorre is on a roll. Why send an innocent man to the gallows, he asks.

Porfiry turns the tables: "Why should I worry about conscience? Let the murderer worry about conscience." The killer was a coward who didn't even steal valuable items,

Crime and Punishment **helps show why Lorre is one of the greatest horror actors. (Photofest)**

Porfiry explains. Then Raskolnikov addresses Porfiry as Professor because the Inspector "professes" to know something about crime.

These scenes are telling. Lorre's behavior would alert anyone to the fact that something is wrong—but Porfiry, despite Raskolnikov's deprecations, is not just anyone. He is a policeman with years of experience in dealing with the criminal mind. He has planted the idea of conscience in Raskolnikov, a seed that will grow because, despite his philosophy, he still has a conscience more powerful than the abstract ideas that have influenced him. Such a role is hard to play convincingly, but Lorre pulls it off magnificently. These scenes are better than any *Columbo* episode, which operates on the premise of the cop pretending gullibility in order to trap the over-confident murderer. Interestingly, the factual Leopold-Loeb murder case of 1924 progressed in somewhat this fashion, as Artie, a murderer who fancied himself a Nietzschean Superman, volunteered to help police "solve the case." The police inspector was not gullible in that case either, as demonstrated by the quick arrest of Leopold and Loeb on the charges of kidnapping and murder.

Events begin moving quickly. The inspector calls on Sonya, who proclaims Raskolnikov the finest man she ever met. But she has also told Porfiry about what Raskolnikov said about the desirability of the pawnbroker's death.

After another give-and-take with Raskolnikov, the Inspector is increasingly beginning to suspect his friend, especially after Raskolnikov begins throwing money around—buying new clothes and comically dismissing Lushin from the lives of his mother and sister. The money has actually come from an editor's offer to pay Raskolnikov 1,000 rubles for some future writings.

Peter Lorre, Marian Marsh and Edward Arnold (Photofest)

With everything but his conscience going his way, Raskolnikov asks Sonya how she can live the way she does. She answers that she believes in God. Raskolnikov is unimpressed, though he wishes the dead could return to life as Lazarus did. Sonya asks Raskolnikov not to take away her belief, and, tellingly, Raskolnikov asks Sonya not to take away his disbelief. Of course, Raskolnikov must remain an atheist since the alternative is horrifying given what he has done. In these scenes, Lorre subtlly suggests the true import of Raskolnikov's situation and emphasizes one of Dostoyevsky's key themes: Human beings who aspire to be gods sink below the level of humans.

As many murderers do, Raskolnikov returns to the scene of the crime and then runs away. The net of his own conscience is tightening.

Grilov, the man who earlier unjustly fired Antonya, regrets his action and asks Raskolnikov to give a payment to Antonya as expiation for his conscience. Though Raskolnikov refuses to convey the money, the point is made that people who commit wrongs must make up for them.

Finally, Porfiry confronts Raskolnikov with his suspicions. At last, both men know where they stand. The repartee is memorable as Arnold exhibits the cool understanding of the Inspector and Lorre exhibits the knife-edged declining confidence of the killer.

Through a door, Grilov hears Raskolnikov confess the murder to Sonya. He promises Antonya that he will help her brother escape if she will only go away with him. His plan fails and Antonya tells the truth of Raskolnikov's deed to Mother. The world is indeed falling apart for the murderer. All of this and his own conscience move Raskolnikov to

Marian Marsh and Peter Lorre (Photofest)

turn himself in. And because (in some ways) he is still the finest man she has ever met, Sonya promises to wait for his return from Siberia or to even accompany him there if possible.

The last scenes of the film depict Raskolnikov's turning himself in to Porfiry, who simply and sympathetically says, "I've been waiting for you." Lorre raises his glistening eyes to heaven and gives every impression of a man freed from some immense burden.

Von Sternberg's *Crime and Punishment* had competition from a French version of Dostoyevsky's novel. Critics have generally preferred the French version because of its greater exploration of Raskolnikov's psychology. Still, the S.K. Loren screenplay, which was reputedly co-written to some extent by Peter Lorre, is strong enough, especially for 1930s American audiences.

The success of this film is primarily attributable to co-stars Lorre and Arnold and to cinematographer Lucien Ballard. But we must remember that the camera points where the director tells it to point, and the actors do as the director directs. Therefore, Josef von Sternberg must receive high accolades. The film is quickly paced and economically shot. The cinematography is somber in the best film noir or German expressionist style. The camera tracks Lorre along murky, shadowy staircases and streets, artfully realizing the contrast between dark and light central to the film's themes.

Though Lorre was cooperative enough to lose 30 pounds to play the role, Von Sternberg did have some difficulties on the set with the actor. Peter Lorre was addicted to morphine at the time of the shooting, and the director on occasion had to wait till he had "come down" enough to give a good performance. I wonder, though, if some of Lorre's best scenes may not have been fueled a bit by morphine. He plays Raskolnikov as a manic-depressive: the glint in his eyes, the pronounced mood swings—I wonder.

Regardless of whether or not morphine played a role in Lorre's performance, he exhibits all the emotions required of Raskolnikov, performing well as both threat and comedian—as pitiable and as loathsome. He does it all. And that is why Peter Lorre is one of the greatest actors of the horror genre and a formidable figure in filmdom at large. Yes, he could be as sinister as sinister demanded (as in *Mad Love, The Stranger on the Third Floor* and *Island of Doomed Men*; yet he could be as pitiable as pity demanded. And he could do both as he does in *M, Face Behind the Mask* and *Crime and Punishment.*) With his persona and timing, he could even perform as a natural comedian as exemplified by his *Crime and Punishment* scenes with Lockhart. In fact, he is the only actor associated with the horror genre who could do comedy so well, Vincent Price coming in a distant second. Lorre would exhibit his sinister best in such films as *Tales of Terror*, and he would be at his comic best in such films as *Arsenic and Old Lace* and *The Raven* (1963). His performances with Sydney Greenstreet set him apart for special recognition in film history. He could do it all, and, as *Crime and Punishment* demonstrates, *he did.*

CREDITS: Director: Josef von Sternberg; Producer: B.P. Schulberg; Screenplay: S.K. Lauren and Joseph Anthony; Based on the Novel by Feodor [sometimes spelled Fyodor] Dostoyevsky; Cinematography: Lucien Ballard; Editor: Richard Cahoon; Art Director: Stephen Goosson; Musical Director: Louis Silvers. 88 minutes

CAST: Peter Lorre (Raskolnikov); Edward Arnold (Inspector Porfiry); Marian Marsh (Sonya); Tala Birell (Antonya); Elisabeth Risdon (Mrs. Raskolnikov); Robert Allen (Dmitri), Douglas Dumbrille (Grilov); Gene Lockhart (Lushin); Charles Waldron (University President); Thurston Hall (Editor); Mrs. Patrick Campbell (Pawnbroker); Michael Clark (Painter/Prisoner); Johnny Arthur (Clerk); Rafaela Ottiano (Landlady)

MAD LOVE
1935
by Steven Thornton

The 1930s will forever be revered in the minds of fantasy film fans as the golden age of the horror film and for good reason. Led by Universal Studios, that imaginative upstart run by the Laemmle family, Hollywood released a memorable and seemingly endless spate of shockers during this pivotal decade, films whose impact and influence still resonate today.

The horror surplus of that first sound era provided meaty and memorable roles for many flamboyant character actors. Boris Karloff, of course, made his mark in *The Mummy, The Black Cat* and especially as the nightmarish, sewn-together creation of *Frankenstein.* Charles Laughton gave a superlative performances in RKO's splendid *Hunchback of Notre Dame.* Lionel Atwill, the former toast of Broadway, rendered similarly noteworthy impressions in both *Murders in the Zoo* and *Mystery of the Wax Museum.* Even poor Bela Lugosi had his moment in the sun in Universal's *Dracula.* Nearly every Hollywood studio had a performer who made a significant contribution to the twisted thespic delights of this legendary era.

Add to this august list the American film debut of Peter Lorre in Metro Goldwyn Mayer's 1935 shocker, *Mad Love.*

By the mid-1930s, the storm clouds of the Third Reich had begun to envelop middle Europe. Lorre, who had already ventured from Germany to work in the French film *Du Haut en Bas* and Alfred Hitchcock's *The Man Who Knew Too Much,* realized that Hollywood had become the safest haven for artists and performers, to say nothing of its more financially rewarding pastures. So like many European film personalities of the day, Lorre, accompanied by his wife, actress Cecelia Lovsky, set his sights west for the friendlier climes of the United States. His first engagement was to have been at Columbia Studios, for a role in von Sternberg's *Crime and Punishment.* But when the film was delayed, Lorre accepted an offer from suave MGM for the role of lovesick and hopelessly demented Dr. Gogol in *Mad Love,* the studio's latest horror offering.

Based upon Maurice Renard's novel *Les Mains d'Orlac,* the film proved to be a boldly audacious American movie debut for the Hungarian-born film performer. Exhibiting lurid desires and maddening obsessions, Lorre's Dr. Gogol is perhaps the most perverse character of the 1930s horror cycle. But like all the memorable figures from horror films past, *Mad Love's* villain exhibits familiar emotions beneath his depraved exterior. In spite of the sordid sexual compulsions exhibited by Lorre's character and his near insanity by film's end, the sympathy of the audience never completely deserts this lamentable creature whose obsession for the film's heroine is so complete, he is driven to "kill the thing he loves."

Peter Lorre as the obsessed Dr. Gogol.

The film opens with a fittingly evocative set piece. At the Theatre des Horreurs in Paris, patrons have gathered to witness an exercise in Grand Guignol voyeurism entitled *Torturee*. Eccentric Dr. Gogol, a regular visitor, has come again to watch the performance of Yvonne Orlac, star of the macabre drama and object of his secret desires. The sadomasochistic show begins as Yvonne (Frances Drake), cast in the role of a haughty duchess, is forcibly brought to her castle's torture chamber to face a barbarous inquisition. Gogol, hidden away in his private box, peers down upon the perverse scene, his

Dr. Gogol looks pensive while paying his nightly homage to the Theatre des Horreurs.

attention fixed upon the woman who has captivated his heart. As the sadistic tour de force reaches its climax, the crowd roars its approval, while Gogol slowly closes his eyes, alone in the orgasmic bliss of his private fantasies.

Making his way through the empty theater, Gogol nervously asks to see Yvonne in her dressing room. With the theater season drawing to a close, Yvonne casually mentions that her performing days are over and that she will soon be reunited with her new husband, concert pianist Stephen Orlac. The camera draws close to highlight the humiliation of the devastated medico, whose idyllic fantasy has been pricked by the intrusion of cruel reality. Gogol's lament of protest is interrupted when a stagehand implores the pair to join a season end farewell party for the cast and crew. Handing out cake and kisses to the attendees, Yvonne offers a friendly, platonic hug to the doctor when his turn in line comes. But Gogol seizes the moment, grasping his unrequited love in an overpowering embrace and assaulting her with a lengthy and provocative kiss.

Lorre's performance during these early scenes suggests a character who is incapable of expressing human emotions in a normal fashion. With his face half in shadow during Yvonne's performance, his manner is indicative of one who harbors an unhealthy obsession with sexual fantasy. During Gogol's love confessional to Yvonne, Lorre's mood intensifies abruptly when his pleas fall on deaf ears. Given a second chance at the cast party (almost a parody of a wedding with Yvonne as the blushing bride and Gogol as the nervous bridegroom), Lorre again pushes it over the edge, using the festivities as a public forum for his forbidden desires. Understandably put off by his actions, Yvonne Orlac tries to laugh off the incident, correctly inferring that the doctor has a private side that contrasts with his well-respected public persona.

Gogol's detachment from reality is suggested by his infatuation with a wax replica of Yvonne displayed inside the darkened theater lobby. Lorre looks upon the likeness with wistful devotion when entering the performance hall, his blissful mood turning contemptuous when a drunken theater patron dares to flirt with the graven image. Later, when Gogol observes a crew of workmen preparing to cart the statue away to the melting pot, he bribes the workers to deliver the figure to his private study. Defensive of his dark desires, Gogol takes umbrage at the suggestions that his actions are anything less than normal. Lorre is effectively childlike in these scenes, poetically recounting the story of Pygmalion, whose love brought the statue of his beloved, Galatea, to life. Like the Greek legend on which the tale is based, Gogol's desire to possess his Galatea will have dire implications for Yvonne Orlac.

Lorre's physical appearance in this film also hints at Gogol's inner depravity. With his bald pate and pudgy appearance, the actor's look faintly suggests a cross between Max Schreck in the silent vampire classic *Nosferatu* and Lorre's own child predator in 1931's *M*. Impeccably dressed in stylish suits and fur-collared overcoat, Gogol appears quite familiar with the creature comforts and decadent pleasures of the upper class. Lorre's trademark pop-eyed gaze also adds a note of the exotic to his character, giving his crazed love rants an extra degree of intensity. Coincidentally, costar Frances Drake's moon-shaped orbs seem a less exaggerated imitation of Lorre's own peepers, providing a curious affinity between the lead characters in this horror melodrama.

Aboard a passenger train speeding toward Paris, Stephen Orlac (Colin Clive) observes Rollo (Edward Brophy), a circus knife performer who murdered his father, being escorted by the police. Borrowing Orlac's fountain pen, a fellow passenger rushes off to get an autograph from the convicted criminal, who is en route to an imminent appointment with the guillotine. Moments later, as the felon bickers with the celebrity hound, Rollo flings the writing instrument through the air like a switchblade, impaling it into the wall just inches from the autograph seeker's head. Orlac timidly reaches into the compartment to retrieve his writing instrument, fascinated by the murderous hands that are so different from his own.

Soon, word reaches Yvonne that the train carrying her husband has derailed. Speeding to the wreckage site, Stephen's unconscious body is located in an overturned passenger car. Orlac is rushed to a hospital, where a physician informs Yvonne that her husband's hands must be amputated immediately. Desperate for a second opinion, she decides to consult with the world's leading authority on reconstructive surgery, none other than friendly Dr. Gogol. The patient is given a quick examination, but the prognosis is not good. "If I believed it would help, I would gladly give my own two hands," Gogol informs the heartbroken Yvonne. But while preparing to amputate, Gogol conceives of an alternative treatment. A call is placed to police headquarters, and hours later Gogol's assistant congratulates him on successfully transplanting the hands of the recently executed Rollo onto the body of Stephen Orlac.

Any doubts concerning Gogol's sordid appetites are dispelled during Rollo's execution scene. Summoned by the police, the doctor arrives just in time to see the confessed

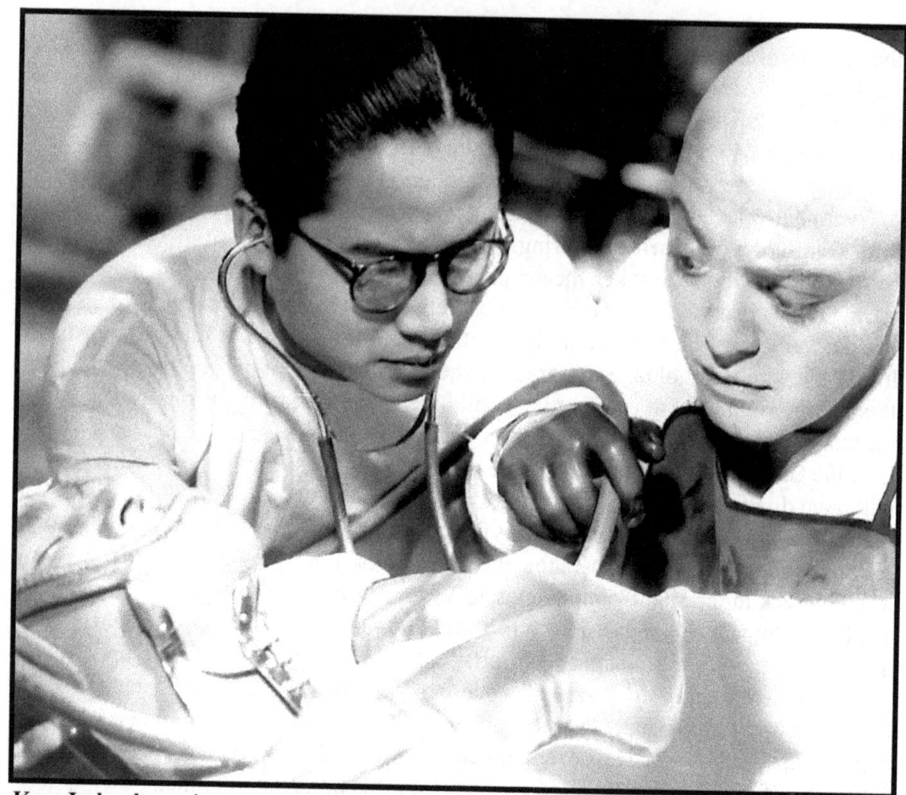

Keye Luke shares important scenes with Lorre in a role that was trimmed by the editors.

killer walk his last mile. Glancing upward at the suspended guillotine blade, Gogol's momentary "thrill" when the machine is set in action is a priceless moment of sadistic voyeurism. Lorre, incidentally, provides an unexpectedly comic moment when the message from the authorities is first received. Tenderly watching over a young patient who is experiencing "her first natural sleep in weeks," Gogol's voice raises to a fever pitch when informed that the death sentence will soon commence, abruptly awakening the slumbering child. So much for bedside manner!

The professional demeanor with which Peter Lorre imbues his character adds another layer of complexity to Dr. Gogol's curious personality. Recognized as an authority in his field, Gogol is authoritative and businesslike in the operating theater, brusquely berating his head nurse when incidental interruptions distract him from his work. Gogol's dedication is evident when he exhibits disappointment over his inability to help the woman he loves, and is reinforced when he envisions how a hand graft can restore Stephen Orlac's lost dexterity (Lorre's eyes light up like high voltage lasers during this inspired moment). Watching his performance, one recalls writer/director Curt Siodmak's sensational claim that Lorre would often frequent operating rooms to observe surgical procedures in progress. Although hard to take seriously, Siodmak's rumor fits well with the notorious, often disconcerting screen presence of this legendary film performer.

Stephen Orlac's difficult recovery commences. Faced with an endless and expensive succession of x-rays, massage treatments, electro-therapy sessions and ultra-violet regimens, Yvonne resorts to pawning her jewelry in an attempt to withstand the onslaught of creditors. But the costly healing process fails to restore Stephen's musical proficiency. When a bill collector threatens to repossess Stephen's keyboard if payment is not made in full, Orlac angrily hurls a pen past his head, lodging it into the woodwork. Yvonne looks back incredulously while Stephen stares at his own hands in disbelief, mentally reliving his brief encounter with Rollo aboard the train.

Peter Lorre imbues Gogol with a layer of complexity.

Desperate for financial help, Stephen swallows his pride and pays a call upon his miserly stepfather, a successful jeweler who bitterly resents his stepson's decision to turn his back on the family trade. Ignoring Stephen's pleas for sympathy, he lewdly suggests that Yvonne find a way to "supplement" their income. Outraged, Stephen picks up a knife and flings it at him, shattering a pane of glass. Shaking his head in horror, he ambles blindly into the city street, oblivious to the automobiles that speed perilously close to his path.

Although Lorre's appearances are minimized in this portion of the film, his presence hovers over it like a bad dream. While the Orlacs are enduring the tribulations of Stephen's difficult recovery, Gogol spends his time primping over his wax replica of Yvonne, pampering it with expensive garments and gently caressing its flowing locks. In spare moments he serenades the figure with hymn-like dirges from his pipe organ and recites tender passages of poetry. Lorre's handling of the character in these scenes recalls a lost and lovelorn child who is overwhelmed by emotions he cannot possibly control.

Even a cursory viewing of *Mad Love* makes evident the sexual symbolism evident in the film's story line. Using his surgical skills to attach the limbs of a dead killer onto his romantic rival, Orlac figuratively castrates Stephen Orlac, corrupting his musical proficiency and driving an emotional wedge between the musician and his frustrated wife. The film's secondary subplots—Rollo's knife-wielding murder of his father and the long-simmering feud between Orlac and his stepfather—further reinforce this symbolic interpretation. When you add to this the film's flamboyant visual style (featuring a preponderance of dreamlike montages highlighted by Gogol's intent gaze, Orlac at the piano and a speeding locomotive), *Mad Love* almost seems calculated to function at least partially on a subconscious level. As such the film resonates with underlying tensions more readily than most of its cinematic brethren from the golden age of film horror.

Gogol's work in the operating room is interrupted when Stephen barges in unexpectedly. In a panic, Orlac demonstrates his newly acquired penchant for throwing knives, implanting scalpels in the wall with surgical precision. Gogol suggests that the problem is all in his mind, the likely result of some unresolved phobia. After the troubled patient exits, Gogol admits to an assistant that he could not acknowledge the true origin of his patient's new hands. "That would probably drive him...," Gogol jests as a demented light goes on in his head, "to commit murder himself."

Encouraged by Stephen Orlac's delicate situation, Gogol informs Yvonne that she must leave her husband before his unstable behavior affects her life. Seeing through the ploy, Yvonne responds with an emotionally devastating verbal assault. This confrontation delivers a trauma to the doctor from which he never fully recovers; from this point forward, Gogol will stop at nothing to possess the woman he loves.

Lorre's performance momentarily becomes more subdued in the film's middle section. During Stephen Orlac's hysterical tirade, Gogol listens with intent fascination, sympathetic to the problem but all too ready to dispense psychobabble in an attempt to placate his patient's fears. Gogol's subtle manipulative tendencies are on full display when he warns Yvonne about her husband's growing instability. Taken aback by her bitter retort, Gogol retreats to the sanctuary of his mirrored recovery room, his reflected images engaged in a fervent defense against Yvonne's accusations. As a disturbing coda to this sequence, Gogol sits motionless in his study while a Venus flytrap captures a doomed insect. Peter Lorre chews the scenery quite thoroughly in this episode, his eyes rolling in emotional torment as his character's tenuous grip on reality begins to slip away.

To lighten the load of *Mad Love's* dark narrative, comic relief is employed with regular frequency. Lorre himself is involved in a few such episodes; one sequence finds him looking askance at the hefty diamond ring of a mother who had moments before expressed concern about the cost of her child's operation. But most of the risible distractions are provided by May Beatty's Francoise, Gogol's chronically inebriated housekeeper who keeps a pet cockatoo absurdly perched upon her shoulder, and Ted Healy's Reagan, the tenacious American reporter who is determined to discover the whereabouts of Rollo's missing body. When Reagan's persistence leads him to question Francoise, she falsely believes that he is seeking the wax replica of Madame Orlac, setting up a predictable (but not altogether disagreeable) exchange involving mistaken identities. Contemporary viewers are inclined to wince at the intrusive comic relief featured in most 1930s horror films (Lee Tracy in *Dr. X* and Charlie Ruggles in *Murders in the Zoo* being the most egregious examples). Like those other "love 'em or hate 'em" performers, today's films viewers may find *Mad Love's* comic performers something of an acquired taste.

Police guard the entrance to the Orlac jewelry shop where Stephen's stepfather has been found murdered. The homicide weapon, a dagger, is found at the scene of the crime and is taken to police headquarters for fingerprints. Meanwhile, Stephen Orlac arrives at a seedy back alley hotel to meet a stranger who promises to reveal the truth about his reconstructed digits. The figure, Gogol in disguise, holds out arms that are encased in surgical steel braces and insists that the missing limbs now belong to Orlac. "When you killed your father, you killed him with my hands," he suggests convincingly. Stephen protests when the stranger falsely identifies himself as Rollo, allegedly brought back to life by the same scientific magic that has given him a new pair of hands. Intent on driving Orlac mad, Gogol offers "proof" of the fantastic claim. "They cut off my head, but that Gogol—HE PUT IT BACK HERE!!!" The camera then focuses in for a ghoulish close-up, giving us a long, horrifying look at the ghastly surgical neck brace supporting the stranger's head. An effectively shocking (although frequently overlooked) vignette, Gogol's masquerade as Rollo remains one of *Mad Love*'s chillingly memorable moments.

Gogol impersonates the dead Rollo.

Stephen returns home to a sleepless Yvonne, now convinced that he committed the murder of his stepfather. As Yvonne tires valiantly to assuage her husband's fears, the police arrive with an arrest warrant. Determined to clear her husband's name, Yvonne returns to confront Dr. Gogol. The doctor's housekeeper, once again heavily soused, takes one look and mistakes her for Gogol's wax dummy lookalike. Forcibly dragging her upstairs, the bewildered maid locks Yvonne in the sanctuary of Gogol's study. Alone in the room, the frightened actress panics, accidentally toppling over her wax doppelganger when she hears Gogol approaching from the hallway outside. The camera takes on Gogol's point-of-view perspective as he sees Yvonne, standing in for the broken figurine. "He thinks he murdered his own father, when it's I who killed him," reveals the crazed surgeon, fully convinced that he is conversing with his still and silent Galatea.

Peter Lorre pulls out all the stops as his Gogol goes over the top in the film's final moments. Laughing maniacally after his appearance as Rollo, it is a wonder he eluded capture by the Parisian magistrates. Back in his study, he continues pouring out his heart to his captive Galatea, his organ playing intensifying into a frenzied toccata. Seeing the crazed look in his eye, one wonders what personal demons the actor was able to conjure to bring his characterization to life.

Although Lorre would enjoy a fine and varied film career, seldom would he have a role that provided such rich and vivid dialogue. Accentuating these plum lines is the unique accent and finely honed vocalization skills that would become the actor's audio signature. "I, a poor peasant, have conquered science, why can't I conquer love," he

Yvonne (Frances Drake) and her fanatical admirer, Dr. Gogol.

protests angrily when Yvonne rejects yet another of his unwanted advances. Later he pulls back on the reins when he sadly admonishes his beloved, "You are cruel, but only to be kind." During the masquerade of Rollo, Lorre's voice becomes a ghastly whisper, while during the film's denouement, it shrieks with crazed and unbridled elation. With such an idiosyncratic command of the spoken word, it is indeed a pity that Lorre did not perform more high-profile roles in the horror films of this era.

At police headquarters, Stephen Orlac pleads his case. His incredible story is lent credence when a fingerprint expert testifies that the prints on the killer's knife match both Orlac and Rollo. With the prodding of news reporter Reagan, the police decide to pay a visit to Dr. Gogol, while Orlac instinctively pockets the knife that was mistakenly left within his reach.

While Yvonne searches desperately for an exit, her face is grazed by the knife-like talons of Francoise's house pet. Seeing a droplet of blood flowing down her cheek, Gogol is exhilarated; like Pygmalion, he believes that his adoration has brought the figure of his beloved to life. As the police arrive, the crazed doctor advances upon the terror-stricken woman. Through a small observation window, Stephen Orlac looks in to see Gogol slumped over his wife, strangling her with her own raven tresses. Orlac pushes the police aside and, recovering the knife from his pocket, takes aim through the narrow opening. With his dying breath, Dr. Gogol looks up to see Yvonne cradled in her husband's arms, safe from the horrors of his obsessively *Mad Love*.

Lorre with Henry Kolker and Ted Healy

The film's shooting script originally called for Gogol to bring Rollo back from the dead temporarily as part of an expanded hand transplant episode (one of many trims made in the editing room). The exclusion of this scene is disappointing on two counts. First, we lose out on the potential thrill of seeing what MGM could do with a Franken-stein–like resurrection sequence. Second, the possibility that Rollo still lives would have added an extra dollop of tension to Gogol's masquerade with Stephen Orlac. It is doubtful that any excised footage from the film is still extant, although the discovery of such a sequence would make a wonderful supplement to future video releases.

MGM, Hollywood's trendsetter for visual glamour, lavished even their most mun-dane features with top-notch production trimmings, and *Mad Love* was no exception. Making his swan song as a director was Karl Freund, the dominating Bavarian who received his cinematic tutelage lensing the stylish German features *The Last Laugh, Variety* and *Metropolis*. He, presumably, was responsible for the film's nifty visual montages and the striking "fist through the window" image that punctuates the film's opening credits. (Oh, to have been a fly on the wall when Teutonic terror Freund made helpful "suggestions" to directors of photography Chester Lyons and Greg Toland!) Guy Endore, author of the novel *Werewolf of Paris*, penned an early adaptation of the screenplay, with last-minute help from John L. Balderston (*Dracula, Frankenstein, The Mummy*, et al.). Handling the art direction (at least officially) was Cedric Gibbons, and providing the music was the great Dimitri Tiomkin. *Mad Love* may have been an ordinary programmer, but the studio had their standards to uphold.

Lorre and Drake in a promotional still used to promote the film.

The cast for *Mad Love* contains a number of recognizable names, although some of them seem like odd choices for a horror film. At the top of the list, Colin Clive gets to once again display his patented reactions of hysteria, this time on the receiving end of a mad doctor's handiwork. Lovely Frances Drake was under contract to Paramount when the call came to play the distaff point of *Mad Love's* twisted romantic triangle. Essaying the role of Stephen Orlac's stepfather was Ian Wolf, an actor whose prickly mood and sourpuss countenance served him well in his appearance as a disagreeable father figure. Rotund Edward Brophy was a questionable choice as Rollo; Brophy's screen image seems far too "likable" to have committed such a ghastly crime. Character actress Sarah Haden was a sly choice for the role of Marie, Yvonne's tart-tongued maid, while Billy Gilbert, an alumnus of Hal Roach comedies, makes a quick appearance as Orlac's boisterous train companion. Turning in a short stint as a cantankerous bill collector was Clarence Hummel Wilson, familiar to genre fans for his appearances in *Son of Kong* and *Son of Frankenstein.* Film fans will also spot Keye Luke, number one son to Sidney Toler's Charlie Chan, as Gogol's surgical assistant, in a role that was trimmed by the film editor's scalpel. The litany of familiar faces makes for entertaining viewing in itself, as cinephiles can take turns saying "guess who that is" when another of MGM's supporting players walks into camera view.

MGM's horror output during the 1930s is a decidedly mixed bag. At the top of the list is *Freaks*, Tod Browning's infamous tale of love and revenge amongst a troupe of circus performers. *The Mask of Fu Manchu* followed, with Boris Karloff lisping away as the insidious Oriental war lord, hell bent on dominating the "white dog" Western world. Then came *Mark of the Vampire*, with an incestuous subplot so daring it failed to survive the cutting room floor. Also out of the closet came *Devil Doll*, a curious tale of vengeance and human miniaturization featuring Lionel Barrymore in drag. Missing out on the atmospheric ambiance of the Universal fright fests, MGM seemed content to focus on the physical horrors and seedy undercurrents of a changing modern world.

Into this milieu, *Mad Love* is an uncanny fit. Belying the film's Expressionist look and Gothic trappings, the real emphasis is on the very human villainy of Lorre's twisted

Orlac (Colin Clive) seeks the help of Dr. Gogol unaware Gogol is trying to destroy him.

Dr. Gogol. And unlike most other horror films of the day, which focused on supernatural elements, the film neatly presages the sexually frustrated, socially maladjusted killers seen in more recent cinematic offerings.

The year 1935 was brutally competitive for horror films. Within months, *Bride of Frankenstein, The Raven, Werewolf of London, Mark of the Vampire* and *The Black Room*, all respectable shockers in their own right, were released to movie theaters, alongside the quirky *Mad Love*. After a surprising sustained and lucrative period, one suspects that this particular horror cycle had finally become long in the fang. These factors, coupled with *Mad Love's* own melodramatic excesses (which must have been way too much for Depression era audiences to handle) spelled certain box-office doom for the release. After experiencing dismal returns in both the domestic and foreign markets, the movie was quickly consigned to the film vaults. There it languished until the early 1970s, when film historians and critics rediscovered and began to reevaluate this interesting and unfairly forgotten example of vintage cinema horror.

Les Mains d'Orlac was first filmed as a 1924 German Expressionist silent starring Conrad Veidt and directed by Robert Wiene. A French version, *The Hands of Orlac* (a.k.a. *Hands of a Strangler*), was released in 1960 featuring Mel Ferrer and Christopher Lee as the principals. The basic idea of disembodied hands that take on a life of their own also influenced the later Peter Lorre feature, *The Beast With Five Fingers*. Although fans of the silent cinema might cast a vote for the Veidt/Wiene rendition, *Mad Love* is the only version that can even remotely be considered a classic horror film.

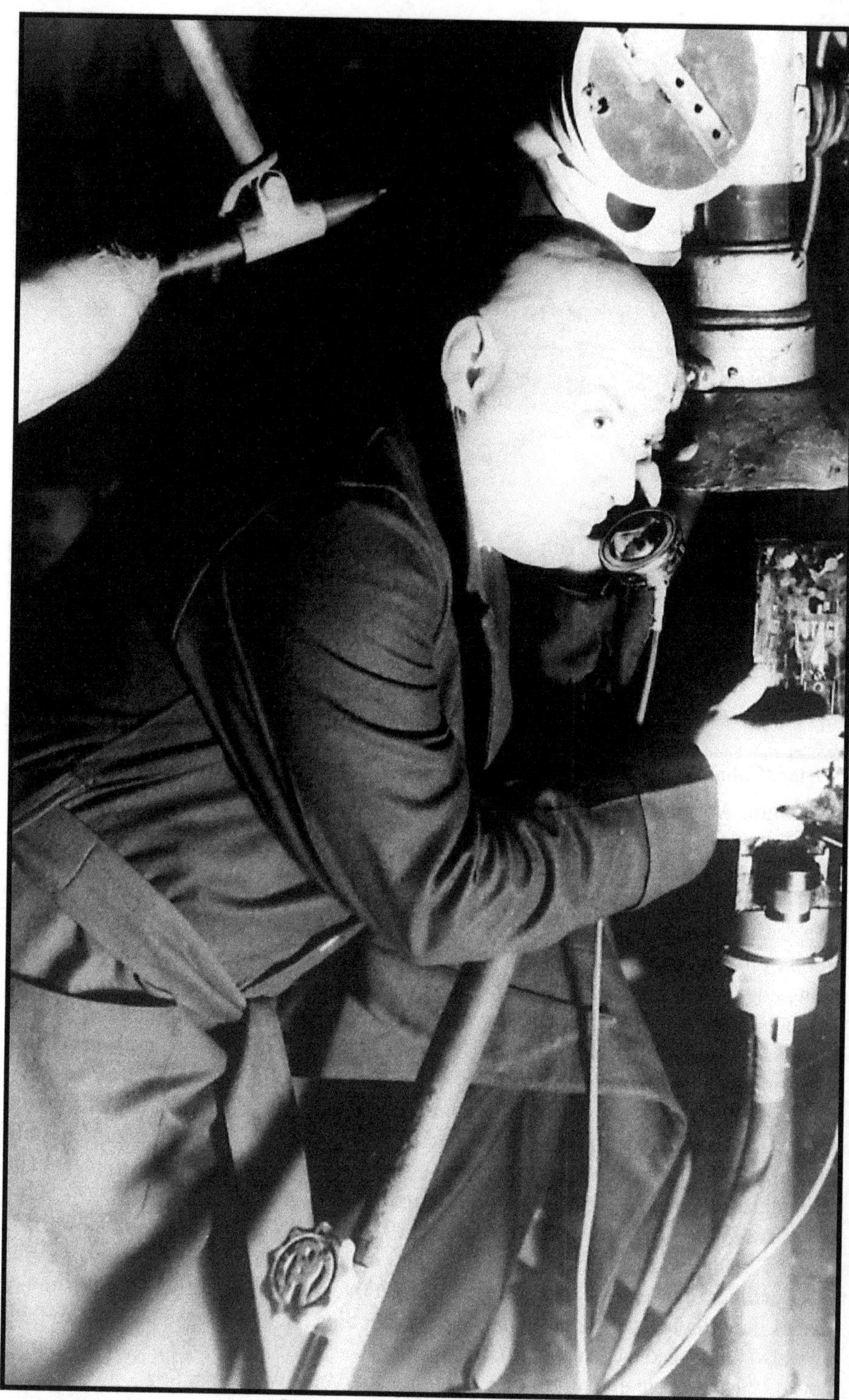

Lorre on the set of *Mad Love*.

After seeing his performance in *Mad Love* according to *Hollywood Cauldron*, Charlie Chaplin called Peter Lorre "the greatest living actor." Exaggerated hyperbole? Unquestionably, but Lorre's work is memorable nonetheless. Like the best horror performers of that decade, Lorre was able to balance his sensitive, skillful playing with an enjoyable touch of overacting, allowing his character to become both genuinely frightening and grandly theatrical. In spite of *Mad Love's* financial debacle, Lorre's nefarious screen presence made an impression on film reviewers of the day. In retrospect, perhaps it is best that the film was not a huge success—becoming pigeonholed as a horror specialist would have surely limited future opportunities for this rare and talented cinematic performer.

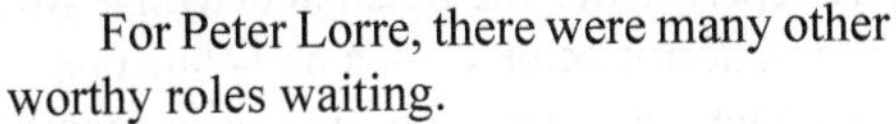

For Peter Lorre, there were many other worthy roles waiting.

CREDITS: Producer: John J. Considine, Jr.; Director: Karl Freund; Adaptation: Guy Endore, Based on Maurice Renard's Novel, *Les Mains d'Orlac*; Screenplay: P.J. Wolfson and John L. Balderston; Cinematography: Chester Lyons and Gregg Toland; Music: Dimitri Tiomkin; Musical Director: Oscar Radin; Art Director: Cedric Gibbons; Editor: Hugh Wynn; Filmed at MGM Studios, Culver City, California, May 6-June 8, 1935; New York City Premier: Roxy Theater, August 2, 1935; Running Time: 68 minutes

CAST: Peter Lorre (Dr. Gogol); Frances Drake (Yvonne Orlac); Colin Clive (Stephen Orlac); Ted Healy (Reagan); Sarah Haden (Marie); Edward Brophy (Rollo); Henry Kolker (Prefect of Police); Keye Luke (Dr. Wong); Ian Wolfe (Henry Orlac); Charles Trowbridge (Dr. Morbeau); May Beatty (Francoise); Billy Gilbert (Man on Train); Clarence Hummel Wilson (Piano Man)

REFERENCES

Everson, William K.: *Classics of the Horror Film*, Citadel Press, Secaucus, New Jersey, 1974
Hardy, Phil: *The Overlook Film Encyclopedia – Horror*, The Overlook Press, Woodstock, New York, 1994
Katz, Ephraim: *The Film Encyclopedia*, HarperCollins Publishers, New York, New York, 1994
Maltin, Leonard: *Leonard Maltin's 1996 Movie & Video Guide*, Penguin Books, New York, New York, 1995
Mank, Gregory William: *Hollywood Cauldron*, McFarland, Jefferson, North Carolina, 1994
Steinbrunner, Chris and Burt Goldblatt: *Cinema of the Fantastic*, Saturday Review Press, New York, New York 1972
Youngkin, Stephen, James Bigwood and James Cabana: *The Films of Peter Lorre*, Citadel Press, Secaucus, New Jersey, 1982

SECRET AGENT
1936
by Alan Warren

Peter Lorre was not, in any meaningful sense, a "horror actor." Out of his 79 films a bare 14 can be classified as horror or science fiction, and this includes such borderline cases as *Stranger on the Third Floor* (1940) and *The Face Behind the Mask* (1941). Moreover, half of those 14 are comedies sending up the genre. It's ironic that Lorre, with his soft-boiled egg eyes and ominous psychotic whine, was used as much to compel laughter as to evoke terror. In addition, he created no single character with which he is identified. (The only series character Lorre reprised was the Oriental detective Mr. Moto—hardly an appropriate signature role for a horror actor, even a part-time one.)

The simple truth is that Lorre was a character actor who appeared occasionally in horror films—admittedly to great effect, as in *Mad Love* (1935) and *The Beast with Five Fingers* (1946)—with no greater frequency than Claude Rains or Basil Rathbone. He is widely applauded by horror fans, more for his inimitable personality and outré appearance than for his actual accomplishments within the genre. There was no one quite like him: Akim Tamiroff and Oscar Homolka were similar in some respects, as was Martin Kosleck, but Lorre was a true original. Not surprisingly, he has had no successors. He worked with great, or near-great directors (Lang, Hitchcock, John Huston and Josef von Sternberg) but none of them—not even Lang in *M* (1931)—completely tapped his full creative resources, which were at their peak in the 1930s.

Following his worldwide success as the child-murderer in *M,* Lorre signed a deal with UFA for several films but the growing political unrest in Germany caused the half-Jewish Lorre to become a political émigré. He went to Vienna and then to France. When he arrived in England in 1934 he was penniless, but made the acquaintance of Alfred Hitchcock, then casting the first version of *The Man Who Knew Too Much.*

Lorre's performance as the leader of a group of international saboteurs helped to establish him with English-speaking critics and audiences, and led to his American film debut a year later in *Mad Love.* (Although the 1934 *Man Who Knew Too Much* is readily available today on tape and laserdisc, it was an extremely rare film for many years; most prints were ordered destroyed when the 1956 version was made.) While *Mad Love* was not successful commercially, it further established Lorre as the screen's foremost purveyor of the unusual.

Following his triumph as Raskolnikov, the student-murderer of Von Sternberg's version of *Crime and Punishment* (1935), Lorre returned to England, where Hitchcock was in the middle of his famed British period. For many years Hitchcock partisans have debated the superiority of this era (1934-1938) over his American period of great

A rendezvous between Lilli (Lilli Palmer) and the General (Peter Lorre). (Photofest)

films (1951-1964) with no clear victor (though his American admirers are clearly in the majority). Hitchcock himself had just completed *The 39 Steps*, the best of his British films (and arguably the best film of his career). He was now teaming Madeleine Carroll, the leading lady of *The 39 Steps*, with John Gielgud and Robert Young in an adaptation of W. Somerset Maugham's stories of Ashenden, the British agent, from Campbell Dixon's play. Lorre received the plum role of "The General," and production began in October 1935.

Secret Agent usually gets short shrift when Hitchcock's "Golden Six" British thrillers are discussed. Unlike *Sabotage*, with its suspenseful boy-with-bomb-on-bus sequence, or *Young and Innocent*, with its incredible crane shot, tracking across a crowded dance hall to move in on the drummer's eyes in close-up, *Secret Agent* has no identifying memory tag, nor is it good enough to stand beside *The 39 Steps* or *The Lady Vanishes.* Donald Spoto blithely describes it as an amalgam of *The 39 Steps* and *Sabotage*, but this is precisely the problem, as those two films are so antipodally opposite that any attempt to combine them must be fatally compromised.

For Peter Lorre, *Secret Agent* was, at best, a mixed blessing. It was his last British film for 17 years (until the unimportant *Double Confession*). It came just a year before his immersion in B films: he made his first Mr. Moto picture a year later; seven more would follow. In the '40s Lorre would be relegated to (mostly criminous) supporting roles in A films and occasional leads in Bs. He would never have the opportunities

Ashenden (John Gielgud) and the General discover the organist has been strangled. (Photofest)

available during the '30s; indeed, with few exceptions (such as *The Maltese Falcon*), his career took a decisive downturn after the mid-'30s. In a brief essay entitled "The Genius of Peter Lorre," reprinted in *The Graham Greene Film Reader*, Greene showed great foresight in prophesying this:

> Lorre—perhaps it is a misfortune—can do almost anything. He is a genius who sometimes gets the finest effects independently of his director (as I have said there is nothing in the script to explain his [*Mad Love* character] Gogol, the seriousness he introduced into the trivial film)...
>
> ...I have a horrible fear that film directors will find it easier to follow in Hitchcock's steps and provide Lorre with humorous character parts than discover stories to suit his powerful genius, his overpowering sense of spiritual corruption. He is an actor of great profundity in a superficial art. It will always be his fate to be cramped, not only by the shortcomings of directors but by the Board of Film Censors. The financiers are not interested in psychological truth, and the Board does not recognize morality.

Sadly but perhaps inevitably, *Secret Agent* was Lorre's last film for Hitchcock.

Secret Agent takes place during World War I. Following a sham funeral in which an attendant lights his cigarette from one of the candles around the coffin, we meet Richard Ashenden (John Gielgud). It was Ashenden's funeral that was faked. He reports to the mysterious "R" (Charles Carson) in an interesting precursor to the M-Bond scenes in the much later Bond films. (Ian Fleming took the idea of a single-letter official from Maugham.) "R" Assigns Ashenden to assassinate a man staying at the Hotel Excelsior in Switzerland. He also assigns him an assistant, known variously as "the Hairless Mexican" and "the General" (Peter Lorre). Lorre's first appearance is preceded by a chambermaid who comes running up the steps, pursued by the lustful General.

"Lady killer, eh?" says Ashenden.

"Not only ladies," "R" replies.

The scene shifts to Switzerland. Ashenden checks into the Hotel Excelsior, only to be told that "Madame Ashenden" has already arrived. In his room Ashenden finds Elsa Carrington (Madeleine Carroll) and the American Robert Marvin (Robert Young). Elsa has been sent by "R." When Ashenden asks her the purpose of their collaboration she replies, "Excitement. Big risks. Danger. Perhaps even a little..." She mimics firing a gun with her thumb and finger. In a way, this encapsulates the film's central flaw: Unlike the devil-may-care *The 39 Steps*, *Secret Agent* asks us to take political assassination seriously, only to evade this question by preventing Ashenden from killing anyone and opting for a conventional ending.

The General arrives. In the film's best-remembered set piece he and Ashenden enter a church, which is echoing with the sound of a sustained organ note. They discover the organist has been strangled. "Nice work—neat, very neat," the General coos. When someone enters they take refuge in the belltower, where they are almost deafened by the bells. (Hitchcock cleverly employs close-ups of their lips and ears as they shout at each other over the clanging of the bells.)

Ashenden and the General meet Caypor (Percy Marmont), Ashenden's intended target. They inveigle him into going on a mountain climb, where he will have an "accident." (The climb looks particularly fake due to rear projection; there's no sense of being outdoors, let alone high in the Alps.) Ashenden has second thoughts and retreats to an observatory, where he witnesses Caypor's death through a telescope. Shortly afterward, they receive a telegram from "R" informing them they have killed the wrong man. Ashenden's real target is Robert Marvin.

Elsa and Marvin leave on a train bound for Greece. Just as Ashenden and the General confront Marvin, the train is attacked by English warplanes. In a convenient *deus ex machina* ending the train crashes and Marvin is killed, though not before he manages to shoot the General, absolving Ashenden of all guilt. Ashenden and Elsa are married. (In Hitchcock's original ending Marvin cries out for water. The General brings him his flask of brandy. As Marvin drinks, the camera holds on his face as he is shot by the General, who then smiles. This ending was unacceptable, presumably because it was judged sadistic.)

For many years after its making, Hitchcock expressed misgivings over *Secret Agent*. In François Truffaut's seminal book-length interview with the director, Hitchcock remarked that:

> ...the public must be rooting for the main character; they should almost be helping him to achieve his goal. John Gielgud... has an assignment, but the job is distasteful and he is reluctant to do it... Therefore, because it's a negative purpose, the film is static—it doesn't move forward.

Maugham's moral dilemma—whether Ashenden is justified in killing a man—places the novel in the company of John Le Carré or Graham Greene, yet Hitchcock's film is a *jeu d'esprit*, clearly not equipped to bear the weight of a serious moral question. Expediently, the film sidesteps the question by having the villain killed not by Ashenden but by chance. Even more fortuitously, the dying villain eliminates the General, whose cheerful amorality clearly cannot go unpunished. Ashenden and Elsa are thus free to marry at film's end, undercutting the entire moral dilemma. (Intriguingly, both Truffaut and Hitchcock misremember the ending: Truffaut says "the villain dies accidentally, but before dying he shoots the hero," and Hitchcock agrees. Raymond Durgnat compounds the error by asserting that "the villain is shot by the Mexican.")

One of the more intriguing aspects of *Secret Agent* is its casting. Robert Donat, the charismatic hero of *The 39 Steps*, is here replaced by John Gielgud. One of the great stage actors of the 20th century (he had a notable rivalry with Olivier), Gielgud was not the conventional leading man type, and he and Lorre make a bizarre, yet oddly endearing, duo. Initially, Hitchcock had tempted Gielgud by describing his role as that of Hamlet in modern dress, but as Charles Bennett's scenario moved away from Maugham's stories, Gielgud's role became noticeably smaller as attention was divided evenly among the four main characters. Nor did Gielgud relish the experience. "I found filming terribly exhausting," he wrote in his memoirs.

> I had to get up very early in the morning and was always fidgeting to get away by five or six for the evening performance [in *Romeo and Juliet* onstage], so I grew to dislike working for the cinema. Of course, I was paid more money than in the theatre, but I had a feeling that no one thought I was sufficiently good-looking to be very successful... I did not have much confidence in my talent as a film actor and I thought when I saw the film that I was rather poor.

Gielgud had no great hopes for the film: Despite Hitchcock's assurances, the director had clearly lost interest in the project midway through. Consequently, Gielgud considered it just another thriller, and his role a mere cypher. He was also upset by Lorre's habit of stealing scenes through unrehearsed bits of business and his extended absences from the set. (Reportedly Lorre would hide in the studio rafters to inject himself with morphine, to which he was addicted.)

Nor did Hitchcock make things easy for Gielgud once filming was underway. "Alfred Hitchcock has often made me feel like a jelly and I have been nearly sick

Hitchcock gave Lorre free rein, allowing him to steal the film. (Photofest)

with nervousness," Gielgud told a newspaperman. In response, Hitchcock told another reporter: "His stage experience is no use to him here. I've had to make him rub out everything and start blank. I've had to rely purely on his intelligence." It didn't help that Gielgud was supposedly "terrified" that his homosexuality might be revealed by the big screen.

It would be unfair to judge Gielgud's film acting from this atypical appearance. His claim to greatness rests mainly on his Shakespearean performances. He started in films in 1924, but was mostly onstage until the '60s, when his film and television appearances became more frequent. He excelled in *Julius Caesar* (1953), Olivier's *Richard III* (1956), *Becket* (1964) and Welles' *Chimes at Midnight* (1965).

As the General, Lorre is allowed free rein, stealing the entire film, almost as though Hitchcock were reluctant to impose limits on his performance. He's allowed an (entirely unmotivated) hysterical scene in which he tears up tissue paper and smashes toiletries right and left, screaming, "Impossible! Mad! This is too much! Really too much!

For you, beautiful woman. And what for me—nothing! *Caramba!*" His hair in curls, his skin darkened brown, sporting an earring, Lorre is a comic delight. It's a far cry from his frightening psychopath in *The Man Who Knew Too Much*, and, surprisingly, this works well in contrast with the more dignified, even dour, Gielgud. Lorre's manic energy drives the film; he's the comic engine that makes it work.

That said, there's a down side to the General's antics, through no fault of Lorre's. While he chews the scenery with great abandon (you can hardly take your eyes off him), after a while you begin to wonder to what purpose all that comic energy is being put. It seems somehow extraneous, added on, and it distracts attention from the serious moral question underlying all else. It also distracts attention from Ashenden, and since he is, rightly or wrongly, the focal character, the inevitable result is a blurring of that focus. Moreover, we're never quite sure how to take the General. In one scene he's shrieking and whooping with comic gusto; in another he's pushing Caypor off the mountain to his death. And his reaction to the news that they've murdered the wrong man—he bursts out laughing—is hardly endearing. His oddly schizophrenic character seems to sum up *Secret Agent*'s schism all too clearly.

The most surprising casting of all is Robert Young as the villain. Audiences weaned on *Father Knows Best* will be nonplused to see Young as a German agent, though it's actually rather predictable, since he's in the film so much, romancing Madeleine Carroll, that there has to be a payoff. The more conventional casting would have been Gielgud as the villain and Young as the reluctant hero, and this upsetting our expectations is quite effective. It also fits in with Hitch's oft-expressed preference for an attractive villain.

Donald Spoto, in *The Art of Alfred Hitchcock*, somehow manages the astounding feat of reading Young's character as gay: "Apparently infatuated with Elsa, he is also associated with a veiled homosexuality." Admittedly, Hitchcock used stereotyped homosexuals as villains (one thinks of *Strangers on a Train* and *North by Northwest*), but Robert Marvin is conceived and played strictly as a conventional romantic figure straight out of a '30s drawing room comedy, solely for the surprise of unmasking him as the villain. (One of Spoto's clues is Marvin sending telephone kisses to Ashenden in one scene; in actuality, Marvin thinks Elsa is on the other end. Spoto's other examples are equally whimsical.) There is certainly no attempt on Young's part to portray the character as gay; had Hitch intended this he would have given more tangible, albeit discreet, indications of the character's ambiguity (Young spends nearly the entire film making passes at Elsa). Actually, it seems more plausible that Ashenden and the General are a gay couple, although admittedly it seems unlikely Hitchcock intended this inference either.

Madeleine Carroll, one of the most beautiful women of '30s cinema, is as suave and vivacious as in *The 39 Steps*. She prefigures the cool blondes of Hitchcock's later films, including Grace Kelly and Tippi Hedren. (Reportedly, Gielgud was nervous about Hitchcock favoring Carroll during the shooting.) There's some attempt at character development, with Elsa starting out as a callow innocent excited by the prospect of killing, only to be disillusioned by Caypor's death, and finally goaded into action. (She tries to stop Ashenden from killing Marvin.) Carroll isn't subjected to the rough and ready handling she received in *The 39 Steps*, though she was reportedly exposed to several rude practical jokes off-camera. This love/hate relationship with actresses persisted throughout Hitchcock's long career.

The rest of the cast includes veterans of other Hitchcock films. Percy Marmont, seen in *Rich and Strange* (1932), appears as Caypor, and there's a brief glimpse of a young Tom Helmore in a steamroom scene. Helmore would play Gavin Elster in *Vertigo* 22 years later. There's also a bit by Michael Redgrave, the hero of *The Lady Vanishes* (1938).

Secret Agent has received mixed reviews over the years. Donald Spoto is one of its staunchest defenders, arguing that the film "offers new riches at each viewing" and calling it "[p]rofoundly disturbing, yet irresistibly amusing," adding that "[t]he fact that the film takes place in 1916, does not lessen its significance for the international situation of 1936, nor, indeed, for any era in which politics and the waging of war exact such a terrible price from humanity. To have accomplished the statement of this theme without propaganda and without arch moralism is rare and admirable. To have accomplished it with such wit and style is the sign of genius." Raymond Durgant, in *The Strange Case of Alfred Hitchcock*, notes that:

> *Secret Agent*... Goes through the looking glass of first-class tourism into an espionage world which resembles it as 'la zone' resembles the real world of *Orphee*. In a few scenes, and moments within the scenes, a black hard mood catches this eerie and unwelcome alloy of freedom and guilt.

Hitchcock's other British films have been analyzed at some length, yet *Secret Agent* remains curiously neglected. It may well be the least well-remembered of the lot, but this is probably due to its avoidance of set pieces comparable to *Saboteur*'s fall from the Statue of Liberty or *North by Northwest*'s cropdusting scene. For all its hesitancies of tone, and despite its reluctance to address the moral question at its center, *Secret Agent* is, of all Hitchcock's British films, perhaps most in need of reassessment.

CREDITS: Director: Alfred Hitchcock; Producers: Michael Balcon and Ivor Montagu; Screenplay: Charles Bennett; From the Play by Campbell Dixon, From the Stories "Triton" and "The Hairless Mexican" in the Book *Ashenden*, by W. Somerset Maugham; Dialogue: Ian Hay; Continuity: Alma Reville; Additional Dialogue: Jesse Lasky, Jr.; Director of Photography: Bernard Knowles; Set Direction: Otto Werndorff and Albert Jullion; Music Director: Louis Levy; Editor: Charles Frend; Recordist: Philip Dorte; Costumes: J. Strasser; 83 minutes; Gaumont British (1936)

CAST: Madeleine Carroll (Elsa Carrington); Peter Lorre (The General); John Gielgud (Richard Ashenden); Robert Young (Robert Marvin); Percy Marmont (Caypor); Florence Kahn (Mrs. Caypor); Lilli Palmer (Lilli); Charles Carson ("R"); Michel St. Denis (Coachman); Andrea Malandrinos (Manager); Tom Helmore (Captain Anderson); Michael Redgrave

MR. MOTO
1937-1939
by Joe Guilfoyle

It has been 35 years since Peter Lorre passed away, but for film fanatics, including the newest generation of fans, he still walks tall. He continues to fascinate. We examine his films over and over for he was a true original—James Dean as seen through the eyes of Charles Addams. Peter Lorre acted on the fringe, even his mainstream characters were quirky, odd or mysterious. Lorre is perhaps best remembered for his work in classic films, but he appeared in a number of B films, most notably in a series of programmers following the adventures of the Japanese sleuth, Mr. Moto.

Lorre had considerable film experience by the time he starred in *Think Fast, Mr. Moto* in 1937. This was the first in what would become a series of eight Mr. Moto features produced by Twentieth Century-Fox. Lorre, who was born in 1904, had been featured in 17 pictures before beginning the Moto series for Fox. Author John Marquand reportedly based Mr. Moto in part on the exploits of a real Japanese detective. Marquand, an accomplished writer, won the Pulitzer Prize in 1937 for *The Late George Apley* but often tried to distance himself from his most famous literary creation. In 1959, the year before his death, he said:

> Mr. Moto was my literary disgrace. I wrote about him to get shoes for my baby. I can't say why people still remember him.

Despite Marquand's feelings about the novels, they were fine mysteries which benefited from the author's skill as a writer and his ability to create an intriguing character who captured the public's imagination. Mr. Moto, in print and on film, was a mystery within a mystery. He is, as described by one character, "a very accomplished gentleman." Moto acknowledges the apt description:

> I can do many things. I can mix drinks and wait on tables and I am a very good valet. I can navigate and manage small boats. I have studied at two foreign universities. I also know carpentry and surveying and five Chinese dialects. So many things come in useful...

Moto is also a master of disguise, proficient in judo and excellent with firearms. In short, he is the embodiment of the perfect sleuth—part Sherlock Holmes, part Charlie

Peter Lorre as Mr. Moto

Chan—although still a unique character. In retrospect, it is difficult to imagine a better choice for Moto than Peter Lorre (particularly since the chance of Hollywood putting a Japanese actor in a lead in a movie in 1937 was on a par with Ed Wood receiving a lifetime achievement award from the Academy of Motion Picture Arts and Sciences). He was, however, a bit of a chance for studio executives who would have preferred a sure thing. Lorre was not a typical leading man, and ironically, the Moto series may have convinced Hollywood that his unique skills required careful casting. Film historian David Shipman once said that Lorre did not know how to make good interesting. He was not a conventional hero in terms of looks or style, he was far better at exposing and exploring the flaws in his characters than their strengths. Over the years, some film critics have argued that Lorre was rarely selected for roles which would have shown his true range of talent. But, in truth, Lorre's physical traits, and the peculiar quality of his voice, made him difficult to cast. In the final analysis, it is remarkable that he left behind such a distinguished body of work. Lorre was a unique presence and a very creative actor (and accomplished scene-stealer). He was, in the parlance of his profession, an actor's actor. Even the great Charlie Chaplin was impressed with the actor's skill, once telling a critic that Lorre was "the greatest actor alive."

Despite often being typed in sinister roles, Lorre was a personable man with a great sense of humor. When actress Debra Paget was at the Memphis Film Festival in the summer of 1997, she was questioned about Lorre, with whom she appeared in 1962 in *Tales of Terror* for director Roger Corman. (They had no scenes together because they appeared in different "tales.")

> Peter was a sweet man and quite a practical joker who was known for his pranks and foolishness on the set.

Paget also remembered a story director Corman had related about watching Lorre work (or work over) Boris Karloff:

> Lorre drove Karloff "nuts." They, of course, were friends, but Peter loved to improvise. He never did a reading or a line the same way twice. He even would change bits of business with props while they were filming.

Paget laughed remembering the story:

> Poor Boris. He was such a perfectionist. He always knew his lines and expected actors to perform the scene the way it was rehearsed. But, of course, that wasn't Peter. The camera would roll and you could almost see Boris brace himself for the worst.

Although this is a sweet story about an accomplished ham, there was a method to his madness which Lorre shared with many great, if wildly insecure, actors. They were all camera hogs who were skilled at getting the audience to notice them, even when the focus of a scene was on another actor. Claude Rains could literally maneuver an actor out of the camera's view by the way he positioned himself and moved within in a scene. Peter Lorre was also a master with props. For example, in the fifth entry in the series, *The Mysterious Mr. Moto,* Lorre has a field day with his eyeglasses. He takes

In the Mr. Moto films Lorre would have a field day with his eyeglasses, using them to call attention to his character.

them off and puts them back on throughout the picture for no apparent reason except to keep the focus on him. In one scene, in which he discusses strategy with an undercover agent, he takes his glasses off, puts them back not once but twice while the two exchange several lines of dialogue. Such gestures may be subtle, but they are comical when you look for them. It is enjoyable to watch Lorre with the volume turned down on the television to see him silently weave his own peculiar spell.

Twentieth Century-Fox was the home of *Charlie Chan.* Fox began the series in 1929 and it remains the big dog of detective programmers with more than 40 features produced before the series ended at Monogram Studios in 1949. However, the studio wasn't looking for a successor to Chan when they optioned Marquand's novel. It wasn't until they measured the public and critical reaction to *Think Fast, Mr. Moto* that they knew they had a winner and began plans to continue Moto with Lorre in the lead. Although Lorre

is the heart of the series, the films benefited from the workman-like contribution of director Norman Foster. Programmers like Chan or Moto were never afforded the budget, schedule or studio talent to make great movies, but Foster helped create a series which is of interest some 60 years after he directed the last feature. Foster, who co-wrote and directed six of the eight films in the series, began his career in Hollywood as an actor appearing in a number of forgettable features like *Skyscraper Souls* and *I Cover the Waterfront* (which he also directed). From 1937, until his death in 1970, Foster only directed and worked on screenplays. Besides the Moto series, Foster directed *Charlie Chan at Treasure Island* (one of the best of the Chan series and arguably Sidney Toler's best outing as the detective), *Journey into Fear* (a fine noir thriller which featured Orson Welles among others), *Rachel and the Stranger* (a family drama with a terrific cast which included Robert Mitchum, William Holden and Loretta Young) and *Davy Crockett* (the Disney feature starring Fess Parker which helped launch a merchandising craze).

Production on *Think Fast, Mr. Moto* began at the end of 1936 with Foster as director and a cast which included the wonderful character actor J. Carrol Naish who, in the 1950s, would play Charlie Chan in the television series. In fact, the entire series is blessed with contributions from some of the finest character actors of Hollywood's golden age, including Ward Bond, John Carradine, Keye Luke and Lon Chaney. The plots to all the Moto films are straight-forward, allowing for a good deal of action in the standard one hour–plus running time. *Think Fast, Mr. Moto* opens in San Francisco with the detective in disguise as a street peddler on the trail of some gem and narcotic smugglers. The investigation leads to an ocean steamer bound for Shanghai where Moto successfully rounds up the international crime ring. Lorre often appeared in disguises throughout the series but required little or no make-up as Mr. Moto relying instead on slicked back hair and a pair of round eyeglasses (which gave him an owl–like appearance). Most great screen actors can express more with a look than a page of dialogue and Lorre was no exception. In revisiting these films, we are reminded of Lorre's strong screen presence. He understood the power of the camera to convey the actor's emotion with the most subtle move or shift of the eye. However, it is possible to get too much of a good thing. In *Mr. Moto's Gamble* director James Tinling repeatedly tracks in on Lorre's mug, especially during the scenes at the boxing matches, so the actor can cue the audience as to what's going on in the story. It was a wrong decision, forcing Lorre to react to something he obviously couldn't see from his vantage point at the match.

Like Charlie Chan, Moto is also a fountain of wisdom when prompted for his observations about the human condition. In *Think Fast, Mr. Moto*, the detective reminds the audience that, "Half the world spends its time laughing at the other half and both are fools." Later he counsels a fun-loving associate that, "Beautiful girls are confusing to a man."

Many critics believe that *Think Fast, Mr. Moto* was the best film in the series. The trade paper *Variety* was very complimentary of Lorre's work in the film noting that, "He's no longer a bogeyman. When he smiles, it is not a wry, warped grimace. The new Peter Lorre will probably be rated as a find by others who heretofore knew him only as a dyed-in-the-wool villain." For the briefest of moments, Lorre appeared to be heading toward a new type of leading man, but fate and seven more Motos would cast his career in a different direction. Hollywood was not yet ready to accept the character actor as star. It would be another 30 years before the likes of Gene Hackman, Robert Duvall, Al Pacino and others would change the star paradigm in Tinseltown. In 1937, stars looked like Robert Taylor, not Peter Lorre.

Lorre as Mr. Moto in disguise for *Think Fast, Mr. Moto.*

Twentieth Century-Fox released the second

Peter Lorre and John Carradine in *Thank You, Mr. Moto.*

entry in the series, *Thank You, Mr. Moto*, in November 1937. The success of the first feature prompted the studio to authorize a larger budget for the picture than typically afforded such programmers, and it shows in the sets and overall presentation. In the story, Moto is competing with a gang of thugs to recover all six pieces of an ancient scroll that indicated the whereabouts of the treasure of Genghis Khan buried somewhere in the Gobi Desert. *Thank You, Mr. Moto* is the most bittersweet entry in the series. When Moto is unable to prevent the torture and murder of Madame Chung who had hired him to secure the scrolls or stop her son from taking his life in a ritual suicide, Moto promises that justice will be served. He tracks down their killers and destroys the scrolls because he knows they will only lead to more suffering and death. If the

Moto series provided a nice change of pace for Lorre, it rarely pushed him as an actor. However, Lorre's approach to the scene in which he comforts the dying Prince (Philip Ahn) affords a glimpse into the actor's depth and range. Lorre is able to convey both his compassion for the fatally wounded Prince and his inner rage at the men who committed the crime. The feelings are not in the pedestrian dialogue but rather in the actor's tone, the way he uses his hands and facial expressions. It's a moment for a great actor at the top of his game and one of Lorre's best scenes in the series. *Thank You, Mr. Moto* is my favorite feature in the series because this haunting story of duty and regret nestles at the border of film noir without the hackneyed humor that became an unwelcome requisite in future Moto adventures.

When Warner Oland died in 1938, Twentieth Century-Fox had already completed the script for his next feature in the series, which was to be titled *Charlie Chan at the Fights*. The Chan series was very popular with audiences of the day and studio executives were quick to instruct writers Charles Belden and Jerry Cady to rewrite their script for the next Mr. Moto. The result, entitled *Mr. Moto's Gamble*, is a disagreeable blend of comedy and mystery. Belden and Cady elected to keep Keye Luke in the story playing Lee Chan (Charlie Chan's son in the series) as a student studying criminology under Mr. Moto. The writers also pay homage to Chan in an exchange of dialogue between Moto and a police lieutenant. Moto acknowledges, "We are all but floundering amateurs in contrast... (to Chan)." In the story, Moto finds the murderer of a boxer who is killed in the ring under mysterious circumstances. The mystery elements of the story are on par with the first two features of the series, but the writers have left in the lame comedy bits which would mar, if not destroy, the latter Chans. In particular, all the scenes featuring Lee Chan (Keye Luke) and Wellington (Maxie Rosenbloom)

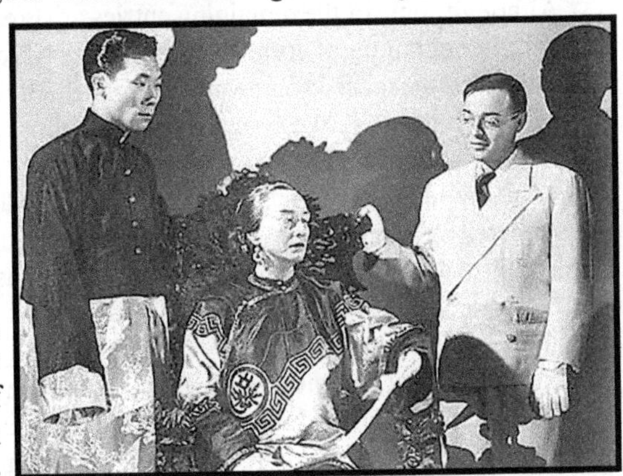

Philip Ahn, Pauline Frederick and Peter Lorre in Thank You, Mr. Moto.

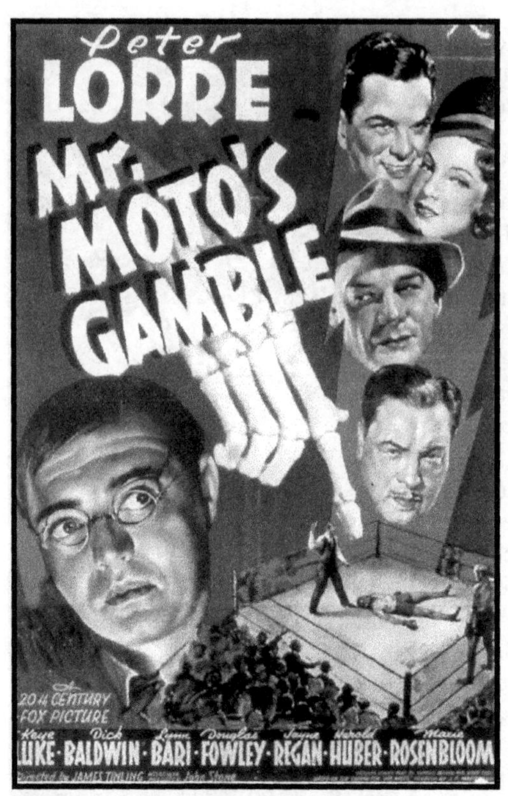

are pain-inducing. Their playful high jinks are one step removed from throwing pies at each other. In what can only be described as the worst sequence in the series, Chan and Wellington are jailed as desperadoes by a small-town sheriff whose procedures don't include checking the prisoners for firearms before putting them in the clink. As they ponder their fate, Wellington encourages Chan to hit him repeatedly in the head to help him remember an important clue in the case. The sheriff, hearing the commotion, arrives in time to engage in some goofy chatter that results in the boys escaping while locking up the lawman in the hoosegow.

This material wouldn't draw chuckles from Larry, Moe or Curly but, more importantly, it diminishes Moto by his association with such low-rent stooges. Lorre has little screen time in this entry. With his dialogue reduced to "Ah So" or something equally as inane in a number of scenes, Lorre goes wild with props. He sharpens pencils, plays with his hat and uses a program from the fights for multiple purposes. Certainly Michael Curtiz or another established director would have reigned in the diminutive actor but James Tinling, who was directing his one and only Moto film, let Lorre work the camera. *Mr. Moto's Gamble* is nearly a complete misfire and the low point in the series.

Although some of the remaining entries are great fun to watch, *Mr. Moto's Gamble* marked the beginning of formula filmmaking which would doom the series to the B track. Perhaps the most disagreeable component of this formula was the comic sidekick. Long a staple in the B Western, Hollywood chose also to burden their more famous sleuths with comic deadweight whose chief function seems to be getting in the hero's way. The brand of humor is always so juvenile that sidekicks make Jerry Lewis seem sophisticated by comparison. Most series had a regular sidekick, but Moto got different comic help with each feature. This is not to say that some of these sidekicks weren't capable actors, but their characters were so inept that the suspense and story- telling inevitably suffered.

Norman Foster returned to direct and co-author the screenplay for the fourth entry in the series, *Mr. Moto Takes a Chance*, which was released in early 1938. Although *Variety* found the film, "too melodramatic in its implausibilities to stack up well with predecessors," director Foster focused his attention on the mystery elements in the story and minimized the slapstick comedy that all but sunk *Mr. Moto's Gamble*. In

Robert Kent, Rochelle Hudson, Lorre and J. Edgar Bromberg in *Mr. Moto Takes a Chance.*

the story, Moto poses as an archaeologist working with an undercover British agent to discover the location of munitions in Indochina before they are delivered to the wrong hands. In what is surely intended as a tongue in cheek remark, character actor Chick Chandler tells his friend, "If he were casting horror pictures, I would have him (Moto) play the murderer." Lorre's role is better developed in this entry than in *Mr. Moto's Gamble* where he filled in for Charlie Chan, but this isn't a good film. The story does afford Lorre the opportunity to wear heavy make-up as an aged holy man, but even his reliable effort can't overcome the ludicrous plot development.

The Mysterious Mr. Moto (a.k.a. *Mysterious Mr. Moto of Devil's Island*), released in 1938, was based on the Marquand novel *Mr. Moto's Last Warning*. As was often the case during the series, the feature opens with Lorre in disguise, this time as a convict who escapes with a master criminal from Devil's Island to try to infiltrate the "League of Assassins" who are plotting evil doings in London. Although some critics at the time found this a "tired" entry in the series, it is, in retrospect, a satisfying mystery with a fine B cast including Leon Ames and Henry Wilcoxon. The feature has a great deal of atmosphere with smoke-filled pubs, streets in shadow and even a Holmesesque band of bad guys, the "League of Assassins."

It would be an omission in reviewing the series not to mention the racial stereotypes that were common in Hollywood films of this period. It has been well documented that black actors, like the talented Mantan Morland, were reduced to playing well-behaved domestics or fools afraid of their own shadow, but in more subtle ways, Hollywood's international trio of sleuths, Chan, Moto and Mr. Wong faced a similar bias. In all their films, the popular threesome were asexual characters who not only didn't get the girl,

Peter Lorre takes a break from filming the Mr. Moto series.

they weren't even allowed to appear interested in the opposite sex. At a time when other popular series of the era like *The Falcon*, *The Saint* or *Bulldog Drummond* featured white leading men with healthy libidos, Moto and company were allowed to be clever and even honorable, but running with the ladies was a cinema taboo. It was assumed by studios of the period that audiences would not accept or sit still for sexual horseplay from a non-white leading man (even when a *white* actor was playing the role).

Mr. Moto's Last Warning is probably the best-known feature in the series because it is the only title in the public domain and has been available on video for years. Unfortunately, it is the only series entry that is readily available. Over the last decade Turner Classic Movies and American Movie Classics have done an exemplary job of reviving the popular detective series from the 1930s and 1940s like *The Saint, The Falcon, Boston Blackie* and *Charlie Chan.* These films are often shown in restored prints with some appropriate fanfare, but not, as of this writing, Mr. Moto. I have been unable to

Warren Hymer, Peter Lorre, Robert Lowery and Richard Lane in ***Danger Island.***

discover whether the problem is ownership rights or the availability of suitable prints, but hopefully Mr. Moto will soon be rediscovered.

Mr. Moto's Last Warning is clearly a fun entry in the series. It features an exceptional cast including Ricardo Cortez, George Sanders and, in his second appearance in the series, John Carradine. The story opens with an associate and fellow detective impersonating Mr. Moto so the real detective can remain undercover while investigating a band of international bad guys who plan to blow up the Suez Canal. The villains prove to be quite successful, killing both the man impersonating Moto, and another detective assigned to the case (Carradine). The thugs also manage to capture Moto, and like an unwanted cat, he is tossed in the ocean tied in a burlap sack. Of course, the resourceful detective escapes the near-death experience and rounds up the evildoers in a fast-moving 71 minutes. By this point in the series, Lorre could put his performance on autopilot, but this isn't the case. *Mr. Moto's Last Warning* is a B quality good time with Lorre in fine form. Lorre's best work as Moto can be found in the features with the better scripts, including the first two Mr. Moto films and *Mr. Moto's Last Warning.*

The seventh film in the series, *Danger Island,* benefits from a strong story, although it is not based on one of the Marquand books. The source instead was a novel written by John Vandercook entitled, *Murder in Trinidad: A Case in the Career of Bertram Lynch.* In fact, the novel had been filmed first in 1934 as *Murder in Trinidad* and was

Lorre, Lionel Atwill and Joseph Schildkraut in *Mr. Moto Takes a Vacation*.

remade in 1954 as *Caribbean Mystery*. The picture is the last feature in the series not directed by Norman Foster. The studio assigned the job to Herbert Leeds who was a competent director of second features. Unlike Tinling, who directed the most atypical feature in the series, Leeds understands the formula and directs the action accordingly. Author Vandercook adapted his own novel and changed the setting to Puerto Rico where Moto is tracking gem smugglers who have murdered the last investigator assigned to the case. The story has several good plot twists although *Variety* gave the production a lukewarm review: "There is a sameness about the Mr. Moto pictures yet the plot of each new story surrounding the detective's adventures is always intriguing."

In retrospect, Mr. Moto is a good series but not in the same league with the better Holmes or Chan features. This is unfortunate since it could have offered so much more. All the popular detective series of the period used the same formula. The only real difference was the particular talents of the star and how the studio chose to use him. The Holmes series played to Basil Rathbone's strengths as an actor, allowing him to create a screen persona which has survived him. Unfortunately, Twentieth Century-Fox did not do the same for Lorre. The fault is less in the lackluster writing as in the failure to give the actor a chance to weave his dark spell. It is clear the studio was trying him out as a leading man in something light and playful. Perhaps Lorre could have given the character of Moto the edge he deserved if the formula hadn't gotten in the way.

Virginia Field, Lorre as Mr. Moto and John Davidson in *Mr. Moto Takes a Vacation.*

Peter Lorre's last appearance as the detective was in *Mr. Moto Takes a Vacation.* It was shot in mid-1939 and was not intended to end the series, but by the time of its release, the studio was becoming aware of the anti-Japanese sentiment growing in the country just prior to the outbreak of Word War II. The studio had signed Lorre to play Moto at least through 1940, which, at the pace of production, would have meant at least three more features, but that was not to be. The executives at Twentieth Century-Fox had their collective thumb on the pulse of the American audience and felt the detective had overstayed his welcome. Following the completion of *Mr. Moto Takes a Vacation*, the mysterious sleuth was allowed to slip quietly into film history. Peter Lorre would also leave the studio in 1940, choosing to freelance rather than be tied down by a studio contract.

Although *New World Telegram* gave this final feature a healthy whack, even complaining that Peter Lorre "plays the bland detective blandly," *Mr. Moto Takes a Vacation* is not without interest. In the feature, Moto is pursuing a murderer who is intent on stealing the recently excavated Queen of Sheba's jeweled crown. Moto is particularly interested in the case because he believes there is a Moriarty-esque prince of crime behind the evildoings. The chase ends at the museum where Moto unmasks this

super criminal and laments that a vacation is not in the cards for him. Lorre's Moto is an engaging footnote in an unusual career. It was not his best work but, given the limitations of a B series, he was able to create a memorable character.

Walking the Shark is a web page devoted to the offbeat life of Peter Lorre. The author notes that Lorre has become a fixture in our pop culture. He is mentioned in the novel *Catcher in the Rye*, numerous cartoon characters mimic his voice and a kid's cereal bears a logo of his likeness. On a ghoulish note, he mentions that two attempts have been made to steal the late actor's ashes from the cemetery, once by a group of airheads who were convinced that Lorre possessed supernatural powers which they were going to tap into by bringing the actor back from the dead. By all accounts, they were unsuccessful and Lorre has recently been allowed to rest in peace. But as an actor and screen personality, Peter Lorre is alive and well. He was a pixie who escaped from a Gothic fairy tale. He was also a hell of an actor. His performances have become the heart of a mystery we are still discovering.

Think Fast, Mr. Moto
CREDITS: Producer: Sol M. Wurtzel; Director: Norman Foster; Screenplay: Howard Ellis Smith and Norman Foster; Based on the Novel by John P. Marquand; Photography: Harry Jackson; Twentieth Century-Fox, 1937

CAST: Peter Lorre (Mr. Moto); Virginia Field (Gloria Danton); Thomas Beck (Bob Hitchings); J. Carrol Naish (Adram)

Thank You, Mr. Moto
CREDITS: Producer: Sol M. Wurtzel; Director: Norman Foster; Screenplay: Norman Foster and Willis Cooper; Based on the Novel by John P. Marquand; Photography: Virgil Miller; Twentieth Century-Fox, 1937

CAST: Peter Lorre (Mr. Moto); Pauline Frederick (Madame Chung); Thomas Beck (Tom Nelson); Philip Ahn (Prince Chung)

Mr. Moto's Gamble
CREDITS: Producer: Sol M. Wurtzel; Director: James Tinling; Screenplay: Charles Belden and Jerry Cady; Photography: Lucien Androit, Twentieth Century-Fox, 1938

CAST: Peter Lorre (Mr. Moto); Keye Luke (Lee Chan); Douglas Fowley (Nick Crowder); Maxie Rosenbloom (Wellington); John Hamilton (Philip Benton); Lon Chaney (Joey); Ward Bond (Big Moran

Mr. Moto Takes a Chance
CREDITS: Producer: Sol M. Wurtzel; Director: Norman Foster; Screenplay: William Cooper, Norman Foster, Lou Breslow, and John Patrick; Photography: Virgil Miller; Twentieth Century-Fox, 1938

CAST: Peter Lorre (Mr. Moto); Rochelle Hudson (Vicki); Chick Chandler (Chick Davis)

The Mysterious Mr. Moto
CREDITS: Producer: Sol M. Wurtzel; Director: Norman Foster; Screenplay: Philip MacDonald and Norman Foster; Based on a Novel by John P. Marquand; Photography: Bernard Herzbrun and Lewis Creber; Twentieth Century-Fox, 1938

CAST: Peter Lorre (Mr. Moto); Leon Ames (Paul Brissac); Henry Wilcoxon (Anton Darvak)

Mr. Moto's Last Warning
CREDITS: Producer: Sol M. Wurtzel; Director: Norman Foster; Screenplay: Philip MacDonald and Norman Foster; Photography: Virginia Miller; Twentieth Century-Fox; 1939

CAST: Peter Lorre (Mr. Moto); Richard Cortez (Fabian);Virginia Field (Connie); John Carradine(Danforth); George Sanders (Eric Morvel)

Danger Island
CREDITS: Producer: John Stone; Director: Herbert L. Leeds; Screenplay: John W. Vandercook, John Reinhardt, George Bricker and Peter Milne; Photography: Lucien Androit; Twentieth Century-Fox, 1939

CAST: Peter Lorre (Mr. Moto); Jean Hersholt (Sutter); Richard Lane (Commissioner Gordon)

Mr. Moto Takes a Vacation
CREDITS: Producer: Sol M. Wurtzel; Director: Norman Foster; Screenplay: Philip MacDonald and Norman Foster; Photography: Charles Clarke; Twentieth Century-Fox, 1939

CAST: Peter Lorre (Mr. Moto); Joseph Schildkraut (Bayard Manderson); Lionel Atwill (Professor Hildebrand)

ISLAND OF DOOMED MEN
1940
by Steven Kronenberg

A famous anecdote about Peter Lorre is recounted by Patrick McGilligan in his excellent book *Fritz Lang: The Nature of the Beast* (St. Martin's, 1997). In the wake of his startling performance as the child murderer in *M*, and as Hitler was rising to power, Lorre fled Germany for Paris. When UFA Studios begged him to return, he cabled a response: "There is not enough space in Germany for two murderers like Hitler and me."

Lorre knew a psychopathic tyrant when he saw one—and in *Island of Doomed Men*, he got to *play* one. In *Island*, Lorre portrays the shady and sinister Stephen Danel, who cons paroled *ex*-cons into traveling with him to his island with false promises of jobs and new leases on life. Instead, Lorre's Danel brutally enslaves the jailbirds with no means of escape. The diminutive Danel lords over the island like a schizoid Napoleon, until he is finally done in by his long-suffering wife (Rochelle Hudson) and an undercover agent, Mark Sheldon (Robert Wilcox) who is sent to Danel's Dead Man's Island to expose and capture the evildoer.

Lorre is a joy to behold in *Island*, but the little B film is also an important entry in Lorre's canon: It is arguably the first film to feature the smarmy, shady Lorre of the 1940s—the one Lorre perfected in *The Maltese Falcon* (1941), *Casablanca* (1942) and *Invisible Agent* (1942). The Lorre of the 1930s was an entirely different breed, characterized by chilling yet oddly sympathetic turns in *M* (1931), *Mad Love* (1935) and *Crime and Punishment* (1935). Lorre's portrayals in these three films were among his most complex and memorable performances. But it is the sneaky, corrupt Lorre of the 1940s that etched the actor's place in mainstream Hollywood. And *Island of Doomed Men* gives us a look at the genesis of Lorre's 1940s style.

Throughout the film, Lorre adopts a decadent, perverse look highlighted by his famed hooded eyes, parted lips and leering, toothy grin. Lorre's Danel struts his island like a decadent dictator, immaculately dressed in white suit and pith helmet, calmly and indifferently puffing a cigarette. And Lorre's sad eyes (which evoke sympathy even for the dastardly Danel) contrast with his sadistic glee as his Danel orders one of his ex-con/slaves whipped while calmly intoning: "I hope we'll hear good reports on your conduct in the future."

Island also allowed Lorre to convey his trademarked sense of evil coated with a decadent, blasé attitude—a style seen in Lorre's later 1940s work. In one scene, he shrugs off his wife Lorraine by indifferently muttering: "I had a very annoying afternoon." In another, he apathetically tells the island's degenerate, drunken doctor (perennial Three Stooges foil, Kenneth MacDonald): "You really ought to keep your

Don Beddoe, Robert Wilcox, Charles Middleton and Peter Lorre (Photofest)

hands cleaner." In scenes like these, we see the genesis of Lorre's ability to understate dialogue—an art which the actor continued to polish throughout his career.

But Lorre's skill at understatement is best displayed in his scenes with Rochelle Hudson. It is clear that Hudson's Lorraine Danel is just as much a prisoner as the island's hapless parolees. Note Lorre's indifference and lassitude as Hudson, obviously frightened, attempts to play a piano piece for her sinister spouse. Amidst the music, Lorre's Danel impassively stares into space, and then, with half closed eyes and wicked smirk, tells Hudson she is doomed to remain on the island with him. He then compounds Hudson's torment by suavely and unctuously lighting one of his ever-present cigarettes. The scene is capped when Lorre turns to Hudson and, affecting that famous toothy smile, says: "What I own I keep!" When Lorre orders Hudson to her room, she immediately goes—because *we* know that *she* knows that she had *better* go! Note, too, Lorre's dazed, almost distracted indifference as he calmly confronts Lorraine and Sheldon attempting an escape by night: "You forget, Lorraine, I'm a very light sleeper." And watch his slow, deliberate lope after he stands eye-to-eye with Hudson's Lorraine, listening to her tell him how much she hates him. In this scene, Lorre's eyes display a fascinating combination of apathy limned with sadness. And when Hudson's Lorraine tries to conceal the fact that she is aiding Wilcox's Sheldon, she tries to phony-

Rochelle Hudson and Peter Lorre in a studio pose for the film. (Photofest)

up a happy face and attitude for Lorre: "I'm just happy because my husband's home!" Lorre's sinister, threatening reply: "I don't like it when you talk like that!"

Lorre affects that same sense of petulant decadence with *Island's* other supporting players. When MacDonald's Doctor asks Lorre what he plans to do about undercover agent Sheldon, Lorre's face breaks into a sinister sneer as he says: "I have many plans for (him)..." And watch Lorre as he finally corners the cagey Sheldon and demands a confession. As Sheldon resists, Lorre delightedly tells his sadistic overseer (Charles Middleton, who played the equally sadistic Ming in Universal's *Flash Gordon* serials): "I'm afraid you will have to use your *ingenuity* on him, Captain."

But in portraying Danel, Lorre's calm exterior belies a penchant for sudden and startling mood swings. In his final confrontation with Lorraine and Sheldon, Lorre calmly tells the two to stand "... close... very close," as he softly tells Sheldon about his wife's beauty. Then, immediately and effortlessly, Lorre turns angry and bitter, as he glares at Sheldon and mutters: "Then *you* came. You *touched* my wife!" Lorre's memorable style was marked by his ability to convey frightening anger, seething beneath a veneer of calm and charm.

Indeed, Lorre's skillful mood swings dominate the second half of *Island.* Watch his composed mood shift into blind rage as he confronts the primate pet of ex-con Siggy: "Keep that *monkey* away from me!" In fact, Siggy's simian is a constant source of torment for Lorre. Whenever the creature is underfoot, Lorre's mood shifts furiously: "I *told* you I didn't want da monkee in da house!" Lorre's palpable anger in these scenes is delightful—until, in an act of irrational fury, he grabs the animal and shoots it. With the deadly deed done, Lorre's mood comes full circle *again,* as he dazedly struggles to calm himself. It is a scene that amply displays Lorre's gift for emotional range—and his ability to startle us with extreme contrasts in mood.

But no scene in *Island* better displays Lorre's talent for mood contrast than the film's conclusion. After being fatally shot by Siggy, who avenges the murder of his monkey, Lorre's voice takes on a pitiful wail as he moans: "Everything on this island belonged to me!" With that scene, Lorre, with wide eyes and upturned mouth, beautifully conveys Danel's greed, frustration, and sadness.

In addition to being a precursor to Lorre's 1940s style, *Island of Doomed Men* is one of Columbia's finest B efforts. The film is well-cast with familiar character veterans like Charles Middleton, George E. Stone and Kenneth MacDonald. The picture was helmed by Charles T. Barton, who later directed *Abbott & Costello Meet Frankenstein* (1948). Barton and cameraman Benjamin D. Kline shot the film in dark, atmospheric tones conveying a sense of oppression reminiscent of 1932's *The Most Dangerous Game.* Still, *Island of Doomed Men* is clearly Peter Lorre's show—and it's a fascinating example of the actor's ability to modulate moods and etch a portrait of evil tempered by subtlety and sadness. It's also an excellent guidepost to the later portrayals for which Lorre would be loved and remembered.

CREDITS: Producer: Wallace MacDonald; Director: Charles Barton; Screenplay: Robert D. Andrews; Cinematography: Benjamin D. Kline; Editor: James Sweeney; Music Director: M.W. Stoloff; Art Design: Lionel Banks; Costume Designs: Robert Kalloch; Released in 1940 by Columbia Pictures; Running Time: 70 minutes

CAST: Peter Lorre (Stephen Danel); Rochelle Hudson (Lorraine Danel); Robert Wilcox (Mark Sheldon); George E. Stone (Siggy); Charles Middleton (Captain); Kenneth MacDonald (Doctor); Don Beddoe (Brand); Stanley Brown (Eddie); Earl Gunn (Mitchell); Don Douglas (Official); Bruce Bennett (Hazen); Sam Ash (Ames); Eddie Laughton (Borgo); John Tyrrell (Durkin); Richard Fiske (Hale)

STRANGE CARGO
1940
by David H. Smith

Filmmakers have always been drawn to the compelling mystery of ambiguity and of gray areas. The certainties of black and white are best left to the clergy.

1940's *Strange Cargo* blurred the boundary lines between the two fields, fanning to flame a smoldering controversy regarding movies' tacit agnosticism. The tinderboxes of risqué banter and the implied liaisons were all too much, even though the sacrosanct finale did its best to extinguish it all.

Strange Cargo was controversial before its first showing. The National Legion of Catholic Decency claimed it "present[ed] a naturalistic concept of religion contrary to the teachings of Christ, irreverent use of Scripture and lustful implications in dialogue and situations." (So weighty was the Legion's censure that leading American distributors did not show a singe condemned film from 1936 to 1943.)" After compliant producing studio MGM made a few adjusting cuts, the film's rating was upgraded to "A-2" (unobjectionable for adults); but even so, the picture was banned in Detroit and Providence as well as in many other cities.

Distribution snags notwithstanding, *Strange Cargo* still managed to provide Peter Lorre with a characterization that audiences and casting directors would associate him with for the majority of the 1940s: the jittery informer. As time went on and scripts were doled out, in everyone's eyes but his, Lorre was at his best as the resident lowlife stool pigeon.

Based on the 1936 Simon & Schuster bestseller *Not Too Narrow... Not Too Deep* by Richard Sale, *Strange Cargo* related the story of the escape of six (reduced from the book's 10) desperate men from an unnamed convict island in the Caribbean. A motley crew (in the truest sense of the cliché) of murderers, thieves and lechers, they determine to risk their lives on a wild gamble.

The fugitives are joined at the last minute by another prisoner, an enigmatic, philosophical stranger none of them has seen before. Together, they struggle not only to escape the horrors of a convict island and the treachery of the sea, but also to free themselves from the shackles of guilty consciences.

Strange Cargo was Clark Gable's follow-up to *Gone With the Wind* (1939), and as such there was a great buzz of anticipation about the movie. Released less than four months after David O. Selznick's epic Civil War romance (the longest and most expensive—$4.25 million—film ever made) and its eight Oscar wins still in the offing, a skittish MGM decide to ensure *Strange Cargo*'s success by casting him with Joan Crawford yet again (for the eighth and final time), still trading on the notoriety of the pair's well-publicized affair in *Possession* (1931).

Peter Lorre as M'sieu Pig and Joan Crawford as Julie in *Strange Cargo*. (Photofest)

At the time, MGM was less happy with Crawford, whose career was in decline (her last box-office year was 1936), yet she was still hounding the studio for more substantial parts. Too, it couldn't have done much for ego when publicity materials ballyhooed that her wardrobe for the movie consisted of three ready-to-wear dresses which cost under $40 (never mind the sequined, backless little number she wears as the local jungle chanteuse!). Crawford regarded *Strange Cargo* as another setback.

The most noteworthy performance in *Strange Cargo* comes from former stage and silent-film actor Ian Hunter as the mysterious "Cambreau." Usually cast as a decent, self-sacrificing man, it is the Afrikaner actor's mild features and genial manner that form the basis for the mystery at the heart—or perhaps the soul—of the movie.

At times the clues as to Cambreau's true identity are subtle; at other times the hints are so conspicuous as to invite audience groans (note his symbolic crucifixion pose as he hangs onto a piece of driftwood during a gale). In Sale's book, christened with the first name Jean, Cambreau's initials made his presence all the more redolent of the Only-Begotten.

Billed fourth, Peter Lorre was on familiar stomping grounds. Devil's Island was the most southerly of the Iles du Salut, in the Caribbean Sea off French Guiana. It was the site of a penal colony from 1852 until 1951, and used mostly for political prisoners. Lorre had masqueraded as a Devil's Island prisoner in *Mysterious Mr. Moto*, and within two months of *Strange Cargo*'s release would appear on the silver screen as the pith-helmeted owner of the similar Dead Man's Isle in *Island of Doomed Men*; demoted, he would even play a bona fide escapee in *Passage to Marseille*.

Here, in *Strange Cargo*, Lorre essays a minor though pivotal role with the unflattering appellation of "M'sieu Pig." Though some texts and reference works supply him with the surname "Cochon" (the French word for "pig"), he is never referred to as that; the character does not even exist in the book.

Lorre plays the character like the name denotes, a craven whiner who preys on the mistakes of others to make ends meet. As a tipster whom even the authorities loathe ("...vermin like him," grumbles warden Frederic Worlock), Pig lurks in shadows around the local nightclub and collects the bounty on recaptured convicts. Swooping down like some porcine parasite, he even propositions a hard-bitten cabaret singer (Joan Crawford) as she finds herself on the verge of being deported for consorting with a prisoner (Clark Gable).

Forced to choose between the grinning convict with the pencil mustache and the sweating stoolie with the bulging eyes ("You're the one man in the world I could never get low enough to touch!"), Crawford's character throws in with the escapees.

M'sieu Pig disappears for the middle portion of *Strange Cargo*, detailing the torturous jungle escape and debilitating sea voyage to the distant mainland. But Lorre returns for the frenzied denouement, surprisingly holding his own in a knock-down, drag-out fight with the rugged Gable, and even winning (through default) the privilege of Crawford's (*ahem!*) company.

But Gable's character sees the light, figuratively and literally, and meets up with Crawford at the end as he surrenders to serve out his sentence. Lorre is left to look moon-faced and Bambi-eyed and... well, forgotten, really. His fate is never revealed, an unsatisfying misstep for a movie that had, until that moment, dealt so carefully with the repercussions of crime and cowardice. (One resource used makes mention of M'sieu Pig's suicide, an act frowned on by the Production Code, so this may be among the last-minute conciliatory cuts made by MGM before release.)

In spite of the abbreviated, bookending nature of his part, Lorre received several good reviews for *Strange Cargo*. The unidentified reviewer in *Variety* noted he "has a particularly despicable role, and pops out of shadows at such odd times that audiences will accept him as a ten-twent-thirt villyun [*sic*]."

Howard Barnes, in his critique of the movie in *The New York Herald Tribune*, cited each actor in turn, finishing with, "Then there is Peter Lorre, that greatly neglected and fine actor, in the part of a slimy stool pigeon."

Film Daily said the acting was "high-grade," mentioning "Peter Lorre is M. Pig, and most expressive about it." *Time* magazine recognized that *Strange Cargo*, derived part of its strange power "from the fact that all the actors... are perfectly typed."

Gable is the unshaven epitome of machismo. Unapologetic for his crimes as a thief, unbroken from weeks of solitary confinement, Gable swaggers, sweats and sweet-talks (he never calls Crawford's character anything but "babe" or "baby") throughout *Strange Cargo*, coasting on his estimable movie star charisma.

At the time of the movie's release, Clark Gable was the biggest male star of the day, the so-called "King" of Hollywood, and would prove to be box-office gold for another 20 years. Tragedy struck in 1942 when third wife Carole Lombard died in a plane crash while returning from a War Bond Drive. Deep in mourning, Gable joined the Army Air Corps, returning triumphantly to the screen in 1945 for *Adventure* ("Gable's back and [Greer] Garson's got him" trumpeted the ads). In his three decades of stardom, the only complaint his female co-stars ever raised was that his breath was occasionally bad.

As Julie, Crawford is the cliché "fallen woman," alluringly photographed through the haze of a diffusion filter that would have made Doris Day proud. Her character has resigned herself to a loveless life, fending off the advances of men she deems too disreputable even for her marginal standards. As the elements take their toll on her during the escape, she becomes disheveled and unbuttoned, all but revealing her "ninny pies" (as the off-screen Crawford referred to women's breasts), but still earthy enough to stir the libidos of her cohorts.

Soon after *Strange Cargo* and a handful of other pictures, MGM would write Joan Crawford off as "box-office poison" and terminate her contract, casting her adrift in the Hollywood sea. Ambitious and remarkably adaptable, Crawford became a star at Warner Bros. playing in women's pictures. It was mostly soap opera stuff ignored by critics, until she earned raves and won an best actress Oscar in 1945 as a sacrificial mother named *Mildred Pierce*.

It was a plum year for hulking character actor Albert Dekker, here cast as Gable's rival for leader of the escapees. Soon after *Strange Cargo*, Dekker would assume the monocular title role in the science-fiction classic *Dr. Cyclops*, directed by Ernest Schoedsack, one of the creators of *King Kong* (1933). A three-strip Technicolor triumph of mattes and back projection, the part of the giant mad scientist would endear Dekker to genre fans for years to come (who, no pun intended, turned a blind eye to his transvestite death in 1968).

Born Pal Lukàcs aboard a train while his mother was traveling to Budapest, Paul Lukas was only three years away from winning a best actor Academy Award for his portrayal of an anti-Nazi underground fighter in *Watch on the Rhine*. He shared a common thread with Lorre by earning good notices under the direction of Alfred Hitchcock for 1938's *The Lady Vanishes*, much as Lorre had with his English-speaking début four years before that in *The Man Who Knew Too Much*; Lukas and Lorre would be reunited in *20,000 Leagues Under the Sea* as a cold, intellectual professor and his naively inquisitive valet.

The semi-religious theme of *Strange Cargo* is unique among films of the era, but typical of what Peter Lorre could expect of his nascent Hollywood studio career.

Strange Cargo. Strange movie.

CREDITS: Producer: Joseph L. Mankiewicz; Director: Frank Borzage; Screenplay: Lawrence Hazard, Based on the Book *Not Too Narrow... Not Too Deep* by Richard Sale; Musical Score: Franz Waxman; Recording Director: Douglas Shearer; Art Director: Cedric Gibbons; Associate: Daniel B. Cathcart; Set Decorations: Edwin B. Willis; Make-Up Created by Jack Dawn; Director of Photography: Robert Planck, A.S.C.; Film Editor: Robert J. Kern; Copyrighted 1940 by Loew's Incorporated; Released by Metro-Goldwyn-Mayer on March 1, 1940; 113 minutes

CAST: Joan Crawford (Julie); Clark Gable (André Verne); Ian Hunter (Cambreau); Peter Lorre (M'sieu Pig); Paul Lukas (Carl Hessler); Albert Dekker (Henry Moll); J. Edward Bromberg (Rudolph Flaubert); Eduardo Cianelli (Jesus Telez); John Arledge (Jacques Duford); Frederic Worlock (Grideau); Bernard Nedell (Marfeau); Victor Varconi (Fisherman); Paul Fix (Louis Benet); Francis McDonald (Moussenq); Betty Compson (Suzanne); Charles Judels (Renard); Jack Mulhall (Dunning); Dewey Robinson (Georges); Harry Cording, Richard Alexander, Budd Fine, James Pierce, Hal Wynants, Christian J. Frank, Mitchell Lewis (Guards); Gene Coogan, Eddie Foster, Frank Lackteen, Harry Semels (Convicts); Art Dupuis (Orderly); Stanley Andrews (Constable); William Edmunds (Watchman)

STRANGER ON THE THIRD FLOOR
1940
by Mark Clark

Crazed Dr. Gogol cackling in his weird neck harness. Intense Joel Cairo training a pistol on Sam Spade. Disillusioned Janos Szabo studying his horribly scarred features in a mirror.

These are a few of the famous faces of Peter Lorre. In my recollection, however, one image stands out above all others: The nameless stranger with the curious grin, winding his long, white scarf around his neck.

For me, *Stranger on the Third Floor* remains the quintessential Peter Lorre movie. Part of the reason for this is purely personal. I first saw the film on late night TV when I was maybe 10 years old, in those halcyon days before home video. It petrified me. For some time afterward, I became unnerved any time I met a man wearing a scarf.

Many years passed before I saw the movie again, and in the interim I forgot the name of the film I had seen. For years, I believed the movie I had watched that midnight long ago was Fritz Lang's *M*. Then at last I saw *M* and realized I was mistaken. Finally, about 10 years ago, I caught *Stranger on the Third Floor* on American Movie Classics. When Lorre appeared, sporting that white scarf, chills immediately shot up and down my spine.

Unlike many movies I loved as a child, *Stranger* held its own against my fond memories. I discovered (or rediscovered) an even better film than I recalled. I have seen *Stranger* probably a dozen times since, and each time I unearth in it a new delight. However, my principal joy remains the same: Lorre's exquisite performance.

Despite extremely limited screen time, Lorre dominates the film. He packs every line, every gesture with meaning. This is boiled down, highly concentrated Peter Lorre. Never again would the actor accomplish so much with so few lines, not even in his memorable *Casablanca* cameo.

The movie unspools for 20 minutes before Lorre makes his first appearance. In the meantime, testimony by reporter Michael Ward (John McGuire) helps convict accused murderer Joe Briggs (Elisha Cook, Jr.), despite the defendant's desperate pleas of innocence. Ward's girlfriend Jane (Margaret Tallichet) believes Briggs. The young reporter suffers the first of two harrowing night sequences.

Lost in his own thoughts, Ward barely notices the Stranger when they first meet. But immediately the audiences' eyes seize on Lorre. He is slumped on the steps to Ward's apartment building, with his hat cocked sideways on his head, nervously fidgeting with a long white scarf. The Stranger looks up at Ward with his round, tormented eyes, then

Peter Lorre stars as the tormented Stranger.

stands, smirks and tips his hat. Lorre has no dialogue in this sequence. He's all shifty looks and diabolical grins, but makes a powerful impression nonetheless. "What an evil face!" Ward "thinks" (in voice-over narration) as the Stranger saunters away.

Later that evening, the Stranger returns and (off-screen) murders Ward's snooping neighbor. Ward gets blamed for the crime, and this time he is falsely convicted. No one except Jane believes his story about a strange man "with thick lips, bulgy eyes and a long, white scarf." She begins canvassing the neighborhood on a frenzied but fruitless search for the Stranger. Along the way she encounters a host of colorful character players in memorable walk-ons, especially Robert Dudley's postman.

Exhausted and disheartened, she stops at a diner. While she catches her breath, Lorre's hands come into frame with his face off-camera and he speaks his first line of the film. It's appropriately bizarre: "I'd like a couple of hamburgers, and I'd like them raw." Clever director Boris Ingster knew audiences would recognize Lorre's voice at once. As Lorre speaks, Jane has her head down. Viewers want to call to her, "Look up! It's him!" This Hitchcockian device is just one of several brilliant turns by Ingster.

Jane turns and comes face-to-face with the Stranger. For the first time we realize how shabby looking his clothes are. Jane follows him into the street, where he feeds the raw hamburger to a stray dog. "He followed me for two blocks, I had to get him something to eat," the Stranger explains.

This tiny scene quickly humanizes Lorre's bogey-man. He and the dog are two of a kind, both strays. "I wish I could keep him," he laments, "but I have no home to give him."

After seeming smug and malevolent earlier, Lorre now acts fragile and frightened. "Why are you looking at me like that?" he asks as Jane stares at him. He bids her goodnight and, as he walks away, reveals his scarf from under his jacket. Jane immediately recognizes the Stranger is, in fact, the man for whom she's been searching. She bolts after him.

"What do you want? Why are you following me?" the Stranger asks. Lorre's phrasing suddenly becomes formal, almost aristocratic. The softness in his voice just moments before disappears. Subtly, he is demonstrating the way his character's fractured psyche weaves between emotional states. The Stranger agrees to walk the girl home, but grows suspicious again when she begins discussing the recent murders.

"Did they send you to take me back?" he asks, his voice suddenly hushed.

"No! Who?" Jane asks.

Lorre, now panicky, looks around with feverish paranoia. "Don't you know?" he asks. "The people who lock you up!"

Shortly afterward, when he complains that "the people who lock you up" also "put you in a shirt with long sleeves and pour ice water on you," it becomes clear that the Stranger is as much victim as victimizer.

Jane calms him by reminding him that they wouldn't send a woman after him. The Stranger chuckles, relieved.

"The only person who ever was kind to me was a woman," he says. Suddenly all emotion drains from his face. His voice grows dreamy and remorseful. "She's dead now," he adds.

The Stranger is terrified he will be sent back to the asylum, and confesses he committed the second murder (the one for which Ward was convicted) because "he said he was going to report me. I *had* to kill him." Lorre delivers the line with so much conviction that its mad logic seems inescapable.

After Jane fails in an attempt to call for help, the Stranger realizes he has been duped. Lorre grows chillingly calm. He places a hand on the girl's shoulder and asks softly, "Why did you lie?" An instant later he is boiling with rage, choking her and snarling, "I'll not go back there!"

Jane (Margaret Tallichet) asks the Stranger (Lorre) to walk her home.

She breaks free from him and dashes across the street. The Stranger gives chase and—in a convenient *deus ex machina*—is run over by a truck. Before he dies, he confesses to a policeman that he committed the murders for which Ward and Briggs were convicted. "But I'm not going back," he adds, as his voice grows dreamy again. For Lorre's Stranger death represents a macabre victory (much like Paul Newman's demise in *Cool Hand Luke*).

Many writers have invested great significance in the fact that before finding his niche as an actor, Lorre studied psychiatry. Some contend this gave him special insight into his mad characters. This is probably an overstatement. But certainly Lorre's interest in psychiatry, paired with the charitable work for the mentally ill which he quietly performed throughout his life, demonstrates that the actor had profound empathy for people with troubled minds.

That empathy allows Lorre to create realistic, three-dimensional personalities instead of typical fright flick caricatures. For comparison's sake, imagine how Bela Lugosi or John Carradine might have handled Lorre's part in *Stranger*. Lorre saw his characters as infirm rather than evil. He always emphasized the redeeming traits of even the vilest villain (as in the scene with the puppy and the hamburger).

As in his star-making turn in *M*, along with other pictures such as *Mad Love* and *The Beast with Five Fingers*, his characterization here is believable menacing, yet he

Lorre brings a brutal intensity to his role as the Stranger when he tries to strangle Jane.

generates as much pathos as fear. In fact, his performance in *Stranger* could serve as a sort of Cliffs Notes for Lorre's entire catalog of movie madmen.

If you will excuse another diversion into personal recollection, I enjoyed Lorre's performance in *Stranger on the Third Floor* for one final reason. For decades my father has battled bipolar disorder (what they used to call manic-depression) and has at times been institutionalized for brief periods. Unlike Lorre's Stranger, my father is not at all violent. However, of all the actors among all the thousands of screen portrayals of mentally ill characters that I have viewed, Lorre alone captures the look of panic I have seen in my father's eyes at the prospect of being hospitalized again. The Stranger's haunted stare is heartbreakingly authentic.

Lorre's brilliant portrayal is just one component (granted an integral one) of an endlessly fascinating film. Many film historians credit *Stranger on the Third Floor* as the first film noir. It certainly contains all the noir trademarks, although I consider film noir a movement or a trend rather than a genre and it takes more than one of anything to represent a trend.

Most of the other critical laurels bestowed on the film these days arise from an amazing nightmare sequence, where Ward imagines himself being tried, convicted and executed for his neighbor's murder. This imaginative, almost surreal, tour de force ranks among the most effective screen dreams in cinema history. Director Ingster, art director Jan Nest Polglase and cinematographer Nicholas Masuraca (who later worked with Val Lewton) pull the scene off masterfully. If bungled, the same sequence could have sunk the film with unintentional laughs.

Frank Partos' script is first rate, as is Roy Webb's score. The acting is consistently credible. McGuire and Tallichet are particularly good, along with the always interesting Cook.

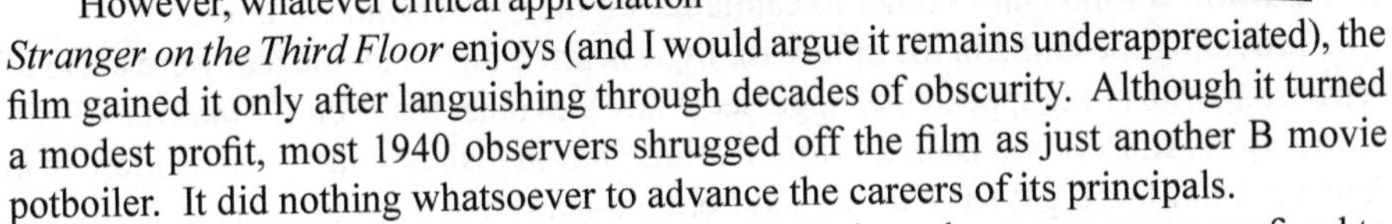

However, whatever critical appreciation *Stranger on the Third Floor* enjoys (and I would argue it remains underappreciated), the film gained it only after languishing through decades of obscurity. Although it turned a modest profit, most 1940 observers shrugged off the film as just another B movie potboiler. It did nothing whatsoever to advance the careers of its principals.

I am unaware of another starring role for McGuire, whose career was confined to smaller supporting parts thereafter. Tallichet married famed director William Wyler and retired. The film marked Ingster's directorial debut. He waited nine years to direct again and helmed only two more films, both forgettable.

Although Lorre's career continued with unabated success, the star never received the accolades for this performance that his work deserved. Nevertheless the Stranger belongs in that elite society of personages who represent the very finest roles of Lorre's career, an exclusive club which also includes Dr. Gogol, Mr. Cairo and friends.

If you're quite, you can hear them laughing.

CREDITS: Producer: Lee Marcus; Director: Boris Ingster; Story and Screenplay: Frank Partos; Musical Score: Roy Webb; Director of Photography: Nicholas Musuraca; Special Effects: Vernon L. Walker; Art Director: Van Nest Polglase; Associate Art Director: Albert D'Agostino; Set Designer: Darrell Silvera; Editor: Harry Marker; Wardrobe: Renié; Running Time: 64 Minutes; Released 1940 by RKO

CAST: Peter Lorre (the Stranger); John McGuire (Michael Ward); Margaret Tallichet (Jane); Charles Waldron (District Attorney); Elisha Cook, Jr. (Joe Briggs); Charles Halton (Mr. Meng); Ethel Griffies (Mrs. Kane); Cliff Clark; Oscar O'Shea; Alec Craig; Otto Hoffman; Charles Judels; Frank Yaconelli; Paul McVey; Robert Dudley

YOU'LL FIND OUT
1940
by Jeff Thompson

Because the old, dark house subgenre of horror movies was so prevalent in the 1920s and 1930s, it was only a matter of time before somebody played the concept for laughs. Peter Lorre played his part straight in one of the earliest such horror/comedy hybrids. *You'll Find Out* was the second of seven films to star popular bandleader Kay Kyser, famous for *Kay Kyser's Kollege of Musical Knowledge* on NBC radio. Although this film was originally titled *The Old Professor* (Kyser's nickname), RKO changed the name to *You'll Find Out* in order to capitalize on the mystery/horror angle.

Providing the chills in his otherwise light-hearted big band musical were a trio of terror stars who never appeared all together in any film other than *You'll Find Out*—Peter Lorre, Boris Karloff and Bela Lugosi. Karloff and Lugosi, of course, made more than half a dozen films together; Karloff and Lorre co-starred in three together, but this was Lorre, Lugosi and Karloff's only three-way appearance.

Peter Lorre was 36 when he made *You'll Find Out,* which followed his Mr. Moto series and was just before his pairing with Sydney Greenstreet. Lorre received second billing in *You'll Find Out,* Lugosi received fifth billing and Karloff received final billing. The screenplay was written by James V. Kern before he began his long television directing career. Director David Butler had helmed five Shirley Temple films, three Kay Kyser vehicles plus *Just Imagine* (1930), *Road to Morocco* (1942) and *Calamity Jane* (1953).

You'll Find Out is generally a straightforward suspense drama with the silly antics of Kay Kyser and his band members Harry Babbitt, Sully Mason and Ish Kabibble (and his dog Prince) providing the merriment. Janis Belacrest (Helen Parrish of *X Marks the Spot*) is a beautiful young heiress who has recently escaped some close calls in the form of "accidents." Janis engages Kyser's band to play at her 21st birthday party to be held at her ancestral home—the gloomy Belacrest Manor. The dark, forbidding mansion stands on a craggy island accessible by a single bridge—which is promptly struck by lightning and demolished after the guests and band arrive. The house itself is a typically weird place of revolving walls, hidden staircases, secret passageways, peepholes, trap doors, dungeons, and voodoo memorabilia.

Even weirder is the bizarre group of people Kyser finds in the house. Janis' spinster aunt Margo Belacrest (Alma Kruger of *Saboteur*) is obsessed with communicating with the dead and spending most of the Belacrest money on seances and spiritualist demonstrations by her houseguest, the exotic, turbaned Prince Saliano (Bela Lugosi). Also present are Aunt Margo's soft-spoken attorney Judge Spencer Mainwaring (Boris

Peter Lorre, Bela Lugosi and Boris Karloff team up to terrorize in *You'll Find Out.*

Karloff) and a peculiar man (Peter Lorre), whom Mainwaring introduces as Professor Karl Fenninger, a psychic researcher, seemingly out to debunk "Prince Saliano."

Lorre enters the action 39 minutes into the film. His character of Fenninger previously is described as "the psychic expert who exposed all those fake mediums." When introduced to the crowd by Mainwaring, Lorre as Fenninger rises serenely from a high-backed chair. He wears evening clothes and puffs slowly on a long cigarette holder. This suave Lorre is not the pudgy little man of later films; he is slender and svelte. His small frame and slicked-back hair make his saucer eyes seem even larger.

Lorre, Karloff and Lugosi do not appear all together in the same shot for another 39 minutes after Lorre's first entrance, but the audience learns the connection between

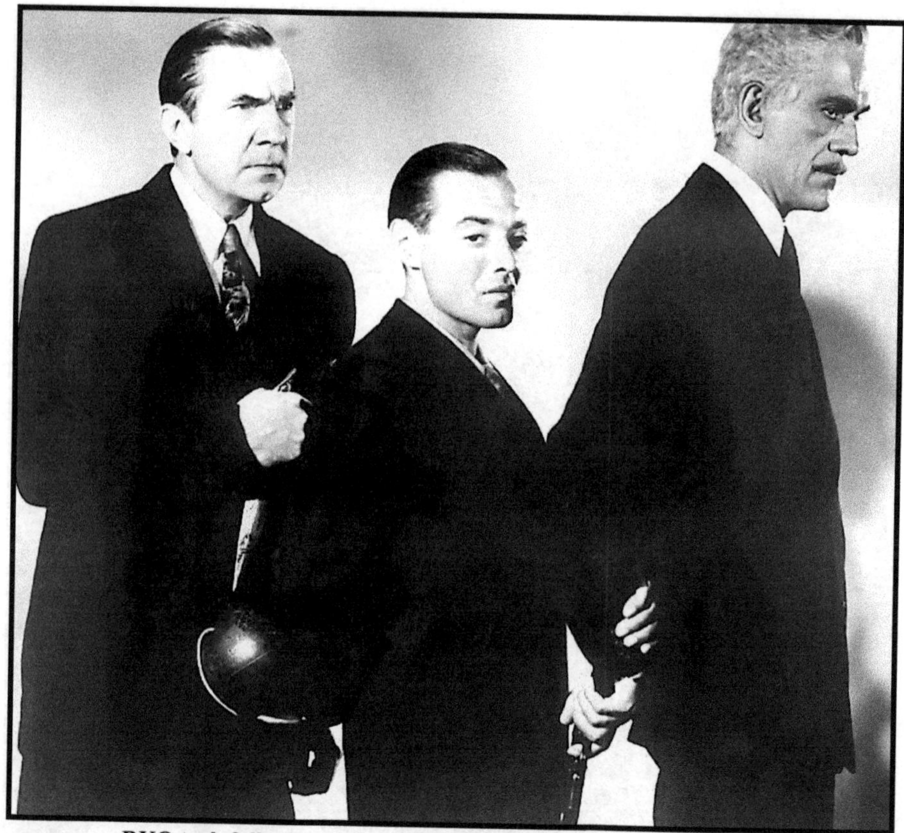

RKO took full advantage of the horror trio in this publicity photo.

the threesome almost immediately. Kyser takes a bit longer to catch on. "I took one look at [Fenninger] and I knew I could trust him with my life!"

The most memorable scenes in the film are Prince Saliano's elaborate seances during which objects fly around, drums beat, the wind howls and the ghost of Janis' father appears to wail at his daughter and his sister. Fenninger watches the proceedings with a detached and superior air. In an eerie, electromagnetic voice, Elmer Belacrest encourages Janis and Aunt Margo to trust Saliano implicitly. But someone in this old dark house is not to be trusted, for the attempts on Janis' life continue. The heiress barely escapes a poisoned dart and a falling chandelier.

After a bumbling trip through secret tunnels and amusing encounters with collapsing stairs, a stuffed grizzly bear and other typical haunted house trappings, Kyser finds a hidden control room with switches for the fake seances. Further sleuthing reveals that Prince Saliano, Fenninger (an impostor) and Mainwaring are conspiring to kill the lovely Janis before all of the Belacrest money—now being controlled by Aunt Margo and thereby Saliano and his confederates—is given to Janis on her 21st birthday.

Kyser and Lugosi have a fistfight (only partially done with stuntmen) before Kyser exposes the treacherous trio. When last seen, Lorre, Lugosi and Karloff run for their lives as Ish Kabibble's dog Prince chases them with a lighted stick of dynamite. The trio are seemingly blown to bits (off-camera) with only the phony prince's turban left behind. Janis is safe in the arms of Kyser's band manager Chuck Deems (Dennis O'Keefe of *The Leopard Man*) and Kyser cannily appropriates "that gadget that talks like the wind" for use with his band.

The final scene of the film is one of several entertaining musical numbers featuring the Kyser band, songs by Jimmy McHugh and Johnny Mercer and the musicians' use of that "new miracle of electricity," the Sonovox, a machine which electrifies voices and makes musical instruments talk. A similar technique was used later by musicians such as Alvino Rey, Peter Frampton, Styx and the Alan Parsons Project.

Sheet music for a song from the film features Karloff, Lugosi and Lorre.

For horror fans the main attraction of *You'll Find Out* is the rare teaming of Lorre, Karloff and Lugosi. Although they are supporting players in a musical comedy featuring Kyser, the terror stars play their scenes straight and bring believability and suspense to an otherwise light-hearted romp. *You'll Find Out* is one of those rare truly successfully horror comedies whose comedy is amusing and whose horror is scary (at least by 1940 standards). The two seance scenes are creepy with the Sonovox adding a macabre touch. Perhaps the most chilling moment is a treat for Lorre fans when, during the seance, Fenninger calmly smells a flower while waiting for death to strike Janis. Lorre is so memorable because he constantly surprises his audience with his versatile performances.

Another unforgettable moment is a scene in the dungeon control room when all three horror stars are huddled together and planning their next nefarious move. Yet, overall, Lorre himself is the singular highlight in this auspicious company. Perhaps because Lorre had not made nearly as many horror films as Karloff and Lugosi, his performance in *You'll Find Out* is fresher and more genuinely unsettling than the equally fine but predictably menacing performances of his higher-profile horror compatriots.

CREDITS: Producer/Director: David Butler; Screenplay: James V. Kern; Story: David Butler and James V. Kern; Special Material: Monte Brice, Andrew Bennison and R.T.M. Scott; Music: Jimmy McHugh, Johnny Mercer, Roy Webb, George Duning; Cinematography: Frank Redman; Editor: Irene Morra; RKO; November 1940; 97 Minutes

CAST: Kay Kyser (Himself); Peter Lorre (Professor Karl Fenninger); Boris Karloff (Judge Spencer Mainwaring); Bela Lugosi (Prince Saliano); Helen Parrish (Janis Belacrest); Dennis O'Keefe (Chuck Deemes); Alma Kruger (Aunt Margo); Joseph Eggenton (Jurgen); Ginny Simms (Herself); Harry Babbitt (Himself); Ish Kabibble (Himself); Sully Mason (Himself)

THE FACE BEHIND THE MASK
1941
by John Stell

The best villains are those who are multidimensional, the ones you know could honestly succeed in the world if they really tried. You actually feel a bit sorry for them, even though they commit terrible deeds. In the 1931 classic *M*, Peter Lorre, in his breakthrough role, played such a character: a brutal child-murderer who, in his impassioned appeal to his potential executioners, explains that he cannot help what he does. His "defense" rings true. But in *The Face Behind the Mask*, we meet the villain (a master thief) before he decides on a life of crime. And it is because of this establishment of character that the story of Lorre's Janos Szabo is so tragic. Although *The Face Behind the Mask* may be only a small B picture, the film features one of Lorre's most heartfelt, and best, performances.

Janos Szabo (Peter Lorre) arrives in New York City eager to begin his new life in America. He has a sweetheart in his native Hungary waiting to join him. Unfortunately, a fire breaks out in the hotel where Janos is staying, and his face is disfigured. Unable now to find work, his thoughts turn to suicide.

As "luck" would have it, however, Janos meets Dinky (George E. Stone), a petty criminal who befriends the lonely immigrant. When Dinky gets sick, Janos steals to get money for medical attention. Realizing he might be able to afford an operation to fix his own face, Janos begins his journey to becoming one of the city's most sought-after criminals.

Janos gets a temporary mask from his doctor, but is eventually told that his face is beyond repair. Leaving his doctor's office in despair Janos meets Helen Williams (Evelyn Keyes), the first woman who treats him kindly. It turns out she is blind, but she can see the warm person that once was Janos Szabo. They fall in love, and Janos quits his gang. Unfortunately, one of his former partners, Jeff (an appropriately smarmy James Seay), thinks (incorrectly) that Janos has double-crossed them. He and the gang track Janos down to his rural home, and rig a bomb in his automobile. But it is Helen who is killed. Finally beaten, Janos strands the assassins, along with himself, in the desert, where they all perish.

For years, Lorre had been cast in either supporting roles or sinister ones. And he excelled in them. He was certainly one of the most reliable character actors that Hollywood had during this time of his career. But rarely was Lorre given the chance to play characters of immense range. Even in his most-known films—*M*, *Mad Love*, *The Maltese Falcon*, and *Casablanca*—Lorre was not the top-billed star. Comparing him to the leading men of the time, he may not have been viewed as "top-billable" material. In other words, his leading roles in the American film industry were few and far between.

***The Face Behind the Mask* gives Peter Lorre the spotlight.**

But *The Face Behind the Mask* gives Lorre the spotlight: He is in nearly every scene. He must carry the film, and he does this effortlessly. More impressively, his Janos character never becomes a cliché. Janos is always evolving. First a naïve émigré, he learns harsh lessons in life and falls into despair. But friendship does give him hope again, even though he finds himself living a life that is abhorrent to his nature. His fortune changes yet again when he meets Helen, and we see a momentary return of the exuberance he possessed in the first scene. Fate, sadly, has one more cruel twist in store for Janos, and it is the final tragedy he cannot stand. Lorre is completely convincing in this character's evolution, and he proves to be just as deserving of complex roles as his peers.

The once gentle Janos embraces Jeff (James Seay) gangster–style.

At one point in *The Face Behind the Mask*, Janos tells Dinky, "You can't do wrong and find happiness in life. Never." If only Janos had realized how prophetic his words would turn out to be. Although Janos finally manages to come back to the world of upstanding citizens, his wrongs return to haunt him. If Janos had been like every other gangster or jewel thief in the movies, such an end might be deemed poetic justice. But since we knew Janos when he was so hopeful, so enthusiastic about his future, the ending stings, and stings badly. Janos' revenge is especially brutal: deliberately isolating his gang in the hot sun of the desert, knowing they will suffer greatly before their deaths. He knows they are "cowards" who will not take their own lives. It is hard to believe that this is the same Janos we met as he arrives in New York, praising the beauty of the Statue of Liberty.

Lorre is grand in his very humorous opening moments. "Excuse me, please. Could I trouble you for a match?" he asks the ship's attendant, who happily obliges. "Thank you very much, I do not smoke. What time is it, please?" he continues, without pause. The attendant tells him, only to see Janos take out his own pocket watch. "So it is," Janos agrees. The attendant is only briefly miffed as Janos quickly tells him, "I am practicing my English." At the risk of sounding patronizing, Janos is absolutely cute and adorable here. His enthusiasm is child-like; he is totally open to the new experi-

Janos imagines himself as something "grand and noble."

ences that America has to offer him. He is so eager to please, so eager to begin an honest life. He can't wait to bring Marie over so they can start their life together and have five watchmaker sons.

After getting directions to a hotel, he suddenly cannot find his money. "Mr. Policeman, I'm gangstered!" he shouts. "I'm stolen!" Luckily Officer O'Hara, played by Don Beddoe in a sympathetic, non-clichéd performance, helps Janos find his money. Later, when O'Hara finds out about Janos' hotel burning down, he hands the nurse his business card to give to Janos. "He was so… hopeful," he tells her. Sadly, O'Hara, who feels responsible for the "little guy" for sending him to the hotel in the first place, inadvertently plants the seed of Janos' final fall. It is O'Hara's business card that Jeff finds, and erroneously concludes that, since O'Hara is working the thefts, Janos has sold out the gang.

Although a watchmaker by profession, Janos eagerly takes a job washing dishes. Just watch the absolute joy Lorre brings to Janos as he scrubs away at the dirtied dishes: His face beams, his voice sings out. It is doubtful anyone has ever enjoyed a busboy job, in the movies anyway, as much as Janos. Even after the fire, just as the doctor is unwrapping the bandages, Janos is still excited, his arms flailing about. "I am a mechanical genius!" he tells the surgeon. He can do anything with his hands. But only a few seconds later does he catch a reflection of himself in the mirror. Janos is crushed. Instead of being filled with the joy of living, Janos is now filled with anger: He explodes into fury, and must be subdued, crying out his beloved Marie's name. It is the first of several heart-breaking moments in the film. He writes to Marie telling her he has met someone else and that she must forget him. Later he realizes no one

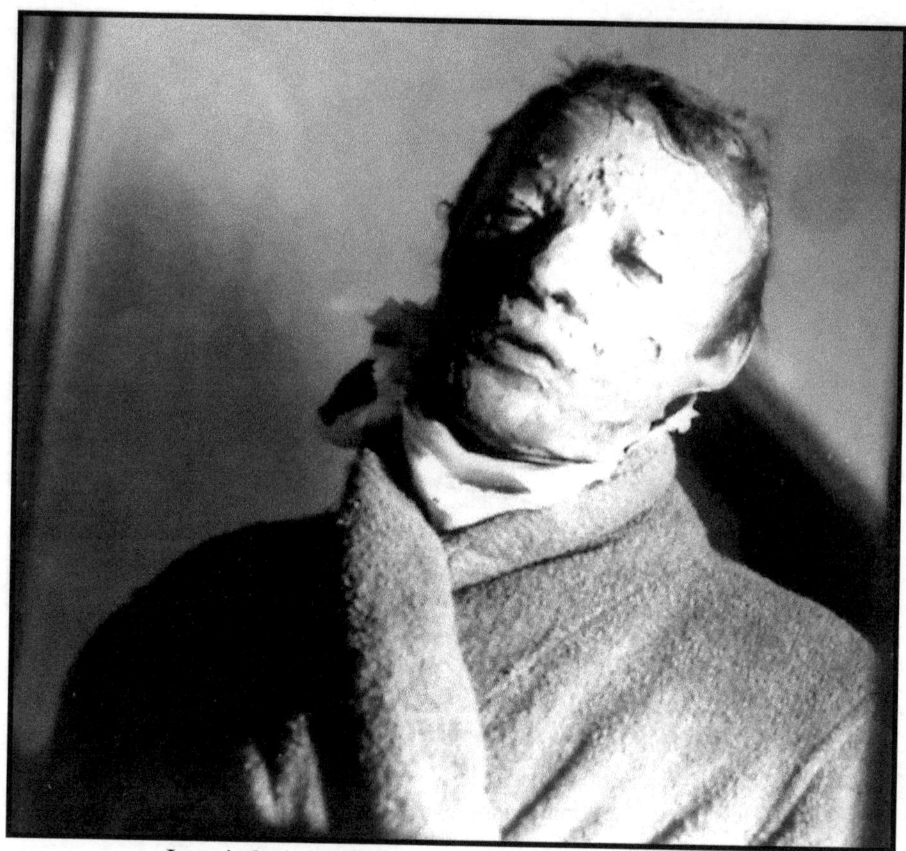

Janos is denied work because of his horribly scarred face.

will hire him because of his face. "My face makes no difference how I can work with my hands!" he pleads to closed ears and minds. Janos turns to crime reluctantly, and does not exhibit anywhere near the same excitement he showed while working in the kitchen. Only when he sees a future of honest work do Janos' spirits again rise. "We've gone a long, crooked road together, Dinky, you and I; a crooked road. But this is where I take the turn-off."

Even though Janos finds happiness again, albeit briefly, when he meets Helen, Janos is never the same as he was when he first arrived. A lesser actor might have tried to show Janos the same as he was before the tragedy, thus overplaying the obvious. But Lorre allows for Janos to be haunted: haunted by the lie he had to tell his fiancé about finding another woman, and haunted by the crimes he has committed. While Lorre clearly shows Janos loves Helen, he also shows it is a love that did not come without a steep price.

Furthermore, Lorre communicates that Janos' turning to crime has destroyed him internally. "Sometimes I wish I could see the world the way you do," he tells Helen softly. "Maybe then I would imagine myself as something grand and noble." Despite Helen's insistence that Janos is such a person, he still judges his worth based on his appearance. "Always you see things the way you want to... If you could see my face,

Robert Florey directs Lorre on a set for *The Face Behind the Mask.*

you would feel sorry for me! People who look at me, they see a mask, artificial. But the face behind the mask, it's mutated, hideous, a horrible nightmare out of which I can never awake." Lorre delivers these lines with a soft-spoken intensity, revealing for the first time his character's belief that his life is a nightmare. His relationship with Helen proves to be an all-too-brief awakening.

Ironically, despite the tenderness of Janos and Helen's romance, Helen presents a small weakness in the film in that her attitude toward her blindness is a bit too positive to be totally believable. There are several scenes where she talks about how wonderful it is to be blind, being able to imagine things as she wishes them to be, for example. Since she has been blind from age four, she has moved past the bitterness and angry stages that a sudden loss of sight would no doubt bring about. But the film would have been even stronger if there had been a bit more edge to Helen, if she had confessed to Janos her own frustrations that may lurk beyond her perky surface. The two would have truly needed each other. This is no fault of actress Evelyn Keyes, mind you, who essays the role very well and sounds convincing in her beliefs. But the truth is that had Janos not entered her life, Helen would have survived. But Janos would not have been redeemed without Helen, although, interestingly, he might have survived. These are two characters who are victims of forces beyond their control: Janos is harmed in a fire he did not start, and Helen is killed when she turns on the car radio. They are true innocents.

Peter Lorre commands the film from beginning to end.

Janos' only other true friend in the film is Dinky, and Lorre and George E. Stone have a nice chemistry as two down-on-their-luck types. Their friendship provides some nice quiet moments, with Dinky always having a smile for Janos. Dinky literally saves Janos from himself, and he is the first person who doesn't judge Janos based on his face. Later Janos returns the favor, although he must steal to do it. When Janos realizes Dinky is getting better, it is the first time since the doctor's office scene where Janos sounds happy. "None of us can do without friends," Janos tells him. This relationship, too, ends in tragedy, as Dinky is tortured and left for dead after the assassins learn where Janos has moved.

Wisely director Robert Florey (who later directed Lorre in 1946's *The Beast With Five Fingers*) never uses Janos' disfigured face for cheap shocks, or as the real source of the film's "horror." Instead, it is the constant tragedy in Janos' life that lends a truly haunting quality to *The Face Behind the Mask*. In fact, we are shown Janos' face only once: in the scene where Janos sees his "new" reflection for the first time. For the rest of the film Lorre is shown wearing his mask, or is shot from behind or over the shoulders. In the scenes with Dinky, Lorre must use his voice and mannerisms to communicate what he is thinking and feeling. Not too many actors would enjoy turning *away* from the camera!

For a low-budget picture, *The Face Behind the Mask* boasts an impressive amount of sets in which Florey manages to capture the dual nature of a big city such as New York. On the one hand, it can seem populated and friendly. There are the scenes of Janos arriving and seeing the city from the ship; his journey through the busy streets, meeting friendly folk ready to help him start his new life; and the later scene of Janos attending an opera as his "boys" carry out his latest burglary. On the other hand, the city can also seem desolate and cold. Janos is virtually alone at the pier, and he and Dinky are by themselves at the junkyard. This duality of the city's nature is a nice visual representation of Janos' duality, as he goes from someone who enjoys the hustle and bustle of life, to someone who feels alone and unwanted. Later, Janos and Helen move to the happiness and warmth of the country. But once again, Janos will find himself in a desolate and deadly place: the desert. This time, however, Janos will not be alone. His partners in crime will die with him. "Strange, isn't it, how a little switch can cause death to someone who is always trying to give happiness?" he asks them in a nicely ironic line, since he "switched" places with their pilot in order to strand people who give unhappiness. He leaves a note for O'Hara, which includes repayment of the money O'Hara loaned Janos when they first met. "I did not forget you," the note says. And as for his former cohorts, he simply explains, "I did not forget them, either." It would appear that Janos hadn't totally lost his sense of humor after all.

In addition to the varied locales, director Florey also employs some familiar trappings from films of yesteryear. Newspaper headlines tell of the baffling series of thefts, including a daring daylight jewel heist. A super-imposed hourglass shows the passage of time as the thieves burn in the hot desert sun. There's the scene where O'Hara's boss chews him out for being unable to apprehend the criminals, even though O'Hara is in no way the comical, ineffectual detective sometimes found in films that focus on the villains. And some of the names Jeff calls Janos are a bit dated to be effective today ("Why that no good rat…"). But the film's swift pace and ironic touches, along with the performances and the story itself, remain fascinating to behold.

While Lorre's resume certainly contains a list of classic A+ pictures like *Casablanca* and *The Maltese Falcon*, one of his best performances can be found in the modestly budgeted *The Face Behind the Mask*. His Janos Szabo is a memorably tragic figure that Lorre brings to life in a way only he could: combining gentleness and bitterness in a believably balanced performance. As a B movie, *The Face Behind the Mask* is a model of its kind. As a showcase for Peter Lorre, it provided the actor with the opportunity to command the film from its first scene to its last, and he is more than up to the task. It remains one of Lorre's finest hours.

CREDITS: Producer: Wallace MacDonald; Director: Robert Florey; Screenplay: Paul Jarrico, Allen Vincent, and Arthur Levinson, Based on a Play by Thomas Edward O'Connell; Cinematographer: Franz Planer; Art Direction: Lionel Banks; Editor: Charles Nelson; Released by Columbia Pictures 1941, 69 minutes

CAST: Peter Lorre (Janos Szabo); Evelyn Keyes (Helen Williams); Don Beddoe (Jim O'Hara); George E. Stone (Dinky); John Tyrrell (Watts); Stanley Brown (Harry); Al Seymour (Benson); James Seay (Jeff); Warren Ashe (Johnson); Charles C. Wilson (Chief O'Brien); George McKay (Terry Finnegan)

THE MALTESE FALCON
1941
by Gary J. Svehla

The Maltese Falcon, released by Warner Bros. in 1941, became an early yet extraordinary example of the emerging film noir style, concerned with the theme of moral ambiguity and of honor and loyalty in a cold-hearted, hard-boiled world where the police finger innocent victims, innocent women never are, private detectives have affairs with their partner's wives and honor among thieves is an unheard-of concept. The film boasted plenty of firsts worth remembering: the directorial debut of young John Huston, the emerging hard-boiled persona of Humphrey Bogart—and it was the first film on Peter Lorre's Warner Bros. contract (which would be terminated in 1946 after completing *The Verdict*).

So much has already been written of *The Maltese Falcon*, but the movie cements Peter Lorre's screen persona as being both quirky and mesmeric. It established a classical screen pairing of "the fat man" and the gardenia-fragranced eccentric—Greenstreet and Lorre.

But for many, the most interesting aspect of *The Maltese Falcon* is its complex investigation of the theme of loyalty and how "the stuff that dreams are made of," the black bird itself, becomes the cinematic catalyst of this theme.

It all begins with a dame in hard-boiled noir drama, in this case a "Miss Wanderly" (aka Brigid O'Shaughnessy, marvelously performed by Mary Astor) who comes into the private investigative offices of Spade and Archer claiming she is looking for her innocent kid sister who has run off with the worldly Floyd Thursby. At first speaking alone to monetarily interested Sam Spade (Humphrey Bogart), partner Miles Archer (Jerome Cowan) enters in the midst of things and immediately becomes sexually sizzled by O'Shaughnessy. "I'll look after it myself," the lustful Archer volunteers when the innocent-appearing client asks for help getting her sister away from the clutches of Thursby. Spade advises O'Shaughnessy to meet Thursby in the hotel lobby where he is staying and that the unseen Archer can take over from there. "I'll see you all right," the goo-goo-eyed detective coos. As soon as the young client leaves the office, Archer interjects, "Maybe you saw her first, Sam, but I spoke first," laying his claim to the young woman's attentions. However, in the sequence immediately following, Archer is staking out the hotel watching it from the edge of deserted Bash Street, when someone approaches him, and at almost point blank range, pulls out a pistol and plugs a hole through his heart, killing the unsuspecting detective who rolls backward down a hill. All the events in the movie which follow are initiated by this brief sequence.

Sam Spade (Bogart), Joel Cairo (Peter Lorre), O'Shaughnessy (Mary Astor) and Casper Gutman (Sydney Greenstreet) with "the stuff that dreams are made of."

First, to explore the theme of loyalty, we need to look at the relationship between Spade and Archer, co-partners in a detective agency. Almost immediately, it becomes apparent that Archer and Spade do not like one another, and it is Archer's wife Iva (Gladys George) that again is at the heart of the problem. Spade is having an affair with his partner's wife, and Miles will not grant his wife a divorce. Thus, Miles' sexual interest in Miss O'Shaughnessy in the presence of his wife's adulterer only points out that Archer himself is not above flirtatious relationships with other women. And when Spade gets a courtesy call, in the middle of the night, from his police cronies telling him his partner Archer has been found shot to death, he dutifully rises from bed, dresses and ventures to the murder scene, asking for details about the crime (discovering Archer was shot at close range and that his pistol remained unfired in his overcoat pocket), but when the police ask if he wants to walk down the hill to look at the corpse, Spade answers candidly, "no." The police add that Miles must have had his good points too, but Spade answers, "I guess so," matter of factly. It is soon revealed that Thursby, the man Archer was tailing, was also found dead, shot four or five times in the back. Spade, who phoned his secretary Effie (Lee Patrick) before he left for the murder scene, told her she had to notify Archer's wife of his death, and he further insists rather forcefully, "Keep her away from me." The next morning, Effie tells Spade that Iva is in the office waiting for Spade, and Spade is noticeably annoyed that Effie did not manage to keep her away, but the interested secretary asks Spade point-blank, "Sam, did you kill him!??? I'd thought you said if it wasn't for Miles you'd...," but Spade cuts her off (the intent being he killed Archer to be free to marry Iva). Spade firmly blurts out, "I am sorry I ever laid eyes on her," making it crystal clear to Effie that he never intends to marry Iva. After abruptly dispatching the widow, Spade just as unemotionally tells Effie to phone someone to change the office glass, to take Miles Archer's name off the glass, and add "Samuel" to Spade (oh, and have someone take out Archer's desk as soon as possible). Later when speaking to O'Shaughnessy who praises Miles Archer and mourns his loss—"so hearty, so solid"—Spade interrupts her in mid-sentence. "Stop it! He knew exactly what he was doing. That's the chances we take. He had a $10,000 insurance policy, a wife who didn't like him and that's the way it was."

Sam Spade is a hardened private dick who knows all the ins and outs of his job; he is a brutal realist, unsentimental, and he doesn't really miss his partner or seem too upset by Archer's violent death. Spade knows only too well Archer's marriage was an unhappy one and that he had an illicit affair with his partner's wife. Thus Spade's loyalty toward his partner is merely professional and superficial, as evidenced by the lustful relationship he executes with Mile's wife, making an unhappy marriage a disastrous one. Spade does not appear to like or even respect his partner, but later, we learn he does respect his partner's professional position.

Second, the loyalty existing between the police and Sam Spade, chiefly his friend Detective Tom Polhaus (Ward Bond) and Tom's boss, Detective Lieutenant Dundy (Barton MacLane), becomes complex. Remember, when Archer was found murdered, Polhaus called Spade immediately and filled him in on the details of the case. Dundy is another type of cop altogether, all protocol and getting his man, at any cost. Dundy suspects immediately, without any actual foundation, that Spade killed Miles Archer. But Dundy is also the straight shooter telling Spade early on, "You know me, Spade, if you did it or if you didn't do it, you'll get a square deal from me and most of the breaks... but that won't stop me from nailing you." To which Spade agreeably answers, "Fair enough." A private detective like Spade, who skirts the subtlety of the law and will take any short-cut to solve a case, needs to have breathing room from the police, but once Dundy tries to finger Spade, feathers do ruffle.

Later in a pivotal sequence where Spade, at his apartment, is meeting with O'Shaughnessy and Joel Cairo, the police try to barge in, having been directed to Spade's apartment by a distraught Iva Archer, who reveals the facts about her affair with Spade and thus establishes Spade's motive for killing his partner Miles. "Talk going around about you and Archer's wife... anything to it?" the police question. To which Spade lies, "Not a thing!" Suddenly in the background, chaos erupts as furniture is overturned and a frenzied male voice screams. The police, waiting for any excuse to go inside, smile and declare, "I guess we're going in." Fast thinking and a ridiculous story concocted by Spade—with a little leg-pulling on Spade's part—prevents the police from arresting any of the assembled crew, now bloodied and screaming at one another. Soon Dundy tells Spade that the District Attorney wants to question him about the murder, but Spade angrily sputters he won't cooperate, that the only way he can clear his name is to bring in the murderer himself, all tied into one neat little bundle, and that he cannot operate if the police keep crowding him. Ever time the police invade his turf, he wearily tells them to search the joint, "as long as you have a warrant," and when they try to act as friends acting in his interest, he abruptly gets rid of them. However, at the movie's end, Spade is innately aware of having a "fall guy" for the police since the current fall guy is him (the obvious choice, since a motive has been clearly established for his shooting Miles). And once Spade has the case cleared up, he happily turns Gutman and his crew over to the police, warning them to be particularly careful of the kid Wilmer. And at the very end, he delivers, almost ruthlessly, a fall "guy" to the police.

Sam Spade confronts Joel Cairo in the hotel lobby.

In other words, the relationship between Spade and the police is love-hate, and generally Spade, who feels claustrophobic when he's under investigation by even his friend Detective Polhaus, more out of self-preservation than loyalty, turns in people to the police who deserve to be. But also emanating from Spade comes a core of common decency that always compels him to do the right thing, even if he seems heartless and ruthless when he's doing it. Not quite motivated by loyalty, Spade understands the complex, symbiotic relationship that exists between the police and private detectives, and in order to buy a little margin of peace and quiet from the police, he sometimes has to throw the coppers a bone or two.

Honor among thieves, or is there? How does this theme of loyalty play among the criminals? Kasper Gutman (Sydney Greenstreet) and his cronies Joel Cairo (Peter Lorre) and Wilmer Cook (Elisha Cook, Jr.) appear to have either a father/son style relationship, or perhaps, even a homosexual one (but homosexual in the Hollywood stereotype, not in the realistic sense of homosexuality in society at large). To add support to this charge, when Cairo first enters Spade's office, he offers Effie a calling card that is gardenia scented, and as Spade's eyebrows rise, the musical score adds a silly (almost humorous) mood-breaking motif, seemingly announcing that Joel Cairo lives an alternative lifestyle. Cairo's fastidious grooming and dress and his dainty politeness seem to reek of stereotyped Hollywood gayness. The gunsel, Wilmer, seems to be sharing the apartment with Gutman, and while this very well may be for protection, Gutman constantly carries on about how Wilmer is like a son to him, but the sado-masochistic nature of Wilmer contrasted to the European charm and politeness of Gutman seem to cast that father-son relationship into the deepest Freudian shadows of speculation. But it is master thief Gutman, who announces he must be off to catch another ship for Istanbul in his final sequence, delighted that the race for the Falcon is still on, who almost seems to prance out of the office, waving his hands and fingers good-bye, in a most frilly fashion. Again, this twisted nuclear family quickly disintegrates. When Spade announces, as part of his payment, he needs someone to take the fall for the murder of Miles Archer, he literally tells Gutman, "Let's give him the gunsel. He actually did shoot Jacoby and Thursby, didn't he? He's made to order for the part!" Gutman, reacting with tittering and broad laughter, rejects the idea several times, one time saying, "I feel towards Wilmer here exactly as though he were my own son. Really I do." However, when Spade is insistent, Gutman speaks to Wilmer, who is slowly regaining consciousness after being punched out by Spade. Gutman, with only a small parcel of remorse, tells Wilmer, 'If you lose a son, it's possible to get another. But there's only one Maltese Falcon..." In other words, it would be abhorrent for a regular parent to fathom the thought of sacrificing his/her own flesh and blood, but since Gutman almost merrily announces, one can get another "son," we have to question Gutman's definition of the word son and guess at what exactly their relationship has been. One might sell out a lover for money (the Falcon), but never one's flesh and blood.

Loyalty seems to mean very little in a criminal world where money means everything. Gutman illustrates this with his relationship to Sam Spade, a man he believes can acquire the Maltese Falcon. During their initial meeting, where everything begins with politeness and fine manners, Gutman offers Spade a drink, toasting, "Here's to plain speaking." Gutman asks Spade if he's a closed-mouth man, declaring, "I distrust a closed-mouth man. He generally picks the wrong time to talk and says the wrong things. Talking is something you can't do judiciously, unless you keep in practice... I am a man who likes talking to a man who likes to talk." Such dialogue reveals Gutman to be cultured, intelligent and intuitive, but also shows this obsessed man to be a windbag who enjoys the sound of his own voice. Gutman, on the subject of loyalty, wants to know whom Spade represents: Cairo or O'Shaughnessy, but Spade wisely evades the issue by declaring he's out for himself. And Gutman has to commend such an answer by ranting: "I do like a man who tells you right out he's looking out after himself." But soon the polite chatting begins to crumble. Spade claims he knows where the Falcon is, but that Gutman knows what it is and why it is so valuable, but Gutman confesses he is not sure he is ready to reveal what he knows. "I must tell you what I know, but you won't tell me what you know. Hardly equable, sir. I don't think we can do business," Gutman says laying his cards on the table. Spade, erupting into anger, rises abruptly and shouts, "Think again and think fast. I told that gunsel you'll have to talk to me before you're through. You'll talk to me today or you are through," breaking his glass against the table. Spade gives Gutman until five o'clock to share his information. However, storming outside Gutman's apartment, Spade's face breaks out into a broad smile, signaling the fact that his performance inside was calculated. As this interchange easily illustrates, there can be no sense of loyalty when manipulation and scheming appear to be the chief motivation for men conducting business.

And this leads to Peter Lorre's fourth-billed performance as Joel Cairo, easily the quirkiest performance in the movie, somehow upstaging Elisha Cook, Jr.'s wound-tight psychopath and Sydney Greenstreet's cultured jewel thief. Lorre's Cairo is just as esoteric and foreign as his name implies, and while he tries to approximate the cultured manners and jovial spirits of his mentor Gutman, Lorre's performance always smolders and displays the childish anger and violent emotional eruptions that lie just under the surface. Cairo is a Gutman wannabe, but his inability to pull off such a charade makes his performance multidimensional because Cairo is a walking contradiction.

As Cairo enters Spade's office, he offers sincere condolences for Spade's partner's death (overdressed in a tight-fitting suit with a bow-tie, curly short-cropped hair, white gloves—which he slowly and carefully removes—and a white cane). Cairo slowly reveals his intentions: "I am trying to recover an ornament that, shall we say, has been mislaid. I thought and hoped you could assist me. The ornament is a statuette, a black figure of a bird... I am prepared to pay, to the rightful owner, $5,000 for its recovery... no questions will be asked." Of course, Gutman later reveals that the Maltese Falcon is worth perhaps as much as a million dollars. Effie buzzes in that she is leaving, and Spade asks her to lock the office door on her way out. Turning back to Cairo, the diminutive man's cheerful mood has abruptly changed, as he produces a gun and asks more than demands, "You will clasp your hands together at the back of your neck... I intend to search your offices, Mr. Spade. I warn you, if you attempt to prevent me, I will most certainly shoot you." When he asks Spade to walk to the center of the room so he can search the detective for concealed weapons (Cairo's hand wanders first to Spade's rear), Spade suddenly spins around, smiling, grabs the weapon and slaps Cairo and then punches him. Smiling more broadly, Spade delivers a hard right which sends Cairo unconscious to the office couch. Searching Cairo's wallet, finding $200 in cash and three international passports, Cairo eventually awakens and cries, "Look what you did to my shirt," looking in the mirror. Bogart, still calm and obviously amused by the shenanigans of this limp-wristed adversary, cynically declares, "Sorry, but imagine my embarrassment when I found out that $5,000 offer was just hooey." To which Cairo, getting his emotions quickly under control, says, "Mr. Spade, my offer is genuine... do you have it?" Cairo fabricates the story that he was simply trying to save his employee the expense money of having to purchase the bird, when Spade asks who he works for. "Mr. Spade, you will forgive my not answering the question!" Soon, Cairo tries to offer Spade a $100 retainer, but Spade insists upon $200 and adds, you are hiring me to get the bird back in "an honest and lawful manner." To which Cairo adds, "In any case, with discretion." Then with his droopy, sad eyes, Cairo asks for his pistol back, and Spade readily hands it over. Then, in extreme stupidity, Cairo again turns the gun against Spade telling him to clasp his hands behind his head, that he intends to search the offices, to which Spade calmly complies, "Why sure, I won't stop you," laughing all the way, obviously convinced Cairo will find nothing, and that if he needed to, he could punch out this man's lights at a moment's notice.

Soon, Spade arranges for O'Shaughnessy to meet with Joel Cairo to discuss getting the bird back. "Madame, I am delighted to see you again." Cairo says, emphasizing he is only minutes away from producing $5,000 during banking hours if O'Shaughnessy can produce the Falcon for his benefactor. But O'Shaughnessy glumly admits, she doesn't have the Falcon, but she will have it within the week. She tells Cairo that Floyd hid the bird, but Cairo states, since she knows where the bird is hidden, why do they have to wait a week? Then Cairo's eyes get expressive and wide and he asks, "And why are you willing to sell it to me?" O'Shaughnessy admits she is afraid and that the fat man is nearby. Cairo quickly rises out of his seat and states, "Is he here?" Spade is aware that the now-unknown Wilmer has been tailing him and is waiting outside his apartment, which leads to some juicy innuendo dialogue delivered by O'Shaughnessy to Cairo. She tells Joel he may be able to get around the boy outside, just like he did to the boy in Istanbul (implying some sort of relationship occurred between Joel and that boy); incensed, Cairo rises, his eyes bulging, his anger flaring, and he counters, "You mean the one you couldn't get to..." implying a physical relationship of a different sort. O'Shaughnessy rises and slaps Cairo hard across the face. When he slowly stands and raises his hand over his head to counter the blow, Spade intercedes, holding Cairo's arm back. When Cairo reaches for his weapon, Spade, as usual, knocks it away, but Cairo is now livid. "This is the second time you laid your hands on me!!!" To which Spade delivers the classic line, "When you're slapped you'll take it and like it," and then he slaps Cairo again. The doorbell buzzes, and Spade is occupied with the police outside in the hall until the fury between O'Shaughnessy and Cairo brings the police into the apartment, something Spade was trying to avoid. Cairo, his forehead a bloody mess, screams like a baby, "Look officer at what she did!" O'Shaughnessy claims when they were alone he tried to attack her, and she was merely defending herself. Now worked up to an emotional fever pitch, Cairo blurts out, "You dirty, filthy liar. It isn't true. I've come up here in good faith." As mentioned earlier, Spade's fast talking keeps all of them out of the cooler. But seeing Cairo the next morning return to the front desk at the Hotel Belvedere, looking the worse for wear having been grilled by the police most of the night, Spade wants to talk with him. But Cairo, in his usual polite tone, refuses: "No, our private conversations have not been such as I'm happy to continue them. Forget my speaking so bluntly, but it's the truth!"

Of course Cairo's character is designed to illustrate the shrewd viciousness that lurks just beneath the surface of well-dressed and polite obsessive thieves and murderers. Cairo is revealed early-on to be an utter idiot, a fool, but his attempts to be polite and urbane contrast well with his childish outburst of emotion and anger. Lorre's final sequence in the movie, after Spade delivers the bird, smuggled into the country by Captain Jacoby (an unbilled cameo portrayed by John's father, Walter Huston), into Gutman's hands, is classic. Gutman, stroking the phallic bird with his exposed blade, cries out it's lead, it's a fake. And Cairo's emotional outrage is classic. "It's you who bungled it. You and your stupid attempt to buy it... no wonder we had such an easy time stealing it. You imbecile! You bloated idiot! You stupid fat head!" Cairo sputters, quickly erupting into overblown tears, finally collapsing into his chair. However, seconds later, when Gutman, all smiles again, states we can cry over this or return to Istanbul, Cairo, smiling immediately, chimes in, "I'm going with you!," as though nothing had happened. Loyalty does not exist between the company of thieves, but loyalty to the dreams of riches and wealth keep them together, ignoring all "bloated idiot" comments. Peter Lorre's performance here contains all the elements for which he is

Loyalty does not exist in this search for the elusive Maltese Falcon.

remembered: the polite European exterior housing the short-fused, temper-tantrumed child/man within.

The theme of loyalty finally becomes almost ridiculous when explored between the private detective and the femme fatale, or, in this case, the not-so-innocent client. Even from the get-go, when Miss Wanderly reveals she lied, that she is really Bridget O'Shaughnessy, Spade smiles and admits, "We believed your $200, not your story." When O'Shaughnessy begs Spade to protect her and help her get the bird, Spade wants to know "what it's all about." To which her tone gets quiet and innocent and she pleads, "I can't tell you now... I will later, when I can. You have to trust me." But Spade, still obviously amused, tells her honestly, "You won't need much of anybody's help. You're good. Chiefly your eyes and the throb you get in your voice... you are dangerous." Amused with O'Shaughnessy's thinly disguised methods, much as he was amused by Cairo's similar deceptions, Bogart asks for all the cash she has, $500. When she only offers $400, stating she needs money on which to live, Spade snaps back and asks if she has jewels to hock. When she admits he does have jewelry, Spade insists on having all $500.

Director John Huston with Lorre, Astor and Bogart.

In a later sequence, O'Shaughnessy admits "I haven't lived a good life. I've been bad. Worse than you could know." To which Spade admits, "That's good because if you were actually as innocent as you pretended to be, we wouldn't get anywhere." Admitting that Cairo offered her $5,000 for the black bird, O'Shaughnessy states, "More than I could ever offer you if I had to bid for your loyalty." Spade quickly counters, speaking on the theme of loyalty, "That's good coming from you. What have you ever given me besides money! Have you ever given me any of your confidence, any of the truth? Haven't you tried to buy my loyalty with money and nothing else!" When she asks what else can I buy you with, Spade answers with his lips, kissing O'Shaughnessy hard and long. She then asks, "Can't you trust me a little longer" and adds, "I trust you completely." To which Spade literally throws up his arms and cries, "Not again." But Spade speaks from the hip: "You don't have to trust me as long as you can persuade me to trust you." Apparently, unlike sap Miles Archer, O'Shaughnessy never manages that one little trick.

Spade carefully figures out that O'Shaughnessy setup and murdered his partner Miles Archer: "He would have been ready for Thursby—but not you... he would have gone up there with you, Angel. He was just dumb enough for that. He would have looked you up and down and licked his lips, grinning from ear to ear. Then you could have stood as close to him as you liked in the dark and put a hole through him!" Refusing to play the fool for O'Shaughnessy, he tells her: "Yes, Angel, I am going to send you over... you're taking the fall. I won't play the sap for you. You've never played square with me for half an hour at a stretch since I've known you. I don't care who loves who, I won't play the sap for you... You killed Miles and you're going over for it." Then bursting through Spade's hard-boiled ruthless exterior comes that seldom-seen ray of decency. "When a man's partner is killed, he is supposed to do something about it. It doesn't make any difference what you thought of him. He was your partner and you are supposed to do something about it. And it happens you're in the detective business. And when one of your organization gets killed, it's bad business to let the killer get away with it. Bad all around... I have no earthly reason to think I can trust you... you'll have something on me you can use whenever you want to. Since I've got something on you, I couldn't be sure you wouldn't put a hole in me someday."

By movie's end, Samuel Spade has revealed his loyalty not to the mob, not to the police, not to his partner, not even to his lady friends, but mostly to his profession, his career—his identity—and to himself. He is too cynical and world-weary to believe in lust's illusion; instead, common sense dictates that a "fall guy" must be sacrificed to the police, and that the guilty-as-sin O'Shaughnessy is the only logical choice.

The Maltese Falcon comprises the beginning of the Hollywood A movie era for émigré Peter Lorre, and working with actors Humphrey Bogart, Sydney Greenstreet and Mary Astor, anchored with a screenplay written and a film directed by John Huston, Lorre's Warners premiere was perhaps the pinnacle of his Hollywood career. *The Maltese Falcon* is simply a momentum-building intelligent slice of propulsive cinema, and Peter Lorre's fourth-billed contribution as Joel Cairo established the little man as a strange character player, but one that mesmerized the screen with energy, subtlety, over-exuberance and charisma.

CREDITS: Executive Producers: Henry Blanke and Hal B. Wallis; Director: John Huston; Original Music: Adolph Deutsch; Cinematography: Arthur Edeson; Editing: Thomas Richards; Art Direction: Robert M. Haas; Costume Design: Orry-Kelly; Make-up: Perc Westmore; Sound: Oliver S. Garretson; Dialogue Director: Robert Foulk; Screenplay: John Huston, Based upon the Novel by Dashiell Hammett; Released by Warner Bros., 1941

CAST: Humphrey Bogart (Sam Spade); Mary Astor (Brigid O'Shaughnessy); Gladys George (Iva Archer); Peter Lorre (Joel Cairo); Barton MacLane (Detective Lieutenant Dundy); Lee Patrick (Effie Perine); Sydney Greenstreet (Kasper Gutman); Ward Bond (Detective Tom Polhaus); Jerome Cowan (Miles Archer); Elisha Cook, Jr. (Wilmer Cook); James Burke (Luke); Murray Alper (Frank Richman); John Hamilton (Attorney Bryan)

ALL THROUGH THE NIGHT
1942
by Anthony Ambrogio

Director Vincent Sherman worked with Peter Lorre only once, on *All Through the Night* (1942).

> From Peter's behavior I surmised that he had given up hope of ever doing serious and meaningful work in Hollywood and had made up his mind to earn as much money as possible, enjoy life, and "make faces." I sensed a bitterness and cynicism hidden inside, which finally resulted in a mockery of himself. Late one afternoon I was shooting a simple scene in which he has to run down a corridor and try to get into a room where [Humphrey] Bogart and [William] Demarest have just locked themselves in. Peter draws a gun and shoots at the lock, as Judith Anderson comes down the corridor yelling, "Was ist loss?" Peter replies in German and the scene ends. I called out, "Cut," but not "Print," thinking I might be able to get a better take. Peter spoke up.
>
> "That's all, brother Vince," he said. "I can only do this kind of crap once a day. Besides, it's six o'clock. Time to go home." (Vincent Sherman, *Studio Affairs: My Life as a Film Director* [Lexington, KY: The University Press of Kentucky, 1996], p. 101)

What conclusions can we draw from this anecdote? (1) Actors are not the best judges of their own work. (2) Never believe what an actor tells you at quitting time when he wants to knock off for the day. (In this, Lorre may have been following his buddy Bogart's lead: Bogart, "during his years of stardom would have written into every contract that he would leave the set promptly at six" [A.M. Sperber and Eric Lax, *Bogart* (New York: William Morrow and Company, Inc., 1997), p. 67]).

All Through the Night is neither the greatest movie Peter Lorre ever made nor the film that contains his greatest performance. It is, however, a minor masterpiece, and Lorre is a major factor in its success.

Peter Lorre starred with Conrad Veidt in *All Through the Night*. (Photofest)

By now—by rights—*All Through the Night*'s reputation should be enormous, if only for its pivotal position in Humphrey Bogart's filmography. Following his acknowledged 1941 classics, *High Sierra* and *The Maltese Falcon*, this important transitional movie cemented Bogart's star status a year before *the* acknowledged Bogart classic, *Casablanca* (1943), set his superstardom in concrete. *All Through the Night* was popular at the time of its release ("its box-office receipts were even better than those of *The Maltese Falcon*," report Sperber and Lax, *Bogart*, p. 180), it has a stellar cast whose fame has grown greater over the years, and it is, in many ways, a kind of "trial run" for *Casablanca*. Working against *All Through the Night* is the fact that it *isn't Casablanca*; it lacks that film's credentials and "seriousness of purpose."

For years, I've noticed *All Through the Night*'s affinities with *Casablanca,* and I always hoped to be the first to enumerate them in print—but Sperber and Lax beat me to it: "What began as an unpretentious little comedy—though with a budget twice that of *The Maltese Falcon*—was in some ways a zany dry run for *Casablanca*" (*Bogart*, p. 172).

All Through the Night remains an unpretentious little comedy, but its composition and circumstances elevated it to something more—all the more reason to wonder why it's never been given its cinematic due.

Consider that stellar cast, consisting of future *Casablanca* stars Bogart (as a cynical hero not quite as world-weary as Rick Blaine), Conrad Veidt (as a Nazi spy as civilized and sinister as Major Strasser) and Peter Lorre (reteaming with his *Maltese Falcon* co-star, playing a psychotic hitman). In addition, Ludwig Stössel, who has a significant supporting role as Mr. Miller in *All Through the Night*, turns up (uncredited) in *Casablanca*, as the memorable émigré Mr. Leuchtag, who practices his English at Rick's café. ("What watch?" ..."Such watch!"). Later, Stössel was a regular ("Ludwig") on the short-lived *Casablanca* TV series (1955).

All Through the Night has many reliable contract players who *don't* appear in *Casablanca* but nevertheless give *All Through the Night* the same excitement and richness that Claude Rains, Sydney Greenstreet, S.Z. Sakall, Leonid Kinskey, Dan Seymour, et al. bring to *Casablanca*: Frank McHugh (Bogart's sidekick and chauffeur, who gets married early in the film and is then frustrated in his attempts to have a honeymoon), Jane Darwell (Bogart's very Irish mother, whose intuition fuels the plot: "When I've got a feelin', I've got a feelin'!"), Barton MacLane and Edward Brophy (Bogart's "business" associates), Wallace Ford (a fast-talking lawyer), James Burke (a dumb flatfoot) and Martin Kosleck (a Goebbels-like Nazi; *all* his Nazis were Goebbels-like. He himself played Goebbels three times: in *Confessions of a Nazi Spy* [1939], *The Hitler Gang* [1944], and *Hitler* [1962]). *All Through the Night* is further distinguished by a trio of later (now late) TV greats: a pre-Uncle Charlie (*My Three Sons*) William Demarest (as the unfailingly pessimistic "Sunshine"), a pre-Sergeant Bilko Phil Silvers (as a near-sighted waiter) and a pre-Ralph Kramden Jackie Gleason (as the double-talking Starchie). Sherman cast Silvers and Gleason at Jack Warner's request because Warner was "tired of paying these guys $250 a week to do nothing but sit on their ass" (quoted by Sherman, p. 99). For good measure, Judith Anderson (*Rebecca*'s Mrs. Danvers herself) turns up as a very lady-like, very English Nazi.

All Through the Night was Sherman's first A picture after a number of Bs. His directorial début was *The Return of Dr. X* (1939; Bogart's only horror film); his most recent movie had been *Underground* (1941), a melodrama about German resistance to Nazism (featuring Martin Kosleck as a Goebbels-like Nazi). If Sherman were a more prestigious director, *All Through the Night*'s reputation would be enhanced (since *All Through the Night* is arguably his best work).

The movie tells the story of "Gloves" Donahue (Bogart), a New York City gambler who's not above stacking the odds in his favor. When Mr. Miller (Ludwig Stössel), the German baker whose cheesecakes are the only kind Gloves eats, is killed, Gloves' mother (Jane Darwell) involves him in the murder investigation. Gloves' reluctant participation turns earnest when he learns there's a *femme* to *cherchez*: Leda Hamilton (Kaaren Verne), who sings at a night spot owned by Gloves' rivals, Marty Callahan (Barton MacLane) and Joe Denning (Edward Brophy). While Gloves is at the club, Denning is murdered, and Gloves is accused of the crime. In the course of clearing himself and fingering the real culprits, Gloves and his sidekicks Sunshine (William Demarest) and Barney (Frank McHugh) uncover a nest of Fifth "Colyumists" (as Gloves calls them) operating in Manhattan and thwart a plot to blow up a battleship in the Brooklyn Navy Yard.

On the surface, this plot sounds nothing like *Casablanca*, but in several significant ways it is, albeit in modified, comic form. Like *Casablanca*, *All Through the Night* features a shady, apolitical protagonist who forsakes neutrality in favor of socially conscious engagement—spurred on (at least in part) by the love of a good woman. That good woman, as in *Casablanca*, is "a mysterious European woman running from a past she can't explain" (*Bogart*, p. 173), but the comparison stops there. *All Through the Night* lacks *Casablanca*'s strong and compelling female lead. German-born Kaaren Verne, who plays Leda Hamilton, is pretty but no Ingrid Bergman. And the role of Leda is much more light-weight than that of Ilsa Lund, though I always suspected that she was meant to be an Ingrid Bergman type, an impression confirmed by Sperber and

Lax: "Hal Wallis settled for her after he was unable to get his first choice, David O. Selznick's recent discovery, Ingrid Bergman" (*Bogart*, p. 173).

Second-choice Verne probably got the nod because she had starred in Sherman's *Underground*. Verne's best year in the movies proved to be 1942; besides *All Through the Night*, she also appeared in *King's Row* and *Sherlock Holmes and the Secret Weapon*. (She also met Peter Lorre on the set of *All Through the Night*, fell in love and began an affair, culminating in their 1951 marriage after Lorre divorced his first wife. They subsequently divorced.) Her later, limited credits include *The Seventh Cross* [1944], *The Bad and the Beautiful* [1952, uncredited] and *Ship of Fools* [1965].

All Through the Night lacks *Casablanca*'s tragi-romantic dimension: the love triangle that complicates and adds dramatic depth to the story, wherein disappointment in love effects the hero's initial withdrawal from engagement and the return of his lover allows him to renew his activism. This raises the issue of *class*—both in the caste and aesthetic sense. There's no doubt that *Casablanca*'s romantic couple is classier than its equivalent in *All Through the Night*, adding another dimension to the movie. There is no self-sacrifice at the end of *All Through the Night*. There are no lines comparable to "The problems of three little people don't amount to a hill of beans in this crazy world" or "We'll always have Paris." (Instead, the final exchange between the heroine and hero in *All Through the Night* is "I … feel it's about time someone knocked the Axis back on its heels," and "Excuse me, baby. What she means is it's time somebody knocked those heels back on their axis." —Funny, but certainly not as *classy*.)

Of course, the world situation changed dramatically between January 1942, when *All Through the Night* came out, and January 1943, when *Casablanca* went into wide release, adding yet another dimension to the movie. Because it was filmed before Pearl Harbor, there's nothing in *All Through the Night* that can possibly have the portentousness or the resonance of Rick Blaine's "If it's December 7 in Casablanca, what time is it in New York? …I bet they're asleep in New York; I bet they're asleep all over America." So we really can't fault Warner Bros. for spinning a comic yarn of "mother love" and "Fifth 'Colyumnists'" rather than a grimmer fable of war.

Like *Casablanca*, *All Through the Night*'s multinational factions (here represented by rival gangs—Donahue's and Callahan's—and an assortment of ethnic types, including Wyoming cowboys, a Jewish waiter, a Chinese laundryman and a black servant) unite against a common, ruthless enemy. But *All Through the Night* also lacks *Casablanca*'s "seriousness of purpose." As satisfying as its climax is, wherein the diverse groups and "warring" factions ("The people you said you would split into angry little groups. You can't beat them, Ebbing") band together to break up the Nazis' meeting, it cannot compare to the emotional shivers *Casablanca* still creates when Victor Lazlo (Paul Henreid) leads Rick's band in a stirring rendition of "La Marseillaise," drowning out the Nazis' singing, or when Captain Renault (Claude Rains) finally declares himself on the side of the angels by telling his men to "Round up the usual suspects."

All Through the Night is a Bogart vehicle (giving him ample opportunity to strut his grown-up Dead-End-kid stuff), but it is not *just* a Bogart vehicle: He takes everybody else along for the ride. It actually is an ensemble piece, sparked by Bogart and Demarest and Bogart-Demarest-McHugh performing as a wise-cracking comedy duo/trio in their scenes together, and marked by a colorful cast of supporting characters spouting the

Sunshine (William Demarest) , Donahue (Humphrey Bogart) and Pepi (Lorre) help make up the ensemble cast of All Through the Night. (Photofest)

kind of rapid-fire dialogue that distinguished so many golden age Warner Bros. films. (The double-talk scene, wherein Gloves and Sunshine confuse the Nazi spies with their verbal flim-flammery, is particularly memorable.)

All Through the Night is not a Lorre vehicle. Nor is his role in it so flashy that it overshadows everyone else's. Instead, it's an integral, memorable part of an ensemble cast, standing alongside the other performers' turns. In this sense, it recalls and anticipates his work in *The Maltese Falcon* and *Casablanca*, both ensemble pieces. Although the villains interact with the good guys, usually individually but sometimes in pairs, they share several scenes together, in which their personalities (as varied as the Gutman-Cairo-Wilmer trio in *The Maltese Falcon*) clash: Veidt's Ebbing—cold, controlled, but obviously smitten by Leda Hamilton; Anderson's Madame (a more thankless role; she doesn't even have a name)—aloof, imposing (even when Bogart calls her "sister"), jealous of Leda and carrying a torch for Ebbing; and Lorre's Pepi—homicidal, pragmatic and in love with himself.

Lorre's first scene occurs some eight minutes into the picture: He's delightfully menacing as the yet-unidentified Pepi who strolls into Mr. Miller's shop, wearing a funny-looking hat, humming a tune and munching a bag popcorn. He addresses the little proprietor familiarly ("Hello, Papa Miller. How's everything?"), immediately establishing for us his relationship with the shopkeeper: both intimate and condescending. "Hello!" Mr. Miller replies in a tone that clearly means "Good-bye." Pepi draws a long face and mimics Miller ("Hello!'") then criticizes his rudeness ("You're not very polite today. You didn't ask me how I am")—until he spies a jar on the counter: "Look! The candies I like," he rhapsodizes. "I'll take a few—" he grabs a fistful. "You don't mind?" he adds, as a rhetorical, *fait-accompli* afterthought. Pepi tells Miller he's been waiting for him all morning; Miller says he's been out on deliveries: "A man must make a living." "Of course," Pepi agrees, "but *I* must make a living, too," he says significantly, sampling the icing from some pastry.

In some ways, in its effect on the audience, one could compare Lorre's character here to Joe Pesci's in *Goodfellas* (1990). Both short men appear comical at first, but soon their actions belie that impression.

Pepi's pretense of camaraderie fades as Miller begins to cross him. "Then you got the information from Schiller?" "No. I won't do this work for you anymore." "Perhaps you need a little encouragement," Pepi suggests. Miller says the wrong thing: "You don't frighten me." "*Frighten* you…" Pepi mutters, as if that's the farthest thing from his mind (as if *frighten* were *all* he was going to do). Lorre casts a wary sidelong glance toward the front to make sure there are no witnesses before following Miller into the back room. When Miller remains defiant ("You are criminals, murderers!"), Pepi shoves him backwards (that'll teach Miller to call him a criminal), and—when Miller threatens to go to the police—Pepi slugs the old man down the cellar stairs, then advances on him, gun drawn (that'll teach Miller to call him a murderer).

The close-up of Miller, pleading helplessly, "No!—" dissolves into the spinning tire of Gloves' car as he speeds to the shop in response to a call from his mother—thus bringing the joint Gloves/Pepi introductions around "full circle," so to speak.

First the good guy, then the bad guy enters, in succeeding scenes, and Mr. Miller is the link that ties the two together. Initially, both emanate an aura of menace, but, subsequently, the picture makes clear that Gloves' menace, unlike Pepi's, is more style than substance. Gloves gets bellicose when Louie (Phil Silvers) serves him a "reasonable facsimile" of Miller's cheesecake because the restaurant hasn't yet received its daily supply: "When I order cheesecake, I don't expect to get mucilage!… You tell Charlie to take his cheesecake from Miller's only—or else." However, almost immediately, belligerence turns to benevolence. Mr. Miller arrives and attributes his tardiness to "a little pain in my back." Gloves tells him to "See Dr. Lechelle, and tell him I sent you," then buys an entire basket of flowers from a street-vendor whom he knows by name, throws a bunch of bills at her and gives the bouquet to Miller for Ma Donahue. The scene ends as Herman looks approvingly after Gloves; a dissolve from the "Miller Home Bakery" sign on Miller's truck to the same sign on his shop window takes us across town as Miller arrives with the flowers for Mrs. Donahue, and then Pepi shows up (without flowers for anyone—although he does pause to smell the blossoms before he badgers, bullies, and then butchers Miller).

(A later incident underscores Pepi's nonchalant brutality. In Ebbing's office, when another reluctant collaborator balks at stealing sensitive drawings, he casually smashes the man's knuckles: While the hapless fellow is making his excuses to Ebbing, the camera follows Pepi's hand as he slides a wooden case forward and then slams it on the man's outspread fingers. "And the next time I break your neck," Pepi growls, for good measure. The wounded man leaves, and Pepi, all smiles, reveling in a job well done, tells Ebbing, "I'm sure he'll bring them now.")

The anticipated Bogart-Lorre confrontation comes 25 minutes into the picture, at the Duchess Club. Pepi turns out to be a pianist, accompanying Leda Hamilton in her singing (and keeping an eye on her). He is suspicious of Gloves' attention to his reluctant collaborator and interrupts their tête-à-tête.

This confrontation pales by comparison to the more famous Bogart-Lorre scenes in *Falcon* and *Casablanca*. In those films, the Bogart-Lorre clash also served to introduce Lorre's character. Here, we've already seen him in action, so—since we already know his murderous capabilities—we perhaps expect something more than we get. In all three films, Lorre plays the "straight man" to Bogart, who gets the better lines—though for a movie that otherwise bristles with snappy dialogue, the exchange between Lorre and Bogart here is disappointingly flat. ("I'd like to finish my drink, please," says Leda. "But we have to rehearse," Pepi insists. "Didn't you hear her? The lady said she'd like to finish her drink," interjects Gloves. "And I said we have no time," Pepi retorts. Scintillating!)

Lorre's confrontation with Bogart in *All Through the Night* cannot match his one-to-one run-ins with him in *The Maltese Falcon* (wherein a fey Joel Cairo, after being disarmed by Spade, finally gets the drop on him and persists in his search of Spade's office) and in *Casablanca*, with its much more memorable dialogue (e.g., "You despise me, don't you, Rick?" "I would if I gave you any thought."). Lorre tugs at Leda, and Bogart advises him not to do that, but the hostilities are cut short before they start by the intervention of Joe Denning and two bouncers, who eject Gloves from the club. There's no drag-out fighting as in *Falcon*, wherein Lorre gets slapped by Mary Astor and Bogart prevents him from retaliating. ("When you're slapped, you'll take it and like it.")

The film's early juxtaposition of the protagonist and antagonist and the pair's subsequent confrontation lead the viewer to believe that Bogart and Lorre will square off again by picture's end. However, that climactic confrontation never comes to pass (which may be another reason for *All Through the Night's* diminished reputation): *All Through the Night*'s big finish involves Bogart and Nazi bigwig Conrad Veidt on a speedboat filled with dynamite, *after* Lorre's ignominious demise.

Most of the rest of Lorre's screen time in the movie consists of short bursts—a fleeting glimpse on-screen or a line or two of dialogue (frequently in German). After Gloves is bounced, Pepi takes Leda back to her dressing room and berates her (in German) for fraternizing with Gloves, then shoots Joe Denning (off-screen) when he interrupts their argument. Later, he kidnaps Sunshine when Sunshine and Gloves are exploring a toy warehouse. (The image of Lorre gagging and pulling back the much taller William Demarest could be laughable, but it happens fast and works in context.) He alerts Madame to Gloves' presence at their antique auction, lurks in the shadows, about to shoot Gloves when the latter draws a gun on Ebbing (Leda sees him and conks Bogart with an *objet d'art* before Pepi can shoot), chases Bogart through a building and Central Park, and discovers him infiltrating the Nazi meeting, but—except for a brief exchange when Pepi tells a (supposedly) trussed-up Donahue that he's to be taken to New Jersey in a crate—the two share no other dialogue scenes. Which is not to say that Lorre doesn't deliver some marvelous dialogue elsewhere (even when his dialogue isn't marvelous, his delivery is), as when he describes Donahue to Ebbing: "Oh, he's a Broadway big shot. Very belligerent personality"—ironic, coming from Pepi. (For his part, Donahue describes Pepi variously as "that squirt" and "a goggle-eyed little rat.")

Lorre gives Pepi a unique perspective, as exemplified by two wonderful moments in *All Through the Night*. During the chase through Central Park, Ebbing comes across Pepi leaning against a tree, gun arm akimbo. "What are you standing here for?" he asks. "Oh, we'll never find them. They are gone," Pepi replies. He doesn't mind chasing and killing easy-to-find victims, but he's not about to overexert himself (despite Ebbing's "We must find them" imperative).

Lorre and Judith Anderson share a scene. (Photofest)

At the end of the movie, after the good guys have invaded the Nazis' hide-out and broken up their meeting, Ebbing orders Pepi to come with him: They'll blow up the battleship themselves. "What? The two of us alone?" Pepi can't believe his ears. "Yes," Ebbing answers, already on the move. Pepi follows him, though only to protest: "But that's silly. I'm not going." (I love this line from Peter Lorre's lips: the Nazi who won't follow orders.) "What did you say?" This time, Ebbing can't believe *his* ears. (You'd think, given Pepi's earlier Central Park remark, that Ebbing would be used to Pepi's recalcitrance. But he isn't. Ebbing is a true Nazi, devoted to the cause.) "I'm not going," Pepi repeats; "Suicide is not for me." So Ebbing shoots him (it's murder instead of suicide), then delivers Pepi's eulogy: "*Schwine!*"

Compare these delightful "humanizing" touches (if such an adjective can be applied to a cold-blooded killer like Pepi) to Joel Cairo's childish, child-like outburst, calling Gutman a "fathead" and "idiot" upon discovering the Maltese Falcon has been replaced by a fake. Such language and actions distinguish Lorre's villain from the usual run-of-the-mill psychotic. Note, too, Vincent Sherman's assertion: "Lorre often came in with ideas and lines that were better than the script, and I used them" (p. 100). Sherman doesn't say *which* ideas and lines Lorre came up with, but I strongly suspect that Pepi's behavior in Central Park and just before he gets shot are two examples. Obviously, Lorre was doing more than merely mugging his way through his roles, even if he didn't consider his Hollywood work serious and meaningful.

Which brings us full circle. Peter Lorre may have claimed he was making "crap" when he was filming *All Through the Night*, but he made it elegant crap. And he came out smelling like a rose.

He also made money and enjoyed life—often at other people's expense:

> Charlie Lederer and I once made a bet of a hundred dollars. I swore I could make Mayo [Methot, Bogart's third wife] and Bogey have a tremendous

fight within five minutes, starting from scratch. I invited Mayo, Bogey, and Lederer to my house one night. As I was walking through the bar carrying some drinks, I said, more or less to myself, "General MacArthur." That was all I said. Within three minutes Bogey was hitting her over the head with a glass and she was biting and scratching him. She was for MacArthur and he was violently against. (Lorre, quoted in Ezra Goodman, *The Fifty Year Decline and Fall of Hollywood* [1961; rpt. New York: McFadden Books, 1962], p. 252)

Bogart was constantly battling with Mayo when he and Lorre were shooting *All Through the Night* (and *The Maltese Falcon*—and *Casablanca*), but this story probably post-dates that film.

A story that doesn't post-date *All Through the Night* is one that Vincent Sherman relates: "Peter liked to tease [Judith Anderson] and got a big laugh every time he left her dressing room by pretending to zip up his fly. When she found out about it, she went after him with a hairbrush" (Sherman, p. 103). The fly gag was either popular with Lorre or apocryphal because Aljean Harmetz and Sperber and Lax—all apparently basing their information on Mary Astor's autobiography, *A Life on Film*—recount a similar incident from *The Maltese Falcon.*

Encouraged by John Huston, who shared the same nasty sense of humor, they [Bogart and Lorre] embarrassed any visitors the publicity department brought onto the set of the Falcon with practical jokes that included Bogart's calling Sydney Greenstreet a fat old fool and Lorre's coming out of Mary Astor's dressing room with his fly unfastened (Harmetz, p. 204)

Outsiders were made unwelcome. "We didn't want anyone looking over our shoulder," Astor said, and the cast assured it. A midwestern women's

> club was greeted by a scene played for its benefit. Peter Lorre swaggering out of Astor's trailer, buttoning his fly and calling back, "Bye, Mary." (Sperber and Lax, pp. 160-161)

My urban-folklorist friend would argue that the similarity of these two stories calls the veracity of both into question.

Also worth questioning is the conclusion of Vincent Sherman's "crap" story:

> "Just a minute, Peter," I replied, pretending to be angry. "Don't talk to me about crap—how did you do all those Mr. Motos at Fox?"
>
> "I took dope!" he said without hesitation. We all laughed, and I called it a day.
>
> Months later, Hedda [Sherman's wife] and I were invited to a dinner party at Rudi Fehr's house. He was the editor of All Through the Night and one of the best. I told the story about Peter merely to provide a laugh.
>
> "But he did," said Rudi. "He took dope all during the making of the series." The laughter stopped. We were stunned. (Sherman, p. 101)

There's no indication as to how Rudi Fehr *knew* that Lorre took dope, and—given the actor's penchant for practical jokes—we can't know for sure if he wasn't pulling someone's leg. But, if the story *is* true, does the fact that Lorre didn't need dope to get through *All Through the Night* mean that he felt it really *wasn't* as crappy as he pretended? (I'd say so.)

CREDITS: Director: Vincent Sherman; Producer: Jerry Wald; Executive Producer: Hal B. Wallis; Scenarists: Leonard Spiegelgass and Edwin Gilbert, From an Original Story by Leonard Q. Ross [Leo Rosten] and Spiegelgass; Cinematographer: Sidney Hickox; Editor: Rudi Fehr; Music: Adolph Deutsch (score); Original Songs: Johnny Mercer and Arthur Schwartz ("All Through the Night") and Lillian Goodman ("Chérie, I Love You So"); Orchestration: Frank Perkins; Assistant Director: William Kissel; Art Direction: Max Parker; Special Effects: Edwin DuPar; Sound: Oliver S. Garretson; Released January 10, 1942; Warner Bros.; B&W; 107 minutes

CAST: Humphrey Bogart (Alfred "Gloves" Donahue); Conrad Veidt (Franz Ebbing); Kaaren Verne (Leda Hamilton); William Demarest (Sunshine); Frank McHugh (Barney); Jane Darwell (Mrs. Donahue); Peter Lorre (Pepi); Judith Anderson (Madame); Jackie Gleason (Starchie); Phil Silvers (Louie); Wallace Ford (Spats Hunter); Barton MacLane (Marty Callahan); Edward Brophy (Joe Denning); Martin Kosleck (Steindorff); Jean Ames (Annabelle); Ludwig Stössel (Herman Miller); Irene Seidner (Mrs. Miller); James Burke (Officer Forbes); Ben Welden (Smitty); Hans Schumm (Anton); Charles Cane (Spence); Frank Sully (Sage); Sam McDaniel (Deacon, Gloves' Valet)

THE BOOGIE MAN WILL GET YOU
1942
by Bryan Senn

A HORROR-AND-FUN-FILLED FREE-FOR-ALL
...WITH GLEE FOR ALL!—*The Boogie Man Will Get You* poster

"He was a delightful man; I miss Peter terribly.
A truly original actor, there was no one like him."
—Boris Karloff shortly after Peter Lorre's death in 1964

In the summer of 1936 Peter Lorre signed a contract with Twentieth Century-Fox, thinking that studio head Darryl F. Zanuck would provide him with a chance to escape his "creep" persona and broaden his thespic horizons. Instead, the studio gave him false eyelids and shoved him into a series of low-budget films as the Japanese detective, Mr. Moto. In 1939 Lorre obtained his release from Fox (where he'd become sorely disaffected with the studio's reluctance to further his career with anything other than B-budget *Moto* entries) and began freelancing. (Just prior to his release, Fox had intended to revive his fiendish film persona by putting Lorre into *The Gorilla* opposite the Ritz Brothers; but when the actor balked, they cast Bela Lugosi instead.) Lorre's subsequent flurry of freelance activity attracted the attention of Columbia executive Irving Briskin, who assigned producer Wally McDonald the task of finding vehicles that would exploit Lorre's sinister screen image. The result was three very different programmers: the tasteless terrors found on the *Island of Doomed Men* (1940), the sensitive trauma suffered by *The Face Behind the Mask* (1941) and the farcical horrors of *The Boogie Man Will Get You*.

Usually looked upon as the "poor relation" of Columbia's Mad Doctor family (whose "legitimate" members consist of *The Man They Could Not Hang, The Man With Nine Lives, Before I Hang* and *The Devil Commands*)—or at best thought of as a "crazy uncle" that nobody ever talks about, *The Boogie Man Will Get You* was made by Columbia to capitalize on the phenomenal success of the Broadway play *Arsenic and Old Lace*, starring Boris Karloff. With Karloff still owing the studio a fifth and final film on his short-term contract, the play's producers reluctantly agreed to let their name star take a brief hiatus from the show to fulfill his screen obligation. With the desperate savvy borne of being the smallest of the eight "major" studios, Columbia rushed out a look-alike script to take advantage of Karloff's current gig. (Columbia was also cognizant of the fact that the proposed movie version of *Arsenic and Old Lace* could not contractually be filmed until after the play had closed on Broadway, thereby allowing Columbia to beat Warner Bros. to the cinematic punch with their ersatz variation.)

Larry Parks, Jeff Donnell, Maude Eburne and Boris Karloff watch Lorre as Dr. Lorencz.

Weary of his repetitive mad doctor series at Columbia, Karloff commented that:

> Being a bogey-man—like baggage-smashing and truck driving—is apt to be a rather exhausting occupation. I know, because I've tried all three. On the whole, I think I would prefer truck driving to house haunting.

It must have been a relief, then, when he returned from his lengthy and highly successful Broadway stage engagement in *Arsenic and Old Lace* to find that the final film on his Columbia contract was going to be a comedy. (Upon completion of his movie commitment, Karloff immediately returned to the stage in a 66-week tour of *Arsenic and Old Lace.* Ironically, when it finally came time to turn the play into a motion picture, Karloff was unable to appear in it due to his stage engagement—whereas Lorre [who was never *in* the play] *did* appear [to excellent comic effect] in the film.) And Karloff must have been even more pleased to learn that his co-star would be his friend and fellow "boogie man," Peter Lorre. Ironically, while *The Boogie Man Will Get You* was intended (and is still generally thought of) as a vehicle for Karloff, it is Lorre who steals the show.

Early in his film career, Peter Lorre commented that, "When I am studying a part and working out its shades and nuances, I become so absorbed that I'm in a fever pitch.

Professor Billings (Karloff) tries to create another superman to aid the war effort.

I take my work with the utmost seriousness." Thanks to continued typecasting, however, by the 1940s this "seriousness" had long given way to a professional resignation that the actor frequently alleviated with a self-mocking humor, both on-screen and off.

Lorre held no pretensions about his work during the late 1930s and early '40s. He labeled his many B-films of this period, "nice little thrown-together quickies that kept studios happy at the box office and paid off a lot of our bills." Lorre's straight-faced, self-deprecating humor was legendary. Due to his on-screen persona, Lorre began receiving some rather unusual fan mail in the early 1940s. When one fan wrote, "Dear Master: I would love to be tortured by you," Lorre answered: "You have been tortured enough by going to see my pictures!"

Even when performing in films that were obviously beneath his talents as an artist, Lorre was a thorough professional who stamped his unique brand of charisma and (when appropriate) humor on whatever he did. "He was very precise," remarked Leon Ames (*The Films of Peter Lorre*), who appeared with Lorre in *Mysterious Mr. Moto*.

> All of his business and everything that he did in front of the camera was very studied. He was sharp. That man never missed a word or a line in his performance, ever. He was like a computer. I saw no evidence of him ever being influenced by anything

other than his job. He was a technical actor, and
you had to be good to cope with him.

Perhaps Peter Lorre saw *The Boogie Man Will Get You*, with its underlying war effort/anti-Nazi theme, as a comical poke in the nose to Herr Hitler… or perhaps he considered it just another "thrown-together quickie." Either way, Lorre injected enough comic life into his portrayal to make *The Boogie Man Will Get You* worth watching—but only just.

Top-billed Boris Karloff plays Professor Nathaniel Billings, "doctor of biochemistry, Century College—before it went under." Billings owns the historic Billings Tavern, a run-down rural inn. With no time for innkeeping, he leaves the day-to-day details to his chicken-loving housekeeper, Amelia (Maude Eburne), and the pig-farming handyman, Ebenezer (George McKay), while the Professor spends his time in his basement laboratory trying to transform unwary door-to-door salesmen into "supermen" to aid the war effort. ("I'm merely toying with a few physiodynamics," explains the Professor, "shaking the unshakable laws of existence, so to speak.") Along comes naïve Winnie Leyden (ingenue Jeff Donnell), followed by her skeptical (and still-adoring) ex-husband Bill (Larry Parks), who wants to buy the old place and turn it into a charming hotel. The Professor is only too happy to sell, wishing only to be allowed to continue his experiments in the cellar. Enter Peter Lorre as Dr. Lorencz, M.D., whose shingle (hung outside his house) reads:

JUSTICE of the PEACE
MAYOR
CORONER
LOANS and INSURANCE
NOTARY PUBLIC

Lorencz holds the lease on the dilapidated inn, and has a financial interest in just about everything in the small New England town. With the transaction made, Lorencz learns of the Professor's experiments and sees a sizable profit potential in the proceedings (even though, as of yet, the experiment has failed—with five perfectly preserved corpses hidden in a secret room serving as testament to the Professor's determination if not his efficacy). Soon bodies are found—and disappear—by the uncomprehending Winnie and Bill; a suspicious boarder arrives and begins poking around; Amelia wanders about clucking like a chicken; and another traveling salesman shows up and volunteers for the experiment (Maxie Rosenbloom doing his usual amiable idiot routine—"Am I unconscious yet?" he asks after sniffing from a bottle of ether). It all winds up (in a painfully "zany" fashion) with the latest experiment interrupted by both the police and "a fascist aviator who just escaped from the prison camp in Canada" (Silvio Bacigalupi). The aviator has 40 kilos of dynamite in his knapsack with which to blow up the nearby munitions plant, and holds the principals at bay. The five hidden "corpses" revive (they weren't dead after all, they were just in a state of suspended animation), the terrorist's bomb is a dud, and the two deputies round up all the parties and prepare to take them away:

Professor: "Where are you taking us?"

Deputy: "To a nice quiet little place called Idlewild Sanitarium."

Professor: "But that's the asylum."

Dr. Lorencz (grinning): "So it is, so it is. But don't worry, Professor, I'm the chairman of the board of directors up there."

Obviously "inspired by" (to use a more charitable term than "copied" or "stolen from") the then-current hit stage play *Arsenic and Old Lace*, *The Boogie Man Will Get You* (like most copies) lacks the crispness of the original. It also takes *Arsenic*'s more linear and plausible (and much funnier) concept of two kindly old ladies "doing good" by painlessly putting lonely old men out of their misery (resulting in a baker's dozen of corpses buried in their Brooklyn home's cellar) and replaces it with a crackpot scientist (Karloff) and his mercenary helper (Lorre) trying to create a "superman" to aid the war effort (resulting in a basement morgue full of *ersatz* cadavers). The superman angle (complete with ludicrous lab machinery and silly headgear) turns *Arsenic*'s clever take on euthanasia into a serial-like farce, and the "human bomb" fascist aviator who pops up for no particular reason at the end adds an air of everything-but-the-kitchen-sink desperation. Furthermore, in *Arsenic and Old Lace*, nobody ran around acting like a chicken (as the fowl-obsessed Amelia does)—which comes off as just silly rather than funny. True, *Arsenic* featured a character (Teddy) who thought he was President Theodore Roosevelt (and who dug the cellar graves thinking they were the locks to the Panama Canal), but that's a lot more dignified (and amusing) than a barnyard animal. When finally filmed in 1944 by Warner Bros., *Arsenic and Old Lace* ran nearly two hours—but watching that clever and at times howlingly funny movie seems to take half as long as viewing *Boogie Man*'s tepid 65 minutes.

While top-billed Boris Karloff is obviously supposed to be the prime comic character, Peter Lorre (playing his sidekick, of sorts) is really the main event, fleshing out his supporting role with bits of physical humor and ad-libs that surpass whatever the pallid script limply offers.

Lorre is always engaging in some amusing bit of business, casually picking bits of lint off his trousers, for instance, or absentmindedly drumming his fingers on his chest. Upon greeting someone, he invariably lifts his big-brimmed hat in a speedy and perfunctory manner, its rapidity making the simple gesture quite comical. And he always carries a Siamese kitten in his coat pocket (!), a living prop that he puts to amusing use.

Lorre's deadpan, distracted, even dismissive demeanor makes the marginally amusing dialogue quite funny. For example:

> Karloff: Have you brought the filthy thing with you?
> Lorre: What filthy thing?
> Karloff: The mortgage—the *leech* you placed upon my neck.
> Lorre: Oh, the leech; yeah, I have it."

Lorre, the local sheriff, throws in with the Professor's plan while trying to keep things under control.

Lorre's mild and accepting tone as he casually admits to having the "leech" while he fishes the papers out of his pocket gives the exchange its comical punch.

It is apparent that many of Lorre's quips are unscripted ad-libs that the diminutive actor sneaks into the pauses in Karloff's dialogue. (By all accounts this was something Lorre did more and more as he got older and more disillusioned with his less-than-weighty film assignments.) Karloff, trained in the old school of stage acting, didn't like to deviate from the written screenplay and generally failed to react to Lorre's impromptu asides, making them that much funnier—jokes that only Lorre and the viewer are in on, as it were. For example, when Karloff shows Lorre the secret room that houses the "perfectly preserved" corpses, the following exchange occurs:

> Karloff: "This is where they used to store the wines and the choice cheeses. Now it enshrines the simple men that have chosen to be martyrs to a great cause." (At this, Lorre rapidly lifts his hat off his head and just as quickly replaces it, the comically perfunctory gesture serving as visual punctuation for Karloff's droll dialogue.)
>
> Lorre (inspecting the sheet-draped bodies): "Very neat, very orderly. Uh, Professor, they are superbly preserved. As a coroner I must say you

have already outmoded formaldehyde. Congratulations. But as a sheriff, I would like to know, how did you keep anyone from—from missing any of your—your *martyrs*?"

Karloff: "Well, we have a great many door-to-door peddlers in this neighborhood. They never have any friends, poor fellows." (Lorre, thumbs hooked in his lapels and fingers lightly drumming his chest as he dreamily half-listens, seemingly awakens from his reverie and shakes his head slightly before emitting a soft, distracted "no" in sympathy.)

Karloff continues: "See, this one sold alarm clocks—" (Here Lorre abruptly breaks his melancholy musings to glance at Karloff a moment before looking at the corpse Karloff gestures toward, and gives a low "oh" in acknowledgment.)

Karloff (pointing): "—there, neckties—" (While Karloff takes a breath before delivering his next line, Lorre turns to where he's pointing and interjects, "Yeah, that's how he looks.")

Karloff (gesturing again): "—hosiery—"

Lorre (jumping in quickly): "He probably didn't have any priority anyway."

Karloff (obviously unaware of Lorre's ad-libs, since he finishes his line while Lorre is still speaking): "—and, uh, let me—oh yes, encyclopedias."

Lorre: "Oh, I'm sure he didn't mind very much."

Throughout the exchange, Lorre's contemplative earnestness and mannerisms, coupled with his quick interjections, make the scene entirely his—despite Karloff receiving the lion's share of the dialogue and *scripted* humor.

This is not to say that Boris Karloff fails to contribute or convince (quite the opposite, for his mild-mannered moral innocent is both a likable and amusing character), just that Lorre, when "on," overshadows all—if for no other reason than to see what little bits of physical or verbal humor he'll perform next.

It is a delightful and unpredictable performance, highlighting this "boogie man's" flair for comedy (a talent that most often went sorely untapped by Hollywood). It's rather a shame that it was in a second-rate copycat vehicle like *The Boogie Man Will Get You.* While not a bad film, and one that is admittedly amusing in spots, it's also not a *good* film, and one that is largely unmemorable.

The Boogie Man Will Get You (deservedly) fared poorly with the critics. *The New York Herald-Tribune* reviewer complained: "With Mr. Karloff is Peter Lorre, another

What smiles the film manages to provide are courtesy of Lorre.

of cinema's bizarre individuals. He too seems overwhelmed by the mass of trite situations, and becomes neither scary nor funny." (An inaccurate criticism, in my view, since Lorre is one of the few things that *are* funny in this warmed-over comedy.)

The *Hollywood Reporter* was a bit more generous: "As a production, even in supporting spots, the film is largely a waste of the talents of Boris Karloff and Peter Lorre, its costars, and of Lew Landers, its director. Fortunately, none will be embarrassed by the efforts they expend to put it over. The intentions are far better than the material provided."

The Boogie Man Will Get You was released in Great Britain in early 1943, where *Kinematograph Weekly* called it a "screwy comedy melodrama, a wild incursion into the macabre. Most of the characters are completely barmy, but somehow their insanity is a little too studio to promote spontaneous thrills or laughter."

Indeed, no thrills (and precious few laughs) are inspired by this *Boogie Man.* But what few smiles can be found come courtesy of not only one of the screen's most celebrated "boogie men," but one of cinema's most underused natural comedians—Peter Lorre.

CREDITS: Producer: Colbert Clark; Director: Lew Landers; Screenplay: Edwin Bum; Adaptation: Paul Gangelin; Story: Hal Fimberg and Robert B. Hunt; Photography: Henry Freulich; Editor: Richard Fantl; Art Director: Lionel Banks; Associate: Robert Peterson; Interior Decorator: George Montgomery; Music Director: M.W. Stoloff; Sound Technician: C. Althouse; Assistant Director: Seymour Friedman; Released October 22, 1942 by Columbia Pictures; 65 minutes

CAST: Boris Karloff (Prof. Nathaniel Billings), Peter Lorre (Dr. Lorencz), Maxie Rosenbloom (Maxie), Larry Parks (Bill Leyden), Jeff Donnell (Winnie Leyden), Maude Eburne (Amelia Jones), Don Beddoe (J. Gilbert Brampton), George McKay (Ebenezer), Frank Puglia (Silvio Bacigalupi), Eddie Laughton (Johnson), Frank Sully (Officer Starrett), James Morton (Officer Quincy)

CASABLANCA
1942
PASSAGE TO MARSEILLE
1944
THE CONSPIRATORS
1944
by Cindy Ruth Collins

By the early 1940s, Hollywood had dashed most of Peter Lorre's hopes. He had arrived on the West Coast hoping to play diverse roles, but the studios instead reinforced his villainous image. When he finally got to play a hero, in *Mr. Moto*, Lorre despised the series enough that he later claimed he'd taken dope just to get through it.

Not until John Huston took a chance on him in *The Maltese Falcon* did the actor find himself once again playing a delicious role in a great picture. *The Maltese Falcon* raised Lorre's stock at Warner Bros., made him lifelong friends with Humphrey Bogart and Sydney Greenstreet and raised the actor's hopes that perhaps Hollywood might yet have a place for him, at least in excellent character parts.

On the strength of the *Falcon*, the studio put Lorre on the "Tentative Cast List" for another film ("If works out with Universal commitment")—a list which (on April 29, 1942) did not yet include Paul Heinreid as Victor Laszlo, nor Sydney Greenstreet as Ferrari (*Round Up*, 159). Lorre's role as Ugarte would be a brief, two-scene character stint, playing the catalyst for the film's action.

Let's try a bit of understatement here: The end-product, *Casablanca*, was never an under-appreciated film. It got a huge publicity boost from the American liberation of Casablanca a month before the film opened, great reviews in major newspapers and excellent box office. Even Philip T. Hartung noted in his unpublished analysis for the U.S. Office of War Information that he believed the film would "stand up in years to come."

Naturally, Warner Bros. capitalized on this success. The studio cloned two imitators—*Passage to Marseille* and *The Conspirators*—from *Casablanca*. These three films freely recycled plot elements and cast. They also allowed Lorre to renew his fight against the Nazis.

As we all must certainly know, *Casablanca* centers around refugees hoping to get passage to Lisbon and hence America. The most prominent of these refugees are Czech Resistance leader Victor Laszlo and his wife Ilsa Lund (Ingrid Bergman), a woman

Humphrey Bogart, Michael Curtiz, Peter Lorre and Hal Wallis on the set of *Passage to Marseille.*

who, we learn in flashback, had an affair in Paris with Rick Blaine (Humphrey Bogart). Lorre's character, Ugarte, has killed two German couriers to get letters of transit to sell to Laszlo and Ilsa, but with the heat on he gives those papers to Rick (a now-cynical café proprietor). With Ugarte's inevitable capture, Rick confronts the moral decision of what to do with the letters: whether to keep them and hence avenge himself on Ilsa, who ripped his heart up when she left him; whether to take off with Ilsa and the letters; or whether to give them to Laszlo and Ilsa, so that Laszlo might escape and forge Resistance to the Nazis abroad. The idealism lurking beneath Rick's cynicism finally wins out when he sets Laszlo and Ilsa on the plane for Lisbon, and goes off himself to fight with a Free French regiment.

In *Passage to Marseille*, we again travel to an exotic location and again get to cheer on the Free French. Apparently using the logic "If one flashback was good, then three will be better," this film outdoes its progenitor by literally using a flashback-within-a-flashback-within-a-flashback to tell the story of a Free French Air Force squadron, comprising escaped convicts from Devil's Island. Three flashbacks down from the framing story, incidentally, we get another Parisian romance between Humphrey Bogart and a beautiful woman, who this time becomes his wife.

Here Bogart plays Jean Matrac, a Parisian journalist whose criticism of Nazi-sympathizers in the government lands him in prison on a trumped-up murder charge. In his jungle prison, he meets a group of patriotic convicts who escape in order to fight the Nazis, and who are rescued from the ocean by a French ship traveling to Marseilles. (Lorre appears as Marius, one of these would-be Free French). Though Matrac goes along with them, his mistreatment in the jungles of French Guyana has left him so embittered that he has no intention of taking up arms to help France, hoping instead to reunite with his wife. When news arrives, however, of the Nazi occupation

Lorre, Victor Francen, Hedy Lamarr, Paul Henreid and Sydney Greenstreet in *The Conspirators*. (Photofest)

and the French government's capitulation, his patriotism revives as he and the other convicts fight fascist supporters (led by Sydney Greenstreet) for control of the ship. In the end, Matrac becomes a bombardier for the Free French Air Force, and is killed while heroically serving the cause of freedom. (Marius dies earlier, manning the guns in a sea-battle with a Nazi plane.)

If these films have one message, it is this: Resistance is not futile. *The Conspirators*, in fact, tries to show the inner workings of the Resistance, featuring Paul Heinreid as Vincent Van der Lyn (a renowned Resistance leader), Sydney Greenstreet as Quintanilla (leader of a Resistance cell in Lisbon) and Peter Lorre as Bernazsky (a member of that cell). This time Heinreid's character is Dutch instead of Czech. This time an opening montage shows him actually sabotaging and blowing German things up. This time he makes it to Lisbon before, not after, the film's action. And this time he's the romantic, not the second, lead. But he's still basically Victor Laszlo… or at least a lovesick Victor, who hasn't yet got his Ilsa.

In *The Conspirators*, Van der Lyn quickly meets with his Resistance contact (Bernazsky) once he arrives in Lisbon, but by chance he first encounters the mysterious and beautiful French woman Irene (Hedy Lamarr), with whom he immediately becomes infatuated. Like an alcoholic on a binge, Van der Lyn starts missing important meetings with Resistance colleagues and flounces about the Portuguese countryside with his new playmate. This "morning after" has unusually serious consequences though: The agent set to meet him in his rooms is instead murdered by Nazis, while he himself faces charges for the murder. Though Van der Lyn believes Irene set him up, the Resistance cell thinks him the killer. Fortunately, he daringly breaks prison, learns that his beloved also belongs to the Resistance and ultimately discovers her German husband to be the traitor who framed him. (In a perversely convoluted double/counter-agent scenario, we find a German Embassy worker posing as a German Resistance fighter who proves

Sydney Greenstreet and Peter Lorre in *The Conspirators*. (Photofest)

in the end to match his public persona: a German loyal to his government!). Van der Lyn clears himself, exposes and kills the traitor (who conveniently happens to be his romantic rival), gets the girl and then puts his romance on hold by taking the murdered agent's place on a dangerous mission. The End.

Sound ridiculous? Well, suffice it to say that the author of the novel on which the film was based wrote a letter to the editor of *New Republic* calling the film's plot "preposterous rubbish" and marveling at the "mentality which can concoct such nonsense with a straight face" (*Motion Picture Guide*).

Even worse for our purposes: This film makes poor use of Peter Lorre. As Jan Bernazsky, Lorre serves as Van der Lyn's guide. He lurks in corners, smokes cigarettes, provides information and even takes Van der Lyn to his leader. But Bernazsky falls flat.

In the first Berlin review ever written on Lorre, Kurt Pinthus marveled at the actor's ability to move his character between impassivity and hysteria. None of that ability shows up here. Bernazsky is almost wholly impassive. Imagine Ugarte's level of passion as he asks the gendarmes' permission to cash in his chips. Imagine such "passion" in scene after scene, with never a hint of Ugarte's shrieks for Rick to come to his rescue, and you'll have a pretty clear idea of the emotional range this role allowed Lorre to play.

Sure, there are some hints at a passionate nature. We learn that Bernazsky once blew up a room full of Nazis who wanted to send his antique clock collection back to Berlin, and his voice seethes with irony as he describes the Nazi appreciation for art. But, aside from this irony, Bernazsky never *shows* any passion. He only tells. Clearly, the problem lies more in the script than in Lorre's performance. In *The Conspirators*, Bernazsky serves merely a plot function—first as Van der Lyn's connection/guide, and later as a red herring in the double-agent subplot. His character has really nothing to

Lorre as the doomed Ugarte in *Casablanca.*

do except pass on information and stand watch, then wait for Lorre's screen persona to draw our suspicion automatically to the character he portrays once we learn the Resistance has a traitor in its midst.

Yes, in his one piece of extended dialogue, Lorre does invest Bernazsky with some semblance of life, yet the irony in Bernazsky's voice may finally reveal more about Lorre's own feelings toward the Nazis than about the material the writers have given him to work with. Lorre seems mostly to sleepwalk through this role, but Bosley Crowther, at least, absolves him in his *New York Times* review. Crowther writes that director "Jean Negulesco has pitched the whole thing in [such] a mood of scowling solemnity" that "the players literally clench their fists and teeth. Under such antiquated direction, it is not surprising that… Sydney Greenstreet, Peter Lorre, Victor Francen and all that mob should mugg like fools."

Lorre, needless to say, fared better under the direction of Michael Curtiz, teaming first with the director on *Casablanca*, then later on *Passage to Marseille*. These two men—both Hungarians, both Jewish—respected one another's talents. Curtiz gave Lorre the freedom to bring his characters to life on-screen, and he in turn so impressed the actor that Lorre later proclaimed Curtiz not only to eat but to "excrete" pictures (*Round Up*, 185). Despite Lorre's appreciation, Curtiz and his set became the target of innumerable gags during the *Casablanca* shoot.

Some directors, like Alfred Hitchcock and John Huston, had allowed Lorre's legendary sense of humor free reign. Teamed again with Humphrey Bogart, his *Maltese Falcon* pal and off-screen partner-in-crime, Lorre not surprisingly used his four brief days on this shoot to create mischief, and even humorous havoc. Paul Heinreid recounts one prank in which Lorre disrupted production on *Casablanca* by interfering with cinematographer Arthur Edeson's shots:

> Lorre would wait until the stand-ins had left… then he'd sneak onto the set while the actors were being called, erase the original chalk marks and put new ones a short distance away. Unsuspecting, we actors would step up to the new marks and Edeson would look into his camera, then shake his head angrily. "That's all wrong! Are you on the marks?" (quoted in *Behind the Scenes*, 152).

Lorre had more madness where that came from, directing his most notorious gag right at Curtiz himself. In *Casablanca*, as we know, Captain Renault (Claude Rains), coerces sexual favors from young women by promising to grant them exit visas. Like Renault, Michael Curtiz frequently used breaks in shooting to take sexual advantage of young starlets. One can easily imagine what he might have promised in return. In response to Curtiz' assignations, Lorre is said to have "persuaded the sound staff to plant a hidden microphone in the director's favorite studio tryst nest and run a loudspeaker back to the set." Even better, Curtiz apparently never found out that the entire cast and crew had heard his sexual encounters broadcast (*Behind the Scenes*, 152).

French poster for *Casablanca* featuring Lorre.

Lorre staged these gags with seeming impunity. Nevertheless, his sense of humor *had* gotten him in trouble years earlier with German authorities. Obviously, as a Jew, he would eventually have needed to flee Nazi Germany. Additionally, as the man who brought child-killer Hans Beckert to life, he sometimes faced threats from unsophisticated filmgoers who equated the actor with the killer. Once, an angry Berlin mob threw stones at him, in one of several *M*-related incidents which prompted him later to remark to Andre Sennwald that Germany was "too small for two such monsters as Hitler and myself."

A Vichy gendarme closes in on Ugarte in *Casablanca.*

In the early days of Hitler's power, though, Lorre had yet a third, and more immediate, strike against him: his satirical sense of humor, and his tendency to direct it at Nazis. He bravely used improvisational performances on the Berlin stage as a chance to taunt Nazi brownshirts in the audience. Though several different reports exist on what, precisely, caused him to flee Hitler's Germany just days before the Reichstag fire, one such report claims that he was forced out after "making fun of a pamphlet he had been asked to read at a Nazi rally" (*As Time Goes By*, 143).

Like Bogart's characters Rick and Matrac, Lorre clearly had an anti-Nazi past. In fact, with the exception of anti-Nazi youth leader Helmut Dantine (*Casablanca*'s young husband, Jan), Lorre had perhaps the strongest anti-Nazi credentials of any cast members in Curtiz's Resistance films. Little Peter Lorre had boldly engaged the Nazis first-hand, from the stage, long before there was a war. Not surprisingly, he continued to follow developments from America, as Hitler rose in power. He listened, "obsessively" it is said, to Hitler's speeches on the radio. Once, during the filming of a Moto movie, he balked at leaving his dressing room to shoot a scene, fuming at director Norman Foster that "the whole world is falling apart, and you want me to make a picture!" (*Films of Peter Lorre*, 41).

Lorre's antic exterior covered a passionate interior, one which cared deeply about the trouble in Europe, and now the world. Of all his characters in these films, Marius in *Passage to Marseille* most clearly reveals these two poles to Lorre's personality. Yes, Bernazsky does have one humorous (even slapstick) moment, when he upsets a waiter's tray at precisely the right instant to prevent a Nazi from trailing Van der Lyn; and Ugarte, of course, tries humor to insinuate himself into Rick's favor. But Marius combines a consistently ironic and self-mocking air with an underlying passion.

In Marius' first scenes, Lorre conveys his character almost entirely through physical acting. Marius, limp as Raggedy Andy when he's pulled from the ocean, never opens his eyes when first given drink. Instead, he smells the cup, rolls his head as if being roused from stupor, grabs the cup from the inside and lifts it to his mouth in a gesture which hints more at animal instinct than human consciousness. Later, when ordered to stand at attention by Sydney Greenstreet's fascist Major, Marius tugs at his shirt in an exaggerated manner, signaling his displeasure and resentment.

Our first impressions of Marius are of a deeply instinctual and resentful man. Yet, when he finally gets the chance to introduce himself, he proves charmingly clever and witty, blithely comparing his ability as a safecracker and pickpocket to that of a musical virtuoso. That lighthearted air carries over during a flashback to the prison. While his patriotic friends offer sentimental images of the France they would fight for (the France of the countryside, the France of history, tradition, and monuments), Marius unsentimentally offers up the gay Parisian lifestyle instead.

Nevertheless, when fellow convict Renault remarks, "I would fight and die gladly to make France free," Marius suddenly becomes intensely serious. To him it is not

Rick Blaine (Humphrey Bogart) and Ugarte have a conversation in *Casablanca.*

even a question. *He* suggests that the presumed patriot Matrac lead them to freedom, *he* gets word to Matrac (currently in solitary), and *he* gets himself put into a position of responsibility so that he can help the group escape. Later, on the ship, he instinctively grabs the guns, twice, when a gunner is shot; and he ultimately dies after heroically trying to shoot down a Nazi warplane. Beneath his glib façade, Marius is a true patriot, fighting unselfishly for a free France and never thinking of consequences before he acts. Our first impressions, of a man who carries deep resentments and operates on instinct, prove true. But the resentments are directed at Fascism, and the instinct is to fight it.

Marius proves an excellent role for Peter Lorre. Not only does Lorre get to play a character who in many ways resembles himself (a character one writer describes, in fact, as "easily the most likable of the five convicts" [*Films of Peter Lorre*, 163]), but Lorre gets almost as much screen time as Bogart, and even gets to use his well-honed physical skills to convey his character more through gestures than words. It's just too bad that the multiple-embedded-flashback structure undermines many great performances, from a cast which *Variety* termed "box-office in itself."

No such scripting problems exist in *Casablanca.* There are, of course, a few errors in the dialogue, with Ugarte getting one of the most glaring (letters of transit signed by Free French General DeGaulle would not carry much weight with either the Germans or the Vichy French). But overall the film showcases nearly non-stop virtuoso writing.

We find in Ugarte a perfect example of the symbiosis in this film between the writing and the acting. Peter Lorre has two scenes in *Casablanca,* and yet Ugarte becomes one of the more memorable characters in this film. We really know little about him. The dialogue in his first scene reveals that he has been in Casablanca longer than Rick; that he deals in exit visas; that he offers cheaper rates than Captain Renault; that he himself hopes to leave Casablanca, even though he does good business in preying upon the refugees' hopes; that he has killed two German couriers for their letters of transit; and that he yearns for Rick's approval perhaps even more than he desires money. There is a whole story to tell here. And the writers never tell it. They short-circuit it instead by having Ugarte get captured and ultimately killed.

By circumventing audience anticipation (or at least audience hopes), the writers make Ugarte all the more fascinating. He becomes one of the film's great mysteries. What the writers leave out becomes every bit as important as what they leave in. We never learn exactly why Rick despises Ugarte yet allows him into the casino. We never even learn the exact circumstances of Ugarte's death.

We do learn, of course, that he died in custody, and that our charmingly corrupt Captain Renault is in a quandary about what to write on his death certificate. However, neither Renault nor the Nazis would have summarily executed Ugarte. They would first have wanted to know what he did with the letters, and they would certainly have interrogated, and probably even tortured, him for that information. Yet Ugarte clearly dies without turning in Rick. Renault only *suspects* the letters to be in Rick's possession. The most logical conclusion? That Ugarte dies under torture… without breaking.

Ugarte certainly knows he is a dead man when he shrieks at Rick to help him. Why does this mercenary not buy an easy death by giving the Nazis the information they want? Is he more loyal to Rick than Rick is to him? Does his sleazy underhandedness merely camouflage another idealist who—though he would gladly profit off of Laszlo—wants even more to see the Resistance leader escape to fight the Nazis? We simply do not know. And, unlike the characters whose mysteries we do penetrate, we will never know.

Belgian poster for *Casablanca.*

Great writing makes Ugarte a potentially fascinating character, but writing alone could not realize that potential. Lorre's performance does that. Lorre has the difficult job of setting the action in motion, and quickly bringing a sketchy character to life. Naturally, he again uses his physical skills to accomplish this task.

Ugarte's face tells how desperately he wants to impress Rick, long before his dialogue broaches the issue. Nearly each of Ugarte's attempts to engage Rick in conversation ends in a rebuff; and with each rebuff, Ugarte's face falls. He tries various strategies to engage Rick, feigning a casual air by laughing and leaning over the table. Finally, when he does draw Rick's attention with the letters of transit, he tries to force intimacy by leaning closer and looking Rick directly in the face. His gestures in this first scene establish the character so well that audience tension mounts when Ugarte must manically run for his life, only to be apprehended by the gendarmes and abandoned by Rick—to whom he shrieks out one of the most famous cries for help in cinema history.

In four brief minutes, Lorre creates a fully-realized (if short-circuited) character, and indelibly prints Ugarte on the American filmgoer's consciousness.

Variety took note, listing Lorre among the "lesser players" that it called "superb." So did *The New York Times*, claiming that Warner Bros. gave this film "a top-notch thriller cast of Humphrey Bogart, Sydney Greenstreet, Peter Lorre, Conrad Veidt and even Claude Rains." And, of course, moviegoers have noticed for over half a century, immortalizing Ugarte's "Reeck! Reeck!" in countless imitations.

Of these three war films only *Casablanca* stands as a legend, or even a classic. But in 1942-1944, all three films served a "higher purpose" than artistry. They boosted wartime morale. Audiences flocked to see even a critically panned flick like *The Conspirators*, clearly appreciating its message of Resistance to Nazis against whatever odds. As for *Casablanca*… well, a year after the film's release the Office of War Information dug deeply for its propaganda value, noting feverishly that in the end "our side triumphs" when Laszlo and Ilsa escape.

These films, whatever their other merits, all gave Lorre a chance to contribute to the war effort here on the home front. Whether playing a "cut-rate parasite" or a French or Polish patriot, whether serving in a plumb assignment as Ugarte or doing latrine duty as Bernazsky, Peter Lorre fought the Nazis, once again, during WWII… in front of a much wider audience than the Berlin stage could ever have afforded him.

Casablanca

CREDITS: Producer: Hal B. Wallis; Director: Michael Curtiz; Writers: Julius J. Epstein, Philip G. Epstein, and Howard Koch (Based on the Play "Everybody Comes to Rick's" by Murray Burnett and Joan Alison); Cinematographer: Arthur Edeson; Music: Max Steiner; Editor: Owen Marks; Art Director: Carl Jules Weyl; Set Designer: George James Hopkins; Musical Director: Leo Forbstein; Orchestrations: Hugo Friedhofer; Gowns: Orry-Kelly; Make-up: Perc Westmore; Special Effects: Lawrence Butler, Willard Van Enger; Montages: Don Siegel, James Leicester; Technical Adviser: Robert Aisner; Music/Lyrics: M.K. Jerome, Jack Scholl ("Knock on Wood," "That's What Noah Done," "Muse's Call"), Herman Hupfield ("As Time Goes By")

CAST: Humphrey Bogart (Richard "Rick" Blaine) Ingrid Bergman (Ilsa Lund Laszlo); Paul Henreid (Victor Laszlo); Claude Rains (Captain Louis Renault); Conrad Veidt

(Major Heinrich Strasser); Sydney Greenstreet (Senor Ferrari); Peter Lorre (Ugarte); S.Z. Sakall (Carl, the Headwaiter) (as S.K. Sakall); Madeleine LeBeau (Yvonne); Dooley Wilson (Sam); Joy Page (Annina Brandel); John Qualen (Berger); Leonid Kinskey (Sascha); Curt Bois (Pickpocket); Helmut Dantine (Jan Brandel)

Passage to Marseille
CREDITS: Producer: Hal B. Wallis; Director: Michael Curtiz; Writers: Casey Robinson, Jack Moffitt (Based on the Novel *Men without a Country* by Charles Nordhoff, James Norman Hall); Cinematographer: James Wong Howe; Music: Max Steiner; Editor: Owen Marks; Art Director: Carl Jules Weyl; Set Designer: George James Hopkins; Costumes: Leah Rhodes; Special Effects: Jack Cosgrove, Edwin B. Du Par, Byron Haskin, E. Roy Davidson; Music/Lyrics: Max Steiner, Ned Washington; Make-up: Perc Westmore

CAST: Humphrey Bogart (Matrac); Claude Rains (Captain Freycinet); Michèle Morgan (Paula); Philip Dorn (Renault); Sydney Greenstreet (Duval); Peter Lorre (Marius); George Tobias (Petit); Helmut Dantine (Garou); John Loder (Manning); Victor Francen (Captain Patain Malo); Vladimir Sokoloff (Grandpere); Eduardo Ciannelli (Chief Engineer); Corinna Mura (singer)

The Conspirators
CREDITS: Producer: Jack Chertok; Director: Jean Negulesco; Writers: Vladimir Pozner, Leo Rosten (Based on the Novel by Frederic Prokosch); Cinematographer: Arthur Edeson; Music: Max Steiner; Editor: Rudi Fehr; Art Director: Anton Grot; Set Designer: Walter Tilford; Gowns: Leah Rhodes; Musical Director: Leo Forbstein; Special Effects: Willard Van Enger, William McGann, James Leicester

CAST: Hedy Lamarr (Irene); Paul Henreid (Vincent Van Der Lyn); Sydney Greenstreet (Ricardo Quintanilla); Peter Lorre (Bernazsky); Victor Francen (Von Mohr); Joseph Calleia (Capt. Pereira); Carol Thurston (Rosa); Vladimir Sokoloff (Miguel); Eduardo Ciannelli (Almeida); Steven Geray (Dr. Schmitt); Kurt Katch (Lutzke)

Sources: "Noted for the Record: Fragments of Recollection Culled from a Recent Visit to the Film City" by Andre Sennwald, in *The New York Times*, 4 August 1935, Section 9: 3; Office of War Information File on *Casablanca*, analysis by *Commonweal* critic Philip T. Hartung (4 November 1943), on file in the Motion Picture Reading Room at Library of Congress; "Casablanca" by Bosley Crowther, in *The New York Times*, 27 November 1942: 27; "Casablanca" in *Variety*, 2 December 1942: 8; "Passage to Marseille" by "Sten.," in *Variety*, 16 February 1944: 10; "The Conspirators" by Bosley Crowther, in *The New York Times*, 21 October 1944: 15; *The Films of Peter Lorre* by Stephen D. Youngkin, James Bigwood and Raymond G. Cabana, Jr, Citadel, 1982; *The Motion Picture Guide*, by Robert Nash and Stanley Ralph Ross, Cinebooks, 1985-1987; *Casablanca: As Time Goes By* by Frank Miller, Turner, 1992; *Casablanca: Behind the Scenes* by Harlan Lebo, Fireside/Simon and Schuster, 1992; *Round Up the Usual Suspects: The Making of Casablanca—Bogart, Bergman, and World War II* by Aljean Harmetz, Hyperion, 1992

INVISIBLE AGENT
1942
by Scott Allen Nollen

In early 1942, Universal announced plans to film "The Invisible Spy," a third sequel to James Whale's 1933 classic *The Invisible Man.* And to rise from the nadir to which the series had sunk with *The Invisible Woman* two years earlier, producers Frank Lloyd and Jack Skirball intended to market the project as an A feature with good production values and a notable cast. Having co-produced Alfred Hitchcock's *Saboteur* a few months earlier, Lloyd and Skirball again chose to support the war effort with a timely depiction of nasty Nazi espionage. However, Skirball soon bowed out, to be replaced by *Wolf Man* director George Waggner.

Spurred by the Office of War Information (OWI), the Hollywood studios were attempting to work Axis heavies into every film, actually depicting Tarzan battling the Nazis for jungle turf. An entire subgenre of World War II horror films emerged, with such absurd productions as Columbia's *The Boogie Man Will Get You* and Monogram's *Black Dragons* (both 1942) showing mad scientists (Boris Karloff in the former; Bela Lugosi in the latter) producing "genetically superior" supermen. And Universal, having acquired the rights to Sir Arthur Conan Doyle's Sherlock Holmes stories, depicted the Great Detective tracking down Nazi saboteurs.

German émigré Curt Siodmak (billed in the film's credits as Curt*is* Siodmak), who previously had penned *Black Friday* (1940), *The Invisible Man Returns* (1940) and *The Wolf Man* (1941) for Universal, wrote the stridently anti-Nazi screenplay for *Invisible Agent*, often resorting to painting the enemy as inept buffoons (much as Charles Chaplin had done in *The Great Dictator* [1940], more than a year before the United States entered the war).

Signed to portray Baron Ikito, a Japanese secret policeman, Peter Lorre joined Ilona Massey, Sir Cedric Hardwicke, J. Edward Bromberg, Albert Basserman, Holmes Herbert and Jon Hall (in his first of two appearances as the Invisible Man). Though Lorre already had established his reputation as a master of menace, *Invisible Agent* is the only Universal horror film in which he appears (and here the "horror" is political rather than supernatural). After his effective performances in *The Maltese Falcon* (1941) and *All Through the Night* (1942), this uneven espionage "thriller" may have been quite a comedown for the actor, though he is excellent in the role. Universal undoubtedly cast him on the strength of his eight Mr. Moto films and his Chinese character in MGM's *They Met in Bombay* (1941).

Lorre appears as Ikito in the opening scene of *Invisible Agent*, accompanying the German agents with whom he has a precarious alliance. When the grandson (Hall) of

Sir Cedric Hardwicke, Peter and an unidentified player in *Invisible Agent.*

original invisible man Frank Griffin refuses to sell the secret formula to the Axis, the Nazis and Ikito, who has been experimenting with a guillotine-like paper press, threaten to chop off his fingers. Telling them that he will give up the chemical mixture, young Griffin instead knocks out a light and escapes from his printing shop.

The United States government also loses out in its bid for the formula—until Pearl Harbor is bombed. Now Griffin agrees to use it on himself and parachute into Germany to learn the date that the Nazis will strike American soil. Following a romantic entanglement with Allied counter-agent Maria Sorenson (Massey), whom he mistakenly comes to believe is a Nazi spy, and several dangerous incidents with Gestapo agents Conrad Stauffer (Hardwicke) and Karl Heiser (Bromberg), Griffin agrees to help the latter escape in exchange for the information he needs. Heiser then admits that a German suicide squad will attack New York City while Nazi agents sabotage industry and utilities.

But before Griffin (who has been aided by carpenter and underground revolutionary Arnold Schmidt [Basserman]) can escape to England with Marie, he is waylaid in the film's most horrific scene. Caught in a net, he is impaled by dozens of razor-sharp

Peter Lorre, Sir Cedric Hardwicke and Jon Hall share a scene.

fish hooks placed by Ikito and his henchmen. After he is carted away in a coffin (a nice macabre touch), the Gestapo men grill the unfortunate Schmidt. In one of wartime cinema's most brutally memorable sequences, the carpenter asks what document the Nazis have placed in front of him.

"Our common form of release," he is told. "It merely states that you've been well treated and that no one has harmed you."

"I, I can't sign it," Schmidt replies.

"You *won't*?"

"I *can't*," he painfully insists. "*You've broken my fingers*!"

These fish-hook and finger-breaking scenes provide a stark contrast to the buffoonery that precedes them. (In one scene, the invisible Griffin dumps food onto Heiser's uniform; in another, he boxes a group of Nazi guards who stumble around the room, grabbing at thin air.) While some critics considered the befuddling of the Germans "highly amusing"[1] and providing "sufficient levity,"[2] others, such as *The New York Times*' "T.S.," found it offensive:

> *Invisible Agent* is as obvious a breach of taste as the screen has provided... the author has concocted an irresponsible tale that blithely mingles gauche attempts at comic satire with

> melodramatic sadism.... *Invisible Agent* takes the ruinous point of view that maniacal brutes may be simultaneously shown as laughable dolts. It is as incredible as a joke told in a nightmare.[3]

With the title character involved in comic high jinks (as well as being played by the lackluster Hall), Ikito emerges as the highlight of the film. For once, studio publicity told the truth: When referring to Lorre's characterization, the pressbook notes that he is "Mild-seeming, unobtrusive... cold steel beneath a purring exterior."[4] Indeed, he admirably underplays the entire part, proving that he could be a very subtle performer. Iniquitous but well-mannered, powerfully sinister yet subdued, Ikito lives by the Japanese code of honor, vowing to die if he makes a mistake. Near the film's end, after stabbing Stauffer to death and wiping his dagger with the Nazi's swastika armband, he commits hari kari. Though the actual knife thrust is kept in darkness, a subsequent, chilling shot shows both Axis enemies lying dead on the floor—another of the film's most effectively horrifying moments.

The supporting players (including future *Return of the Vampire* [1943] werewolf Matt Willis and B-Western favorite Lane Chandler) all give adequate performances, but Lorre, as usual, is unique. At one point, Griffin makes the racist statement, "I can't tell you Japs apart, but that voice haunts me."

Essentially a villainous variation on his Mr. Moto characterization, Lorre was praised by *The New York Herald Tribune* as "exud[ing] an abundance of treachery and cunning,"[5] while *Variety*'s "Walt" considered him "excellent."[6] During the war, Universal could have chosen to depict Ikito as the stereotypical slant-eyed, bucktoothed Nip monster, but instead created a real character for Lorre.

The most outlandish aspect of the film is the Invisible Man. In two generations, the transparent Griffins have transformed from an anti-establishment madman to the ultimate, Nazi-fighting spy! But the war was a grim reality, and even fantasy had to propagandize the real horror being perpetrated on those fighting abroad.

Two connections to James Whale's *Invisible Man* are a hay-filled barn onto which Griffin parachutes and the obligatory scene of a cigarette traveling through the air as he puffs away. However, the concept of food remaining visible inside his transparent body was ignored by Curt Siodmak, since Griffin heartily dines with Maria.

John P. Fulton's special effects are perhaps a bit sub-par, but the cigarette scene and an innovative sequence involving the Invisible Man lathering up in Maria's bathtub are well executed. Unfortunately, showing him smearing cold cream on his face, rather than wearing the original Claude Rains/Vincent Price bandages and goggles, is totally absurd. *Newsweek*, however, reported that "the familiar camera legedermain is still thrilling after a relaxing fashion."[7] Griffin is not only a lackadaisical spy, but also Siodmak's anti-Nazi mouthpiece. Aside from creating situations to expose the ineptitude of the Gestapo and the German Army, he launches into a long-winded propaganda speech while confronting Heiser in the doomed officer's jail cell. At one point, he sharply remarks, "I pity the Devil when you boys start arriving in bunches."

Obviously ashamed of what his former countrymen had become under Hitler's fascist Reich, Siodmak turned nearly all his propaganda firepower against the Nazis, while including only a few blatant swipes at Ikito. In fact, the Japanese are not shown

Lorre as Baron Ikito.

as barbaric until late in the film, when the fish-hooked net engulfs Griffin. Ikito is even depicted breaking with the Nazis because he does not approve of Stauffer's methods.

Director Edwin L. Marin actually filmed a scene written by Siodmak in which Griffin kicked Hitler in the ass, but it was cut from the final print. Though the *Invisible Agent* pressbook claims that a ban had been enacted on cinematic attacks on dictators, other films did not follow suit. Released the following year, the ludicrously awful *Hitler: Dead or Alive* depicts Ward Bond and his fellow commandos sneaking into Germany to cut off Der Führer's mustache!

Top-billed Massey is her usual lovely, exotic self, portraying an amazing female character, considering the social standards of the period. She proves both a spy and a capable pilot: She not only flies Griffin away from the landing strip as he drops bombs on the Nazis, but also saves them both after he falls asleep, failing to radio the British. Grabbing a parachute and Griffin, Maria floats safely to the ground.

Hardwicke and Basserman are excellent, but Lorre—even though his screen time is limited—takes top acting honors. Given a character unlike the typical one-dimensional, fanatical World War II stereotype, he lends Ikito restraint and a degree of unlikely ambiguity. But of course, being a sinister enemy of the Allies, his destiny is unpleasant death; and being a dishonored Japanese, he meets it at his own hand.

CREDITS: Director: Edwin L. Marin; Producer: Frank Lloyd; Associate Producer: George Waggner; Screenplay: Curtis Siodmak; Suggested by the Novel *The Invisible Man* by H.G. Wells; Director of Photography: Les White; Editor: Edward Curtiss; Assistant Director: Vernon Keays; Special Effects: John P. Fulton; Art Director: Jack Otterson; Musical Score: Hans J. Salter; Previewed at the Hillstreet Theatre, Los Angeles, July 29, 1942; Released July 31, 1942, by Universal Pictures; Running Time: 81 minutes

CAST: Ilona Massey (Maria Sorenson), Jon Hall (Frank Raymond [Griffin]), Peter Lorre (Baron Ikito), Sir Cedric Hardwicke (Conrad Stauffer), J. Edward Bromberg (Karl Heiser), Albert Basserman (Arnold Schmidt), John Litel (John Gardiner), Holmes Herbert (Sir Alfred Spencer), Keye Luke (Surgeon), Philip Van Zandt (Nazi SS Man), Matt Willis (Nazi Assassin), Mabel Colcord (Maid), John Holland (Spencer's Secretary), Marty Faust (Killer), Alberto Morin (Free Frenchman), Henry Guttman (Storm Trooper), Wolfgang Zilzer (Von Porten), Ferdinand Munier (Bartender), Eddie Dunn, Hans Schumm (SS Men), John Burton (RAF Flier), Lee Tung-Foo (General Chin Lee), Milburn Stone (German Sergeant), Michael Visaroff (Verichen), Walter Tetley (Newsboy), Pat West (German Taxi Driver), Leslie Denison (British Radio Operator), William Ruhl, Otto Reichow (Gestapo Agents), Bobby Hale, Wally Scott (English Tommies), Mabel Conrad (Housekeeper), Charles Flynn, Phil Warren, Paul Bryar, John Merton (German Soldiers), Lee Shumway (Brigadier General), Henry Zynder (Col. Kelenski), Ferdinand Schumann-Heink (German Telephone Operator), Victor Zimmerman, Bill Pagan (Storm Troopers), Lane Chandler, Duke York, Donald Curtis (German Sentries), Charles Regan (Ordnance Car Driver), Sven Hugo-Borg (German Captain), James Craven (Ship's Radio Man), Pat McVey (German)

[1] *Harrison's Reports*, 15 August 1942.
[2] *Variety*, August 1942.
[3] *The New York Times*, 6 August 1942, p. 23.
[4] *Invisible Agent* pressbook, Universal Pictures, 1942.
[5] Ted Sennett, *Masters of Menace: Greenstreet and Lorre* (New York: E. P. Dutton, 1979), p. 153.
[6] *Variety*, August 1942.
[7] *Newsweek*, 17 August 1942.

BACKGROUND TO DANGER 1943 by Dennis Fischer

Peter Lorre was one of the most distinctive actors of his, or any other, generation. His nasal, sinister or near-hysterical voice served as an open invitation to hundreds of imitators, and its lasting influence can still be felt in such creations as Ren, the Chihuahua from *The Ren and Stimpy Show*. (Lorre-like mad scientists had terrorized Bugs Bunny and Daffy Duck in some Warners cartoons, and Paul Frees did a frantic rendition of "My Old Flame" for Spike Jones in an overdone Lorre accent.)

However, when Lorre first came to the United States under contract to Columbia, he was hoping to tackle serious dramatic roles such as Raskolnikov in *Crime and Punishment* more than the madman roles for which he came to be typecast. Long-time friend Bertolt Brecht (1898-1956) tried to develop projects specially designed for his talents (Lorre had starred as Galy Gay in Brecht's *Mann ist Mann* at the Staatstheater), but they consistently were unable to find sponsorship and never became produced.

Born Laszlo (Ladislav) Löwenstein in a small town about 150 miles northeast of Vienna in Austria-Hungary, Lorre is not, as some writers have maintained, Hungarian, but rather an Austrian who spent much of his early life in Vienna. To satisfy his father, he was an unhappy bank clerk before launching his acting career. Despite his father's disapproval, Lorre was drawn to the stages of Breslau, Zürich, Vienna and finally Berlin, to which he moved at the age of 21. There he appeared in minor film roles until Fritz Lang cast him as the child molester/murderer in *M*, a tour de force performance that manages the magnificent task of winning audience sympathy for the most despised of men.

Lorre married his first wife, Celia Lovsky (with whom he had lived earlier in Berlin), in London while working on Alfred Hitchcock's *The Man Who Knew Too Much* (1934). (Lovsky, who was known as Cäcilie Lvovsky in Europe, had a long career of her own in American movies and television, and is most often recalled these days for having playing Spock's regal mother, T'Pau, on *Star Trek*.)

Lorre met wife number two, the German actress Kaaren Verne, while filming *All Through the Night* (1942) and married her in 1945, shortly after divorcing Celia. Ever since a serious operation as a young man in Switzerland, for which he had been given morphine, Lorre had struggled with a drug problem. His ongoing morphine addiction helped break up his marriages. In fact, he had met his last wife, Anne Marie, while in a German sanitarium for his drug problem. Billy Wilder complained about Lorre's drug use when they roomed together in Los Angeles back in the late 1930s. It was due to Lorre's illness that stuntman Harvey Parry was hired to double Lorre as Mr. Moto during judo and other fight scenes.

Peter Lorre and George Raft in *Background to Danger.*

Lorre's career was saved by John Huston's casting him as the malefically amiable Joel Cairo in the classic *The Maltese Falcon*, which also cemented a future partnership with experienced stage actor but film neophyte Sydney Greenstreet as well as establishing a strong friendship with fellow practical joker Humphrey Bogart. Like Bogart, Lorre loved to puncture pretense and would refer to acting as simply "making faces."

Though both Lorre and Greenstreet appeared in the Michael Curtiz classic *Casablanca*, they had no scenes together, and the pair were reteamed for *Background to Danger*, adapted from the Eric Ambler novel. *The New York Times'* Bosley Crowther praised the pair as "experts at espionage and intrigue." Together, they were masters of menace, appearing in eight films together, with directors delighting in their physical contrast. Lorre at the time was thin, short, delicate but intense, while Greenstreet was massive, imposing, yet laid-back.

Eric Ambler, who was 89, revolutionized the art of the spy novel with a style that set a new standard for a generation of writers including Len Deighton and John Le Carré. He wrote 21 published novels during his life, as well as his autobiography, amusingly titled *Here Lies*, in 1985.

Ambler's novel of *Background to Danger* (aka *Uncommon Danger*) involved his hero battling the Pan-Eurasian Petroleum Company, an unscrupulous corporation. It possesses the standard Ambler ingredient: international skullduggery, exotic locales and mysterious characters of ambiguous loyalties. The enemy was changed to Hitler for the film version, in which Greenstreet plays Colonel Robinson, an American Nazi agent who seeks to get Turkey to ally itself with Germany by planting phony invasion plans that would convince the Turks that the Russians are preparing to invade. "Our task," announces the suave and assured Robinson, "is to present Turkey with a match that will inflame the people against Russia."

Joe Barton (George Raft) is an American agent posing as a salesman who is simply traveling by train to Ankara, Turkey, when he meets a frightened Ana Remzi (Osa Massen) who, fearing that she will be searched, asks Barton to hold an envelope containing "securities" until she can meet him in Ankara. Barton is puzzled when he later examines the contents and finds photographs of oddly marked maps. He discovers that he has become a target both for the Germans, who wish to publish the documents in the Turkish press, and the Russian agents who seek to destroy them.

However, things go from bad to worse when he finds Ana dead in her hotel room and thereby becomes implicated in her murder. Fortunately, he is able to conceal the envelope before Nazi agents capture him and escort him to Colonel Robinson. The colonel is determined to recover the plans by any means and prepares to torture Barton, when Russian agent Nikolai Zalenkoff (Lorre) comes to his rescue.

Zalenkoff is one of Lorre's "colorful" foreigners, given to eccentric outbursts who when frustrated sits on the floor and exclaims, "I want my vodka!" Though toned down, he is akin to Lorre's even more eccentric Mexican general in Hitchcock's *Secret Agent*. He proves a somewhat unreliable ally who keeps altering his story, confusing Barton as to whether Ana was a Russian or a German agent.

Zalenkoff is working with his sister Tamara (Brenda Marshall) and together they convince Barton to hand over the plans. He agrees to meet them at the Soviet embassy; however, Barton discovers that the plans have been stolen and suspects his erstwhile compatriots. To ameliorate his suspicions, they produce a signed confession that clears him of Remzi's murder.

After a lot of scuffling and rushing around, Barton finds himself confronted by Robinson, who holds a gun on him and has brought the fake plans to a traitorous Turkish newspaper publisher. With a wide grin, he announces in Greenstreet's inimitable way, "A dead man on the floor. A doomed man in front of me. A Strauss waltz on the radio. What could be more entertaining?"

Barton is surprised to discover that the Zalenkoffs are apparently Robinson's partners; however, Robinson informs them, "We Nazis do not relish failure!" and takes the

Zalenkoffs prisoner, only for them and Barton to escape with the Nazis in hot pursuit. Lorre's character dies bravely, shot to death while attempting to escape; however, Zalenkoff's sacrifice allows Tamara and Barton to make good their escape.

Once free, Barton informs the Turkish authorities and he then catches up with Robinson and forces him to incinerate the false plans. Faced with extermination should he return to Berlin, Robinson decides to head off with Tamara for Cairo hoping to "cement Russian-American relations."

Jack Warner did not care for Lorre, and in his book *My First Hundred Years in Hollywood* described the actor as "a plump little fellow with a deceptive baby face, who deliberately upstaged other actors because there was no one way he could compensate for his lack of height and good looks." This apparently stemmed from the fact that the chain-smoking Lorre liked to use a cigarette as a prop and on occasion began to blow smoke in George Raft's face. Raft asked him to stop several times, but Lorre persisted.

"Peter, if you hit me with that smoke once more, I'm going to let you have it," threatened Raft. Lorre promised to stop his antics, but the next day when shooting resumed, he once more wafted smoke into Raft's eyes. Raft socked the diminutive thespian in the jaw, knocking him out for five minutes. Warner remarked, "He never tried the stunt again."

Ambler's novel was adapted by the great crime writer W[illiam] R[iley] Burnett, author of *High Sierra, Little Caesar* and *The Asphalt Jungle*, as well as scripting such crime classics as *Scarface, This Gun for Hire* (from Graham Greene's *A Gun for Sale*) and *The Great Escape*, with some uncredited rewrite work by literary great William Faulkner.

Director Raoul Walsh was one of the greatest action directors of all time, as well as helming two of the most unusual and elaborate fantasies ever made (*Thief of Bagdad* [1924] and *The Horn Blows at Midnight*). He had worked as an actor under David Wark Griffith, and later directed such classics as *They Drive By Night, High Sierra, Objective Burma!, Captain Horatio Hornblower* and *White Heat*. Though entertaining, *Background to Danger* must be counted as one of his minor efforts.

Commented film critic James Agee, "*Background to Danger* has plenty of danger, in lively motion at that, without a background keenly drawn enough to make it really dangerous. Short of the really 'creative' men, Raoul Walsh is one of my favorite directors; but—besides thoroughly enjoying it—you could use this film for one kind of measurement of the unconquerable difference between a good job by Hitchcock and a good job of the Hitchcock type."

CREDITS: Director: Raoul Walsh; Producer: Jerry Wald; Screenplay: W. R. Burnett; From the Novel by Eric Ambler; Director of Photography: Tony Gaudio, A.S.C.; Editor: Jack Killifer; Art Direction: Hugh Reticker; Music: Frederick Hollander.

CAST: George Raft (Joe Barton); Brenda Marshall (Tamara); Sydney Greenstreet (Colonel Robinson); Peter Lorre (Zalenkoff); Osa Massen (Ana Remzi); Turhan Bey (Hassan); Willard Robertson (McNamara); Kurt Katch (Mailler); Daniel Ocko (Rashenko); Pedro de Cordoba (Old Turk); Frank Puglia (Syrian vendor); Steven Geray (Rader)

ARSENIC AND OLD LACE
1944
by John Stell

At the heart of most, if not all, horror comedies is spoofery—making fun of those reliable clichés (thunderstorms, secret passages in cobweb-filled mansions, etc.) found in many horror films. But merely mocking the familiar may prove only mildly amusing. The great horror comedies usually contain a "legitimate" piece or pieces of horror history: the actual Kenneth Strickfaden sets from *Frankenstein* used in *Young Frankenstein*, or the appearances of Bela Lugosi, Lon Chaney, and Glenn Strange in *Abbott & Costello Meet Frankenstein*. Think of what these films would be like without them. Thus, one of the primary joys in viewing *Arsenic and Old Lace* is seeing Peter Lorre having fun with the "dastardly henchman" role, a role he played for real in, for example, *The Maltese Falcon*. Certainly known as a "heavy" *(M, Mad Love)* Lorre, by 1941, the year *Arsenic and Old Lace* was filmed (although it wasn't released until 1944), had played a "good guy" in the Mr. Moto quickie mysteries. And while Lorre's other spoofs, such as *You'll Find Out* and *The Boogie Man Will Get You* (both also featuring Boris Karloff, whom Raymond Massey is supposed to resemble in *Arsenic and Old Lace*) failed, in varying degrees, to reach their potential, *Arsenic and Old Lace* is an unqualified bull's-eye.

Cast as "Dr. Einstein," partner in crime to Raymond Massey's Jonathan Brewster, Peter Lorre is the seemingly hardened criminal with the heart of a pussycat. A supposed jailbird-doctor who is squeamish at the sight of blood and violence, Dr. Einstein possesses a mild talent for plastic surgery. Now traveling with the escaped Jonathan, he gives the psychotic Brewster brother the occasional face-lift, although the scars are obvious. The deadly duo return to Jonathan's boyhood home one Halloween evening, and discover, to Jonathan's shock and Dr. Einstein's great amusement, that Jonathan's aunts Abby (Josephine Hull) and Martha (Jean Adair)—"Two of the dearest, sweetest, kindest old ladies that ever walked on the earth."—have 12 bodies in their cellar, 11 of which they have poisoned. "That's wonderful Johnny," Einstein says, unable to stop laughing. "You've got 12, they've got 12." Jonathan needs a 13th victim to best his aunts.

Potential victim number 13 comes in the form of Jonathan's brother Mortimer (Cary Grant), who has just married Elaine Harper (Priscilla Lane), a preacher's daughter no less. Unfortunately Mortimer has been unable to begin his honeymoon since discovering the very recently poisoned Mr. Hoskins in the window seat. Hoping to commit his aunts and brother "Teddy Roosevelt" (John Alexander) to Happy Dale Sanitarium without tipping off anyone about the bodies, Mortimer finds himself in a black comedic game of "chicken" with Jonathan and Einstein.

Mortimer (Cary Grant) confronts Jonathan (Raymond Massey) as Dr. Einstein (Peter Lorre) looks on.

Although a supporting player in a cast of top-flight talent, Peter Lorre makes his Dr. Einstein role something to remember: Lorre plays Einstein as anything but dangerous. Despite his association with the lethal Jonathan Brewster, the doctor doesn't really wish harm on anyone, even trying to warn Mortimer at one point of what his brother has in store for him. In fact Einstein seems to be as frightened of Jonathan as everyone else. "Not the Melbourne method!" he exclaims when Jonathan tells him how they'll kill Mortimer. Heck, the doc even seems to be afraid of his own shadow: Einstein trips in the dark and finds himself in the window seat, whining, "Where am I? Oh, here I am." When the Brewster sisters admit to being frightened by a Boris Karloff picture, Einstein tells them, "I saw that picture too...I was intoxicated." Karloff made such an impression that the doc gave Jonathan the horror icon's face!

Even when confronted with the eccentric "Teddy Roosevelt" Brewster, Einstein willingly goes along. "My how I've changed," he tells Teddy after being shown a picture of "him" [Teddy thinks Einstein's a general he's worked with], sounding as if he really does think that is an old photo of him. When asked to accompany the president to "Panama" [the cellar] to bury another "yellow fever victim" [the aunties' poisoned gentleman], Einstein willingly obliges ["Well... bon voyage!"], even donning a pith helmet. He gets a big kick out of the fact that a grave has been "readied" in advance for Johnny's latest victim ["That's hospitality, huh?"]). In fact, Dr. Einstein gets a kick out of almost everything he sees in and learns about the house of Brewster ("Yes, Johnny, it's a good hideout," are his first words.)

Dr. Einstein is amused when Teddy Roosevelt Brewster (John Alexander) offers him a pith helmet, much to the annoyance of Jonathan.

As enjoyable as some of Lorre's later spoofs are (the jealous sorcerer in *The Raven*, an unwilling murderer in *The Comedy of Terrors*, his tongue-in cheek turn as a jilted spouse in *Tales of Terror*), he frequently seems to be a bit grouchy. Part of that has to do with the character he is playing, of course. But the truth is Lorre didn't look kindly upon these latter-day roles. Luckily there is not an ounce of grouch in his Dr. Einstein. Quite to the contrary, he's positively giddy.

After years of playing sinister types—top bananas and second fiddles—one might have expected Lorre to merely recreate one of his villainous roles and be done with it. In some ways, for example, Dr. Einstein is similar to the General from Alfred Hitchcock's *Secret Agent* (1936). Lorre's slightly mad portrayal of a ruthless spy jarringly alternates between moments of ingratiating warmth and moments of pure ruthlessness. In *Stranger on the Third Floor* (1940) Lorre's mad killer seems absent-minded, as if he were moving through life in a daze. In 1941's *The Face Behind the Mask*, Lorre goes beyond the call of duty in creating a truly sympathetic character (Janos), full of humor and vigor, only to have his life hinge on the possibility of plastic surgery! *The Maltese Falcon* finds him a polite, potentially dangerous, but easily overtaken opponent for Humphrey Bogart. But his interpretation of Dr. Einstein is never as vicious as the General or the Stranger. Nor is he as naïve as Janos, or as threatening as Joel Cairo. No, Dr. Einstein may be rough around the edges, but he's a true comic character who seems to be enjoying himself as much as anyone watching *Arsenic and Old Lace*.

Still, Lorre actually manages to pull off a couple of impressive feats here. Although he no doubt comes from the "wrong side of the tracks," he is the most jovial presence in the picture. Mortimer is stressed out because of his aunts' dreadful deeds. Jonathan is too consumed with thoughts of revenge to get a moment's rest. The sweet aunties are upset about Jonathan coming home. Poor Elaine can't figure out why all the romance has suddenly been drained from Mortimer. Meanwhile, Einstein just sits back and watches all this occur. Despite the occasional disagreement with Johnny, Einstein maintains a positive attitude no matter what obstacle gets thrown in his way. He actually seems to like every member of the Brewster household he meets. Meanwhile, his goals are simple: Get rid of the latest body, and fix Johnny's face. Einstein concerns himself with little else.

More importantly, the doctor serves as Johnny's "compass," although certainly not a moral one. Einstein grabs Johnny's arm as he's about to go after Teddy for blowing his bugle. He establishes the "rules" about how many bodies Johnny can include in his death tally, authoritatively voiding the one who died of pneumonia. In fact, Einstein knocks Johnny out just as he's about to kill a police officer. By the end of the film, Einstein is something of a hero!

One unsurprising element of Einstein's character is a clichéd love of drink. Just seconds after arriving at the new hideout he takes a swig from his flask. On two separate occasions he almost inadvertently drinks the poisoned elderberry wine. But Lorre basically treats this cliché as a throwaway and never overplays this aspect of his character. In fact, compared to the over-the-top nature of the film overall, Einstein's "weakness" is positively subtle. Furthermore, Einstein is usually whispering, in contrast to everyone else who is endlessly screaming. Thus Lorre's performance not only generates frequent laughs, but acts as a nice balance to the fever-pitched performances of many of the cast members.

Still, many of Lorre's best moments do involve physical comedy. There's his fall into the window seat, at which point he "loses" himself. Finding out about the aunts' "charity," Lorre plops down on a stool, and, with chin on fist, starts laughing uncontrollably, shaking his head back and forth in disbelief, amusement and adoration. The scene where Jonathan and Einstein take stock of Johnny's victims, with Lorre counting them on his fingers, is a riot. When Cary Grant tries to grab Einstein for questioning him about the bodies in the cellar, Lorre makes a quick and cowardly move to hide behind Johnny. Frequently Einstein will try to warn Mortimer of the danger, starting and stopping his sentences, as if he were an excited two-year-old trying to tell you about his latest toy. Unable to find the words to describe what "horrible things" Johnny does, Lorre sums it up with a motion to his own throat.

Lorre's high point, however, is actually his last scene in the film. With Jonathan in custody and policemen all about, Einstein is on his way out the door when the phone rings. As the description of Jonathan's partner is being given, Einstein is sure he's caught. His body sags, his head hangs low and, when the officer mentions "pop eyes," his eyes squeeze shut. He looks like a child caught with his hand in the cookie jar, about to be spanked. But luck is on his side as he manages to leave the house unrecognized. He cannot help but give one last, quick laugh.

It is Lorre's greatest gift as an actor that makes Einstein such a winning character: Lorre's uncanny ability to make his underdog characters so sympathetic. In the classic

Dr. Einstein and Jonathan ready the homemade grave for their next victim. (Photofest)

film, *M* (1931), he plays a despicable child murderer and still, in his heartfelt final scene, makes us feel for sorry him. We certainly hate what he did, but he is not simply evil personified. His memorable performance as Dr. Gogol in *Mad Love* (1935) shows a man committing horrible crimes, not for power or money, but for love. "I have conquered science...why can't I conquer love?" Even his murderous Hilary in *The Beast With Five Fingers* (1946) is a much-abused secretary who's finally driven over sanity's edge. And one would be hard-pressed to find a more sympathetic "villain" than Lorre's turn as Janos in *The Face Behind the Mask*. Thus, in *Arsenic and Old Lace*, Lorre is once again playing the underdog: the one who gets abused by his bossed, threatened by the hero proper, and yet still manages to ride to victory in the end. Since we are never told the exact nature of Einstein's crimes (he doesn't seem to be a real doctor) except that he follows Johnny around, we never see him as some sort of hissable villain. Lorre's charisma here is effortless. Since he has moved us when playing truly bad characters, it is not at all surprising that he instantly wins us over in his first scene in a film that is certainly not meant to be taken seriously.

It would be unfair, of course, to ignore the other talents involved in this classic piece of dark comedy. The screenplay itself is chock-full of zingers and sight gags. Sworn bachelor Mortimer is author of the bachelor's bible, *Marriage: A Fraud and A Failure*, and the upcoming *Mind Over Matrimony*. Insanity doesn't just run in his family, "it practically gallops." In fact, the murderous Aunt Abby doesn't just walk about the house—she trots. After Mortimer accuses Aunt Abby of offing another gentleman, she denies the charge: "That man is an impostor...you don't think I'd stoop to telling a fib?" she shouts, then runs tearfully to her sister. Meanwhile brother Teddy always "Charges!" the steps thinking they represent San Juan Hill. Jonathan and Einstein almost drink the poisoned wine until they're startled by Teddy's horn blowing and drop their glasses. The cupboard in the dining room is full of men's hats. And it takes only Mortimer's kisses to make Elaine forget about the 13 bodies she finds in the cellar.

Director Frank Capra keeps the events in *Arsenic and Old Lace* moving at a lightning-fast pace. The film opens with a fight at Dodger stadium that has nothing to do with the rest of the story. ("From hereon, you're on your own," the title card tells us.) Then Mortimer attempts to get a marriage license incognito so his "crime" won't be discovered. In no time at all, however, Mortimer discovers the body in the window seat and his happy future is no more. Grant frantically tries to get everything he needs to have his aunts and brother committed: signatures, transportation, witnesses, etc. Meanwhile, poor Elaine Harper whistles, "Here Comes the Bride," the code they agreed upon to signal she's ready to leave for Niagara Falls, to no avail. In spite of all this, Aunt Abby and Aunt Martha continue to make wedding reception arrangements, Teddy continues to charge up "San Juan Hill," and the cab driver waits, albeit impatiently, to chauffeur the newlyweds to the airport. Capra even throws in one genuinely scary moment: As the aunts move toward the window seat to remove Mr. Hoskins, the curtain suddenly is parted from the outside (accompanied by a very loud musical cue) by Jonathan, who gives the ladies and the audience a fright. But Capra lets the camera linger on Jonathan and the musical cue continue long enough so that we find ourselves laughing. Also, watch for the eerie scene in the cellar, where Einstein is "speaking" with the shadow of Johnny's head.

There are no slouches in the cast, either. Grant has never been funnier (save for *His Girl Friday*), as the exasperated Mortimer Brewster, who's too busy to be scared. Priscilla Lane is a sweet and winning, appropriately flustered wife. Josephine Hull and Jean Adair are perfection as the sweet aunties. John Alexander always finds a hilarious facial expression or tone of voice for Teddy ("Taft!"). And Raymond Massey is the next best thing to Boris Karloff (who played the role on Broadway) for playing a demented killer. (Massey's best moment comes when, not realizing how Einstein hid their body, Massey introduces the doctor, his voice cracking for the only time in the movie, as, "something of a magician.") *Arsenic and Old Lace* features one of the best all around casts ever assembled for a black comedy.

In sizing up Peter Lorre's list of comedies, *Arsenic and Old Lace* easily tops the chart. Lorre's Dr. Einstein is an immensely likable leech whose seemingly villainous intentions mask a really sweet guy who sticks by his pal Johnny despite his better judgment. He gets the last laugh, sneaking out the door at film's end. No doubt his first stop was the nearest bar.

CREDITS: Producers: Frank Capra and Jack L. Warner; Director: Frank Capra; Screenplay: Julius J. Epstein and Philip Epstein, Adapted from the Play by Joseph Kesslring; Cinematographer: Sol Polito; Art Direction: Max Parker; Editor: Daniel Mandell; Music: Max Steiner; Released by Warner Bros., 1944, 116 minutes

CAST: Cary Grant (Mortimer Brewster); Priscilla Lane (Elaine Harper); Raymond Massey (Jonathan Brewster); Jack Carson (Officer O'Hara); Edward Everett Horton (Mr. Witherspoon); Peter Lorre (Dr. Einstein); James Gleason (Lt. Rooney); Josephine Hull (Abby Brewster); Jean Adair (Martha Brewster); John Alexander ("Teddy Roosevelt" Brewster); Grant Mitchell (Reverend Harper); Edward McNamara (Brophy); Garry Owen (Taxi Cab Driver); John Ridgely (Saunders); Vaughn Glaser (Judge Cullman)

HOLLYWOOD CANTEEN 1944 by David H. Smith

If a tree falls in a forest and no one is there to hear, does it make a sound?

Honing the same axiom, if Peter Lorre appears for only one minute in an all-star cavalcade of a movie, is it truly a Peter Lorre movie?

A pleasant though dated piece of wartime propaganda, *Hollywood Canteen* is based on the authentic refuge for World War II servicemen. In 1942, actor John Garfield, still several years away from his part in the classic *Body and Soul*, was quite outspoken about the much-discussed idea that actors should be given deferments to make morale-building and propaganda films. If famous folk like Ted Williams and Jimmy Stewart could refuse the coin of celebrity to buy them favors, so could he. "We'll go when we're called," Garfield said, "just like everyone else," a statement that inspired an invitation to the White House and special thanks from the president. But the Army found that Garfield had a heart murmur, which earned him a 4-F classification and a good case of humiliation. He wrote an article for *Theater Arts* urging actors to become involved selling bonds and entertaining troops. Garfield did both.

Garfield went still further. "One day, just after the start of World War II," Bette Davis wrote in her book *This 'n' That*:

> [I]n the Green Room, our dining room at Warner Bros., Johnny Garfield sat down at my table during lunch. He had been thinking about the thousands of servicemen who were passing through Hollywood without seeing any movie stars. Garfield said something ought to be done about it. I agreed, and then and there the idea of the Hollywood Canteen was born.

The idea was inspired by Garfield's work at New York's Stage Door Canteen. But, as Swindell wrote, "he was better in coming up with an idea than in carrying one through." However, he did know who did have enough clout and initiative to get such a project started—Bette Davis.

Garfield had picked the right woman. Davis was an organizer, a catalyst and an inspirer. Working with people like Bob Taplinger, who headed public relations at Columbia; Alfred Ybarra, an MGM art director; Jules Stein, head of the Music Corporation of America, and his wife; Milani (a chef); and assisted by members of 42 Hollywood unions, Davis found an abandoned nightclub one block off Sunset Boulevard.

For its grand opening on October 17, 1942, the Canteen had bleachers on either side of the entrance. People paid $100 each to sit there and watch 3,000 soldiers, sailors and marines enter. (Civilians, including the stars, entered by a separate entrance.) A sign over the entrance read, "Through these portals pass the most beautiful uniforms in the world."

From old movie fan magazines and the biographies and autobiographies of the stars, it is clear just about everyone in Hollywood put in an appearance at the Canteen at one time or another, performing, dancing with the soldiers, working in the kitchen or acting as host or hostess.

Davis also persuaded the stars to contribute money. Some donated their scale salaries from such films as *Thank Your Lucky Stars* (1943), an earlier Warner Bros. cameo-studded movie associated with the Canteen, and *Hollywood Canteen* itself.

The latter movie is notable today only because of the number of World War II-vintage stars in it. In addition to the principals—Bette Davis, John Garfield, Robert Hutton, Dane Clark and Joan Leslie—it included dozens of stars in cameo appearances or doing a song, dance or musical number.

The nominal story centers around Slim (Robert Hutton), the millionth GI to come through the Canteen. (The real millionth GI to come through the Canteen was one Sergeant Carl Boll, who was given a four-day tour of Hollywood and its nightspots during which he was accompanied by a series of starlets.) On sick leave, Slim dances with hostess Joan Leslie, falling in love and wanting a date with her before returning to active duty in the Pacific. Today, *Hollywood Canteen* can only be recommended as a nostalgic trip down memory lane for members of that generation, but, even then, with reservations.

Peter Lorre and Sydney Greenstreet as ghoulish volunteers at the *Hollywood Canteen.*

Peter Lorre's brief screen appearance in *Hollywood Canteen* comes about 45 minutes into the movie. When an overzealous soldier (James Flavin, a real-life West Point graduate) tries to sweep a hapless Patty Andrews, the youngest of the Andrews Sisters harmony trio (they played themselves in 15 films), off her feet, their dance floor gyrations bump them into moonlighting maître d' Sydney Greenstreet and busboy Peter Lorre. The soldier's facetious vow to dance her hips "right outta their sockets" inspires Messrs. Greenstreet and Lorre to stereotypical rumination:

"Say, Sydney," Lorre says, "doesn't that constitute mayhem?"

"Definitely, Peter," Greenstreet rumbles in agreement.

"Besides, it would be very gruesome," Lorre ventures in his most dulcet tones.

"Horrible sight," Greenstreet concurs.

The soldier tries to stammer an explanation, dismissing his braggadocio as a figure of speech, like "tearing a guy limb from limb," which makes Greenstreet's eyes gleam. Interrupting, Lorre invites the man to step outside. Thoroughly terrified, the GI reneges on his dance with the singing star and hurries to rejoin his outfit.

Lorre is crestfallen, saying, "All I wanted to ask him was to join me in a cigarette."

"He didn't trust us, Peter," Greenstreet explains.

"But we are such gentle people," Lorre insists.

Greenstreet's eyes bulge. "Are we?" he asks rhetorically, causing an uneasy Lorre to edge furtively away. The pair disappear from the rest of the proceedings.

Lorre and Greenstreet, on-screen for only slightly more than a minute, merely trade on their most familiar personae in *Hollywood Canteen*, with Greenstreet's "character" conspicuously relishing the prospect of gory shenanigans. Lorre, as crafted in the two men's 10 screen pairings, played the confederate, the impudent and imprudent man-child, his most innocuous overture mistaken for villainy. It strains neither man's talents, and makes for an engaging bit of humor. Leonard Maltin called their cameo among the two "best bits" in the movie (along with a violin duet performed by Jack Benny and Joseph Szigeti).

However, that modern endorsement hardly echoes contemporary reviews. Joan Crawford, unsheathing her claws and furthering her famous feud with Bette Davis (the origins of which seem to reside in Davis' having had an affair with Franchot Tone—who was married to Crawford at the time—when they co-starred together in 1935's *Dangerous*), called *Hollywood Canteen* "a very pleasant pile of shit for wartime audiences." (Crawford agreed to appear in the film only when she learned that the billing would be alphabetical—"C," of course, precedes "D.")

Although the critics didn't go so far as that, their reviews were, by and large, rather noncommittal. A typical example came from the unnamed reviewer in *Variety*, who said, "There isn't a marquee big enough to hold all the names on this one, so how can it miss? Besides, it's basically solid."

However, Kate Cameron, in *The New York Daily News*, did not like *Hollywood Canteen* much at all, saying it was presented "in such a patronizing manner as to make one blush for its complete lack of reserve in singing the praises of Hollywood. It boasts screen personages unashamedly and without a flicker of humor. The players in the picture seem constantly awed by their own gracious and hospitable entertainment of the servicemen."

Echoing her sentiments, GIs themselves were none too happy with the movie either. One group of enlisted men wrote Warner Bros. that *Hollywood Canteen* was "a slur on the intelligence and acumen of every member of the armed services." Fast realizing its outmoded plot and situations, the studio parodied the movie not long after V-J Day, in the 1946 "Looney Tune" *Hollywood Canine Canteen.*

John Garfield persisted in trying to have his draft classification changed, and finally succeeded, being notified that he would be called within 90 days. But before he received his "Greetings" from the Army, he had a heart attack while working, appropriately, at the Hollywood Canteen. (Garfield suffered a life-ending heart attack in 1952, primarily, a friend said, because he had been blacklisted by the Hollywood studios, not because he was thought to be a Communist but because he had refused to cooperate with the House Committee on Un-American Activities.)

But Bette Davis stuck with her Canteen to the end; as the war went on, she, like a middle-aged professor with an eye for the pretty young coeds in his class, noted that the boys who came to the Canteen "were all much younger, and less robust."

As actor Jack Carson revealed to Davis' biographer Lawrence J. Quirk, "There were some real lookers at the Canteen... knockouts...[b]ut Bette was the one they clustered around." Carson remembered asking one marine what it was about Bette Davis that attracted such a crowd, and he said quite candidly: "I hear she screws like a mink." It may be difficult for the fans of today to see Davis inspiring such salacious comments; after all, in the 1960s, after starring in such Gothic fare as *What Ever Happened to Baby Jane?* (1962), *Hush... Hush, Sweet Charlotte* (1964) and *The Nanny* (1965), she referred to herself as "Boris Karloff in skirts."

Whatever their intentions, everyone at the gala closing of the real Hollywood Canteen on November 22, 1945 agreed that it had been a genuine and moving experience for the stars who had done their bit. It is understandable that Bette Davis would say, "There are few accomplishments in my life that I am sincerely proud of. The Hollywood Canteen is one of them."

Today, the Hollywood Canteen itself is a four-story garage at 1415 Cahuenga Boulevard, but the organization survives as the Hollywood Canteen Foundation and continues to perform charitable work.

Outside of his 30-second cameo in his sophomore film *Bomben auf Monte Carlo* (1931) and his unbilled one-liner in *Meet Me In Las Vegas*, Peter Lorre's role in *Hollywood Canteen* is the most meager in his filmography, but worth it for those fans equipped with videotape and, most importantly, a fast-forward button.

With that in mind, *"Tim-ber-r-r!"*

CREDITS: Original Screen Play: Delmer Davies; Producer: Alex Gottlieb; Director: Delmer Davies; Musical numbers created and directed by Leroy Prinz; Musical Director: Leo F. Forbstein; Director of Photography: Bert Glennon; Film Editor: Christian Nyby; Art Director: Leo Kuter; Sound: Oliver S. Garretson and Charles David Forrest; Wardrobe: Milo Anderson; Make-up Artist: Perc Westmore; Set Decoration: Casey Roberts; A Warner Bros.–First National Picture; Released by Warner Bros. Pictures, Inc on December 30, 1944; 124 minutes

CAST: Laverne Andrews (Herself); Maxene Andrews (Herself); Patty Andrews (Herself); Jack Benny (Guest); Joe E. Brown (Himself); Eddie Cantor (Himself); Kitty Carlisle (Herself); Jack Carson (Himself); Dane Clark (Sergeant); Joan Crawford (Guest); Helmut Dantine (Himself); Bette Davis (Herself); Faye Emerson (Herself); Victor Francen (Himself); John Garfield (Himself); Sydney Greenstreet (Himself); Alan Hale (Himself); Paul Henreid (Guest); Robert Hutton (Slim); Andrea King (Herself); Joan Leslie (Herself); Peter Lorre (Himself); Ida Lupino (Guest); Nora Martin (Herself); Joan McCracken (Herself); Dolores Moran (Herself); Dennis Morgan (Guest); William Prince (Himself); Joyce Reynolds; John Ridgely (Himself); Roy Rogers & Trigger (Themselves); S.Z. Sakall (Himself); Zachary Scott (Guest); Alexis Smith (Guest); Barbara Stanwyck (Guest)

THE MASK OF DIMITRIOS
1944
by Dennis Fischer

The second and best of Peter Lorre's Ambler films, as well as his second best pairing with Greenstreet after *The Maltese Falcon*, was *The Mask of Dimitrios*. Lorre, over Jack Warner's strenuous objections, was given a heroic, starring role, and he makes the most of it with a subtle, layered performance that proves endlessly fascinating to view as he constantly confounds expectations.

The Mask of Dimitrios was but the second feature of its director, Jean Negulesco (1900-93), who was born in Craiova, Rumania. Negulesco would carve out a reputation for creating sentimental melodramas, but his best work was seen in such Warners films as *Dimitrios, Three Strangers, Johnny Belinda* and *Road House*, in which he used his talents to conjure up a world with the glamour of cynical, worldly people who exchange offhand, knowing dialogue. Negulesco later switched to 20th Century-Fox where he made mostly forgettable, CinemaScope, Deluxe-colored melodramas.

A competitor of John Huston's, Negulesco claimed to have prepared *The Maltese Falcon* for filming, only to have Huston take the assignment away from him while he was off on another assignment. Anatole Litvak recommended Eric Ambler's spy thriller *A Coffin for Dimitrios* (the American title of the book) as an ideal project for filming, and Negulesco intended to use Lorre and Greenstreet from the outset. However, the pair almost sabotaged the project during the screen test stage because, as Negulesco recalls, "Peter was a joker—he and Humphrey Bogart were a great pair of clowns—forever perpetuating gags. ...Lorre and Greenstreet monkeyed around during most of the test," causing producer Henry Blanke to consider canceling the project. The puckish pair shaped up the subsequent day and allowed Negulesco to continue now that the clowning was out of their systems.

Lorre specialized in intelligent and cultured characters, usually with sinister purposes, but *Mask* affords him a rare opportunity to play a hero who isn't an Asian detective. One of the aspects of Lorre that continues to fascinate is that his characters were so often full of contradictions. He often seemed a weary genius frustrated by all the sanity and insanity of the world. *Mask of Dimitrios* is a film to be savored because not only does it tell an involved, intricate and interesting story, it also allows Lorre to essay a character who is much like his actual self rather than yet another emotionally crippled madman.

Director Jean Negulesco in *The Celluloid Muse* had nothing but praise for Lorre's talent, perceptively commenting:

Playing against type, Lorre (with Sydney Greenstreet) is the mystery writer searching for Dimitrios. (Photofest)

Lorre was the most talented man I have ever seen in my life. If you watch *The Mask of Dimitrios*, you'll find that the whole picture, its entire mood, is held together by him. Without him, you're a little bored by it.

I think his chief asset lay in the element of surprise. When you expected him to be quiet, he was loud. When a scene in *The Mask of Dimitrios* threatened to run down, for example, this little man would shout for no reason at all; and as you were slowly recovering from the shock he'd ask mock-innocently: "Did I scare you?"

He was wonderful. When they were measuring his distance from the camera with a tape measure—and everybody was just sitting there bored stiff—he would scare the bejeezus out of the man measuring with a sudden yelp and the poor guy nearly dropped the tape; that's the kind of thing he did with his scene in *The Mask of Dimitrios*.

I allowed Lorre complete freedom to improvise. Sometimes he went too far, and then I think

> it's the role of a director to step in and say: "I think it's wonderful, it's very funny, but it's not in keeping with the mood and the style of the rest of the film."

In *The Mask of Dimitrios*, probably because of his Germanic accent, Lorre's character is transformed from an Englishman into a Dutch mystery writer, Leyden, who is on holiday in Istanbul. Lorre looks at his best in the role, having lost his baby fat and prior to his weight gain following his illness. He is given distinguished silver streaks at his temple and looks every bit the continental intellectual. The film, after its opening credits written in an open book, begins with the following written foreword:

> For money, some men will allow the innocent to hang.
> They will turn traitor... they will lie, cheat, steal...
> They will kill.
> They appear brilliant, charming, generous!
> But they are deadly.
> Such a man was Dimitrios.

The story opens in Istanbul on a beach where a young girl runs forward and then screams as she spies a dead body washed up on shore, the only clue as to its identity an I.D. card. Colonel Haki (Kurt Katch), head of the local secret police, subsequently announces the case closed.

Director Negulesco then cuts to a subjective shot of a man receiving an invitation from Madame Elise Chavez for an evening of music on the 21st of November, 1938. There the man, who proves to be Leyden, meets a fan of his work in Colonel Haki, who admits to Leyden that he plays the fool because it is expected, setting up the film's themes of deception and cunning.

Screenwriter Frank Gruber omits Haki's idea for a mystery book and, while being generally faithful to Ambler's work, pares down all non-essential material as much as possible, keeping the pace fairly sprightly without getting bogged down in details. This was Gruber's finest work, though most of the best dialogue comes directly from Ambler's novel. Gruber would later create the *Tales of Wells Fargo* TV series and also scripted *Terror By Night* and *Dressed to Kill* (1946) as well as having several of his Western novels adapted into films.

Colonel Haki explains that the body of master criminal Dimitrios Makropoulos (Zachary Scott in his film debut) has washed up on a beach, stabbed to death. He explains that Dimitrios was involved in an assassination—not as the assassin himself, but as one of the men who hired the assassin. In one of the film's more memorable pieces of dialogue, Haki maintains, "To me the most important thing about an assassination is not who fired the shot, but who paid for the bullet."

To entertain the author, Haki begins to relate what little he knows of Dimitrios' background. Haki became acquainted with Dimitrios when Dimitrios was a fig picker with a criminal past in Smyrna. Desperate to leave, he convinced a colleague to rob a pawnbroker. Instead, Dimitrios murders the man with a knife with his compatriot's help, but as the pair are celebrating in a tavern their ill-gotten wealth, the police arrest the compatriot while Dimitrios escapes. The robber confesses to the robbery, but maintains that Dimitrios did the actual killing. He is nonetheless sentenced to death while Dimitrios flees the country. This sets up a pattern of murder, treason, and betrayal of his partners that persists throughout Dimitrios' life story.

Fascinated, Leyden decides to investigate and calls for a ticket to Athens to try to put together the missing pieces of the Dimitrios puzzle. The desk clerk who answers Leyden's call is approached by Peters (Greenstreet) who inquires about Gollos, and then heads off for the morgue as well.

Never having been to a morgue or seen a dead body, Leyden goes to the morgue to do some firsthand research. He sees in Dimitrios a potentially interesting character for a novel. After viewing the body, Leyden resolves to trace the footsteps of this clever criminal. Leyden's very ordinariness allows the audience to identify with him, share first his curiosity and later his fear as he sets about answering such questions as "Who is Dimitrios?," "Why did he die?" and eventually "Is he really dead?" (There also remains the possibility that Ambler's plot provided the inspiration for Orson Welles' *Mr. Arkadin* a.k.a. *Confidential Report*, in which a rich rogue hires a reporter to investigate his background in order to uncover and eliminate anyone who knows the real truth about himself.)

Lorre's Leyden is a man who has considered murder mostly in the abstract and is little prepared for the grim reality of an actual crime. When at the Athens records office, he uncovers that Dimitrios was wanted on a charge of robbery and attempted murder, he exclaims gleefully, "That's Dimitrios, all right!" before the baffled clerk.

However, Negulesco uses his visuals to remind viewers of the literal darkness of the subject matter. Regarding his visual style, Negulesco noted:

> In *The Mask of Dimitrios*, I established a somber, low-key mood that I followed in a number of subsequent films. I learned that the public loves to share the actor's situation, to be a vicarious part of the action. It's curious that when you see actors moving and talking in semi-darkness, it's always more exciting than seeing them plainly, because you identify with them more.

Mask's cinematography is filled with such murky lighting courtesy of cinematographer Arthur Edeson, whose work has graced such films as *All Quiet on the Western Front*, *Frankenstein*, *The Invisible Man*, *The Maltese Falcon* and *Casablanca*. With its dark shadows and night-time settings, *The Mask of Dimitrios* can be considered film noir, though its European subject matter runs counter to that of most noir films.

Throughout the film, Negulesco also makes use of railroad sounds to build atmosphere, and for the initial meeting between Peters and Leyden, he creates a moody train station. Peters enters Leyden's sleeper coach and blusters about how all men are brothers and all languages beautiful. Leyden is less interested in this new companion than in getting some sleep before he arrives in Sofia, and so turns over to sleep while Peters contents himself with reading from a book entitled *Pearls of Everyday Wisdom*.

The next morning as Leyden leaves, Peters recommends a hotel and declaims, "That's the trouble with this world. There is not enough kindness." (In a nice character touch, Greenstreet wanly waves his hand to say good-bye to Leyden after the writer has already left and cannot see the gesture.)

In Sofia, a friend, Marukakis (Eduardo Ciannelli), takes Leyden to a cafe run by Irana Preveza (Faye Emerson), a kind of low-rent Marlene Dietrich type, who upon hearing Dimitrios' name, orders the pair out of her establishment and then to sit down ("If you will explain, Madame, how we can get out without standing up we should be grateful," Marukakis says acidly). She relents to tell them her story privately after lamenting upon learning that Dimitrios died penniless as he owed her money, that she is certain never to see again.

Negulesco initiates a flashback showing Irana returning from a drive with her married, well-to-do lover. Dimitrios, a thorough cad who lives in the same seedy hotel as Irana and owes the landlord for his rent, coerces Irana into giving him food and then he uses his knowledge of their relationship to blackmail Irana's lover. After Dimitrios is arrested, a "friend" secures Dimitrios' release from Bulgarian prison in exchange for his assistance in an attempted assassination. The attempt is a failure, and Dimitrios forces Irana to provide an alibi and more funds before leaving his brokenhearted lover.

In one of the film's finest scenes, when Leyden returns to his room, he finds it in extreme disarray. It has been searched by Peters, who holds a gun on the mild-mannered writer. Quoting one of Ambler's most florid speeches in the book, the eccentric Peters lifts the volume that Leyden had been reading (and into which he had inserted his notes on Dimitrios), and observes, "A book is a lovely thing. A garden stocked with beautiful flowers. A magic carpet on which to fly away to unknown climes."

Lorre does a terrific job of conveying Leyden's astonishment at finding this peculiar, pedantic character who has invaded his personal space and is holding a gun on him. Leyden lifts his hands up in surrender half-heartedly while exclaiming, naturally enough, "What are you talking about?"

However, Lorre's real brilliance is pulling off the unexpected reaction. Faced with this absurd character holding a gun on him, Lorre's writer wearily removes his overcoat and announces, "I'm tired, I'm going to bed." He ignores the threat and stops to consider the figure confronting him:

> What in truth are you doing here? Last night I met you on the train and you said you were going to Bucharest, and now I find you here waving this silly pistol in my face. I can only conclude that you are a thief or you're drunk.

Lorre leans forward and smilingly asks in a more polite, less accusatory tone, "Are you drunk, sir? Maybe you're mad. In that case, I can only humor you and hope for the best." Lorre's evident amusement at his character finding himself in such a predicament is very noticeable and adds greatly to the humor of the scene. Despite the pistol, he still does not take the intruder very seriously.

Leyden is intrigued by this impertinent man, and inquires what Peters' interest in Dimitrios is, noting, "Money? He had none. I saw his body at the mortuary, but there certainly wasn't...." Greenstreet moves his bulk forward menacingly, surprised at what Leyden has revealed. Caught off guard, Leyden responds, "What's the matter?" Peters appears dazed.

Recovering, Peters changes his tone, suddenly offering Leyden the name of a man who could supply him with more information on Dimitrios, and inquires about Leyden personally. "Your passport describes you as a writer, but that is a very elastic term. Who are you, Mr. Leyden, and what is your game?" Peters offers to pool resources with the writer, and explains that he has in mind a plan to secure a million French francs.

Peters sends Leyden on to Geneva, Switzerland, where he is to interview Grodek (Victor Francen, a Belgian actor who seemed to specialize in spy dramas), a retired master spy. There, a servant shows Leyden into Grodek's high-ceilinged, Bauhaus–style study complete with roaring fireplace. Lorre once more emphasizes the unexpected reaction. His character, upon seeing two Siamese cats on a sedan, cannot resist kneeling down and fondling them. Lorre chuckles at himself, takes a seat, curls his thumbs into his waistcoat, and then smokes a cigarette, making himself at home.

Grodek enters and inquires about Leyden's relations with Peters, and Leyden laughingly admits that he too is puzzled by his relations with the imposing Swede. Grodek says that he too is a writer. Leyden inquires whether he is writing his memoirs, but Grodek mysteriously responds, "I am writing the life of St. Francis, but I confidently expect to be dead before it is finished." (The reason for this is not explained in the film, but rather refers to the exhaustive amount of material which has already been written on St. Francis that a researcher would have to go through. Grodek has therefore chosen to occupy himself with something that would present no threat to others—he still has enemies as he explains—while filling up his time before his eventual demise.)

Grodek is amused to learn that Peters approached Leyden with a firearm, noting that Peters is quite terrified of firearms. He advises Leyden to go on to Paris to conclude his dealings with Peters, and admits that he was an employer of spy labor, and it was in that capacity that he had known Dimitrios.

Lorre demonstrates his range as an actor in this simple scene as he reacts to Grodek's every utterance, expressing by turns his wish to confide in Grodek, his amusement at the situation, his ability to be charming and disarming, concentrating at Grodek's expression of concern, toasting his host. He is friendly, blinks frequently at his host, and listens with rapt, focused attention.

Grodek's tale transitions to yet another flashback as Grodek explains Dimitrios' methods. Rather than resort to elaborate ruses to infiltrate a Yugoslavian military ministry to retrieve secret information of interest to the Italian government, instead Dimitrios simply enters the ministry, quickly notes the faces of the men who work there, picks a pigeon, and waits for him to leave from work.

Dimitrios' pigeon is Bulic (Steven Geray, looking like a milquetoast Dan Duryea), a lowly clerk whom Dimitrios builds up to feel important. Dimitrios offers the man 20,000 dinar (worth several months' salary) if he will influence which company will receive a contract to provide binoculars for the Marines. Despite Bulic's having no real control, Dimitrios pays off, pretending that the people awarded the contract were his secret subsidiaries, entertaining Bulic and his social-climbing, indolent wife (Marjorie Hoshelle), and eventually convincing him to gamble, leaving him with a large debt to pay off. Using this as leverage, Dimitrios coerces the lowly clerk to do the stealing for

Mr. Peters (Sydney Greenstreet) pulls a gun on Leyden (Lorre). (Photofest)

him. Knowing that he has no real influence, Bulic nevertheless accepts Dimitrios' offer in hopes that if Dimitrios' company happens to be awarded the contract, he could earn several months salary for doing nothing.

Ironically, explains Grodek, Dimitrios double-crossed him as well, taking both the money and the charts to sell to another government. To thwart him, Grodek leaked the knowledge of their having been stolen, resulting in the competing government receiving worthless charts and Bulic putting a bullet through his own head. (Grodek has no pity for the poor Bulic, whom he simply regards as a traitor to his country for having stolen the plans in the first place.)

In the final act of the story, Leyden makes his way to Paris. There, Peters knocks on the door, and Leyden amusingly and approvingly observes, "Oh, you're knocking at doors now. Quite an improvement, quite an improvement." Nevertheless, Leyden remains too trusting and is ill-prepared for such dangerous circumstances. He inquires if Peters brought his pistol with him, and, on being told no, gives Peters a dressing down. Taking the upper hand for once and leaning over Peters, Leyden explains:

> I'm not a violent man, Mr. Peters. As a matter of fact, I hate violence. But there are times when the most peace-loving simply must do it, and this may be one of them. I know who you are.

Leyden has discovered that Peters was once named Petersen and was a co-conspirator with Dimitrios in a smuggling ring (toned down from the Ambler novel's prostitution and drug ring). Dimitrios typically betrayed his comrades by informing the police before safely fleeing with the profits. He suspects Peters of murdering Dimitrios for his money.

The ever-duplicitous Peters then brandishes his hidden pistol while Leyden screams, "I knew it! I knew it! There it is!" Peters takes him to a well-furnished apartment in a seedy part of Paree and explains that the man the police thought was Dimitrios was actually Konstantin Gollos, a fellow co-conspirator who sought to revenge himself on Dimitrios by blackmailing him before Dimitrios stabbed him and left his own identification on the body.

Leyden agrees to blackmail Dimitrios despite the evident danger in such a plan, but declines to share in the profits. (The book's Peters is even more roguish, admitting that he had planned to cheat the writer out of his portion anyway.) When Peters launches once more into his favorite theme, the exasperated Leyden can only respond, "Not that again! Not that 'kindness in the world,' it's coming out of my ears," he complains.

Peters sends out a letter to Dimitrios demanding that he meet with them at the Hotel Ledia. As the pair are about to enter the hotel, Leyden inquires what would prevent Dimitrios from coming up and shooting them both (a good question), but Peters insists that Dimitrios is a very cautious man; however, when Leyden points out that while Peters is planning to disappear, he will still be about as a potential target for the ruthless criminal, Peters tells the writer to obscure his identity and features.

When Dimitrios arrives, Peters chides him for not greeting an old comrade, or even apologizing for betraying him. Peters convinces Dimitrios that his companion can establish Dimitrios' real identity, and the criminal agrees to pay a million francs. After the man leaves, Leyden weighs in with, "It's Dimitrios, all right. Ruthless and primitive. I was frightened." Peters looks after the departing Dimitrios malevolently and confesses that he didn't realize until just then that he hated Dimitrios enough to kill him.

Naturally, Dimitrios arranges to have his persecutors followed, but Peters anticipates that eventuality and the pair elude their follower. In the novel, Ambler has the pair taking elaborate precautions in picking up the money to prevent Dimitrios from simply killing them, thereby saving himself a million francs, including insisting that the money be left by women. In the film, the pair foolishly pick up the swag themselves and return to Peters' apartment to celebrate, with the deadly Dimitrios lying in wait for them.

At first, Peter is oblivious, thumbing through the large stacks of mille notes and smiling in delight until he sees Dimitrios' hat and his face falls (a great Greenstreet moment as his hopes for riches are dashed). Then he holds his money-grubbing hands aloft and trembles. Dimitrios shoots Peters without the slightest qualm.

Agitated, Leyden protests. "He was my friend. No, he wasn't my friend, he was a nice man...compared to you," bravely slapping Dimitrios' pistol away, "you rotten insane brute, do you think you can go on murdering?" Dimitrios chokes him and Leyden responds, "Killer. Let me go, you!" while trying to fend off Dimitrios' attack.

As they struggle, the wounded Peters retrieves the gun and holds it on Dimitrios and tells Leyden to go. "I'll go call the police or something," promises the departing

Leyden. Terrified, Dimitrios begs, "Come back, or do you want this carrion to kill me?"

Negulesco cuts to Leyden outside the apartment and starting to descend the stairs and then stopping when shots ring out. Uncertain, he pauses, and then the door opens slowly. There in the doorway is the wounded Peters. "I'm very glad it is you," says Leyden. "Are you all right? Put that money away. That's all you ever wanted, isn't it?"

"I won't want it now," announces Peters, his character having finally developed beyond his greed. Then, pointing to where the deceased Dimitrios lies, he adds, "I've done what I had to do." He throws the bills in his hands down the stairs in a repudiating gesture as gendarmes come in to arrest him. "You'll be glad to know I killed Dimitrios Makropoulos," he informs them. Then to Leyden, "You wanted to write a book. Write it. Send me a copy. I'll have a lot of time to read it where I'm going."

"Good-bye, *au revoir*," responds the sympathetic Leyden. "I'm sorry you won't be going to the Indies now."

Peters simply shrugs, "You see? There's not enough kindness in the world."

Lorre was fourth-billed in *The Mask of Dimitrios* despite having the starring role. While playing drunks, cripples, and madmen will usually get an actor a lot of attention (note how many Academy Awards have been given for just such kind of performances), true acting consists of playing a normal person realistically and interestingly. Lorre makes the most of this rare opportunity, providing the film with its moral center and serving as an intrepid inquirer to the sordid world of espionage, assassination, and crime.

His attitude toward working at Warner Bros. can be divined from reports that during the shooting of the film, he livened up the cast during coffee breaks and broke up the staff and visitors to the set by putting on a terrific act in which he would begin by pacing up and down nervously, pretending to pull out his hair, and shouting about Jack Warner, demanding to know, "Where is that creep? I sent him out for a bottle of beer a half-hour ago, and he isn't back yet!"

Nevertheless, most of the best lines in the film belong to Sydney Greenstreet. He and Lorre were the Laurel and Hardy of crime and made excellent partners.

The rest of the film is expertly cast as well. Oily, sharp-featured Zachary Scott proves quite promising in his film debut. Steve Geray excels here as the nervous Bulic who gets pressured into playing the bigshot and loses big time. In addition to the decadently suspect Victor Francen, such experienced hands as Eduardo Cianelli, Kurt Katch, John Abbott, and Monte Blue help round out the supporting cast.

Negulesco worked with Lorre and Greenstreet twice more, first on the desultory *The Conspirators*, an unfortunately miscalculated attempt to recapture the atmosphere and flavor of *Casablanca* with Lorre and Greenstreet. Neither Lorre nor Greenstreet were given much to work with, and the menacing pair did much better in their next effort for Negulesco.

John Huston wrote the script of the sardonic *Three Strangers* for Negulesco, another variation on the *Falcon*'s "three conspirators" motif, a group that included both Sidney Greenstreet and Peter Lorre. Huston had intended to shoot the script himself with Humphrey Bogart, Mary Astor, and Sydney Greenstreet, but after leaving the service, Huston went on to other projects and Negulesco took over and put Peter Lorre and Geraldine Fitzgerald in the Bogart and Astor parts. Jack Warner thought Negulesco was crazy for handing the romantic lead to Lorre, but the film's modest budget kept him from worrying too much.

Lorre is quite good as an alcoholic, small-time hoodlum and bank robber in the film, whose life is intertwined with two others who have formed a pact and mutually own a horse race sweepstakes ticket, as it has been foretold that Kwan-Yin, the Chinese goddess of fortune and destiny, will open her eyes and heart to three strangers, allowing them to win good fortune. As a film, the results were not up to the level of *Dimitrios*, though Lorre does expose his guilty cohorts and achieves a nice redemption at the end. *Casablanca*'s Howard Koch was brought in to polish up the script which had also had an uncredited rewrite by famed fantasy writer John Collier, while Arthur Edeson once more contributed some evocative photography.

However, it is Lorre's Ambler films that really stick with the viewer. While modern spy films became absorbed in James Bondian gimmicks and gadgetry, these films evoke a cynical, more realistic world where espionage is more about manipulating people into destroying their lives for one's own selfish ends, leaving tragic consequences in the wake. *The Mask of Dimitrios* stands out for its elaborate, intricate plot and well-realized characters, for the opportunity of its featured players to hold an audience in the absence of traditional leading players. The result is one of the best B films of all time and one of Lorre's finest films and finest low-key performances.

CREDITS: Director: Jean Negulesco; Producer: Henry Blanke; Screenplay: Frank Gruber, (From the Novel *A Coffin for Dimitrios* by Eric Ambler); Cinematography: Arthur Edeson; Sound: Oliver S. Garretson; Music: Adolph Deutsch; Music Director: Leo F. Forbstein; Orchestral Arrangements: Jerome Morross; Art Director: Ted Smith; Set Decorator: Walter Tilford; Make-up: Perc Westmore; Technical Adviser: Michael D. Kadri; Dialogue Director: Herschel Daugherty; Unit Manager: Lou Baum; Assistant Directors: Jack Sullivan and Don Page; Editor: Frederick Richards. Filming completed on January 27, 1944. Released by Warner Bros. June 23, 1944. Running Time: 95 Minutes

CAST: Peter Lorre (Cornelius Latimer Leyden); Sydney Greenstreet (Mr. Peters); Zachary Scott (Dimitrios Makopoulos); Faye Emerson (Irana Preveza); George Tobias (Fedor Muishkin); Victor Francen (Wladislaw Grodek); Steve Geray (Bulic); Florence Bates (Madame Chavez); Eduardo Ciannelli (Marukakis); Kurt Katch (Col. Haki); Marjorie Hoshelle (Anna Bulic); Georges Metaxa (Hans Werner); John Abbott (Mr. Pappas); Monte Blue (Dhris Abdul); David Hoffman (Konrad); Philip Rock, Rita Holland, and Rola Stewart (People on Beach); Georges Ranavent (Fisherman)

CONFIDENTIAL AGENT
1945
by Michael H. Price

From the day of its arrival, at a New York trade screening for theater operators in October 1945, to the immediate here-and-now, Herman Shumlin's *Confidential Agent* has been lamented as a waste of high artistry and star quality in the service of sanctimonious hackwork and studio starmaker politics.

Representative critics at the time spoke gratefully of Peter Lorre's passive but spirited bad-guy role and Katina Paxinou's more flamboyant show of rabid villainy. The press weighed in respectfully on Charles Boyer's tasteful underplaying in the lead. And the reviewers generally acknowledged novice Lauren Bacall's sex appeal while they "chopped me to pieces," to use the actress's own words, in terms of her dramatic worth.

The recent-history narrative milieu struck more than a few of the "crix" of 1945 as "badly dated"—funny, how timeliness becomes an irrelevant concern as a film outlives its original audience. It is, however, as crippling a problem now as it was then that producer Robert Buckner's screenplay captures but little of the ominous passion or military-industrial complexity of Graham Greene's source novel. Even in its shallowness, the picture is superficially verbose and, at 113 minutes' running time, overlong. The most prominent critic of the day, the future novelist and screenwriter James Agee, let *Agent* squeak by as "the best attempt yet, though still inadequate, to make the best of a Greene novel." As a star vehicle for Boyer, the picture today invites dismissal as "a trifle" by the critic and historian Larry Swindell, one of Boyer's more perceptive biographers.

Confidential Agent fared indifferently at the box office, threatening to compromise the faith that Warner Bros. had placed in Bacall. But then, even Warners had thought so little of the project as to hasten *Confidential Agent* into play as a mere stopgap between Bacall's sensational debut film, *To Have and Have Not*, and her troubled but promising second entry, *The Big Sleep*. (Her powerful agent, Famous Artists president Charles K. Feldman, had bullied Jack L. Warner into regarding *The Big Sleep* as Bacall's own vehicle. Thus subjected to extensive, star-conscious tampering and re-shooting, *The Big Sleep* would not be pronounced fit for release until 1946. Not until 1997 would a pre-tampering original cut surface for popular appraisal.)

The emotional heat-lightning that crackles between Bacall and Humphrey Bogart in *To Have and Have Not* and *The Big Sleep* could not have been duplicated between her and Charles Boyer in *Confidential Agent*, for she and Bogart relied on the tart natural chemistry that fueled their mutual attraction in real life. She had hoped to be cast opposite Bogart in *Agent*, which had been announced with Bogart and Eleanor Parker in the leads—but although Bacall was cast as a replacement for Parker, so did Boyer

Denard (Charles Boyer), Mrs. Melandez (Katina Paxinou) and Contreras (Peter Lorre). (Photofest)

replace Bogart. Director Shumlin was but an expendable talent in the development of a picture that was designed to be ephemeral: The former journalist was a Broadway-based producer-director who had helmed only one film, *Watch on the Rhine* (1943), before *Confidential Agent*, which became his last stab at directing in Hollywood.

Confidential Agent found Bacall struggling, as well, with an upper-crust British character assignment that was impossibly beyond her experience and narrow range. Boyer, a versatile leading man who seems to have been incapable of giving an inadequate performance, dealt with the Bacall problem by refusing to "play down" to her limitations. His performance thus renders hers more acceptable, and even makes it seem vaguely plausible that her character should at length forsake a pampered existence to help Boyer fight Fascism.

None of us should be obliged to search so diligently to find saving graces in a film. Boyer is great despite Bacall. Bacall is rescued by Boyer's rock-steadiness. Totalitarianism is a bad racket, and here we have a picture that is not shy about saying so. Praised by faint damnation.

Thankfully, one need only leave it to Katina Paxinou and Peter Lorre to make *Confidential Agent* more genuinely worth watching, more than an incidental curiosity of celebrity-driven marketplace manipulation. They account for the richest and most harrowing moments in a picture that hangs on their peculiar brand of menace—otherwise, it's just a case of Spaniard Republican Loyalist Boyer's reminding us of how wicked those dagnabbed Spaniard Facists are—and even Shumlin's indecisiveness as a director works to their advantage. Lorre and Paxinou seem to sense that no one knows or particularly cares where to take this meandering story, and so they impose upon it as intense a control as their doomed roles will allow.

Humphrey Bogart, Gordon Carveth, and Peter Lorre on the set of *Confidential Agent*

Denard (Boyer), a celebrated composer and musician who has lost his family to wartime treacheries, has abandoned his career to fight against the Fascists in the Spanish Civil War. Deputized to out-bid the enemy in a quest for British coal, the admittedly amateur statesman chances to meet Rose Cullen (Bacall), daughter of an English mining magnate, soon after arriving in England. Bored with an uneventful evening and drawn to the adventurous urgency she senses in Denard, Rose helps him escape from a series of ambushes engineered by a shadowy mastermind named Licata (Victor Francen).

Denard connects early on with a fellow Spaniard, Contreras (Lorre), a sniveling, rumpled agent whose cover is a teaching job in a school devoted to the pacifist gospel of a crackpot "international language." Neither man seems quite ready to trust the other. Mrs. Melandey (Paxinou), a hotel manager who feigns loyalty, but only just, to Denard's cause, is more obviously someone who is bound to want killing before too much longer. Denard befriends Else (Wanda Hendrix), a downtrodden teenage servant who routinely suffers abuse from Mrs. Melandey. Infuriated by Else's daughterly attachment to Denard, Mrs. Melandey shoves the girl to her death from a high window while Contreras looks on, as fascinated as he is horrified—and incapable of intervening. (James Wong Howe's precipitous camera compositions, Franz Waxman's ominous musical prelude and a dizzying job of film cutting capture the murder with a cruel immediacy, darting from the child's cringing progress toward the open window, to Paxinou's scowling ferocity, to Lorre's self-absorbed terror.)

Despite an impassioned plea to the coal-mining industry, Denard finds his mission apparently thwarted. Enraged to learn of Else's slaying, Denard draws a gun on the trembling Contreras, who dies from overexcitement when the weapon misfires. As he prepares to return to Spain in defeat, Denard viciously confronts Mrs. Melandey, demanding that she pay for Else's murder. But the malicious landlady has already been undone by a nosy boarder (Dan Seymour), who had documented a distant witness's account of the crime and alerted the police. Mrs. Melandey has taken poison rather than face up to justice—but Denard manages to give the old bat a couple of good whacks upside the head before she croaks.

The mission seems an exercise in frustration until Denard learns that his bid for coal has been honored, after all. Rose, whose slow-burn romance with Denard has been little more than a subplot, joins up with his cause without ever quite grasping the social commitment involved. "I can't be faithful to people I can't see—like you are—so I came along," she explains.

Katina Paxinou (1900-1973) appeared only sporadically in films. The alumna of the Greek National Theatre had found herself stranded in London and unable to return to her native country upon the outbreak of World War II. Paxinou retrenched in America, debuting on Broadway in *Hedda Gabler* in 1942 and making an indelible Hollywood impression in 1943 with an Oscar-anointed heroic performance in *For Whom the Bell Tolls*. She returned to Greece as soon as circumstances allowed, and with her husband, Alexis Minotis, founded the Royal Theatre of Athens.

"She's wicked! And when she beats me, she's like a madwoman!" So speaks debuting ingenue Wanda Hendrix in describing Paxinou's Mrs. Melandey. Paxinou serves up a marvelously hateful and unapologetic principal villain, mocking Boyer's errand with a chilling speech: "Idealism is a luxury I've never been able to afford. In this world, it's better to be without pity..."

The Paxinou-Lorre combination is vastly more satisfying than the teaming of Boyer and Bacall. Lorre establishes Contreras early on as an obsequious little man suffering from a heart condition, revealing by degrees the character's parasitic attachment to evil. Lorre speaks up assertively only when hiding, as it were, behind the skirts of Paxinou's Mrs. Melandey. Although he makes it plain that he wants no part of dirtying his own hands with an act of violence, Lorre observes Paxinou's sadistic outburts as if bewitched. Later along, he lies about his whereabouts in relation to the servant's murder.

For Lorre's admirers, the salent point of *Confidential Agent* lies in his final confrontation with a vengeful Boyer: "Don't! Don't frighten me!" Lorre gasps while cowering at gunpoint. "I have a bad heart! The doctors've only given me six months to live! They –" Boyer interrupts: "They made a mistake," he barks, intent upon bestowing a quicker death.

Lorre pleads to be heard out as he seeks to excuse his worthlessness. "If you—if you only had six months to live, and—and no hope at all, wouldn't you choose a little comfort and respect?" Boyer pens Lorre in and pulls the trigger, but the weapon only clicks. Lorre collapses as Boyer is distracted by Bacall's arrival. It is a splendid death scene, and as memorable as any moment in Lorre's more substantial Hollywood showcases.

CREDITS: Producer: Robert Buckner; Director: Herman Shumlin; Screenwriter: Robert Buckner; From the Novel by Graham Greene; Photographed by James Wong Howe; Musical Score: Franz Waxman; Art Director: Leo K. Kuter; Dialogue Director: Jack Daniels; Film Editor: George Amy; Running Time: 113 Minutes

CAST: Charles Boyer (Denard); Lauren Bacall (Rose Cullen); Victor Francen (Licata); Wanda Hendrix (Else); George Coulouris (Capt. Currie); Peter Lorre (Contreras); Katina Paxinou (Mrs. Melandey); John Warburton (Neil Forbes); Holmes Herbert (Lord Benditch); Dan Seymour (Mr. Muckerji); Art Foster (Chauffeur); Miles Mander (Brigstack); Lawrence Grant (Lord Fetting); George Zucco (Detective Geddes)

THREE STRANGERS
1945
by Steven Kronenberg

It's somehow fitting that *Three Strangers* followed Peter Lorre's work in *The Maltese Falcon* (1941) and *Casablanca* (1942). While all three films teamed Lorre with Sydney Greenstreet, *Falcon* and *Casablanca* showed us a seamy, dark and corrupt Lorre. *Three Strangers*, the last of them, saw Lorre come full circle as a character capable of evoking sympathy and love.

Three Strangers features Lorre, Greenstreet and Geraldine Fitzgerald as three random characters who meet in London in 1938 on the night of the Chinese New Year. They gather in Fitzgerald's flat to make three separate wishes on Kwan Yin, the Chinese Goddess of Destiny. Simultaneously, all three pool their resources on a lottery ticket, which they also hope will be blessed by the Chinese idol. The fickle goddess deals an interesting hand to each character, but only Lorre's John West emerges with his sanity and his life intact.

When we meet Lorre's West, we are initially fooled into thinking he is just another sleazy, corrupt persona plucked from Lorre's 1940s stable of characters. As Fitzgerald's Crystal Shackleford watches Lorre play her piano, she says: "You can play." Lorre's irreverent response: "Even the piano must be astonished." When Fitzgerald suggests that the three make their wishes on Kwan Yin, a skeptical Greenstreet scoffs at the notion. Lorre smugly and delightedly proceeds to challenge the man's skepticism. In this scene, in particular, Lorre uses his quirky facial movements, sudden smirks and upturned eyebrows to dare Greenstreet into tempting fate. Lorre's animated visage also provides a striking contrast to Greenstreet's gruff, formal style.

But the smarmy veneer of Lorre's West belies a heart of gold and a man of charm and poise. Note Lorre's good-natured appeasement of his greedy landlady—who plagues him with demands for back-due rent. We know he bears the woman no ill will, as he calmly lights a cigarette and appeases her in a low, conciliatory voice.

But Lorre's eyes and mouth convey John West as a troubled, pathetic man. And nowhere in the film is Lorre's pathos more palpable than in his scenes with Joan Lorring, as the woman who shelters and adores him. In his scenes with Lorring, we learn that Lorre's West was an accomplice in a bank robbery which ended in a policeman's murder. We also learn that Lorre is about to be framed for the slaying by the *real* killer. And it is when Lorre's fortunes are at their lowest ebb that his tenderness for Lorring is revealed. In all of his many scenes with Lorring, Lorre displays an extraordinary capacity for warmth, compassion and fragility. Lorring returns the tenderness in equal measure, accentuating the mutual pathos and love that reside in both characters.

West (Peter Lorre) and Icy (Joan Lorring) share a moment. (Photofest)

Yet, Lorre superbly conveys West's desire to stifle any sympathy which Lorring may have for him. On the run from the police, the couple decides to sleep under a bridge. Instead of bemoaning his fate, Lorre coolly tells Lorring: "I like it here. Do you think we'll have to pay the city rent?" And despite the fact that his life is crumbling, Lorre's West delights in the simplest pleasures, as he tells Lorring how he enjoys looking at the lights of London from their new home beneath the bridge. In these scenes, we see those famous hooded eyes gaze lovingly at Joan Lorring. Yet, these same eyes express an inability to cope with the depth of that love—and with the gravity of the situation that fate has handed him.

Indeed, Lorre's penchant for insouciant charm carries the second half of *Three Strangers*. Even after being apprehended, framed for murder and sentenced to die, Lorre is seen calmly sitting on death row, listening to a record. Yet, his ostensibly carefree attitude is touched with a patina of sadness as he bids farewell to one of his partners in crime, who has come to visit him in prison.

But for Lorre's West, the film ends on an upbeat note. A dying confession from the real killer frees Lorre from prison, just in time for him to join Greenstreet and Fitzgerald for the lottery drawing. By this time, Greenstreet, a bankrupt barrister who has stolen a prominent client's trust fund, is pathologically desperate for his share of the winnings. The three, indeed, possess the winning ticket, but Fitzgerald refuses to surrender Greenstreet's share of the money. Watch Lorre calmly and indifferently play piano as

Peter Lorre and Sydney Greenstreet—together again. (Photofest)

the winning ticket is announced, and Greenstreet desperately begs Fitzgerald for his portion of the bounty. Lorre's West refuses to become agitated, even after Greenstreet kills Fitzgerald in a blind rage. In fact, after the murder, Lorre coolly tells Greenstreet to stop panicking and have a drink—all to no avail as we watch Greenstreet run raving into the street, his sanity gone.

Ostensibly, the insouciant attitude of Lorre's West clashes with the sensitivity he displays in his scenes with Joan Lorring. But we see that it is West's casual indifference that has helped him overcome the misfortunes that dog his trail. In his final scenes with Joan Lorring, Lorre's expressive eyes and mouth palpably display a sense of disappointment and frustration: He is no better off now than he was on the night he met Fitzgerald, Greenstreet—and the Goddess Kwan Yin. But he is no worse off either and, in his final scenes with Lorring, Lorre's demonstrative facial movements commingle despair with a touching sense of relief and, finally, love. Indeed, it is Lorre's essential goodness—juxtaposed against the corruption of Fitzgerald and Greenstreet—that allows fate to deal him a benign hand.

Three Strangers is not Lorre's best film, despite a topnotch cast and crew. In addition to Greenstreet and Fitzgerald, Lorre co-stars with Robert Shayne (*Superman's* Inspector

Henderson and 1953's *The Neanderthal Man*), Arthur Shields (1957's *Daughter of Dr. Jekyll*, directed by Edgar G. Ulmer) and 1930s horror veterans Holmes Herbert and Edgar Norton. The film was lensed by another golden age horror stalwart, the great Arthur Edeson—who shot the picture in moody, dark, noirish tones. The film's weakest link is its screenplay, an unexpected disappointment since it was penned by John Huston and Howard W. Koch. Fitzgerald's scenes are marred by soapiness, and Greenstreet's commanding presence is diluted by some unnecessary comedic bluster.

Predictably, *Three Strangers* is redeemed by Peter Lorre's sonorous, modulated performance as John West. Time and again, Lorre displayed an underrated versatility in his work, but *Three Strangers* gives us an opportunity to see him as a fully sympathetic character whose breezy indifference is finally conquered by tenderness and love. The Lorre of *Three Strangers* is strikingly different from the Lorre we know and love to hate—and that contrast makes for a memorably rich performance.

CREDITS: Producer: Wolfgang Reinhardt; Director: Jean Negulesco; Cinematographer: Arthur Edeson; Music: Adolph Deutsch; Screenplay: John Huston and Howard W. Koch (Based on the Story "Three Men and a Girl" by John Huston; Editor: George Amy; Art Designer: Ted Smith; Special Effects: Edwin DuPar; Released by Warner Bros.; Running Time: 95 minutes

CAST: Peter Lorre (John West); Sydney Greenstreet (Jerome K. Arbutny); Geraldine Fitzgerald (Crystal Shackleford); Joan Lorring (Icy); Robert Shayne (Bertram Fallon); Alan Napier (David Shackleford); Peter Whitney (Gabby); Marjorie Riordan (Janet); Arthur Shields (Prosecutor); Rosalind Ivan (Lady Rhea); John Alvin (Junior Clerk); Clifford Brooks (Senior Clerk); Doris Lloyd (Mr. Proctor); Stanley Logan (Major Beach)

THE BEAST WITH FIVE FINGERS
1946
by Scott Allen Nollen

Three years after the release of *Invisible Agent*, Peter Lorre interpreted another of Curt Siodmak's characters, in *The Beast With Five Fingers*, a bizarre, hallucinatory film loosely based on William Fryer Harvey's 1928 short story. By accepting the role of deranged astrologer Hilary Cummins, Lorre also was reunited with *Face Behind the Mask* director Robert Florey, who currently had a short-term contract with Warner Bros.

After reading Siodmak's screenplay, Florey expressed his criticisms to the Warners powers-that-were and received a three-month suspension in return: a curious move, considering that he recently had struck pay dirt for the studio by directing *The Desert Song* (1943) and *God is My Co-pilot* (1945). When Lorre returned to the studio in November 1945, he also was dissatisfied and backed up Florey's objections. Both men agreed that the sets and cinematography should be done in an expressionistic style, and that the story be told through the eyes of Cummins. Though this approach would have been more faithful to Harvey's story, Warners refused, causing both actor and director to dampen their enthusiasm. Nonetheless, benefiting from a 10-week shooting schedule and a $750,000 budget, Florey designed as many unusual compositions, camera angles, panning and tracking shots and weird effects as possible.

Lorre, too, tried to make the best of the material, creating an obsessive performance on par with his unhinged characters in *M*, *Mad Love*, *Crime and Punishment* and *The Face Behind the Mask*. During this period, Lorre cared little for his films, often playing his roles with a tongue-in-cheek, flamboyant style, but his admiration for Florey resulted in one of his most memorable, multilayered characterizations. As he and Florey had done in *The Face Behind the Mask*, they devised a character imbued with pathos who eventually becomes demented due to environmental circumstances.

Beast opens with a Max Steiner *sturm-und-drang* title theme that sets the stage for the bizarre events to come. "Nearly 50 years ago" (which sets the tale in the mid 1890s) in San Stefano, Italy, partially paralyzed pianist Francis Ingram (Victor Francen) is hammering out a left-handed transcription of a J.S. Bach piece prepared for him by con man and would-be composer Conrad Ryler (Robert Alda). Lorre is first shown inside the library, pulling aside the curtains as Cummins peers out the window at the approaching Ryler. Here, Florey and cinematographer Wesley Anderson begin to demonstrate their unusual camera angles designed to accentuate Cummins' obsessive, paranoiac interest in astrology. (Several set-ups foreground Lorre with a large gyroscope.) Cummins immediately indicates his mental instability, declaring to Ingram's beloved and beautiful nurse, Julie Holden (Andrea King), that he will discover a knowledge of astrology

Peter Lorre, J. Carroll Naish, John Alvin, Charles Dingle, Robert Alda and Andrea King

"lost since the burning of the library at Alexandria" (nearly 2,000 years earlier!). The mad seer also reveals that Julie's plans to leave the old man's employ must be averted so he can continue with his important studies.

Following a dinner at which Ingram asks his companions to attest to his sanity, Cummins reports that he has overheard Julie and Conrad making travel plans. Outraged, Ingram attempts to strangle Cummins before ordering him to leave the house. (Here Lorre famously proves that he possessed one of the best hangdog facial expressions in cinema history.)

That night, Ingram ventures out of his room during a raging storm, his wheelchair tumbling down the huge staircase, sending him to his death. When the will is read, his greedy relatives, Raymond Arlington (Charles Dingle) and son, Donald (John Alvin), are unexpectedly shocked to learn that the entire estate has been left to Julie, who accepts primarily to spite them. Cummins is greatly relieved, having told the Arlingtons that the library's voluminous ancient tomes all belong to him. The avaricious pair hire Ingram's lawyer (David Hoffman) to contest the will, but the mercenary attorney is murdered by a mysterious crawling hand. Hearing Ingram's unmistakable music emanating from the main hall, Julie, Raymond and Cummins investigate, finding the late pianist's enormous ring on top of the instrument. Later, Inspector Ovidio Castanio (J. Carroll Naish) and the men venture into Ingram's crypt, where they discover that the deceased has "cut off his own hand." (This scene, with its superb compositions and lighting, is a visual highlight.)

David Hoffman, Peter Lorre and Charles Dingle

When Donald attempts to steal a previous will (which bequeaths the estate to him) from Ingram's safe, the piano begins to play just before the hand throttles his neck. Standing watch, Ovidio arrives in time to save him. Now Cummins starts his true descent into madness, with Lorre subtly increasing his nonverbal reactions as Florey utilizes sharp editing, chiaroscuro lighting and sound effects: A guitar hanging on the wall pops its strings, a clock chimes and the fire crackles loudly before the hand crawls out of its box. Lorre's eye and mouth movement, as well as his rapidly increasing breathing technique, all combine to bring the scene to a fever pitch.

Trapping the hand in the desk, Cummins runs upstairs to alert Conrad and Julie, who of course do not believe his seemingly incomprehensible story, particularly after the drawer is found empty. Left alone in the library once again, Cummins sees a row of books move (a variation on an event in Harvey's story), frantically grabs the hand and brutally nails it to the desktop. Slowly walking upstairs, the astrologer, now in a trance-like state, again attempts to convince Conrad of its existence.

Remembering that the safe's combination corresponds to the number of bones in the hand, Donald opens the steel door, finds the murderous five-fingered stump and runs out in terror. Julie then accuses Cummins of perpetrating the crimes and receives a good throttling in return. But the astrologer is halted when the piano begins to play once more. As Cummins now totally loses his mind, Florey pans between Andrea King and Lorre, cutting off the music when showing her but resuming it whenever the latter is shown (here achieving some of the narrative subjectivity he originally planned for

Julie (Andrea King) and Conrad (Robert Alda) with Cummins (Lorre).

the astrologer). Flipping open a switchblade, Cummins pursues Julie, but she remains calm, telling him that he must destroy the hand. Though he captures it, tossing it into the fire, it climbs back out and strangles him. Florey again presents the event from Cummins' warped perspective: Upon investigating, the others see that he has choked himself to death!

Instead of furthering Florey's expressionistic content, the final scenes of *Beast* feature a pedantic explanation by Ovidio (much like that offered by Dr. Richmond [Simon Oakland] in the closing sequence of Alfred Hitchcock's *Psycho* [1960]). In an attempt to explain away the muddle of events, the inspector prattles on about how Cummins had created the illusion of a disembodied, living hand (he had hidden an Edison gramophone in a suit of armor!); and that a subsequent nervous breakdown accounted for his belief that the crawling member was real. The entire episode seems tacked-on, ending not only with a cumbersome investigative explanation, but also with some forced, unnecessary humor: After a maid sees a white glove on the stairs and promptly passes out, Ovidio adds to the absurdity by noticing a hand (his own) crawling up to strangle him. Florey's expressionist sensibilities should have guided him away from having J. Carroll Naish fall completely out of character to directly address the audience: Since the film was already so fantastical, with some of the action filtered through Cummins' warped subjectivity, such balderdash was not needed to defuse its supposed "seriousness."

Cummins tragically descends into madness.

Florey and his crew used five different methods to achieve the crawling-hand effects. For Anderson's long shots, technicians built a mechanical hand fitted with a toy train–like spring motor: When wound it moved across the set on two tiny wheels. For the long shots set high above the piano, a plastic hand with attached wires danced convincingly across the keys. The arm of pianist Erwin Nyiregyhazi was covered with black velvet for close-ups at the keyboard, which were expertly lit by Anderson.

While a wax hand was manipulated by an actor in some scenes, Florey used his own for the most terrifying shots in which Cummins loses his mind: Sitting under the astrologer's desk, the director thrust his hand through a hole and into the box; throwing open the lid, he then writhed his fingers in a threatening manner. Both Florey and Lorre had wanted to transform Siodmak's scene of Cummins nailing down the hand into one in which the astrologer impales his own, proving that the entire episode was a hallucination generated by his ever-increasing insanity. This aspect, they believed, would clear up the confusion that existed in the script and in the final scenes of the filmed version. But producer William Jacobs thought otherwise, deeming the concept uncommercial and ripe for censorship. Disappointed but undaunted, Florey still managed to convey Cummins' obsession and paranoia during the sequence in which the astrologer is menaced by the crawling "beast."

Though *Time* reported that Florey was "plainly untroubled by considerations of taste,"[1] and *The New York Times* noted his leisurely pacing,[2] many critics liked the film. *Variety*'s "Mike" did criticize "the switches from straight narration to scenes registered by Lorre's deranged mind" (exactly the problem both actor and director attempted to avoid), but he also praised Anderson's camerawork, Siodmak's script, Steiner's score and Florey's direction, describing it as "impeccable."[3] "Often brilliant technically"[4] raved *The Los Angeles Times*, while *Film Daily* pointed out that Ovidio's summing up did little to dispel the effect created by Cummins and the crawling hand, for "the audience... knows more and has seen more than the policeman."[5]

Nearly all the reviews singled out Lorre's performance as the film's most outstanding element. He was "fine,"[6] and "masterly,"[7] particularly garnering admiration for his work in the hand-nailing sequence. While *The New York Times* assured readers that this event was "guaranteed to raise a few goose pimples,"[8] *Variety* added:

> Best and most gruesome parts of the picture are when Lorre is alone with his vivid imagination.

> He chases a ghoulish hand around the library several times, catching it finally and hammering it down in a bloodcurdling scene reminiscent in mood of *The Cabinet of Dr. Caligari*. ...Scenes in which the disembodied hand crawls around the room achieve a surrealistic effect and will surely be labeled among the most scary ever filmed.[9]

Indeed, Lorre carries the last half of the film, depicting Cummins losing his mind as he obsessively seeks "the law that changes unknown fate into predictable fact." No other Hollywood character actor could have matched his performance, the last he would give under his Warner Bros. contract. (A decade later, he would ferociously chew the scenery as Nero in the studio's unbelievably atrocious *The Story of Mankind* [1957], which also features Vincent Price as the Devil and Harpo Marx as Sir Isaac Newton! [What more could you expect from Irwin Allen?]) *Beast* also marked Robert Florey's final film under a studio's repressive wing.

Ironically released nationwide on Christmas Day 1946, *Beast* played to respectable business and later fared even better in Europe. But Florey, frustrated that Warners had butchered his work with script dictates and post-production editing, advised his colleagues to avoid seeing it. For Lorre, the film, one of the few Hollywood horror thrillers produced after World War II, had provided him with one of his last great golden-age roles.

CREDITS: Director: Robert Florey; Producer: William Jacobs; Screenplay: Curt Siodmak: Based on the Short Story by William Fryer Harvey; Director of Photography: Wesley Anderson; Editor: Frank Magee; Special Effects: William McGann, H. Koenekamp; Dialogue Director: Jack Daniels; Musical Score: Max Steiner; Musical Arrangements: Hugo Friedhofer; Assistant Director: Art Leuker; Art Director: Stanley Fleischer; Tradeshown November 19, 1946; Released December 25, 1946, by Warner Bros. Pictures; Running Time: 89 minutes

CAST: Robert Alda (Conrad Ryler), Andrea King (Julie Holden), Peter Lorre (Hilary Cummins), Victor Francen (Francis Ingram), J. Carrol Naish (Ovidio Castanio), Charles Dingle (Raymond Arlington), John Alvin (Donald Arlington), David Hoffman (Duprex), Barbara Brown (Mrs. Miller), Patricia White (Clara), William Edmunds (Antonio), Bette Mitchell (Giovanna), Ray Walker (Mr. Miller), Pedro de Cordoba (Horatio)

[1] *Time*, 13 January 1947.
[2] *The New York Times*, 26 December 1946, p. 28.
[3] *Variety*, December 1946.
[4] *Los Angeles Times*, December 1946.
[5] *Film Daily*, 1946.
[6] *The New York Times*.
[7] *Variety*.
[8] *The New York Times*.
[9] *Variety*.

THE CHASE
1946
by David H. Smith

In 1541, the Countess of Salisbury was executed by Henry VIII of England because she had a faint claim to the throne and a son who was a nuisance to the King. She ran away from the executioner and had to be dragged back.

It was a spirited attempt that failed.

Hollywood studio executives, with the end of World War II, decided it was time for a change of direction, and moved away from the recent years of morale-boosting, colorfully escapist adventures, comedies and musicals. Feeling a financial pinch with reorganization, the majors began farming their highly-paid contractees out to lesser studios.

Already dispirited by the limited roles being dealt him by Warner Bros., Peter Lorre was probably champing at the bit when the word came down. For several years, he had aspired to something new, something different than usual chickenhearted stoolie and cold-hearted gunsel parts that had been his bread and butter for the length of his contract.

While his situation was hardly as dire as the Countess of Salisbury's, it was a chastened Peter Lorre that found himself loaned out to United Artists to once more fill the undemanding role of a gangster's accomplice in *The Chase* in 1946.

But Tinseltown was fast becoming a braver new world for actors and behind-the-scenes personnel. Many of those filmmakers who had experienced wartime service returned to civilian life with a more mature edge to their talent, determined to abandon the upbeat, glamorous look of the pre-World War II movies to delve into the dark and gritty side of life.

Derived from the term *roman noir* ("dark novel") which described English Gothic fiction of the 19th century, film noir reflected the gloomy, post-war mood of the nation in their explorations of corruption and betrayal with characters that stoically faced an inescapable, doom-laden fate. The movies were seen to mirror the starker mood of a country troubled by the newborn nuclear age and (within a few years) the paranoia of the Cold War.

Set in the rain-drenched, shadow-enshrouded mean streets of an urban jungle, *films noir* used expressive contrasts of light and shade, distorted perspectives and new levels of screen violence to achieve their atmospheric results. It was a world of fedoras, trench coats and handguns. Of rats scurrying down rainy alleyways at 2 a.m. Of dark shadows, creepy alley shots and racing car engines. And of ham-fisted bad guys pummeling good guys with walloping haymakers.

Roman (Steve Cochran) and Gino (Peter Lorre) share a drink with Johnson (Lloyd Corrigan). (Photofest)

Some of the better *film noir* efforts came from smaller studios, and United Artists' *The Chase* delivered the goods—straight, but with a strange aftertaste for a chaser.

Indigent Chuck Scott (Robert Cummings) finds a wallet on a Miami sidewalk and, by way of the address on the I.D., hikes out to return it to its owner (no mean feat—the nearest "Hermosa Drive" to Miami is 200 miles away in real life). He is greeted at the mansion door by the suspicious, chain-smoking Gino (Peter Lorre). After a brief interrogation, Gino reluctantly escorts Scott upstairs to his boss Eddie Roman (Steve Cochran).

From the outset, Roman is obviously a gangster, cuffing a clumsy manicurist (Shirley O'Hara) and accepting mysterious phone calls even as he takes his hat off to Scott's naive courtesy. Nevertheless, Gino is contemptuous of Scott's innocent motives, calling him a "silly law-abiding jerk" to his face.

Scott is soon enough hired on as the house chauffeur, which leads to an unexpected infatuation with Roman's willowy wife Lorna (Michèle Morgan), a cliché damsel in distress if there ever was one. Her marriage is a stock miserable one, and she longs to escape across the Florida Straits to Cuba. Naturally, if stupidly, Scott throws in with her, and together they escape to Havana.

Gino pays a visit to Madame Chin (Nina Koschetz) during *The Chase*. (Photofest)

But Lorna is knifed in a crowded *cantina*, and suspicion for her murder falls on Scott. He manages to escape police custody, but his efforts to prove his innocence come undone at every turn. It is revealed it is Gino who is dogging Scott's every move, planting evidence and killing those who could provide Scott with an alibi.

Even as the hopelessness of the situation begins to overwhelm him, Scott awakens back in his chauffeur's room in Florida. Hinted at before, the film makes clear Scott is a shell-shocked veteran. From his nightmare he develops amnesia and seeks out the nearest VA hospital for help. His memory returns in time for him to meet Lorna at the gangplank, even as Roman and Gino are obliterated trying (and failing) to outrace a train at a railroad crossing on their way to intercept the couple.

The Chase was based on the 1944 Doubleday novel *The Black Path of Fear* by mystery writer Cornell Woolrich, itself based on one of Woolrich's stories for the pulps, in this case "Havana Night," from the December 1942 issue of *Flynn's Detective Magazine* (formerly *Detective Fiction Weekly*). The resulting picture has become infamous among fans of the writer for the way director Arthur D. Ripley (1895-1961) and scripter Philip Yordan (b. 1913) scuttled the novel's bleak vision by having all the nightmare events turn out to be just that—a bad dream from which Chuck Scott awakes.

Woolrich (1903-68) was born in New York City to estranged parents, and spent much of his youth in Mexico with his engineer father. After briefly attending Columbia University (he dropped out in his junior year), he began his writing career as an F. Scott Fitzgerald imitator, writing six jazz-age novels that were decently received by the critics (though not by the public).

After that, Woolrich moved to California and served an unsuccessful stint at writing films. Following a disastrous marriage, he moved back to New York City, where he lived with his mother in a succession of hotel rooms for the rest of his life.

But Woolrich was far from the failure he seems from such a superficial biography. After the West Coast fiascoes, Woolrich went on to write a score of mystery novels under his own name (as well as a couple of pseudonyms), and dozens of short stories compiled in over 15 editions, both pre- and posthumously. His work has been a source unparalleled in the mystery genre for adaptations for radio, TV and film. Most famously, *Rear Window* (1954) was a reasonably close adaptation of "It Had to Be Murder," an inventive 1942 short story.

As far as *The Black Path of Fear* goes, the dope dens and sinister Orientals and secret lairs and hair's-breadth escapes (which Woolrich added to the earlier story to make it book-length) don't represent the author at his best, exciting and action-packed though the pages are. But the earlier chapters with their evocations of love discovered and love destroyed, their sense of what it must be like to be alone and hunted through a nightmare city of the mind, furnish reason upon reason for the retroactive view that Woolrich is among the greatest psychological suspense writers who ever lived.

Besides *The Chase*, other media quickly introduced the book to a wider audience. CBS Radio's classic series *Suspense* aired a superb 30-minute version on August 31, 1944, with Brian Donlevy as Scott; the network repeated the same adaptation March 7, 1946, with the even better Cary Grant in the lead.

The movie proper was later adapted into a 60-minute radio play (*This Is Hollywood*, November 9, 1946) with Robert Montgomery and, reprising her screen role, Michèle Morgan. Several years later, it was made into a live hour-long TV drama (*Lux Video Theater*, December 30, 1954), starring Ruth Roman, Pat O'Brien and a pre-*Gunsmoke* James Arness. From the brief descriptions available, these versions apparently had even less relation to Woolrich's novel than did the movie.

Producer Seymour Nebenzal (1899-1961) had a twofold reason for casting Lorre in such a comparatively minor role. As one of the producers of *M* back in 1931, the German émigré naturally knew of the actor's ability to project an aura of quiet menace on-camera without resorting to tics and gestures better suited to the stage. Even sitting quietly in a restaurant booth, Lorre's charisma naturally drew the viewer's eyes, anticipating—and even hoping for—the ubiquitous veiled threat or violent response.

Also, Nebenzal was obviously familiar with the screenplay's source novel. In *The Black Path of Fear*, Lorre's character (named Bruno Giordano) is described almost as if Woolrich had the actor's stereotypical role in mind when describing Scott's impression of him:

> Something about him gave me the creeps; I don't know what it was. It was like standing with your face up against a coiled rattlesnake. An inch away, so that the darn thing wouldn't even have to stretch its neck and fang you. You can't even back out, because that might bring it on even faster. That was the kind of feeling.

Nebenzal had christened his production arm of United Artists, as a tribute to the Nero-Film A.G. Studios in Berlin where he and Lorre had gotten their start, Nero Productions.

But United Artists had lately fallen on hard times, and that made mounting a large ad campaign beyond the studio's wherewithal. Released on November 16, 1946 (but not even copyrighted until six days after that), it was perceived as a minor B-picture that received only a handful of contemporary reviews. The unnamed reviewer in *Variety* felt let down by the underhanded finale; beyond that, however, he or she felt it was "a superior production in every department." While finding the actors all "adequate," the reviewer made especial mention of Lorre, "in one of his best roles... with a solid assist as the killer's aide-de-camp."

Of course, the very name of Peter Lorre carries the stigma of "horror," and some writers make wrongheaded assumptions based on his billing in the cast. The eighth issue of the usually astute *Castle of Frankenstein* summarized *The Chase* with a pun better suited to lesser, juvenile film magazines: "Lorre is gory in this neatly-done murder thriller."

As Chuck Scott, health food devotee Robert Cummings was most known for appearing in light romantic comedies, but here is remarkably effective in a heavier, dramatic role. When Eddie Roman facetiously offers him a medal for his honesty, Scott's quiet refusal, saying he already has one (which carries no weight in civilian life), is both heartfelt and heartbreaking. Cummings went on to no little success on the small screen, winning an Emmy Award for a 1954 television version of *Twelve Angry Men*, then returning to his comedic forte in the TV series *Love That Bob* (1955-59) and *The New Bob Cummings Show* (1961-62).

Delicate blonde beauty Michèle Morgan appeared in her first movie at age 15 and quickly became the most popular screen actress in her native France before giving Hollywood a try during World War II. She made several films in the U.S., including *Passage to Marseilles* with Lorre, before returning to Europe. Without missing a beat, she won the Best Actress award at the Cannes Film Festival for *La Symphonie Pastorale* the same year *The Chase* was released.

As the gangster, Steve Cochran, like Lorre, projects an aura of intimidation without resorting to histrionics. He had only made his film début the year before, yet he soon made a name for himself (after a fashion) as an off-screen "boy-toy" of many of Hollywood's most glamorous stars, spanning film eras with the likes of Mae West, Joan Crawford and Jayne Mansfield. His greatest claim to fame, however dubious, came in the tabloids with his passing in 1965, dying of acute infectious edema on his yacht (with his all-girl crew of eight) in the Pacific off the coast of Guatemala.

A sometime screenwriter and director (*The Mysterious Dr. Fu Manchu*, its two sequels, others), character actor Lloyd Corrigan's lone scene in *The Chase* stemmed not from the book but was created out of whole cloth as a showcase to substantiate Cochran's and Lorre's villainy. As a shipbuilder who won't freely relinquish his wares for smuggling, Corrigan's character is guided downstairs to inspect the rarities in Roman's basement wine cellar (an uncommon enough commodity in South Florida with the region's high water table), only to be abandoned in its maze-like milieu and killed by Roman's brutish Great Dane. The grisly stuff kept just off-camera, the copper-colored contents of a broken bottle of Napoleon brandy sluicing against the walls more than suffice.

After unceremoniously dumping the body in the bay and reading about its discovery in the next day's newspaper, Gino laments price inflation when he has to send flowers to their victim's funeral. Sounding world-weary and bored by it all, it just might be a signifier of Lorre's growing disenchantment with Hollywood's one-track- minded casting directors.

CREDITS: Producer: Seymour Nebenzal; Director: Arthur D. Ripley; Written for the Screen by Philip Yordan, From the Book *The Black Path of Fear* by Cornell Woolrich; Director of Photography: Frank (Franz) E. Planer, A.S.C.; Art Director: Robert Usher; Production Manager: Joe Popkin; Special Photographic Effects: Ray O. Vinger, A.S.C.; Set Dressings: Victor A. Gangelin; Sound Recording: Carson Jowett; Make-up: Don Cash; Hair Stylist: Marjorie Lund; Miss Morgan's Gowns: Peter Tuesday; Wardrobe: Bill Edwards; Assistant Director: Jack Voglin; Musical Director: Heinz Roemheld; Musical Supervisor: David Chudnow; Original Musical Score: Michel Michelet; Film Editor: Edward Mann; Associate Producer: Eugene Frenké; Copyrighted 1946 by Nero Pictures, Inc.; Released by United Artists on November 16, 1946; 86 Minutes

CAST: Robert Cummings (Chuck Scott); Michèle Morgan (Lorna Roman); Steve Cochran (Eddie Roman); Peter Lorre (Gino); Lloyd Corrigan (Emmerich Johnson); Jack Holt (Commander Davidson); Don Wilson (Fats); Alex Minotis (Lieutenant Acosta); Nine Koshetz (Madame Chin); Yolanda Lacca (Midnight); James Westerfield (Job, the Butler); Jimmy Ames (The Killer); Shirley O'Hara (Manicurist); Florence Auer (Lady Barber); Martin Garralaga (Cabman); Alex Montoya (Detective)

THE VERDICT
1946
by Gary J. Svehla

The setting is Newgate Prison, London, 1890, as Scotland Yard police superintendent Grodman (Sydney Greenstreet) listens to the prison bells chime as a poor, pathetic man is led by a clergyman to his death by hanging. All the assembled police and prison guards commend Grodman for the excellent police work performed resulting in the guilty's quick and fair execution. But as Grodman states to one constable, the job of a police superintendent is never cut and dried:

> Ours is a profession of disturbing contradiction, Sir. The man who builds a great ship or composes a classic symphony... success means the fruits he tastes are sweet. Thus, success is often measured by the amount of lives we take. The fruit is bitter. I have no personal feelings... like the court that condemns. May his soul rest in peace.

Soon, Grodman receives visitors at the Yard, Inspector Buckley (George Coulouris) and Sir William Dawson, who have startling news: Grodman sent the wrong man to the gallows, and that his entire case, built on circumstantial evidence, falls apart because the condemned man's formerly considered bogus witness has just been found, but found too late to save his life. The condemned man claimed a clergyman he was with at the train station could confirm his innocence, that he could not have been at the scene of the crime the night of July 21. The condemned man claimed the clergyman was taking a train from Waterloo Station to Wales, but everyone knows no train goes to Wales from Waterloo Station. However, what the condemned man failed to understand was that the clergyman was traveling to New South Wales, Australia, where he has been ever since. Suddenly a haze of self-revelation hits Grodman hard as he immediately comes to realize an innocent man is dead for a crime he did not commit. Sir William chimes in, "I shall accept your resignation, with regret." Claiming it is time for a younger man to step up to the plate, Sir William appoints the hardly youthful Inspector Buckley as Grodman's immediate replacement. Buckley tells Grodman, solemnly, he is sorry, but Grodman can see the ambition in his eyes and states: "On the contrary, you're delighted... I shall watch your career with the greatest of interest... perhaps with some amusement." However, the proud police superintendent, looking around his walls to read commendations from even the Queen herself, feels disgraced and empty, very much alone.

Peter Lorre as Victor Emmric in this locked door mystery. (Photofest)

Such is the beginning of Warner Bros.' underrated "locked door" mystery of 1946, *The Verdict*, starring Sydney Greensteet and Peter Lorre in their final movie together. However, it features the directorial debut of Don Siegel, the man who would go on to direct *Invasion of the Body Snatchers, Dirty Harry* and John Wayne's final film, *The Shootist*. Thematically, *The Verdict* has much in common with Siegel's better-known works; stylistically, this Warner Bros. setbound period piece is worlds apart from the on-location shooting of *Dirty Harry* or *Charley Varrick*. Interestingly enough, *The Verdict*, based upon the novel by Israel Zangwill, was thrice filmed: *The Perfect Crime* in 1928 and as *The Crime Doctor* in 1934.

As Greenstreet quoted above, *The Verdict* is a movie of disturbing contradictions, using the mystery genre as a means of forwarding the theme of moral ambiguity. Even the major characters are paired together two-by-two, each becoming the yin to the other's yang, neither extreme becoming a blueprint for the satisfying, effective life but each, when studied side-by-side, illustrates the weaknesses and strengths of one personality contrasted to the other. Grodman, after his fall from grace, will seek almost sadistic pleasure from trying to see his younger upstart disgraced by making even more foolish mistakes in the day-to-day operations of his job. The rotund and stoic policeman, now called *Mr.* Grodman as he corrects one of his officers, decides to devote his life to writing a book highlighting his police career and illustrating the folly in basing police investigation upon circumstantial evidence, his own folly.

Into this mix comes always either slightly or profoundly inebriated Victor Emmric (Peter Lorre), a man who lives to indulge in life's hedonistic pleasures,

Frequent co-stars Lorre and Greenstreet make *The Verdict* snap, crackle and pop. (Photofest)

work coming secondary (with Grodman work is his life). Perhaps the more perfect human being would be the middle ground between Victor and Grodman (whom Victor refers to as Mr. G, transforming the larger than life symbol of police perfection into just another one of the guys); however, each character demonstrates both the strengths and weaknesses of the other so a middle ground is almost impossible to delineate. Victor is introduced pouring wine for the soon-to-be-returning Grodman, while friends gather to cheer him up, ring-leader Victor orchestrating the tone for the party to follow. Victor is concerned about all the medicine bottles he finds that Grodman now takes, calling him a man in a daze, a man obsessed.

The other assembled partygoers include Arthur Kendall (Morton Lowry), the nephew of the murder victim, for whose murder an innocent man died swinging from the gallows. And soon to appear is Clive Russell (Paul Cavanagh), member of Parliament and avowed political enemy of Kendall. Once again we have that "disturbing contradiction" of two affluent men who consider themselves above the common morality. One will later be revealed as a murderer, and the other, a government representative, will find himself blackmailed for having an affair with a married woman. Both men dress to the nines, speak elegantly in polite company, but both men, when dealing one-on-one, display an ugly side. However, each man's digression against conventional morality differs by degrees; one sin is far more serious than the other.

After Grodman returns home and seems to enjoy the camaraderie of the assembled crew (he asks Victor, an artist, to illustrate his massive police book, to which the eager Victor brags, "I can do corpses... exquisitely!" in that unmistakable Lorre voice), the mood is immediately shattered when Russell arrives to eyeball Kendall and the two begin sparring. Russell and Kendall, both men of means and privilege, mix together like oil and water. Russell, defender of the rights of coal miners, is seen as a political opportunist by the quieter Kendall. "I invited you up here to cheer him up, not to have a fight," Victor shouts at both men, but the mood of the moment has been shattered, and Russell and Kendall leave after Kendall wishes lightning would strike Russell's train, which he is catching immediately. Victor, upset that Kendall helped ruin the night for Grodman, says ironically he likes just two things about Kendall: "your tact and your charm." However, as Victor and Grodman continue drinking, outside Russell confronts Kendall by tapping him on the shoulder to get his full attention, stating, "I'm warning you Kendall, this time you've gone too far!" To which Kendall responds that he heard some "things" about Russell which would make "rather juicy reading for the newspapers." Russell's final words are foreshadowing of disasters to come: "If you spread any more lies, I'll take steps to silence you, once and for all." Listening to this entire exchange is Lottie (Joan Lorring), observing all this commotion while sitting in a carriage. She also confronts Kendall, her apparent lover. She tells him the jewelry he gave her is utter trash and, being very upset, Kendall tells her if the jewelry is false, it is appropriate for her. Getting into a screaming match, Kendall hurries off, stating they can settle this tomorrow.

There is absolutely no surprise as to who will be the murder victim, but many plot surprises await as the story unravels.

Having ended their party early, Victor and Grodman exit into the street and observed the fireworks described above, with Victor deadpanning, "The air is full of sinister currents tonight!" Victor continues, "Sorry we can't continue our evening... the night is still young for wine, women and song." It is apparent that while Grodman is ready for bed, his friend is ready for a night of partying until dawn.

Subsequently, the viewer is shown Kendall retiring to his flat, telling his downstairs neighbor Mrs. Benson to please wake him at 6 a.m., after which he enters his apartment, shuts all the windows, lowers the curtains, locks his deadbolt and retires to bed. The next morning, Benson knocks on the door, but nothing stirs from within. Becoming overtly concerned, Mrs. Benson rushes to Grodman's flat, stirs him from bed ("What a filthy morning," he declares), follows him to Kendall's flat, watches as he bangs on the door, forces the door open, and investigates, as Benson remains outside in the hallway. Kendall is found murdered in his bed, a stab would through his heart (but how could the murderer get into a locked room and leave it the same way—the locks and windows tight and secure?).

Buckley immediately goes to work proving he is the fool that Grodman claimed he always was. He hires a convicted breaking-and-entering man to figure out the mystery of the murder in the locked room, but all his solutions are proven false. Victor, who was found wandering aimlessly, actually occupies the room directly above Kendall's living quarters; thus, he soon becomes a red herring. Lorre draws Buckley as the devil with horns, amusing Grodman. "When Constable found me... I was drunk... it was all a little vague." Later Grodman asks Victor what he thinks of Buckley, and Victor chimes back, "I dislike him very much. Wonder how many mistakes he will make?" To which Grodman displays one of his uncommon outbursts of humor: "He's already made one. He's misjudged the size of my britches," as Grodman's huge posterior completely covers the camera lens and both men break out into contagious laughter. It is apparent that both men, of different social rank and disposition, complement and amuse each other and share a special friendship.

Lottie, Kendall's lover, is caught by Buckley breaking into Kendall's flat searching for some missing article, a watch with a good luck charm embedded. Lottie insists that even though she quarreled with Kendall the night before his murder, they were the best of friends. Soon Buckley finds Mrs. Benson also peeping through the keyhole, a snoop of a different sort. Once again the screenplay by Peter Milne juxtaposes opposing types, this time a young, sexy tart and an old fuddy-duddy busybody, each attracted to Kendall and each extremely jealous of the intentions of the other. Benson snarls that Kendall was never the same after he began to see "this creature." Lottie retorts calling Mrs. Benson "you old hag" and the two women almost come to blows. Mrs. Benson claims the high road stating she is only protecting Kendall's name. But both women have their own agendas and each is just as sneaky and dishonest as the other.

But since Buckley has not recovered the watch, he orders the corpse of Kendall exhumed since the coroner cannot remember burying the corpse with the watch. In a rather ghoulish sequence, photographed at night, the coffin is dug up, as Victor enters the sequence, along with Grodman and Buckley. "Good evening, lovely night, isn't it," Victor proclaims. "I've always had the suppressed desire to see a grave opened... especially at night... it's exciting," Soon finding the watch, buried on the body, Benson screams and cries for the assembled to leave, to "let him lie in peace." Victor, acting the eccentric with spunk and delight, adds, "I do so want to see what Kendall looks like," but Grodman, perplexed, can only ask, "Why Victor?" However, on the body is found a photo of Mrs. Benson with the inscription, "from one who loves you from afar." Buckley adds that Mrs. Benson was a tad too eager to accuse Lottie of the murder. Victor, upset that Buckley has kept Lottie arrested for one week, calls the new police superintendent "a strange man" who "simply wants to keep people under arrest." When Grodman asks Victor about his interest in the case, in this macabre setting, he innocently responds, "simply one of an artist."

But such a simple line demonstrates again the dichotomy between Grodman and Victor, Grodman the dedicated and obsessed career man, always the science of his job foremost in his mind. On the opposing end we have the laissez-faire artist, the eccentric, the low-key and beloved weird observer, a man who never allows the pressures of the everyday job to frazzle or disorient him. The next morning, for instance, we see Victor reading the morning paper with Grodman. "Come Victor, I have a delightful stabbing for you to illustrate." With those hound-dog eyes that only Lorre could flash, he responds: "Oh, no, I've done three stabbings in a row. How about a nice strangling!" Yes, Victor is only playfully responding in his usual "what the hell" philosophy of everyday life, but his humor and irony is always being contrasted to Grodman's obsession and seriousness in both solving the case and embarrassing his police successor.

Soon, upon Lottie's release from prison, Grodman and Victor, who are sitting in the audience watching her risqué saloon-singing at a nightclub and are referred to in their drunken state as "big bubbles and little bubbles," discover Kendall knew of a mistress that Russell kept, a Lady Frieda, whom Kendall always threatened to expose to the media. Russell always threatened to silence Kendall if the news ever leaked out. All the while Grodman and Victor are plying Lottie to spill her guts, Victor is drawing a caricature of Lottie on the tablecloth, and both are declaring their unending friendship for one another. "Bravo," Victor shouts at the end of her number, wildly applauding. Realizing that Kendall was "a bad lot," Lottie in her funk states, "I guess I always get the bad ones, right." Rising to the noble occasion at hand, fueled by those bubbles, Victor chivalrously announces, "I assure you Lottie, I'm very good!" But Lottie responds, "No such thing as a good man." And as we have observed throughout the movie, every man we have observed is indeed flawed and so are the women.

The next day Victor runs into Grodman on the streets, and states he just saw "our friend," referring to Buckley. "Lately, he has gone quite balmy. Thought he was clever, trying to draw me out about Lottie—so it cost him a lot of his liquor!" Victor tells Grodman that Buckley claims he knows every movement Lottie's made since he released her. Grodman repeats, "Every movement?" Victor then adds, "That's a very disturbing thought," and both men erupt into bawdy laughter.

Returning home for another sequence of macabre humor, Victor is greeted by Mrs. Benson, who advises him to wear a whistle for protection. Never missing the opportunity for eccentricity, Victor politely asks, "How would you blow a whistle if someone cuts your throat?" Benson looks utterly horrified and proclaims, "I never thought of that." Then, ascending the stairs slowly, Victor mimics the sound of blowing a whistle, smiling. The mood is abruptly changed when a black-gloved intruder attempts to break into Victor's room that very night, but the silhouette of the intruder seems to resemble Grodman. Awakening the household, Victor tells Mrs. Benson to call the police while he searches the house, and once again Benson rouses Grodman from his sleep, but as the rotund figure dresses, two black gloves slip from his bed clothes.

Soon Superintendent Buckley puts all the circumstantial evidence he has mustered together and declares Russell is the murderer. He arrests the man, who stands trial, and is found guilty and sentenced to die at the gallows, in a plot device very similar to the beginning of the film. Grodman attempts to search Europe trying to find Russell's mistress, to use her as the alibi for Russell's whereabouts the night of the murder, but Grodman returns only hours before the execution, claiming he found her too late, she is dead. The execution will continue.

Victor, for once very solemn, is drinking alone at a tavern, and when he is asked if he had enough, he responds, "Sometimes enough is not enough..." and exits the bar, headed for his friend's Grodman's home, when he interrupts Grodman who is writing in his book that he suspected "Victor knew more...," as Victor enters the room. "Come in Victor, I was expecting you," and for once Victor states (mimicking Grodman), "It's a wretched night," when Grodman corrects him, "Maybe it's only you who are wretched!" Grodman announces he is working on his last chapter of the book, dealing with the Kendall murder case. Victor, now not so happy-go-lucky, is trading personality extremes with Grodman, who is strangely outgoing and warm. Victor apologizes and says, "I want a drink. I'd rather work some other time." But Grodman becomes solemn stating, "There will be no other time, Victor." Momentarily remembering the murder case at the movie's beginning, he claimed the murderer took advantage of a friendship and that "no one will ever do that again." When it seems imminent that Victor will be exposed as the murderer, the tables are upturned once again when Grodman declares the only way to save Russell is to disclose the true murderer. "If that were not true, Victor, you wouldn't have come here tonight." Victor declares, "I'm afraid, I'm ter-

Victor with Lottie (Joan Lorring) happily indulges in wine, women and song. (Photofest)

ribly afraid." In a surprise revelation, Grodman admits he wished to make Buckley's humiliation and defeat as bitter as Buckley made Grodman's. Only after Grodman and Victor visit Buckley, and Grodman asks Buckley if he accepts full responsibility for the execution of Clive Russell, only after Buckley, with pride, admits he assumes full responsibility, does Grodman reveal that Russell is indeed innocent. Grodman confesses that he drugged Kendall's drink the night before his murder so he wouldn't awaken at 6 a.m., and when Mrs. Benson called him in to investigate (as he knew she would) and banged at the door, Grodman admits that Kendall was still very much alive when he forcibly entered his room. Since only he entered the flat, he then immediately stabbed Kendall through the heart, killing the ruthless man for his "double murder. First, Kendall murdered his aunt, and second, realizing an innocent man was convicted, sentenced and executed for his crime, he willingly committed a second murder. Grodman admits there was no other way to "bring him to book." With these parting words, Grodman asks Victor to deliver his book to the publisher.

In one of the strangest roles of his movie career, Peter Lorre, playing the eccentric and ghoulish Victor Emmric, seems all the more weird when contrasted to the fastidious and regal Grodman, a professional policeman whose life is dedicated to protecting the innocent and punishing the guilty. However, even with his lackadaisical attitude, Victor reveals himself to be a real friend to his mentor. It seems only he can get Grodman to act silly and laugh, and after his disgrace, it is the concerned Victor who orchestrates the cocktail party for the sole purpose of cheering up his humiliated friend. But things never become too serious for Victor as they become for Grodman, and once again the distinct contrasts in personality only demonstrate flaws inherent in each individual (Grodman's cockiness and ego vs. Victor's lack of commitment to anything worthwhile in life, other than his art, which we only see him address half-heartedly). Victor's character, at first appearing frivolous and weird for weird's sake, soon becomes muli-dimensional and emotionally more expressive in those final sequences with good friend Grodman who decides he has to turn himself in to save the life of the innocent Russell (cad that he might be). Their off-handed and left-of-center friendship seems somewhat alien in this traditional murder mystery, but it is precisely because of these quirks in personality, aided by inspired acting, that make Peter Lorre and Sydney Greenstreet snap, crackle and pop. While Lorre is again committed to another supporting role, it is his enthusiasm and eccentricity with which he imbues his character that makes the role of Victor so memorable and *The Verdict* so outstanding.

CREDITS: Producers: William Jacobs, Jack L. Warner (Executive); Directed by Don Siegel; Musical Score: Frederick Hollander; Cinematography: Ernest Haller; Editor: Thomas Reilly; Art Direction: Ted Smith; Set Decorator: G.W. Berntsen, Jack McConaghy; Costumes: Travilla; Make-up: Perc Westmore; Sound Department: C.A. Riggs; Screenplay: Peter Milne (Based upon the Novel by Israel Zangwill); Released by Warner Bros, 1946

CAST: Sydney Greenstreet (Superintendent Grodman); Peter Lorre (Victor Emmric); Joan Lorring (Lottie); George Coulouris (Buckley); Rosalind Ivan (Mrs. Benson); Paul Cavanagh (Clive Russell); Arthur Shields (Reverand Holbrook); Morton Lowry (Arthur Kendall); Holmes Herbert (William Dawson); Art Foster (Warren); Clyde Cook (Barney Cole); Ian Wolfe (Jury Foreman)

QUICKSAND
1950
by David J. Hogan

The Go-getter

In 1943 a businessman named Sam Stiefel, like Edward G. Robinson's Johnny Rocco in *Key Largo,* wanted *more*. He owned theaters in Baltimore and Philadelphia, and decided he wanted to make movies instead of merely exhibit them. His onetime business partner, Eddie Sherman, had split for the coast and now managed the red-hot careers of Abbott and Costello. To Stiefel, this was big-time stuff, a gold mine. Because he had horse racing interests on the West Coast, he was familiar in general terms with what he probably called the "layout" of L.A. Stiefel was a go-getter, a quick thinker with a glib tongue. But although he had invested heavily in horses, he needed a special kind of horse if he was going to ride into Hollywood.

When top MGM star Mickey Rooney came through Pittsburgh to promote *Andy Hardy's Blonde Trouble* in 1943, Stiefel made a point to meet the 23-year-old actor. Throughout the year, Stiefel worked hard to ingratiate himself not just with Rooney, but with the actor's mother and stepfather. In March 1944 Rooney and Stiefel agreed to form Rooney, Inc., with Mick as president, Stiefel as secretary-treasurer and attorney Mort Briskin as counsel.

Rooney was still under contract to MGM at this time, so Rooney, Inc. was involved less with the actor's locked-up film career than with such subsidiary things as personal appearances, licensing (Rooney even had his own comic book) and race horses and other investments. This arrangement continued while Rooney did Army service from 1944 to the spring of 1946. During that period Stiefel had freely given money to Rooney and to Rooney's folks. Come discharge day, Stiefel and Rooney meet up and Stiefel casually mentions that while Rooney, Inc. is going great, no kidding, the Mick and his parents owe him $100,000. Rooney's jaw dropped. How could this be? Wasn't Rooney, Inc. making money? Well, sure, Stiefel admitted, but the earnings had lessened considerably during Mickey's time in the Army. And anyway, the money that had been loaned to Mickey and to his folks had been *Stiefel's* money, not the corporation's.

Do you have a bad feeling yet? Do you have a sense of where this is going? If Rooney did, he didn't take steps to disengage himself from Stiefel. To the contrary, he agreed to a 50/50 earnings split with his partner. Well, that sounded okay, Rooney supposed. He was still under contract to MGM, and although his "cute" years were behind him (he was now a short—if talented—young adult of pleasing but unromantic, unrugged looks), he had won good notices for his first "serious" MGM vehicle, 1947's

Mickey Rooney and Peter Lorre (pictured with Jeanne Cagney) were forced into this production by Sam Stiefel.

Killer McCoy, a modestly budgeted boxing melodrama that earned a hefty $2 million. The success of *McCoy* suggested to Rooney that he could make the difficult transition from huggable juvenile to leading man.

Simultaneous with Rooney's belief in his future were dramatic changes in the dynamics of Hollywood business. Movie attendance in America had peaked in 1946 and had been on a dramatic downward slide since. Studios were cutting loose many of their contract players, and other stars were leaving voluntarily to set up their own production companies. In such situations, the stars reasoned, they could control not just their artistic destinies but their financial ones, as well. If Humphrey Bogart could do it, why not Rooney?

So Mick confidently allowed the licensing and personal appearances and investments handled by Rooney, Inc. to continue—but there still was that contract with MGM. Egged on by Stiefel in 1948, Rooney engaged studio boss Louis B. Mayer in an acrimonious shouting match and got out of his contract. Or maybe he was tossed from the studio the way an irritated man at midnight tosses a pesky tomcat out the door. Anyway, Rooney was free—free, that is, to take home a paltry $10,000 from each earnest and low-budget melodrama Stiefel planned to put together for him.

Sam Stiefel had the sort of cunning that some might call unscrupulous. Although a key figure in Rooney, Inc., he refused to bankroll the corporation's film productions

Peter Lorre had been a creature of the Hollywood studio system.

with his own money. Instead, he told partner Mort Briskin to drum up outside financing. Nevertheless, Stiefel arranged to award himself 40 percent of whatever profits the films might make.

Rooney finally woke up. Ten thousand free and clear from each picture wasn't going to cut it—not with alimony payments and nights at the Mocambo and the cars and the wardrobe and a place to live that befit America's former #1 box office star. So it was that Rooney made *Quicksand* and another melodrama, *The Big Wheel,* as vehicles to get him *out* of Rooney, Inc., and not as projects that would make the corporation thrive. It had dawned on Mick that if any thriving was to be done, it would be done by Stiefel and, probably, Briskin.

No surprise that when Mickey Rooney began work on *Quicksand* late in 1949, it was with an attitude that was less than enthusiastic.

The Hungarian

Like Rooney, Hungarian-born actor Peter Lorre had been a creature of the Hollywood studio system, having enjoyed five fruitful years as a top character star at Warner Bros., Hollywood's grittiest and most textured major studio. (His first contract picture for Warner was *The Maltese Falcon,* released in 1941.) Like Rooney, Lorre found himself at loose ends after the war: An amusing 1946 psychodrama, *The Beast With Five Fingers,* was Lorre's last under his Warner contract, which was not renewed. Experienced on stage as well as on film, and well known throughout Europe as well as America, Lorre's options seemed wide, certainly wider than Rooney's.

And then Sam Stiefel came along to say hi. When he finished doing that, he gave Lorre the same sort of tap dance he had given Rooney, and so in 1946 Stiefel, Briskin and Peter Lorre formed Lorre, Inc. Blurbs about the Stiefel/Rooney/Lorre plans appeared in *Variety* in June 1946 and again in September 1947. Stiefel confirmed to the paper that Lorre would star in a slate of three independent pictures that would bring the actor considerably more freedom and money than he had enjoyed at Warner Bros. All of that sounded good to Lorre, but what he really wanted to do was produce and direct. Stiefel made sounds suggesting that he thought Lorre's ambitions were terrific. But before we do movies, Stiefel said, let's do a few other things. Lorre shortly found himself on the lecture circuit, on the vaudeville stage (very much a moribund art form by the late 1940s) and making "personal appearances."

Stiefel also lined up radio work for his partner. Lorre had done American radio as early as 1936, and had no trouble toplining *Mystery on the Air,* a 1947 summer replacement for *The Abbott and Costello Show* (the deal was worked out between Stiefel and his old pal Eddie Sherman). Under Stiefel's stewardship Lorre continued to work in radio, but by 1950 the jobs were tailing off. His immediate post-Warner movie work consisted of *My Favorite Brunette* (1947), *Casbah* (1948) and *Rope of Sand* (1949). These were not bad films but they brought Lorre the familiar sorts of Lorre roles: exotic hoodlum, police inspector, glib drunk. None of these pictures were Stiefel productions, though under the terms of Lorre, Inc. Stiefel took a piece of the salaries Lorre earned for appearing in them.

In 1947 Lorre's friend Bertolt Brecht, another émigré from Hitler's Germany, invited Lorre to join his new Berlin theater ensemble. Lorre declined, and without much urging from Sam Stiefel. By this time Lorre had been a Hollywood fixture for 12 years. He had made good money, become a demon tennis player and owned a beautiful home. He was hooked. But still, he hoped to do significant work in Hollywood, in conjunction with Lorre, Inc. He showed Stiefel a script Brecht had written for him, and Stiefel, whose notion of the pinnacle of the filmic art was Abbott and Costello, said uh-uh, not commercial enough. And that was that, because Stiefel had given himself the last word.

Did we mention that Stiefel also gave himself power of attorney vis-à-vis Lorre's affairs? Indeed, yes, and Sam soon managed to completely bollix up Lorre's finances. By 1949 he had mortgaged Lorre's home in order to maintain the illusion of solvency.

But illusion doesn't go far in business, particularly in Hollywood; Lorre, Inc. needed a cash infusion.

In the summer of 1949, then, Rooney, Inc. and Lorre, Inc., two powerhouses of the American entertainment business, came together on Los Angeles locations and on rented stages to shoot a terse little B called *Quicksand.*

Not the Leading Man

Whatever chit-chat had been exchanged between Stiefel and Lorre about Lorre, Inc. developing leading roles for the actor had been forgotten or willfully ignored by the time of *Quicksand.* The film is indisputably a Mickey Rooney vehicle, designed to perpetuate the mild anti-hero persona the actor had fashioned in *Killer McCoy.* Come to that, *Quicksand* was a *Rooney, Inc.* production. For the moment (and for all time, as things developed), Lorre, Inc. had been consigned to the Phantom Zone. Lorre's role in *Quicksand* is large and even pivotal, and also the sort of thing Lorre had done many times before.

Stiefel apparently was not a complete lox, for *Quicksand* is a tight, well-made little thriller that undoubtedly satisfied the double-bill patrons who saw it. Dan Brady (Rooney) is a perpetually broke garage mechanic who lifts 20 bucks from the till in order to date a well-worn cashier named Vera Novak (Jeanne Cagney), the former girlfriend of Nick Dramoshag (Lorre), the sinister proprietor of a penny arcade on the Santa Monica pier.

The date goes well, in a lowlife sort of way, and Dan plans to repay the money with the $20 owed to him by a buddy, with nobody the wiser. Trouble is, the bookkeeper shows up at the garage for his regular audit two days early. The sound you hear is Dan's sphincter letting go. What to do? At a jewelry store up the street, Dan buys a $100 watch on credit and immediately hocks it for $30. He sneaks the missing $20 into the cash drawer and all seems hunky dory until he's visited a day later by a private dick who tells him that to pawn something that doesn't belong to you is grand larceny. Pay off $100 in 24 hours or face the cops.

From here, *Quicksand* more than lives up to its title. Now in for a C-note instead of the $20, Dan is sucked into a vortex and does some bad things: He rolls a drunk and Nick finds out about it; he steals a car from his boss for Nick and his boss (Art Smith) finds out about it; he knocks over Nick's safe and is nearly perforated by a night watchman; Vera blows half the dough on a fur coat, so Dan can offer his boss only half the value of the car; the boss makes ready to call the cops so Dan throttles him; convinced he's a killer with nothing to lose, Dan carjacks a fellow. The carjack victim turns out to be a kindly attorney (Taylor Holmes), who offers free legal advice. Even better, a news report that comes over the car radio says that Dan's boss isn't dead at all—he just has a really sore neck. Accompanied during his final misdeeds by The Sweet Girl Who Really Loves Him (Barbara Bates), Dan looks forward to a year's sentence, or maybe just probation.

That Lorre Style

Actor-turned-director Irving Pichel, writer Robert Smith and cinematographer Lionel Lindon concocted a sharp little film noir, with the requisite shadowplay, crummy locations, no-good dame and loser-as-hero motif. Events unreel with a sickening in-

Dan (Rooney) and Nick (Lorre) tangle in this textbook noir.

exorability. The deeper into trouble Dan gets, and the more entangled with Nick he becomes, the darker and more claustrophobic the film becomes. It's textbook noir, done on the cheap with style and smarts. The falsely happy ending—for which somebody deserved to be cracked on the head with a 2 by 4—is the picture's only real misstep.

Lorre's Nick reminds me of Pepe, the vile little New York Nazi Lorre played in 1942 in *All Through the Night.* Now, after the war and with no more call for fifth columnists, Pepe—heavier but hardly less nasty—has had to go (halfway) legit or starve.

The penny arcade is a dump frequented by sailors, pie-eyed couples and rowdy kids. The place is dingy and looks dark even when the sun outside is blazing. Nick loves money, dislikes his work and hates his customers. To a gaggle of little boys: "I'll save you all the trouble of growing up!" (Say it out loud in your best Peter Lorre voice,

with soft, pregnant menace.) To a swabbie who asks for change for a buck: "Okay, Admiral." (Say this with derision—and don't forget to gyp the sailor out of a nickel.)

Rooney and the vaguely mannish Jeanne Cagney share some amusingly cynical dialogue, but the funniest and most piquant exchanges are between Rooney and Lorre. During a confrontation over the affections of the profoundly unworthy Vera, Nick warns Dan, "I don't like to be pushed around." No, it's not much of a line, but when Lorre says it, watch out, because he's a porcupine who's going to jump on your face. And indeed, the brief fistfight that follows this warning is brutal.

Later, after Nick has discovered that Dan rolled the drunk, he makes an idle phone call:

"You'd better come and see me, or else."

"Or else what?"

"Or else something is going to happen. Happen to you."

The beauty of this is in Lorre's famously unique voice, of course, as well as his fabulously laconic manner. Squinting through a lazy haze of cigarette smoke, he's the ultimate in cool menace. You can see that Nick's been threatening guys all his life, and mostly getting away with it, so a twerp like Dan can be handled without Nick having to come to full wakefulness.

Loser and schemer meet at the arcade and Nick reveals he knows the identity of Dan's mugging victim, and precisely what the drunk was carrying in his kick (wallet): "$50 bills," Nick recites happily. "They talk very loud. What do they say? 'Shorty McCabe. Shorty McCabe...' I'm a businessman. I think I can do business with you very nice. You just get me a new car and I don't know nothing."

Dan is astounded. "You nuts?"

Nick considers. "Nuts? Me? I don't *think* so."

Things to Ponder

Unfortunately, after Dan sees that Nick gets his car, Nick disappears from the movie. That's unwise because we wonder about him. Does he still threaten little kids? How many more nickels will he swipe from sailors? Does he own any suits besides the square-cut double-breasted job he wears to work? Does he ever get off the pier to go to the beach and if so does he wear shorts? Is he happy with the new car? Does he drive it with the radio on or off? These are important questions. But because this is a Rooney movie and not a Lorre movie, a Rooney, Inc. production and not a Lorre, Inc. production, we're not supposed to care about the answers, and are steered away from Nick and away from Mr. Lorre. Nick has been merely a device, a plot pivot. Nick has been *used.*

New Lives

Pushed into bankruptcy by Stiefel, Lorre managed to extricate himself from the partnership immediately after *Quicksand.* By the time the film was released, early in 1950, Lorre was in Germany, where he was in the middle of starring in his sole directorial effort, *Der Verlorene (The Lost One;* 1951), a thematically ambitious film that the actor also co-wrote. Lorre, Inc. was dead, dissolved, and after one more picture, Rooney, Inc. would join it.

Grim and thoughtful, *Der Verlorene* was a box-office bust that mystified critics. But after his return to Hollywood, Lorre found that the freelance life would be good to him. He scaled back his style of living, became a father as he neared 50 and worked steadily in high-profile films until his death in 1964. Today, the Lorre mystique is kept alive via impressionists, animated cartoons old and new (think: *Ren and Stimpy*) and easy availability of Lorre's most popular pictures. *Quicksand* was not one of those at the time of release, and is not one now, but it does capture the compelling actor in prime "Lorre mode"—corrupt, cynical, contemptuous, a master of insouciant menace.

A trade review in the February 24, 1950 edition of *The Hollywood Reporter* was positive, though Lorre was given short shrift with an aside that he was "up to his usual sinister tricks...."

Tricks? Let's say *skill* and *effortless craft* instead. Lorre and Nick Dramoshag remain vivid and full of life.

And me? I hope Nick had a *swell* time with his new car.

Credits: Executive Producer: Sam H. Stiefel; Producer: Mort Briskin; Director: Irving Pichel; Screenplay: Robert Smith; Cinematography: Lionel Lindon; Editor: Walter Thompson; Art Director: Boris Leven; Set Decorations: Robert Priestley; Music: Louis Gruenberg; Musical Director: Emil Newman; Assistant Director: Maurie M. Suess; Production Manager: Lewis J. Rackmil; Make-up: Mel Berns; Hair Stylist: Annabelle Levy; Sound: William Lynch; Unit Manager: Harold Godsoe; Black and White; 79 Minutes; Filmed 1949; Released March 24, 1950; A Samuel H. Stiefel Production; A United Artists Release

Cast: Mickey Rooney (Dan Brady); Jeanne Cagney (Vera Novak); Peter Lorre (Nick Dramoshag); Barbara Bates (Helen); Art Smith (Mackey); Taylor Holmes (Attorney Harvey); Wally Cassell (Chuck); Jimmy Dodd (Buzz); Lt. Nelson (Richard Lane); John Gallaudet (Private Detective Moriarty); Minerva Urecal (Landlady); Patsy O'Connor (Millie); Sidney Marion (Shorty McCabe); Lester Dorr (Baldy); Kitty O'Neil (Madame Zaronga); Frank Marlowe (Night Watchman); Ray Teal, Tom Munro (Motorcycle Officers); with Red Nichols and His Five Pennies

THE LOST ONE
1951
by Michael H. Price

Just as he was beginning to catch on as a formidable presence in the German cinema, Peter Lorre sensed that the emerging Third Reich meant only harm to any soul who could not meet its false standards of correct breeding. The Nazi Party's climactic power grab of 1933 drove the artist formerly known as Laszlo Löwenstein into a frenzied self-exile. Following a satisfying pause in London to grace Alfred Hitchcock's *The Man Who Knew Too Much* (1934), Lorre followed the lead of his own breakthrough director, Fritz Lang—a fellow fugitive from the Hitler mob—and settled in as a citizen of Hollywood.

Almost a generation later, the American film capital had granted Lorre an exalted status that can only be reckoned rare for an actor so thoroughly well associated with overtly strange roles. Lorre was only somewhat less indelibly linked with horror films than his fellow immigrants Boris Karloff and Bela Lugosi, but he possessed a more vividly accented speaking voice than either player. Too, Lorre cultivated a somehow *alien* screen presence that made his Hungarian countryman, Lugosi, look like an ultra-bourgeois Beverly Hills squire by comparison.

The image was pure calculation, though. Among that handful of Depression Era and wartime up-and-comers—Karloff, Lugosi, Lorre and Lon Chaney, Jr.—who found their careers demarcated by their horror movies, only Lorre proved a cunning enough strategist over the long haul to resist the gravitational confinement of the spookers. He held forth as a dangerously heroic star player in the *Mr. Moto* mysteries at Fox, and as a top-shelf villain at Warners (with lesser, weirder, assignments as almost a sideline) during a time when Karloff and Lugosi were treading treacherous waters in low-budget "programmers." Junior Chaney's star was prematurely on the wane as Lorre began a fresh ascent in the post-World War II years.

Hollywood learned, too, from its long association with Lorre that while you can take the boy out of the country, you can't take the country—the Old World, that is—out of the boy. Germany, and the loss of what Germany could have meant to him, haunted Lorre so insistently that in 1949 he returned there to survey the savaged landscape and wrecked human spirit that the Nazis had left behind. He found inspiration, too—a desperately negative inspiration—in the resurgent arrogance of a people so recently defeated.

This cruel muse moved Lorre to deliver a work of embittered genius called *Der Verlorene*, or *The Lost One*. More a merciless lecture on social responsibility than a conventional murder thriller, as much a study in Old Testament damnation as a psychological portrait, this little-seen film boasts one of the most strikingly original scenarios in the history of the medium. It pivots on a leading performance that advances and

Lorre as Dr. Karl Rothe and Karl John as his assistant Hoesch. (Photofest)

develops the arguments of Lorre's earliest defining portrayal in Lang's *M* (Germany, 1931). And it displays a job of directing that mingles an almost documentary naturalism with the dreamlike Expressionism of silent-screen German cinema, heavily influenced by G.W. Pabst and Fritz Lang. That Lorre is responsible for all three key elements (the screenplay is collaborative, from his source-story), is indicative of the pain and passion he brought to the project: He had not directed before, nor would he direct again, but here he became the first filmmaker in postwar Germany to mount an explicit indictment of the Nazis. He was not a storyteller by profession, but rather an interpreter of other people's stories. Only his performance bears much kinship to the personality that his immense audience had come to expect, but it lacks the excitable manner and droll wit that he brought to bear on even his grimmest Hollywood portrayals. Germany removed the twinkle that American stardom had put in those globular eyeballs, returning Lorre to the tormented appearance of his terror-stricken slayer of children in *M*.

Lorre cast himself as Dr. Karl Rothe, who is working under the assumed name of Neumeister (literally, "new master") in a refugees' compound in postwar Germany. A new arrival, variously known as Hoesch and Nowak (Karl John), settles in as Rothe's assistant, intent upon infiltrating the doctor's orbit for sinister reasons. Rothe pegs him as a former antagonist, hazily remembered, from the war years, but Hoesch proposes an

Renate Mannhardt and Peter Lorre

uneasy alliance: He needs Rothe's influence to throw the Allied occupational forces off his trail. Over a round of drinks, Hoesch blatantly reminds Rothe of certain "favors" granted in hiding a crime that Rothe seems unable to remember. Rothe takes Hoesch at his word, agreeing that there is a debt in need of settling.

Flashback to 1943: Rothe was working as a medical researcher for the Nazis, and Hoesch was his laboratory assistant. Hoesch and Gestapo Colonel Winkler (Helmut Rudolph) confronted Rothe with a claim that Rothe's fiancée, Inge Hermann (Renate Mannhardt), has peddled his findings in immunology to British Intelligence. Hoesch, secretly a Gestapo agent, had seduced Inge to test her loyalty to the Reich. Rothe's heartbreak over Hoesch's arrogant revelation had driven the doctor to a tense encounter with Inge. As she pleaded with him for a reconcilement, Rothe lapsed unexpectedly into a trancelike tenderness, caressing her throat and then gripping her in a strangehold.

The barroom, 1949: Rothe still cannot recall committing the murder, but he confides to Hoesch that he senses he must face up to punishment. Hoesch and Winkler had covered Rothe's tracks too well for the authorities to trace him.

In 1943: A young woman (Johanna Hofer) became Rothe's new neighbor in a lodging-house, occupying the very apartment that had belonged to the slain Inge. Rothe found himself attracted to the new arrival, but his dawning affections were undermined by the urge to kill. He fled rather than risk succumbing to the impulse. While regaining his bearings in a pub, Rothe met a prostitute (Gisela Trowe) and accompanied her to her residence. There, she regarded him with growing concern—suddenly becoming terrified without overt provocation and shrieking that he must be a murderer.

Rothe, bewildered by this outburst and desperate for solace, left in haste. He finally caught an after-hours train, where he met Helene (Lotte Rausch), a similarly lonesome soul with a mile-wide streak of nymphomania. Panicked by an air-raid signal, the passengers stampeded off the train—all except Rothe and Helene. Later, her body was found aboard the train.

Rothe wandered on aimlessly, vowing to track down and kill the troublemaking Hoesch, whose meddling had triggered the murderous impulse. Rothe pledged himself to suicide. But Hoesch had vanished, and the war dragged on. Rothe forged a new life under a new name—but now, Hoesch's return has forced Rothe to realize old deeds cannot be ignored.

In 1949: The drinking bout continues. Hoesch, forgetting his need of Rothe's cooperation, challenges Rothe to kill him. Rothe mechanically draws a gun and fires on the informer who had wrecked his life. Rothe walks away from the camp and begins an unnervingly calm stroll down the nearby railroad tracks. A train approaches. Rothe stops in mid-stride, facing away from the engine and covering his face with one hand.

Where Lorre's portrayal in *M* stops short of self-confrontation—what with the character's being too busy dodging both the law and an outraged underworld—his kindred enactment in *The Lost One* charges head-on into this more forbidding psychological realm. The German public was ill-prepared for such heavy going, such a thrashing of the national conscience, and avoided *The Lost One* for reasons quite different from the German critics' hostility: Reviews of the time were more concerned with calling Lorre an imitator of Lang, which was hardly the case. For although the Lang style echoes throughout, in the sheer Kafka-like disorientation and nightmarish fugues of Lorre's Dr. Rothe, *The Lost One* plays out as more of a social-problem picture—a denunciation of the society's desire to cast a blind eye on its thuggish recent past—punctuated by outright terror.

The film might have played more successfully in America, where Lorre was almost unfailingly a box-office draw, but it was scarcely to be found outside Germany. A print in the UCLA film archive, bequeathed by Lorre, was about as accessible as *The Lost One* became to American eyes until 1985, when Fred Pressburger—son of the film's producer, Arnold Pressburger—mounted a restoration and added English subtitles for a surprisingly ambitious theatrical release. The U.S. critics, distanced by more than a generation from the postwar sensibilities of either Allies or Axis, greeted the film as a bold dispatch from an unsuspected frontier. A sporadically available video edition is the nearest most of us can come today to seeing this strange and disturbing film, which is as essential to an understanding of Peter Lorre's artistry as Charles Laughton's one stab at directing, the similarly grim *The Night of the Hunter* (1955), is to a grasp of his vast body of work.

Lorre as a director lacks the easy narrative flow of Lang, although he dwells similarly on metaphoric detail, wordlessly equating the blasted ruins of Hamburg with Lorre's numb and ravaged expression. There are suggestions of Erich von Stroheim's style in the cold orderliness of Rothe's careworn progress, and in a meandering, *cul-de-sac* subplot about a Hitler-assassination conspiracy. Lorre draws a finely etched portrayal of cruelty-with-impunity from Karl John, whose extended "drunk scene" in the framing story is a marvel of vile incoherence. Gisela Trowe shines as the free-spirited prostitute who dissolves in horror upon sensing Dr. Rothe's feral nature. Lorre allows himself to grow animated only when gripped by the strangling frenzy; the shooting of John is an utterly placid moment. The final shot, where Lorre awaits the onrushing train, will stay with the viewer long past the experience of sitting through this fascinating exercise in guilt and gloom.

CREDITS: Producer: Arnold Pressburger; Director: Peter Lorre; Story: Peter Lorre; Screenwriters: Peter Lorre, Benno Vigny and Axel Eggebrecht; Photographed by: Vaclav Vich; Musical Score: Willy Schmidt-Gentner; Associate Producer: Heinz Abel; Film Editor: C.O. Bartning; Art Directors: Karl Weber and Franz Schroedter; Running Time: 98 Minutes

CAST: Peter Lorre (Dr. Karl Rothe); Karl John (Hoesch/Nowak); Renate Mannhardt (Inge Hermann); Kurt Meister (Prefect); Richard Munch (Inspector); Johanna Hofer (Frau Hermann); Lotte Rausch (Helene); Helmuth Rudolph (Col. Winkler); Eva Ingeborg Scholz (Ursula Weber); Gisela Trowe (Prostitute); Hansi Wendler (Secretary); Alexander Hunziger (Drunkard); Josef Dahmen (Bartender)

20,000 LEAGUES UNDER THE SEA
1954
by Bruce Dettman

Coming out of a movie theater in Rockford, Illinois, in the summer of 1954, having seen *20,000 Leagues Under the Sea* for the first time, I was quite certain I had just viewed the greatest motion picture ever made. To be honest, being only four years old at the time, legitimate comparisons were admittedly on the skimpy side. As a matter of fact, the only other film I'd experienced up to that point in my life was the classic western *Shane* (1953), whose nasty main villains, a couple of whiskered brutes called the Ryker Brothers, I somehow managed to confuse with images of various bearded Biblical prophets I'd encountered in Sunday school lessons.

In any case, I also came away from *20,000 Leagues* positive that I would learn everything I could about giant squids which my older brother assured me actually existed in nature, that I would someday grow a beard just like the one sported by James Mason (as Captain Nemo) and that actor Peter Lorre was one of the oddest and most bizarre adults I had ever seen. (For the sake of historical accuracy, I did continue to study the world's largest invertebrates, grew a beard as soon as nature allowed [though it is admittedly no longer as dark as Mason's] and have never faltered in my finding Peter Lorre a most intriguing, peculiar and favorite cinematic figure.)

In retrospect, what I now find most curious about being so impressed with Lorre in this picture is how, due to a recent serious illness which had bloated his trademark features, he exhibits little if any of the celebrated characteristics, mannerisms, inflections and overall quirky yet engaging qualities that made him one of the most recognizable and readily distinguishable actors in such films as *The Maltese Falcon, Casablanca, Crime and Punishment, Three Strangers* and *Arsenic and Old Lace.* It is, I think, a real testament to the actor's unique presence and delivery that even when not at the top of his game he still stood out as something so very unique to a four-year-old boy.

Though *20,000 Leagues Under the Sea* had been filmed before in 1905 and 1916, it was the 1954 Disney version which truly defined Jules Verne's tale in the public's mind. Vastly popular at the time of its 1869 writing and an enduring classic ever since, the book can nonetheless be a rather stilted, mannered and episodic experience, particularly for modern readers. What Disney did, thanks to screenwriter Earl Felton, was to lift the story's most exciting and atmospheric elements—along with adding a few new wrinkles of their own—and engineer a rip-roaring, wonderfully paced and gripping adventure yarn. Most of it worked very well.

Set in 1868, the film recounts the story of Captain Nemo, a scientific genius embittered by war, who designs the *Nautilus,* a futuristic submarine, to help him prevent

Captain Nemo (James Mason), Conseil (Peter Lorre) and Ned Land (Kirk Douglas).

future outbreaks of aggression by attacking and destroying the hostile parties involved. Initially believed to be the work of a marauding sea monster, a shipload of military men and sailors plus marine scientist Professor Arronax (Paul Lukas) and his assistant Conseil (Lorre) are dispatched to destroy the creature. Ultimately attacked and shipwrecked by the *Nautilus*, Arronax and Conseil, accompanied by sailor Ned Land (Kirk Douglas), find themselves taken prisoner aboard the underwater craft. While Arronax is fascinated by Nemo's creation, Conseil and Land, in an uncomfortable alliance, scheme to make their escape. Eventually, after clashes with cannibals, a giant squid and warships, Nemo is critically wounded and along with his loyal crew dies aboard the submarine in what appears to be a nuclear explosion while Ned, Arronax and Conseil manage to flee to safety.

Directed by Richard Fleisher (son of Disney animation rival Max Fleisher of Popeye and Betty Boop fame), *20,000 Leagues* was in its time considered a masterful accomplishment and a real triumph, both artistically and financially, for Disney and Company, who at the time were looking to break away from their cartoon signature products and expand into full live-action work. As a leadoff venture *20,000 Leagues*

Ned and Conseil row toward the *Nautilus*. (Photofest)

would turn out to be just as excellent a selection for them on the big screen as the phenomenally popular Davy Crockett TV series would prove on the small one.

Certainly the cast was impressive. Walt Disney, who throughout his career rarely utilized top stars in his films, selected Kirk Douglas for the role of the swaggering, over-the-top hero sailor Ned Land. As the haunted genius Nemo, James Mason, appropriately urbane, clipped and remote, was a brilliant choice. It is precisely Mason's intellectual detachment and callous disregard for those who oppose his iron will that make his duplicity and painful underlying motives so compelling to watch. Ironically, like most children who first saw the film in their youth, I initially viewed Mason as the quintessential villain and Land (whom I emulated in our backyard by nearly killing off a tree that, much to my father's chagrin and wrath, made a damn fine substitute for a giant squid) a great hero. As an adult, however, I see Land mostly as a bullying, strutting fool, albeit a heroic one, and Mason as the tragically flawed figure of the piece.

For the other two leading roles in the film, veteran leading man and later Hungarian character actor Paul Lukas was chosen for the aloof and conventional Arronax. Lucas, whose continental stiffness and Old World charm had occasionally served him well in such films as *Watch on the Rhine* and *The Lady Vanishes,* was not an ideal selection.

With his static delivery and colorless performance, he is at best adequate. Finally there is Peter Lorre as the Professor's assistant Conseil, Arronax's servant. In the early 1950s Lorre, like so many of his acting contemporaries from the 1930s and '40s, was at an awkward and uncertain phase of his career. He had admittedly lent himself to self-parody in too many lightweight and frivolous films. In doing so he had ultimately come to represent to the general filmgoing public little beyond a strange and rather odd-looking man with bulging eyes and shifty manner, rarely up to any good. Moreover, unlike other actors who made a living out of playing bigger-than-life villains, there was something undeniably unsettling, perhaps even a bit depraved and perverse about the Lorre persona. Whether in heavy make-up or playing exotic or even heroic parts as in the Mr. Moto series, the indelible image remained, and while he occasionally found himself in character parts, he recognized that he, a classically trained actor who had worked with the likes of Brecht and Fritz Lang, was nonetheless perceived by audiences in a very limited way he just couldn't seem to shake. His plight was not perhaps as extreme as Bela Lugosi's, who rarely ended up in a quality production after his heyday. Lorre *was* featured in many excellent movies, but unlike Boris Karloff who could occasionally get away with a benevolent or even vulnerable part, ticket payers expected Lorre to be Lorre no matter what.

In many ways, despite it not being a great role for him, portraying Conseil in *20,000 Leagues Under the Sea* was a breakthrough part to the extent that it suggested and offered a softer and more malleable characterization, which allowed for occasional comedic elements in the script, particularly in his scenes with Douglas. Moreover, the weight gain he had experienced since his illness broadened and expanded his features so that what had once been a rather unsettling and severely offbeat countenance became something of a hang-dog appearance. This droopy, vulnerable look would serve him well throughout the remainder of his career, and while Lorre would never again have a truly great role, his hob-goblin reputation certainly eased up a bit and he was seen more and more as an amusing though certainly slightly oddball old friend.

Lorre's Conseil, despite some rather petulant and occasionally comedic characteristics ("Seems like you can't do anything on this boat without getting wet"), is quite often the most level-headed and balanced one of the four main characters in the film. He is somewhat of a brave child, but certainly not a stupid one. Unflinching in his loyalty to Arronax, he also sees the scientist as naive in his undaunted admiration for Nemo and the latter's scientific achievements, a kind of kid in a toyshop who begins to lose sight of the stern realties of the outer world. Conseil knows he must do his best to keep his mentor out of trouble and protect him while at the same time not sticking out his own neck, which he very much fancies, too far.

Conseil is described by author Verne as a young Flemish boy (actually 30) who is "phlegmatic by nature, regular from principle, zealous from habit, evincing little disturbance at the different surprises of life, very quick with his hands, and apt at any service required of him; and despite his name, never giving advice—even when asked for it," Lorre is actually too old and full of chicanery for the obedient, single-purposed character as created by the Frenchman. In truth, however, it is Lorre's very maturity and vocalized frustration at what is going on around him that makes the part far more interesting than his obsequious literary counterpart and he is largely enjoyable to watch. The only exceptions are those unpleasant scenes in which the loutish Ned Land physically and mentally

Ned Land often abuses the more reserved Conseil. (Photofest)

abuses him ("Don't look at me with those soft-boiled eyes"), unpleasant because Land himself is such a brutish and self-involved figure (as opposed to when Lorre played the sniveling, Joel Cairo in *The Maltese Falcon* and Humphrey Bogart, as the cynical but morally on target Sam Spade, roughed him up). During these moments one cannot help but wish for the old slippery Lorre of grander film days to momentarily re-appear and bury one of the obnoxious seaman's own harpoons in his back but, of course, this never happens.

For the most part, Lorre does a fine job, operating effectively in all Conseil's various moods and posturings. Though some have accused his performance of being disinterested and listless, I consider his energy just about right for the sort of mildly underhanded, slightly world-weary and scheming character the screenwriter Felton envisioned. It is certainly not one of his great performances, but it is nonetheless a solid and intuitive one and certainly better than most give him credit for.

It is unfortunate that *20,000 Leagues Under the Sea*, while to a degree putting him back on the Hollywood success track and opening a few new doors for him, didn't really open the right ones. His post *20,000 Leagues* credits, with a few likable exceptions such as his work for producer Roger Corman in the 1960s, are uniformly poor and nearly forgettable, nothing at all, as is too often the case with Hollywood history, like the actor himself.

CREDITS: Producer: Walt Disney; Director: Richard Fleischer; Screenplay: Earl Felton (Based on the Novel *Twenty Thousand Leagues Under the Sea* by Jules Verne); Cinematography: Franz Planer, Ralph Hammeras, Till Gabbani; Underwater Photography: Till Gabbani; Art Director: John Meehan; Music: Paul J. Smith, Johann Sebastian Bach; Editor: Elmo Williams

CAST: James Mason (Captain Nemo); Ned Land (Kirk Douglas); Professor Pierre Arronax (Paul Lukas); Peter Lorre (Conseil); Robert J. Wilke (First Mate, *Nautilus*); Carlton Young (John Howard); Ted de Corsia (Captain Farragut); Percy Helton (Diver); Ted Cooper (Mate of *Abraham Lincoln*); Eddie Marr (Shipping Agent); J.M. Kerrigan (Billy); Harry Harvey (Shipping Clerk); Herb Vigran (Reporter); Esmeralda the Seal

BEAT THE DEVIL
1954
by Alan Warren

By the 1950s Peter Lorre's career had taken a decided downturn. Instead of starring in films featuring his peculiar persona to advantage (such as *M* or *Crime and Punishment*), or dominating others as the leading heavy (as in *The Man Who Knew Too Much*) or playing the occasional hero (as in *The Mask of Dimitrios*), he had been reduced to supporting roles. Much of the old menace was gone, replaced by a surprising aptitude for comedy. There were at least two reasons for this: For one, Lorre had sustained the greatest debacle of his career—the failure of *The Lost One* (1951), the anti-Nazi film he had directed and co-written, his sole attempt at *auteurism*. Apparently, this failure hurt him personally as well as professionally. Afterward, he adopted a more detached attitude toward acting: With few exceptions, he seemed to be marking time. Second, by the mid-'50s, he had gained nearly 100 pounds, and the pendulous bulk of his formerly svelte frame typed him as a comic heavy. Sadly, Lorre, who started his career so brilliantly as the child-murderer of *M*, finished it as a straight man for Jerry Lewis (in *The Patsy*).

Exceptions to this acting rut were sadly few. Horror fans enjoy his amusingly over-the-top antics in *Tales of Terror, The Raven* and *A Comedy of Terrors*. But his subtlest comic acting, and perhaps his greatest turn as a comedian, came in John Huston's one-of-a-kind *Beat the Devil* (1954). This film, now considered a classic, did not find a wide audience upon initial release. Even Humphrey Bogart, its star, growled that "Only the phonies think it's funny. It's a mess." Bogart's negativism is understandable: He was one of the producers. Lorre himself commented:

> It was a flop in New York. Why shouldn't it be? It was a deliciously sardonic comedy, meant for art houses, and they opened it with a blood-and-thunder campaign. The people just didn't get it.

This isn't surprising. *Beat the Devil,* a self-consciously "hip" film, was conspicuously out of place in the conformist '50s. It took 10 years for films like *What's New, Pussycat?* to be accepted and even applauded for their non sequiturs and absurdist plotting. In addition, the presence of Bogart and Lorre, and Huston as director, naturally evoked fond memories of *The Maltese Falcon.* Anyone expecting another *Falcon* was naturally disappointed, even though *Beat the Devil* was originally intended as a straight thriller. It was based on a novel by "James Helvick," actually a pseudonym for Claud Cockburn. Cockburn did one screenplay deemed unsuitable; a second script

Old friends Bogart and Lorre star in *Beat the Devil.* (Photofest)

by Peter Viertel and Anthony Veiller also proved unsatisfactory, and Huston called in Truman Capote, whose offbeat sense of humor permeates the film. Actually, the basic structure of the Viertel/Veiller script was followed; what Capote did was add jokes and rewrite dialogue, emphasizing the absurd and keeping just ahead of Huston's cameras. "Sometimes scenes that were just about to be shot were written right on the set," Capote remembered. "The cast was completely bewildered... sometimes even Huston didn't seem to know what was going on. It was totally mad, but it was meant to be. I was always just one day ahead, sometimes I was down there in the morning distributing the script to the cameramen and the poor actors." The stars were encouraged to create their own dialogue; Lorre and Robert Morley were rather good at this, but Morley didn't think much of Bogart's attempts: "A nice man, but not much brain, really," he said later. A young actor-mimic named Peter Sellers was engaged to dub four voices, including Bogart's after his tongue was split in an accident in a taxi. Sellers also dubbed several Italian actors who spoke no English and understood not a word of Huston's direction or Capote's script.

Even today, many moviegoers, even Bogart fans, simply don't "get" the film. It's still avant-garde, even by '90s standards, a bit disjointed, threatening to fall apart at any moment (and yet somehow still managing to hang together). Overall, it affords proof

of Pauline Kael's observation that "John Huston is an infinitely more complex screen artist than David Lean. He can be far worse than Lean because he's careless and sloppy and doesn't have all those safety nets of solid craftsmanship spread under him." Kael added that "Huston (like [Norman] Mailer) tests himself, plays the crazy game crazy—to beat it, to win." In *Beat the Devil* Huston wins the crazy game.

The film was shot in Ravello, Italy, a mountainous, nearly inaccessible town south of Naples, now the home of novelist Gore Vidal. Bogart, the unofficial producer, invested $400,000 of his own money, and both he and Huston wanted Lorre for a key role, a bizarre reprise of his Joel Cairo character in *Falcon.* Lorre wanted $25,000; he settled for $15,000 and first-class living expenses. Co-star Morley didn't care for Lorre, "who I always thought was a rather unpleasant character, an unlovely man in every way."

Bogart felt very differently about his frequent co-star. According to the excellent new biography *Bogart*, by A.M. Sperber and Eric Lax, the two were very close. Bogart often slept off a bender at Lorre's house. In turn, Bogart loaned the Hungarian money with no thought of reimbursement because of Lorre's high lifestyle and his (concealed) drug habit. According to Gary Stevens, a friend of Lorre's, Bogart "*loved* Peter—really loved the guy."

The plot, which is full of absurd complications and jagged edges, is the key to much of the film's humorous style. Like many of Huston's films, it involves a band of misfits involved in a failed quest, usually (as here) a crime that goes wrong. Playwright Harry Kurnitz observed that "No matter where you come in during its running, you seem to have missed at least half the picture." For the record, it involves Billy Dannreuther (Bogart), and his wife Maria (Gina Lollabrigida), who are traveling to Africa aboard the steamer *Nyanga*. They meet Harry Chelm (Edward Underdown), the very embodiment of the British stiff upper lip, and his wife Gwendolen (Jennifer Jones), whose specialty is romance at short notice—in brief, a habitual and inventive liar. Dannreuther's "business associates" are a motley crew, comprised of Peterson (Robert Morley, in a variation on the Sydney Greenstreet character in *Falcon*), Ravello (Marco Tulli), Major Jack Ross (Ivor Barnard)—a homicidal little man nicknamed "The Galloping Major"—and O'Hara (Peter Lorre), the screen's unlikeliest Irishman. Through fraud the group intends to buy land in Africa containing valuable uranium deposits. Overhearing one of Gwendolen's "inventions" and believing it to be true, the group kidnaps Harry Chelm. Complications ensue: There's an explosion aboard the *Nyanga,* and the group wind up on a deserted shore where they are captured by Arabs. They are almost home free when a Scotland Yard official (Bernard Lee, "M" of the James Bond films) turns up, investigating the murder of an official, the work of the Galloping Major. Gwendolen tells the detective about the group and they are arrested, leaving Dannreuther, Maria and Gwendolen to join the missing Harry Chelm, who has acquired the land containing the uranium deposits. All of this is accompanied by Franco Mannino's mock-pompous score, perfectly suited to the absurd, and Bogart's pseudo-tough guy narration.

Paradoxically, even though Humphrey Bogart is the star, *Beat the Devil* isn't really a Bogart film. He's curiously diminished by the madness all around him. As the one sane man aboard a ship of fools (literally as well as figuratively), he's burdened with carrying the plot forward and handling the mock heroics (he battles the heavies and gets the girl), which seem jarringly out of place. He provides a center of gravity for all the mad goings-on, but that's about all. Pauline Kael remarked that he "looks rather bewildered, as though he hadn't been let in on the joke." Jonathan Coe went further, stating that Bogart "gives a totally blank performance, leaving a gaping hole at the center of things which the livelier playing of Jones, Morley and Lorre serves to embellish rather than disguise." Even so, he comes off better than Lollabrigida, who's not only not in on the joke but doesn't speak the language. (She recited her lines phonetically, and was dubbed "Lola Frigidaire" by Bogart and Huston.)

The film is really a comic ensemble; it allows for wonderful comic turns for Jennifer Jones, Robert Morley, Edward Underdown and (especially) Peter Lorre. Part of *Beat the Devil's* charm is that it's full of familiar actors doing unfamiliar things, and Lorre, as O'Hara, is the unlikeliest casting of all. (Bogart calls him "my wide-eyed Irish leprechaun.") His hair dyed blond, and puffing on a cigarette in a holder (and rather resembling Truman Capote, though presumably this was unintentional), Lorre shows off his talent for self-parody, and he's seen to better advantage here than in any other '50s film (save *The Lost One*) because he's in on the joke, unlike Bogart. And Capote's dialogue is so memorable and epigrammatic that Lorre is allowed a comic aria. His most quoted speech is delivered stage center: "Time, what is it? The Swiss manufacture it, the French hoard it, Italians want it, Americans say it is money, Hindus say it does not exist. You know what I say? I say time is a crook."

Funny and memorable as this is, Lorre's real side-splitting scene occurs later, when he's assigned to keep Dannreuther busy while Peterson questions Gwendolen Chelm. Barging into Dannreuther's room, O'Hara stalls for time by extemporizing wildly while Dannreuther glares at him, and the scene is a little masterpiece of comic timing and reaction. Keeping an eye on the courtyard outside, O'Hara rambles on:

> I give you my word, Billy, I give you my word, I appeal to you like... an older brother. It's not so much the difference of age, it's... it's probably, yes, the reason is because I come from a culture which is so much older than yours. In my country a child which is six years old is older in his heart than you will be at 60.

"It smokes, it drinks, it philosophizes," Dannreuther growls. "At this rate I'll be 60 before you get to the point."

It's not all Lorre's film, of course. Robert Morley gives one of his drollest performances ("Good laugh does more for the stomach muscles than five minutes' sitting-up exercises. And now that we've had our moment of fun ..."). And there's a memorable cameo by Manuel Serano as the movie-smitten Arab chieftain smoking a hookah and questioning Dannreuther about Rita Hayworth ("You're sure the peerless Rita will like me?"). In addition, a blonde Jennifer Jones gives the best performance of her career as Gwendolen Chelm, ready to invent at a moment's notice. (Whenever she starts to tell a lie she says, "In point of fact.") This is yet another echo of the *Falcon*, recalling Mary Astor as the lying Brigid O'Shaughnessy. (At one point Bogart suggested the film be retitled *The Lady Lies*.) Jean Simmons and Audrey Hepburn were originally considered for the role, but Jones proved an inspired choice. She may well be, as Pauline Kael suggested, the funniest performer in the film.

Beat the Devil presupposes a certain sophistication on the part of its audience. At times it resembles those classic '50s comedies, such as *The Lavender Hill Mob* or *The Lady-killers*, brimming over with audacious one-liners, deliciously underplayed performances and hilariously overdone caricatures. But this resemblance is superficial: Where the Ealing comedies were genteel and good-natured, *Beat the Devil* is more blunt, subversive and devoid of the social niceties. In addition, its dialogue is so eminently quotable, so studded with *bons mots*, that the film may seem at first viewing like an anthology of epigrams, recalling the (perhaps apocryphal) story of the woman who finally saw a play by Shakespeare and complained that it was nothing but famous quotations.

The film's lunacy cuts both ways. At times the film threatens to dissolve into a series of comic vignettes or sketches, but there's a demented logic at work. Unlike the *Nyanga*, the film reaches port through sheer exuberance: The insanity keeps it buoyant. It repeatedly catches audiences off-guard; it keeps threatening to run along familiar channels, only to venture into unexpected and uncharted waters. It's so original that it's no surprise 1954 audiences sat there in shock and growing anger, perhaps wondering if Huston had gone mad. One theater manager wrote a letter stating: "What an awful show... Couldn't understand how Huston directed such a picture and Capote wrote it and Bogart played in it. It should go down as a freak picture in the Museum of Modern Art." Another theater owner in Michigan ran an ad actually *apologizing* for showing the film: "If you don't see this picture you are not missing much. The picture at the Temple did not come up to our expectations. We would like to discontinue it, but are forced to play it until Wednesday. Please accept our apologies. After the first show tonight we will give passes to the first 10 people who tell us they actually liked it." It should be kept in mind that Huston's near-masterpiece *The Red Badge of Courage* was savagely trimmed after preview audiences laughed at it; a similar fate befell Orson Welles' classic *The Magnificent Ambersons*.

Lorre as O'Hara. (Photofest)

Reviews of *Beat the Devil* were surprisingly positive, demonstrating that, despite arguments to the contrary, critics are right more often than moviegoers. *Time* magazine called it "as elaborate a shaggy-dog story as has ever been told... A sort of screwball classic." *Los Angeles Times* critic Charles Champlin called it his favorite Huston film, and wrote: "In its rather quirky way it's about loyalty, and loyalty is a major theme that runs through so much of Huston's work, from *The Maltese Falcon* forward. It is also a celebration of rascals, lowlifes, underdogs and born losers who didn't always lose more eloquently and fondly than John Huston did."

Perhaps the most astute comment came from film historian Eugene Archer in his *Films and Filming* monograph on Huston. He called *Beat the Devil* "a parody within a parody, a private joke, amusing to the initiated, incomprehensible to the uninformed... [I]t is a film for connoisseurs, who treasure it highly—most highly, perhaps, because it is valueless for the layman."

This last rather overstates the film's recherché qualities. Admittedly, you must be on the right wavelength to appreciate its eccentric humor and overall style (just as with James Whale's *The Old Dark House*), but *Beat the Devil* is by no means impenetrable. It was simply too far ahead of its time, and paid the price in terms of commercial acceptance. It quickly became an acquired taste and virtually defines the term "cult film."

But this was all in the future. In 1954 the film's repercussions were unfortunate. Its failure ended the Bogart-Huston partnership. It also marked the final pairing of Bogart and Lorre. Their careers went in different directions: Bogart appeared only in expensive, mainstream Hollywood films from then on (*The Caine Mutiny* earned him an Academy Award nomination and boosted his box-office standing); Lorre continued playing parodies of his former self, mostly in empty, extravagant adventure films (*Voyage*

Gina Lollabrigida and Peter Lorre (Photofest)

to the Bottom of the Sea, Five Weeks in a Balloon) or in comedies (*The Sad Sack, The Patsy*). His career picked up slightly in the '60s when American-International teamed him with Vincent Price, but by then it was too late, and Lorre knew it. "Movies are no longer an *industry*," he was quoted as saying.

> After all, who ever heard of an industry that offered no loyalty to its employees? You see, making movies used to be such great fun in the old days. Of course, I suppose a lot of things in the old days were more fun. It isn't any longer. It's now a very cold-hearted business.

Few opportunities for Lorre lay ahead. Even the American-International films used him for unsubtle comedy relief, and it's obvious Lorre felt his talents were being wasted. Set visitor William K. Everson recalled that Lorre answered a little girl's question as to whether a shambling figure in make-up was a good or bad monster by responding:

"Oh, it's a BAD monster. There are NO good monsters at American-International." By then *Beat the Devil* was 10 years in the past, and there would be no follow-ups, no further efforts to tap Lorre's abilities at subtle, cerebral humor. Pratfalls and lowbrow comedy were the order of the day. (*Beat the Devil* was reissued in 1964, the year Lorre died, though by then it had become a staple at revival houses and Bogart festivals.)

Truly unique movies are rare, and become classics of a kind. After 45 years it's clear that *Beat the Devil* belongs to the small group of films that merit this distinction. Its originality is perhaps, as Pauline Kael suggested, dangerously marginal: A second attempt at this, by Huston or a lesser director, might well have ended in disaster. No matter. As the Fat Man (Sydney Greenstreet) in *The Maltese Falcon* would have characterized it, *Beat the Devil* is *rara avis*—inimitable, unsurpassed, indispensable.

CREDITS: Director: John Huston; Associate Producer: Jack Clayton; Screenplay by Truman Capote and John Huston; Based on the Novel by James Helvick; Director of Photography: Oswald Morris, B.S.C.; Music: Franco Mannino; Editor: Ralph Kemplen; Art Director: Wilfred Shingleton; Music Direction: Lambert Williamson; Production Manager: Bill Kirby; Camera Operator: Freddie Francis; Assistant Director: John Arnold; Location Manager: James Ware; Continuity: Angela Allen; Make-up: Constance Reeve; Hairdressing: Bette Lee; Sound Recording: George Stephenson, E. Law; Chief Production Electrician: Louis H. Lavelly; Dubbing Editor: Stanley Hawkes; Personal Assistant to John Huston: Jeanie Sims; Romulus/Santana/United Artists; Filmed in Italy in Association with Rizzoli-Haggiag; Running Time: 92 Minutes; New York Opening: March 1954 (Original 100-minute version released by Independent Film Distributors in England on November 24, 1953)

CAST: Humphrey Bogart (Billy Dannreuther); Jennifer Jones (Gwendolen Chelm); Gina Lollabrigida (Maria Dannreuther); Robert Morley (Peterson); Peter Lorre (O'Hara); Edward Underdown (Harry Chelm); Ivor Barnard (Major Jack Ross); Marco Tulli (Ravello); Bernard Lee (C.I.D. Inspector); Marion Perroni (Purser); Alex Pochet (Hotel Manager); Aldo Silviani (Charles); Guilio Donnini; Saro Uri; Juan De Landa; Manuel Serano; Mimo Peli

SILK STOCKINGS
1957
by Susan Svehla

The film career of Peter Lorre did not proceed as he would have wished. The sad-faced actor longed to perform in dramatic films but was soon typecast as effeminate gangsters or brutal killers. Eventually, the serious actor, but well-known practical joker, would appear in comedies and musicals. It seems as though Hollywood, while making a commercial success of Peter Lorre, also destroyed his creative career. However, while Lorre may have detested his latter film roles, we can still rejoice in them. Peter Lorre was a top-notch actor and no matter what career or personal problems haunted him, his impish grin and twinkling eyes were always present. Lorre is endearing in the Corman horror comedies but no other Lorre performance can make me laugh more than his Comrade Brankov in *Silk Stockings*.

Peter Lorre was no stranger to musical comedies. Cast alongside Boris Karloff and Bela Lugosi, the trio of terrors teamed up to do in an heiress and claim her fortune in *You'll Find Out* (1940), a musical comedy starring bandleader Kay Kyser. Lorre was still slight and had an air of sinister menace during this stage of his career and made the perfect choice as Fenninger. In 1947 Lorre, based on his supporting roles in noir films, would be teamed up with cinema clown Bob Hope to appear in *My Favorite Brunette*, a detective spoof that also starred Dorothy Lamour and Lon Chaney. Lorre portrays Kismet, a knife-throwing murderer who is out to kill Bob Hope's character. The following year Lorre would portray Inspector Slimane in the Universal musical *Casbah,* which starred popular singer Tony Martin. *Cinebooks* notes the best performance in the film was by Lorre, who should have received an Academy Award nomination.

Lorre, with perhaps one of the most recognizable faces and voices in Hollywood history, would make frequent guest star appearances in films. He would first work with Cyd Charisse, his *Silk Stockings* co-star, in *Meet Me in Las Vegas* where she starred with Dan Dailey. Lorre makes a guest appearance at a blackjack table but is only on-screen a few short moments. Michael Todd added Lorre to his all-star lineup of *Around the World in 80 Days* as a Japanese steward.

In 1957 the death knell could be heard ringing down the curtain on the Hollywood musical. Hollywood wanted nothing more to do with the frothy happy musical of the past. Musicals would take on a harder edge before almost disappearing from the silver screen—*Gigi* (with the underlying kept woman theme), *Carousel* (wife abuse), *The Pajama Game* (workers' rights), *South Pacific* (WWII), *West Side Story* (gang violence), *Cabaret* (Nazi Germany) would become the pick of the day. No longer could

Peter Lorre, Bela Lugosi and Boris Karloff team up for terror in *You'll Find Out.*

audiences disappear into a theater, spend an hour and a half in delightful abandon and exit humming a memorable tune from top-notch composers such as Irving Berlin and Cole Porter. Oh, for the good old days.

Arthur Freed, head of the infamous Freed unit at MGM, battled studio heads for his choice of director—Rouben Mamoulian. MGM considered Mamoulian an unwise choice since his last MGM musical, *Summer Holiday* in 1948, had been plagued with problems and ran way over budget. The film wound up losing over a million dollars. Still Freed fought hard for Mamoulian and ultimately MGM agreed. *Silk Stockings* was given the green light and would be based on the stage musical, which was based on the film *Ninotchka. Ninotchka* starred Greta Garbo and the advertising campaign centered on the line "GARBO LAUGHS!"

Mamoulian, known to horror fans as the director of 1932's *Dr. Jekyll and Mr. Hyde*, was a musical pro who produced and directed what is considered one of the best musicals every made, *Love Me Tonight*, which starred Jeanette MacDonald and Maurice Chevalier. An aging Fred Astaire was cast as Steve Canfield, a Hollywood producer making a film in Paris. Astaire manages to sign a visiting Russian composer, Peter Ilyitch Boroff (Wim Sonneveld), to write the score for his film. Three commissars are sent to bring Boroff back to Russia—Brankov (Lorre), Ivanov (Joseph Buloff) and Bibinski (Jules Munshin). This musical version of the Three Stooges consisted of Buloff, a Broadway star who had appeared in several B musicals including *Carnegie Hall* in 1947 directed by Edgar Ulmer; Jules Munshin brought his comedy and dancing gifts to films such as *Easter Parade* (1948), *Take Me Out to the Ball Game* (1949) and *On the Town* (1949); and Peter Lorre—who couldn't dance and couldn't sing but proved a lovable addition to this trio of Russian miscreants. Peter Lorre was fourth billed under Astaire, Charisse and Janis Paige.

When Boroff and Steve return to the hotel, the three Russians peek from behind a pillar. The sight of Lorre leading the pack with the much taller Munshin right behind him lets viewers know these three are the comic focus in the film. Munshin and Buloff use Russian accents, but Lorre, with his distinct European accent, didn't bother.

> Munshin: We talk to him now.
> Lorre: Be careful, don't frighten him. Smile.
> Munshin: I haven't smiled in 30 years.

Lorre tries to show them how to smile, he tightens his lips and grimaces two times. They all plaster the fake smiles on their face as they approach Boroff.

Munshin, Lorre and Buloff in a studio publicity shot.

Peter Lorre, Joseph Buloff, Fred Astaire and Jules Munshin party with Belita, Tybee Afra and Barrie Chase in *Silk Stockings.* (Photofest)

Steve explains Boroff can make $50,000 for writing the film score. "How much taxes will Russia get off $50,000?" he asks. Lorre deadpans, "$50,000." Steve throws down Hollywood magazines with cheesecake photos of his star, Peggy Dayton (Janis Paige). Lorre edges closer and, propping his arm on the table, remarks in a serious tone, "Um, looks very intelligent."

Soon Steve pulls in three evening-gowned chorus girls for an night of partying with the Russians. Of course, this leads to the first Cole Porter song, the delightful "Too Bad." Lorre's bangs splay across his forehead and the ever present cigarette is in his left hand as his head rests on the shoulder of one of the beauties. Lorre, who enjoyed the finer things in life, seems more used to the bon viviant role than Munshin and Buloff. Champagne flows as the group breaks into "Too bad we can't go back to Moscow." As the rest of the group sing and dance, Lorre places his hands one at a time behind his head and moves his hips while trying valiantly to keep time with the musical beat before sticking a knife between his teeth while crouching down between the table and chair, and begins kicking his legs in time with the music. The chair eventually gets away from him and he falls on his behind but gets right back up and starts over again, still kicking away as the number ends. It appears the chair wasn't supposed to fall, but Mamoulian let the cameras roll.

Nina Yoshenka—or Ninotchka as Steve calls her (Cyd Charisse)—is sent to bring back Boroff and the three commissars. Steve takes Ninotchka on a tour of Paris. At two in the morning the commissars are frantically waiting for her to return. Lorre enters disheveled, lipstick on his cheek and a silly smile upon his face. "I just got your call.

Lorre tries to hold his own with Munshin and Buloff in "Siberia" in *Silk Stockings.* (Photofest)

I was having a manicure." "At two in the morning?" Munshin asks. "I cannot sleep with long fingernails," Lorre says as he chuckles.

Things are going along swimmingly, Steve had wooed the lovely Ninotchka who has given in to the luxuries of the capitalist Paris and the commissars are decadently happy. But when the Russians visit the movie set and see how Steve has turned Boroff's "Ode to a Tractor" into a popular song, they are highly insulted and decide to return home.

The commissars, on a throne room set from the movie, consider their fate with the number "Siberia." Lorre, who seems to have no sense of rhythm, manages to hold his own with musical pros Munshin and Buloff. He's stiff as a board as they sing and dance to "When we meet in dear Siberia..." but the trio manage to pull off this amusing number. At one point they join hands and execute a sort of ballet step that probably made Nijinsky spin in his grave. This is their tour de force number and they make the most of it as they entertainingly strut their stuff.

Back in Russia the commissars have been saved from Siberia by Ninotchka's good report and they get together with her and Boroff in her quarters. This leads to a showcase for Cyd Charisse, who has never been better in any of her film roles. The ensemble breaks into "The Red Blues" as Lorre lifts Charisse onto a piano, kicks a dancer in the rear end and once again the knife is clenched between his teeth as he kicks in time with the music.

Joseph Buloff, Wim Sonneveld, Cyd Charisse and Peter Lorre doing his version of a dance routine in *Silk Stockings*.

Ninotchka is summoned and again sent after the wayward commissars when they are sent back to Paris to sell Russian films. Unfortunately, the roguish trio hasn't sold a single film and an anonymous letter is received citing their scandalous behavior—one night they got drunk and entered a dance contest—and won! Dressed in tuxedoes, the trio greet her with delight and tell her they own the nightclub. Lorre gleefully cries, "We are now rotten Capitalists and if all goes well, we'll be much rottener than we ever dreamed!" He takes her by the hand and leads her to the nightclub where he watches her as she sees Steve on stage and smiles at her reaction.

Ninotchka agrees to marry Steve and the ensemble reprises "Too Bad (We Can't Go Back to Moscow)"—Lorre with a cigar stuck between his teeth and kicking away for dear life as the final credits roll.

Fred Astaire wouldn't do another musical until the wan *Finian's Rainbow* in 1968. Cyd Charisse would do several crime films before reuniting with Astaire in *The Towering Inferno* in 1974. Munshin's film musical career was also over, although he would appear as a Frenchman in several comedies. However, Peter Lorre's musical career was not over. He would appear in a role in American-International's *Muscle Beach Party* in 1964. His role was kept secret and he appeared at the end of the film as the strongest

Ina Balin, John Carradine and Peter Lorre in *The Patsy*. (Photofest)

man in the world and the father of character Flex Martian (Rock Stevens, soon to use his real name of Peter Lupus).

Lorre would revisit comedy again in two Jerry Lewis films—*The Sad Sack* also in 1957 and *The Patsy* in 1964. In *The Patsy* he plays a director whose star performer dies in an accident. He and the other employees of the deceased star decide to create a new comedy sensation—Jerry Lewis. Well, at least the French would laugh. Lorre would die four days after completing this film.

However, no other film role provided the sheer fun and chuckles than his comedic performance in *Silk Stockings.*

Silk Stockings is filled with marvelous musical numbers including "Stereophonic Sound" sung and danced gloriously by Astaire and Janis Paige, and the dazzling "Fated to be Mated" performed by Astaire and Charisse. This song was written specifically for the film and focused exquisitely on the dancing skills of the duo rather than vocals. Charisse's vocals were dubbed by Carol Richards. One of the flaws of the videotape and television showings of *Silk Stockings* is the old pan and scan demon. Unfortunately, since Peter Lorre was often sidelined while the other cast members performed more difficult dance routines, he is often cut out of these versions. Wait for the letterboxed edition to fully enjoy this vastly different Lorre performance. Why was Lorre cast in *Silk Stockings*? I haven't been able to find out. Many of the cast are long gone and Cyd Charisse had nothing to say when asked about Lorre's work in the film. Perhaps it was on the recommendation of Rouben Mamoulian. Hopefully we will find out when Stephen Youngkin, co-author of *The Films of Peter Lorre,* releases his forthcoming definitive biography on Lorre. Whatever the reason, Lorre adds spark and zest to one of the final frothy musicals that ended an era, and for that I am grateful.

CREDITS: Producer: Arthur Freed; Director: Rouben Mamoulian; Assistant Director: Al Jennings; Screenplay: Leonard Gershe and Leonard Spigelgas (From the Musical Play *Silk Stockings* by George S. Kaufman, Leueen Mc-Grath and Abe Burrows which was Based on the Story "Ninotchka" by Melchior Lengyel and the Screenplay by Billy Wilder, Charles Bracket and Walter Reisch); Songs: Cole Porter; Choreography: Hermes Pan (Astaire numbers) and Eugene Loring; Cinematography: Robert Bronner; Editor; Harold F. Kress A.C.E.; Costumes: Helen Rose; Make-up: William Tuttle; Metrocolor; CinemaScope; MGM; Released July 19, 1957; Running Time: 117 Minutes

CAST: Fred Astaire (Steve Canfield); Nina "Ninotchka" Yoshenka (Cyd Charisse); Janis Paige (Peggy Dayton); Peter Lorre (Brankov); Jules Munshin (Bibinski); Joseph Buloff (Ivanov); George Tobias (Commissar Vassili Markovitch); Wim Sonneveld (Peter Ilyitch Boroff); Belita (Vera); Barrie Chase (Gabrielle)

VOYAGE TO THE BOTTOM OF THE SEA
1961
by David H. Smith

Glub.

With *Voyage to the Bottom of the Sea*, the career of Peter Lorre was sinking to new depths, in more ways than one.

As the calendar pages of the 1940s were torn away, without the security of a studio contract and hardly blessed with the chiseled Arrow Shirt features of the leading men of the day, Peter Lorre had to rely on the munificence of producers who remembered him for his abilities and professionalism more than for his looks.

For better or worse, one such producer was Irwin Allen, who had started in radio in the 1940s; later, with the arrival of television he created the first celebrity panel show. He began producing films in 1951, and two years later won an Academy Award for *The Sea Around Us*, a semi-documentary he also wrote and directed for RKO. Allen followed this with *The Animal World* for Warner Bros. in 1956.

Allen hedged his bets on *The Animal World* by reuniting the erstwhile special-effects veterans of 1949's *Mighty Joe Young*, stop-motion animators Willis O'Brien and Ray Harryhausen, for a short dinosaur sequence in this otherwise mediocre feature. So dramatic and exciting was the O'Brien/Harryhausen footage (highlighted by the energetic battle between a horned ceratosaurus and a plated stegosaurus) that the entire publicity campaign for the movie was built around it. ("Two Billion Years in the Making" declared the ads.)

However, unlike the artisans' earlier, solo efforts like *King Kong* (1933) and *The Beast From 20,000 Fathoms* (1953), because of Allen's budgetary restrictions, the dinosaurs were shot using multiple cameras filming the set-ups from different angles in order to provide maximum footage, and the models were quickly animated at two frames per exposure instead of one; some live-action puppets were also used for close-ups; there was no process photography or glass art to lend depth to the miniature terrain.

Due to its documentary nature, *The Animal World* is rarely seen nowadays, though the memorable dinosaur scenes are on view as a prehistoric flashback sequence in *Trog* (1970) and on 3-D Viewmaster reels. The high regard held for that scene, coupled with the gimmick of all-star casting in his follow-up *The Story of Mankind* (with Peter Lorre billed ninth) the next year, plotted the course for Irwin Allen's future projects.

In 1960, turning to full-blown science fiction, Allen chose to remake Sir Arthur Conan Doyle's 1912 fantasy-adventure novel *The Lost World*. The canny producer-director hoped to gain some appreciation from old-time devotees of monster movies by

Lorre as Nero in *The Story of Mankind* enjoys a celebration.

retaining O'Brien in a supervisory capacity. ("Fantastic adventures of an expedition to a lost land of prehistoric animals and fierce headhunters!")

Sadly, for the sake of expedience, Allen was obliged to use magnified chameleons, iguanas and alligators instead of an animated prehistoric menagerie of 49 dinosaurs like O'Brien had created for the 1925 film version (and taken 14 painstaking months to do so!).

Still and all, the remake's formula worked, and audiences (though few hard-core fans) overlooked the shortcut in light of the remake's superior sound, color and its widescreen CinemaScope presentation.

Afterward, Allen turned more toward reality, by "tearing from the headlines" progress being made by the U.S. Navy in the field of submarines. The world's first nuclear submarine, the USS *Nautilus*, had been commissioned in 1954, and had recently made the news (August 1958) by being the first ship to cross the North Pole beneath the frozen Arctic icepack. At 319 feet long, the *Nautilus* was fast eclipsed in size by the *Seawolf* (338 feet long) in 1957.

Ready to go the U.S. Navy still one better, Irwin Allen came up with the *Seaview* for *Voyage to the Bottom of the Sea*. Supposedly 600 feet long (even 40 years later, the world's longest submarines are only 560 feet long), this atomic-powered submarine would be capable of diving farther and faster than any craft in history, and was equipped with a mini-sub, diving bell and Polaris ballistic missiles.

As if to underline the view that there were no half measures about the *Seaview*, even its creator and skipper is an admiral—Admiral Harriman Nelson (Walter Pidgeon), sailor-scientist head of the Bureau of Marine Exploration ("a great man, a great inventor"). His *aide de camp* is Commodore Lucius Emery (fourth-billed Peter Lorre), a world-renowned physicist (and part-time ichthyologist) who acts as the admiral's

Frankie Avalon, Walter Pidgeon and Peter Lorre

chain-smoking sounding board for eccentric theories. On-screen, Emery, wearing rubber overalls in a wading pool, urging a similarly rubber shark ("C'mon, Bessie, let's go!") to recover from an anesthetic is introduced to a cynical congressman (Howard McNear, a co-star from *The Big Circus* two years earlier) and a smarmy psychiatrist (Joan Fontaine) touring the sub on a fact-finding mission.

The plot of *Voyage to the Bottom of the Sea* has the *Seaview*, with sinking (!) chunks of ice (actually, metal frames covered with wire mesh and layers of cheesecloth coated with wax) bouncing off her hull, surfacing from a sub-polar expedition to discover the sky aflame (an impressive effect achieved by running shots of a flame-thrower through an optical printer 57 times) and the Earth's temperature rising at a dangerous rate.

Out of touch with the world for the duration of their dive, a staticky radio contact informs Nelson and his crew that a meteor shower set the Van Allen radiation belt ablaze a couple of days before. The others turn to Emery to verify the theory; he, without so much as a slide rule or missing a beat, mutters, "Theoretically, it's possible," a confirmation as useless as a milk bucket under a bull.

The *Seaview* races at flank speed back to New York City for the esteemed scientists aboard to attend a conference scheduled at the United Nations to discuss the crisis. En route, surviving on a diet of "coffee and cigarettes," Emery and Nelson lock themselves away to try to solve the world crisis ("Oh, you're always so *sure* of everything!" Lorre snipes at one point). Stuffed like 10 pounds of flour into a five-pound sack (undoubtedly exceeding the Navy's 164-pound maximum allowable weight limit for his five-foot, two-inch frame), the rotund Lorre dons his best Navy dress blues and accompanies Nelson and his curvaceous secretary (Barbara Eden) to the chamber floor.

Without hesitating, Nelson proposes his radical theory of launching nuclear missiles to extinguish the stratospheric flames . This speculative option outrages the world's foremost expert (Henry Daniell) on the subject (an extremely narrow field of study, to be sure), who believes the fire, given time, will burn itself out. Reunited with his *Hotel Berlin* co-star, Lorre testily offers to share with Daniell his and the admiral's calculations, then mumbles (possibly improvising) under his breath, "Oh, he irritates me!"

Not granted UN sanction, the Seaview nevertheless gets underway in a race against time to reach the precise longitude and latitude from which to fire Nelson's atomic solution. On the way, the crew encounters a minefield, a squid, a pursuing sub, an octopus and even a religious zealot (swarthy Massachusetts-born Michael Ansara, a co-star from *The Sad Sack*), all trying to stymie the unauthorized mission. It is a foregone conclusion Nelson's theory is right after all, and the missiles are launched just under the wire. The *Seaview*'s deck awash, a beaming, sweaty Lorre emerges from the conning-tower to scan the clearing heavens alongside Pidgeon as the soundtrack swells in triumph. Rightly anticipating boffo box-office (made for $2 million, it grossed over $7 million at the theater), the publicity department at Twentieth Century-Fox blew its ballast tanks—a kind euphemism—and went for broke. There was an authorized comic book adaptation (Dell Four Color #1230) on the drugstore spinneret ("From the green gloom of the ocean's depths to a sky aflame with disaster for all the world, comes a tale of frightening suspense and adventure."), which at least featured a cover photo of Lorre (alongside Eden and Fontaine) looking worriedly out the bow window.

In June, the month before *Voyage to the Bottom of the Sea*'s release, Pyramid books released a novelization. Selling for 35 cents, the paperback featured cover art of a submarine (hardly resembling the *Seaview*) battling a fanged undersea serpent which appeared neither in the book nor in the movie proper.

The dreadfully boring book was written by the late Theodore Sturgeon, who was, along with A. E. van Vogt, Robert A. Heinlein and Isaac Asimov, one of the key figures in the evolution of science fiction during what is termed the "golden age" (approximately 1938-46) with a flood of material in the *Astounding Science-Fiction* pulp magazine.

Best remembered for his novel *More Than Human* and his short stories *It* and *Killdozer* (in among historical novels, Westerns, detective novels and bouts of writer's block), Sturgeon is perhaps most famous for his often misquoted "Sturgeon's Law," derived from a statement he made in the March 1958 issue of *Venture Science Fiction*: "Sure, 90% of science fiction is crud. That's because 90% of everything is crud." Oddly, when cited, the final word is almost invariably changed to "crap."

Tiresome even at a meager 159 pages, the deadly dullness of Sturgeon's novelization is not entirely his fault, since he had to frequently interrupt the narrative flow and spend whole pages backtracking to explain all of the scientific improbabilities (a glass-nosed submarine?), tactical unlikelihoods (shooting electrical charges through the super-sub's hull?) and physical impossibilities (ice sinking?).

Yet, in spite of all that, the book's Commodore Emery emerges as the most human character amid all the technological gobbledygook, as the *Seaview*'s Captain Crane confers with him about their mission's dilemmas:

> Emery was, in Crane's eye, the original Shaggy Man. There was an undefinable quality about the man that always called the name up. It had nothing to do with his appearance, really. Starched, smoothed, pressed (none of which he was at the moment) he would still seem shaggy. Perhaps it was the big-dog friendliness of the man, perhaps his utterly confident lack of respect for formality. He was a man who did not need straight ruled lines and sharp creases to comfort himself in an uncertain world.

The publicity machine at Twentieth Century-Fox also ground its gears to manufacture some interesting views of the film by its cast members. Lorre, according to the exhibitor's campaign manual, was delighted about being cast as a hero (of sorts) for a change. He was quoted as saying, "I get to play a good guy! After playing top brass in every enemy army in the world I finally get a chance to portray a United States commodore." Only in the world of publicity hyperbole. Except for the occasional role as an intelligence officer (*Lancer Spy*), as an Axis spy (*Invisible Agent*) or as a POW camp sergeant (*The Cross of Lorraine*), Lorre never played such parts.

Lorre also shouldn't have been too impressed about playing a commodore either. Reestablished as a naval rank for World War II after a 44-year hiatus, only 147 officers

Peter Lorre, Robert Sterling and Barbara Eden (Photofest)

held it as a temporary rank. By the first day of 1950, no commodores remained on active duty. And *Voyage to the Bottom of the Sea* was supposed to take place in an undated *future*.

During production, Lorre's disdain for his inconsequential part came to a boil. To achieve the sweat-drenched effect everyone suffered (even underwater in a climate-controlled *Seaview*!), one of the crewmen on the set had a seltzer bottle adjusted to deliver a fine mist and would go from cast member to cast member and squirt them. Lorre wanted no part of it; he simply hated being squirted. At that point, grumbling, "The hell with realism," a chase began. Through the elaborate *Seaview* sets he would run with the crewmember in hot pursuit, armed with a squirt bottle.

Reviews then and since, while impressed by the visuals, were rather dismissive of the melodramatics. The unnamed reviewer in *Variety* allowed, "The acting is generally capable, about the best it can be under the circumstances." Co-authors James Robert Parish and Michael R. Pitts, in *The Great Science Fiction Movies*, rued, "A superior cast was forced to mouth rather mediocre dialogue."

Getting more specific, in the second volume of *Keep Watching The Skies!*, Bill Warren lamented, "Peter Lorre is helplessly lost.... he has almost nothing to do"; similar sentiments were echoed by Tim Lucas in a 1994 issue of *Video Watchdog*, who called Lorre "the most interesting cast member," but sighed the actor "has almost no dialogue and is given nothing to do but smoke and pace."

Walter Pidgeon, a 1940s leading man who had graduated to character roles in the 1950s, is, in spite of being twice-nominated for Oscars, probably best remembered as

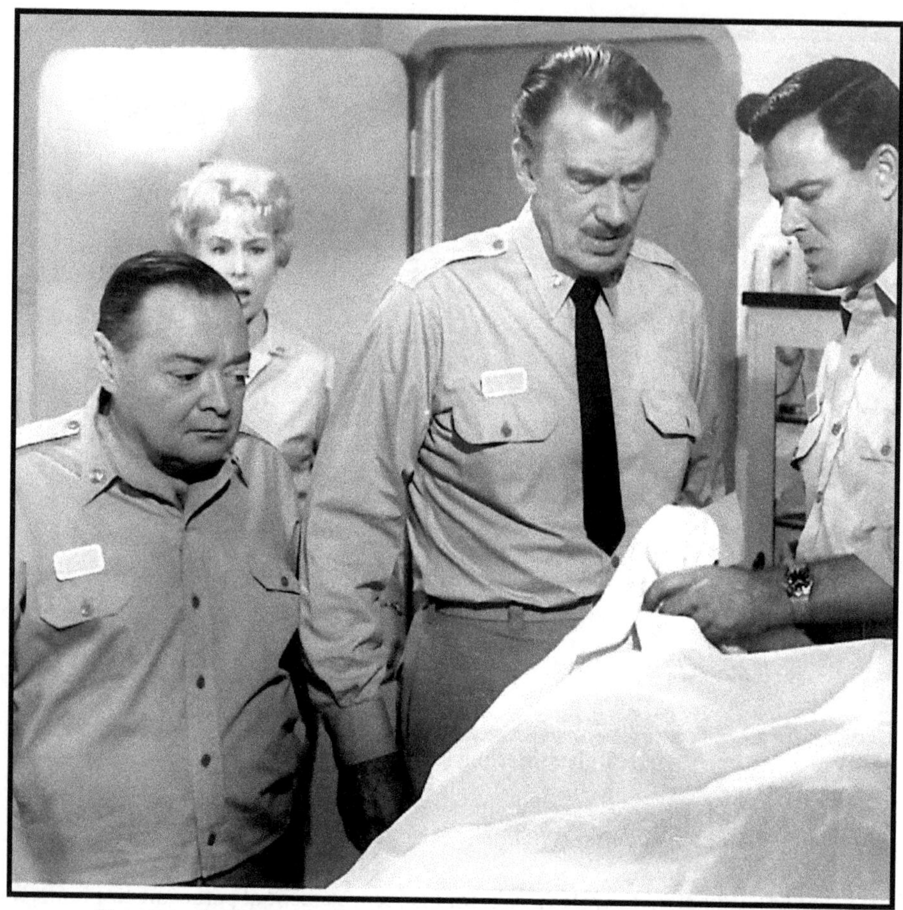

***Voyage to the Bottom of the Sea* wasted Peter Lorre's talents. (Photofest)**

a semi-mad scientist in the classic *Forbidden Planet* (1956). While unlikely lifelong friends as the movie suggests, his and Lorre's camaraderie suggests a mutual respect for one another, perhaps more as real-life actors rather than as make-believe naval officers.

Joan Fontaine, seemingly a lifetime away from her pigtailed teenager role alongside Lorre in *The Constant Nymph*, was revealed at the end to be the mysterious saboteur for equally mysterious reasons (and being inelegantly dunked in Lorre's shark tank as recompense). In her autobiography *No Bed of Roses*, the Oscar-winning actress dismissed *Voyage to the Bottom of the Sea* as "horrendous," doing it only to pad her income.

Saving in production costs, the movie's three sub models (on the surface a 20-foot model was used, an eight-foot one for underwater shots and, for the sequence with a reticent live octopus, a four-foot model was used), sets, costumes, props and reel upon reel of underwater footage were brought out of dry-dock a few years later for a sequel of sorts, 110 episodes of a TV series of the same name.

The freshly cast television crew's mission, though ostensibly scientific research, was to combat threats to world peace from anyone who felt a bit antsy—and that included werewolves, planet-monsters, robots, silver-suited space aliens, ghosts, time travelers, 16th-century pirates and even killer dolls and leprechauns. The feature film's plot (and astronomical pyrotechnics) were recycled for an episode in the series' second season, titled "The Sky's On Fire!" Lorre passed away six months before the series' premiere.

Voyage to the Bottom of the Sea is typical of many titles on Peter Lorre's filmography. It wastes his talents, but, thankfully, not to the detriment of his rich career. He was simply used as a name to be exploited by the producer, who knew Peter Lorre could be counted on to damn the torpedoes—or the poor scripts—and go full speed ahead.

CREDITS: Screenplay: Irwin Allen and Charles Bennett; Story: Irwin Allen; Producer/Director: Irwin Allen; Music: Paul Sawtell and Bert Shefter; Song "Voyage to the Bottom of the Sea" by Russell Faith; Sung by Frankie Avalon; Director of Photography: Winton Hoch, A.S.C.; Art Direction: Jack Martin Smith and Herman A. Blumenthal; Set Decorations: Walter M. Scott and John Sturtevant; Special Photographic Effects: L.B. Abbott, A.S.C.; Underwater Photography: John Lamb; Film Editor: George Boemler, A.C.E.; Assistant Director: Ad Schaumer; Technical Advisor: Fred Zendar; Make-up: Ben Nye; Hair Styles: Helen Turpin, C.H.S.; Costume Designer: Paul Zastupnevich; Assistant to Producer: Al Gail; Sound: Alfred Bruzlin and Warren B. Delaplain; Orchestration: Max Reese; Color by De Luxe; a CinemaScope Picture; Copyrighted 1961 by Windsor Productions, Inc. and Twentieth Century-Fox Film Corporation; Released July 1961; 105 Minutes (Produced under the working title *Journey to the Bottom of the Sea*)

CAST: Walter Pidgeon (Admiral Harriman Nelson); Joan Fontaine (Dr. Susan Hiller); Barbara Eden (Lieutenant Cathy Connors); Peter Lorre (Commodore Lucius Emery); Robert Sterling (Captain Lee Crane); Michael Ansara (Miguel Alvarez); Frankie Avalon (Lieutenant Chip Romano); Regis Toomey (Dr. Jamieson); John Litel (Vice Admiral B.J. Crawford); Howard McNear (Congressman Llewellyn Parker); Henry Daniell (Dr. Emilio Zucco); Mark Slade (Seaman Jimmy Smith); Charles Tannen (CPO Gleason); Delbert Monroe (Crewman Kowski); Anthony Monaco (Cookie); Robert Easton (Sparks); Jonathan Gilmore (Young); David McLean (Ned Thompson); Larry Gray (Dr. Newmar); George Diestrel (Lieutenant Hodges); Art Baker (UN commentator); Dr. John Giovanni (Italian delegate); Kendrick Huxham (UN Chairman); Skip Ward, William Herrin, James Murphy, Michael Ford (Crew Members)

FIVE WEEKS IN A BALLOON
1962
by Don G. Smith

Irwin Allen could not have picked a better time to produce, direct and co-script a film based on Jules Verne's *Five Weeks in a Balloon.* After all, 1962 was the centennial of the book's writing (it was published in 1863). Allen had already made such big-budget science fiction fare as *The Animal World* (1956), *The Lost World* (1960) and *Voyage to the Bottom of the Sea* (1962). By 1963, Allen was used to directing fine actors, among them Peter Lorre, who appeared in such Allen epics as *The Story of Mankind* (1957), *The Big Circus* (1959) and the aforementioned *Voyage to the Bottom of the Sea* .

Lorre had long demonstrated the ability to play both comic characters and villains, and *Five Weeks in a Balloon* called on him to play both in the character of Ahmed, the slave trader. Verne's novel, his first, set the formula for many novels to follow: A scientist or man of genius produces a unique invention for travel and supplies enough scientific information to make it believable to the reader. The scientist then goes on an exciting journey to an exotic location and has a series of adventures. Unlike Verne's novel, the tone of the film adaptation is assuredly comic, an obvious factor in Allen's acquiring Lorre's services.

The plot concerns Professor Fergusson's invention of a huge balloon that can rise or descend without loss of ballast. He and his assistant Jacques Verlain try to interest the Royal Geographic Institute in financing an air expedition to unexplored East Africa. When the Institute is unimpressed, Donald O'Shay, a reporter, convinces his newspaper to finance the trip, as long as O'Shay can go along and report the story. It seems that the British government is also interested in taking advantage of the expedition in order to secure a territory desired by slave traders who are on their way to claim the area. Fergusson and crew are to ride the winds 4,000 miles across Africa to the Volta River and plant the British flag. The adventures soon begin. First, Fergusson is displeased that the British government is sending along Sir Henry Vining, the President of the Royal Geographic Institute, to keep an eye on things. Matters become more complicated when O'Shay insists on risking the lives of everyone by rescuing Makia, a pretty slave girl. Of course, she becomes the fifth passenger. If that were not enough, additional trouble develops when a severe storm forces the balloon down in the city of Hezak, where the natives conclude that the balloon is the moon. At a feast, Ahmed the slave trader arrives, dragging along a captured missionary schoolteacher, Susan Gale.

In these opening scenes, Lorre is the grimacing villain. Swarthy in complexion and rotund in appearance, he makes a rather unsavory entrance dragging along the pretty Susan. Once again, the dauntless O'Shay comes to the rescue by pretending to be the Moon God in order to get Susan released. Ahmed, however, is crafty enough to expose

Peter Lorre, Red Buttons and Barbara Eden (Photofest)

the hoax. Lorre expresses exceptional delight in the comic discovery, which seems to both surprise and amuse the Sultan of Hezak. In scenes that garner a few laughs, the crew and Susan attempt to escape in the balloon. Lorre, however, is in hot pursuit, at least as hot as his weight will allow. As the balloon lifts off, Lorre, with some difficulty, climbs aboard in an effort to retrieve his slave. The scene reminds me a bit of a W.C. Fields scene in *Never Give a Sucker an Even Break* in which the comedian leaps off a plane (rather than onto a balloon) in order to retrieve a lost whiskey bottle.

Lorre, of course, is now a prisoner himself, and the balloon carries seven passengers (eight, if you count Chester the Chimp). As the adventures continue, Lorre's character becomes increasingly endearing. Not only does he abandon his cruel profession as flesh dealer, but he even dons a disguise to help rescue some of his fellow travelers held captive at a Timbuktu slave market. In disguise, Lorre is an interesting figure. Striking a sinister pose, he channels his attention to the matter at hand.

The expedition is finally successful, but only thanks to Ahmed, who skillfully throws a dagger into the last slave trader before the would-be killer can shoot O'Shay. The expedition ironically owes its success to a once-vicious man who was not even supposed to fly along.

When he made *Five Weeks in a Balloon*, Peter Lorre was overweight and suffering from high blood pressure, factors that would end his life only two years later. His weight became a target of humor, however, when he appeared to plug the film on Groucho Marx's television show *You Bet Your Life*. When Lorre announced the title, Groucho raised his eyebrows and asked, "Are you playing the part of the balloon?"

Also plugging the film was a large 12-page pressbook in which one of the press releases hypes Peter Lorre:

> Probably the most imitated character actor in motion pictures is Peter Lorre, whose insidious roles have stamped him a connoisseur's "heavy." But this is not entirely to Mr. Lorre's liking; he would like to play an occasional "good guy." His current screen appearance in the Irwin Allen production *Five Weeks in a Balloon,* the 20th Century-Fox, Cinemascope DeLuxe Color release due... at the... Theatre, is at least a partial realization of this ambition.
>
> In the role of Ahmed the slave trader, Lorre begins *Five Weeks* as a thoroughly evil little man. As the rollicking adventure-comedy progresses, however, Lorre progresses from a heartless dealer in human lives to something of a hero. "You see," comments Lorre, "nobody's *all* bad... even me."

This raises an interesting question. While Lorre was certainly a well-known villain, was he typecast in the usual sense of the word? Well, yes and no. He had made his share of horror films, and with the *Shock Theater* horror revival of the late 1950s and early 1960s a new generation became aware of his considerable contribution to the genre. Of course, he had played many villains in many non-horror films as well, some of which were great, some of which were mediocre, but none of which were downright bad. He certainly played more straight roles than Bela Lugosi did, and though his film output and his screen time dropped off somewhat in the late 1940s and in the early-to-mid-1950s, Hollywood never neglected him like it did Lugosi. Lugosi had his *Return of Chandu* serial, which gave the actor a chance to play a hero, but Lorre had many roles throughout his career in which he played sympathetic and sometimes even heroic characters. And while Lugosi appeared in several comedies, they were usually low-budget junk that simply exploited the actor's horror persona. Lorre's comedies, on the other hand, were substantial films that demonstrated the actor's comic talents, which were considerable. *Five Weeks in a Balloon* was one film that allowed Lorre to strut both menace and comedy.

One reason that Lorre played more villains than heroes was his physical appearance itself. His looks and accent made him perfect for exotic, sinister roles, but he would not have passed a screen test to play Rhett Butler in *Gone with the Wind.*

Five Weeks in a Balloon as noted, was a big-budget film. Pyramid Books released a paperback tie-in as part of the promotion, and Columbia cut a 45-rpm record of the title song performed by the popular Brothers Four. What's more, Lorre is surrounded by a terrific cast. Cedric Harwicke is solidly convincing as Professor Fergusson. Red Buttons is his usual light-hearted self in the role of reporter O'Shay, and Henry Daniell successfully adapts his sinister persona to the character of Sheik Ageiba. Billy Gilbert adds some over-the-top comedy, and young singing idol Fabian is adequate as a lure for star-struck female patrons and as a love interest for pretty Barbara Luna. Barbara Eden comes across nicely as the dedicated missionary schoolteacher, and stiff-necked comedian Richard Haydn draws some chuckles as the ever-so-British Sir Henry Vining. As simian actors go, Chester the Chimp is right up there with Cheetah and Bonzo, his antics reinforcing the film's farcical qualities.

Aimed at audiences of all ages, the film was intended primarily for youngsters. It received mildly positive reviews because its cast and splash are hard to dislike. Still, it is little more than a "popcorn movie," suitable for a few hours of light-hearted entertainment. For Peter Lorre, the film was a job, and not a bad one. He had done better work, and he would do better work in the final two years of his life, but *Five Weeks in a Balloon* is fun, thanks in part to Peter Lorre.

CREDITS: Producer/Director: Irwin Allen: Screenplay: Charles Bennett, Irwin Allen and Albert Gail: Music: Paul Sawtell: Cinematography: Winston Hoch: Art Directors: Jack Martin Smith and Alfred Ybarra: Set Decorator: Walter M. Scott, Stuart A. Reiss and Norman Rockett: Production Illustrators: Maurice Zuberano and George Bloemler: Special Photographic Effects: L.B. Abbott and Emil Kosa, Jr.: Sound: Al Gail: Make-up: Ben Nye; Costume Designer: Paul Zastupnevich: Title Song Written by Jodi Desmond and Sung by The Brothers Four: Hair Stylist: Helen Turpin: Orchestration: Sid Cutner: Main Title: Pacific Title: CinemaScope-Color by DeLuxe. Running Time: 101 minutes

CAST: Red Buttons (Donald O'Shay); Fabian (Jacques); Barbara Eden (Susan Galo): Cedric Hardwicke (Fergusson); Ahmed (Peter Lorre); Richard Haydn (Sir Henry Vining); Barbara Luna (Makia); Billy Gilbert (Sultan-Auctioneer); Herbert Marshall (Prime Minister); Reginald Owen (Consul); Henry Daniell (Sheik Ageiba); Mike Mazurki (Slave Captain); Alan Caillou (Inspector); Ben Astar (Myanga); Raymond Bailey (Randolph)

ROUTE 66
"Lizard's Leg and Owlet's Wing"
1962
by Jonathan Malcolm Lampley

Throughout the 1950s and early 1960s, television provided Peter Lorre with a considerable amount of lucrative exposure. He was the first James Bond villain in a 1954 production of *Casino Royale*, for example, and in 1960 he turned up in "The Man From the South," a classic episode of *Alfred Hitchcock Presents*. But the best remembered TV role of Lorre's career remains "Lizard's Leg and Owlet's Wing," a Halloween episode of *Route 66*. As a matter of fact, this episode seems to be the best remembered of the entire series as well.

Route 66 ran from 1960 through 1964 on the CBS-TV network. Backed by a cool theme song, the show chronicled the adventures of swingin' singles Tod Stiles (Martin Milner) and Buzz Murdock (George Maharis) who cruised along the eponymous federal highway in Tod's Corvette convertible looking for fun, girls and the occasional job. Part of the show's popularity stemmed from the fact that it was largely shot on location; if viewers lived along the road, which stretched from Chicago to the Santa Monica pier, they stood a chance of seeing themselves (or at least familiar local sites) on national TV.

First broadcast on October 26, 1962, "Lizard's Leg and Owlet's Wing" features a script by co-creator Stirling Silliphant, one of Hollywood's busiest scriptwriters and producers of the period. Silliphant, who would go on to win an Oscar for writing *In the Heat of the Night*, dreamed up the idea of reuniting the silver screen's most fear-some bogey-men as a special Halloween treat for the viewers. The story involves Tod and Buzz going to work as convention liaisons at Chicago's O'Hare Inn. The boys are excited about the assignment because a convention of 40 executive secretaries from across the country is in town. Of course, only one liaison can be assigned to each group, so a coin toss decides that it will be Buzz's lucky day. Tod is put in charge of a strange group called the Society for the Preservation of the Gerenuk, which we learn is a rare African antelope.

Unbeknownst to Tod, the Society is actually a cover for a filmmaking concern being founded by three of the world's leading horror stars: Boris Karloff, Lon Chaney and Peter Lorre, each playing himself. The masters of the macabre plan to make a new television series, but they cannot agree on what approach to take. Karloff wants to focus on new ideas and eschew the old familiar ghouls, but Lorre and Chaney insist on featuring the classic monsters of legend that made the terrible trio stars in the first place. Attempting to keep matters focused on the financial and logistical elements of the deal is Mrs. Baxter (Martita Hunt), the formidable business manager of the group. Because a unanimous decision is required, the actors argue back and forth until Tod, accidentally overhearing the plan, comes up with a novel suggestion: Karloff and company will dress up in their old costumes and test the old monsters on a new generation of potential fans—the young women attending the convention for executive secretaries.

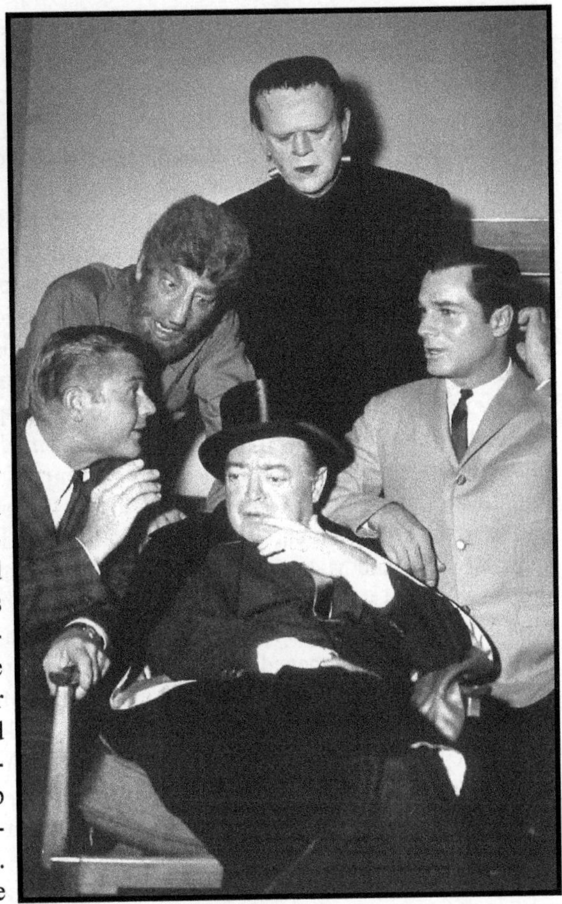

Peter Lorre, Martin Milner, Lon Chaney, Boris Karloff and George Maharis

Soon the boys are up to their old tricks. Karloff stomps around in his Frankenstein Monster get-up, while Chaney does the old Wolf Man bit after abortive runs as the Mummy and the Hunchback of Notre Dame. Since Lorre doesn't really have a monster character, he is content to record the activities of the others, although at one point he dons top hat and cape, evidently to represent some sort of generic ghoul. The experiment is a success: The secretaries, including their hard-nosed chairwoman, Lila (Betsy Jones-Moreland), promptly react by screaming and fainting all over the place. One young woman, however, is seemingly immune to the monster invasion. The beautiful but unhappy Molly Cross (Jeannine Riley), deep in the throes of unrequited love for her boss, Charles Stephenson (Bill Berger), is oblivious to everything else. Even when the hairy-faced Chaney shows up in response to a room service call, Molly is not frightened; instead, she tries to comfort the hapless faux werewolf!

A chance meeting with Molly gives grandfatherly Karloff the idea to call Stephenson and urge him to make haste for Chicago. Later, while Lila is excoriating Molly before the other women as an example of what happens when one gets too close to the boss, Stephenson bursts into the meeting and literally sweeps Molly off her feet. When he pauses on a staircase to kiss her, Molly looks over his shoulder and sees the three monster men watching approvingly. She promptly faints dead away, apparently from the combination of three monster men and the first ever kiss from her beloved. The episode ends with Tod and Buzz receiving the thanks of Karloff, Lorre and Chaney, who now agree that the old monsters are still the scariest.

Route 66 doesn't seem to have the same kind of cultish following other classic television shows of the period enjoy. Unlike *The Andy Griffith Show* or *The Twilight Zone*, there is no plethora of episode guides, cookbooks or other merchandising that would indicate any kind of fan base for the program. It is true that the rise of the Interstate Highway System has rendered the real Route 66 obsolete, but this has inspired a lot of nostalgia and merchandising for the road itself, not the show. But among fans of classic horror, this one episode at least is fondly remembered. How many of us who grew up in the late 1960s and 1970s read about "Lizard's Leg and Owlet's Wing" in the pages of *Famous Monsters of Filmland* or other publications and wished we could see it for ourselves? In the late 1980s cable television's Nick at Nite finally allowed younger viewers a chance to see what all the fuss was about.

Rewatching "Lizard's Leg and Owlet's Wing" recently, I have to admit I am not greatly impressed with it. Like so many projects inspired by the early 1960s monster craze, the episode is played mostly for broad comedic effect—but for me there isn't much to laugh about. There is a faintly patronizing attitude toward the subject that reminds me of the campy approach to another 1960s TV show, *Batman*—and I don't like that show's treatment of its main character either! Whether told by the guest stars or Milner and Maharis, the jokes are mostly groaners. A bit where Tod playfully threatens his pal with Federal anti-trust laws if Buzz doesn't allow access to the girls falls flat. When Buzz first spots Molly, he walks right into a swimming pool and keeps going as if nothing happened—a gag that wasn't funny the first million times somebody pulled it in a movie or TV show. And then there's Molly herself, moping around in a Hamletesque daze, babbling about how sad the world is. This stuff might have worked during the Kennedy administration, but all I could think of is how badly the girl needed some Prozac!

I suspect modern audiences of a more liberal bent will actually be offended by the portrayal of the secretaries, Lila in particular. Betsy Jones-Moreland enthusiastically attacks the role, but as written Lila is clearly meant to be seen as a lonely career gal embittered by her failure to land a successful husband; in the wake of the women's movement, such a stereotype is pretty uncomfortable to watch. And the fact that it is a group of women targeted for a scare, albeit all in fun, would probably raise eyebrows among contemporary feminists.

But what of the old monsters? How do they fare with this material? They make the best of it, just as they all did in many inferior programmers both before and after this gig. Poor old Lon Chaney comes off the worst: He throws temper tantrums when his scare tactics fail on Mrs. Baxter and Molly that are meant to be funny but are just pathetic. Karloff fares much better; the scenes where he moderates the lovers' spat clearly transmits the Englishman's famous inner warmth. However, in other places he strikes me as something of a grouch, such as when he upbraids Chaney for trying to spook Mrs. Baxter.

Peter Lorre comes off best. In fact, his work is the most successful in the piece, although I like Martita Hunt's sarcastic responses to the tomfoolery surrounding her. Lorre's humorous bits are similarly deadpan; his world-weary attitude, complemented with an ever-present dangling cigarette, provides real bite in every line he delivers. Arriving at the hotel under the alias "Retep" (one of the lamest gags in the episode is this one, suggested by Karloff, wherein the actors adopt pseudonyms consisting of their first names spelled backwards), he dryly dismisses the clerk's suggestion that "Mr. Retep" looks like Peter Lorre—then slaps away the bellboy's hand from a bag! Lorre also gets the one unquestionable gem in the episode. In the middle of all the commotion caused by Chaney's Wolf Man "attack," three fleeing women come to a stop before the diminutive actor. Lorre says nothing, offers the ladies a friendly smile—and they faint dead away!

Lorre's performance here is worth noting for a number of reasons. Overall he is the funniest of the three celebrities, and he seems to be having the most fun with his creepy screen image. His genuinely unnerving appearance, his sly humor and his famous voice all combine to convey the sense of personality that made Lorre a star for over 30 years. There are traces of the "star power" once attributed to Karloff and Chaney, but only Lorre fully succeeds in harnessing his greatest attributes.

Although it hasn't aged well, "Lizard's Leg and Owlet's Wing" remains of interest to horror fans for several reasons. It brings together three of the screen's great bogeymen for one last hurrah; never again would Karloff portray the Frankenstein Monster, nor would Chaney play the Wolf Man or the Mummy after this (his brief appearance as the Hunchback seems to be a tribute to his father, as the younger Chaney never interpreted this character before). The episode's shortcomings at least serve to let Peter Lorre shine above his more monstrous co-stars, thus providing viewers with a brief reminder of the actor's ability to evoke laughter as well as screams—often simultaneously! Finally, "Lizard's Leg and Owlet's Wing" makes a point with which fans of its stars must surely agree: Hollywood's classic movie monsters will always be the best.

CREDITS: Executive Producer: Herbert B. Leonard; Producer: Mort Abrahams; Teleplay: Stirling Silliphant; Director: Robert Gist; Director of Photography: Irving Lippman; Music: Nelson Riddle; Special Make-up: Ben Lane and Maurice Siederman

CAST: Martin Milner (Tod Stiles); George Maharis (Buzz Murdock); Boris Karloff (Himself); Peter Lorre (Himself); Lon Chaney (Himself); Martita Hunt (Mrs. Baxter); Betsy Jones-Moreland (Lila); Jeannine Riley (Molly); Bill Berger (Charles Stephenson); Conrad Nagel (Mr. Parvis, the Hotel Manager)

TALES OF TERROR 1962 by Steven Thornton

By 1962, Peter Lorre's acting career was in a noticeable decline. His tutelage in the German stage and film studios of the 1930s was by now a distant memory. The Hollywood studio system, which had created for him a comfortable niche as a respected character performer, had become a thing of the past. Opportunities to find work in the freelance world of modern cinema were becoming increasingly infrequent. Like far too many of his cinematic contemporaries, Lorre had become a victim of the changing times—forgotten by one generation and a stranger to the next.

Lorre, of course, was still active as a performer. Television work was in abundance in the late 1950s, providing the actor with numerous appearances on such diverse teleplays as *Playhouse 90, Climax, Studio 57, Alfred Hitchcock Presents* and *Rawhide*. Radio also helped keep Lorre in the public ear; his distinctive voice could be heard on *The Big Show*, miscellaneous episodes of the short-lived *Nightmare* series and on the *Philip Morris Playhouse on Broadway* presentation of "The Night Has A Thousand Eyes." Even the film world still provided him with occasional bits, as his recent work in *The Big Circus, Scent of Mystery* and *Voyage to the Bottom of the Sea* clearly demonstrated. But, in spite of his trademark moon-eyed gaze and unmistakable speech pattern, Lorre's appearances during this period were largely undistinguished, his work comprising roles that could have been performed by any over-the-hill character actor.

A new opportunity, however, would come from a very unlikely source—the horror films of American-International. Since the mid-1950s, AIP, the Little Film Company That Could, had enjoyed notable success with its energetic, youth-oriented drive-in fare. At a time when the major Hollywood studios saw their profit margins steadily eroded by the upstart medium of television, AIP's cheap but entertaining horror, sci-fi and hot rod movies consistently hit box office bingo. Subtle and sophisticated they weren't, but for the young adult audience of the rock-n-roll era, AIP co-founders James Nicholson and Sam Arkoff provided an entertainment option that could be found nowhere else.

AIP's low-budget, high energy approach to filmmaking worked wonders throughout the late 1950s, but the new decade had raised the bar for genre films. From across the Atlantic, England's Hammer Films and Mario Bava's Italian Gothics were bringing traditional horror back with a visceral vengeance. AIP's own success, meanwhile, had inspired other American filmmakers to flood the drive-in market with similar, low end product. And Alfred Hitchcock's *Psycho* would soon demonstrate that modern audiences had an appetite for sophisticated thrillers with a grisly edge. To continue its successful run, American-International would clearly have to step its game up a notch.

Peter Lorre mugs as Montresor Herringbone in *Tales of Terror*.

The answer to this challenge was found in the works of Edgar Allan Poe. With their universal literary acclaim, faithful period ambiance and titles that had conveniently fallen into public domain, Poe's writings provided the ticket with which AIP would keep a dismembered leg up on the increasingly competitive horror market. The relative failure of prior Poe adaptations was a plus also; although the author's stories had been a fixture of the cinema since the silent days, few filmmakers had mastered the difficult task of fleshing out these abbreviated tales to feature film length. But AIP was ready to tackle the challenge. With a creative team that included frugal but resourceful director Roger Corman and successful writer and television adapter Richard Matheson, the studio embarked on a series of Poe films that became a notable addition to the decade's canon of cinema horror.

1960's *House of Usher*, which established the formula for the films to follow, got the series off to an energetic start. Featuring Vincent Price in the starring role, Poe's tale of madness and tragedy amidst the accursed Usher household was given the full (if relatively austere) AIP treatment. Colorful and convincingly creepy ambiance was

Montresor confronts his put-upon wife (Joyce Jameson).

provided by set designer Daniel Haller, while veteran cameraman Floyd Crosby captured the eerie visuals in eye-catching CinemaScope. On Roger Corman's shoulders fell the unenviable task of disguising the film's budgetary restrictions, in addition to meshing the uneven performances of AIP's inexperienced supporting players with the enjoyable hamming of headliner Price. Richard Matheson's screen treatment also helped, adding a discernible layer of perverse sexuality to augment the underlying tensions of the original text. Original, inventive and quite effective, *House of Usher* was a standout among the many fine horror films of that prolific year.

The success of *Usher* quickly prompted AIP to produce more in the same vein. *Pit and the Pendulum*, again with Vincent Price, was released the following year, with *The Premature Burial*, this time with Ray Milland, close behind. Box-office receipts were respectable, but an unmistakable creative lethargy was beginning to set in. With each subsequent film, the padded plots and repetitive story lines became more apparent. "I was getting tired of the Poe films by this time," Corman remarked in *The Films of Roger Corman: Brilliance on a Budget*, and the lack of on-screen inspiration was beginning to show. It was becoming clear that if the AIP Poe series was to keep from being entombed under the weight of its own success, changes were in order.

With 1962's *Tales of Terror,* AIP experimented with a fresh approach. For this film, multiple short stories were tailored for the screen in an anthology format that minimized the need for story line elaboration. Elements of humor were featured prominently in one episode, a noted departure from the oh-so-serious approach of the initial Poe films.

Wine expert Fortunato (Vincent Price) has a surprise in store for him.

Most significant of all was the decision to utilize well-respected names from Hollywood's golden age in the film's plum supporting roles. For Corman and production head James Nicholson, who actively courted the familiar faces appearing in this film, the strategy was a sure-fire way to buttress the film's marquee value. For film fans, the upside of this approach was that it provided Vincent Price with some talented thespic sparring partners to help enliven the film's episodic stories.

Enter Peter Lorre.

Over the prior decade, Lorre's cinematic output had tapered off to an average of two films per year, ranging from cliché supporting turns to appearances that were little more than cameos. As the mainstream movie market turned more and more to realistic fare, the eccentric roles in which Lorre excelled were in danger of falling completely out of vogue. "If you wanted to stay in the business, you bloody well went into costume pictures," Vincent Price once opined (*The Complete Films of Vincent Price*), and for the actors of his generation those words were now more true than ever. Fortunately for Lorre, the horror boom initiated in recent years was now at its apex, opening the door for performers whose styles hearkened back to an earlier, more flamboyant era. And when the grand make-believe of horror cinema came a-knocking, the aging actor was ready and willing to answer its call.

Lorre, of course, was no stranger to the horror film—he had contributed more than his share of memorable characterizations to the macabre chillers of filmdom's past. Yet

A wine tasting challenge is proposed between Montresor and Fortunato.

the actor's admittedly show-stopping turns in these roles had been supplanted (and, to most filmgoers, overshadowed) by his appearances in such Hollywood classics as *The Maltese Falcon, Casablanca* and *The Mask of Dimitrios*. This versatility allowed Lorre to sidestep the typecasting that had proven fatal to the careers of other performers who made regular visits to the world of cinema horror, most notably Bela Lugosi and Lionel Atwill. Yet when called on to deliver the goods, Lorre's unnerving screen presence was still capable of making the blood run cold. As a result, the actor's appearances in AIP's successful and memorable Poe pastiches became an unexpected gift to fans of the fantastic, giving them yet another reason to appreciate this distinctive film series.

Principal filming on *Tales of Terror* commenced late November 1961 and the film was readied for a May 1962 release. A quartet of Poe tales were adapted for the film's three episodes. The first, inspired by Poe's *Morella*, teamed dependable Vincent Price with Maggie Pierce and Leona Gage in another of AIP's death-guilt-return-from-the-grave scenarios. The closing tale, a reworking of *The Facts in the Case of M. Valdemar*, featured Basil Rathbone as an unscrupulous mesmerist who hypnotizes Price at the point of death, all the while keeping a leering eye out for grieving widow Debra Paget. But it was the penultimate episode, which combined elements from *The Black Cat* and *The Cask of Amontillado,* that provided Peter Lorre with the opportunity to leave his distinctive mark on the AIP Poe series.

"And what is it that happens just before death...," intones narrator Price in the spoken prelude to "The Black Cat" segment. Peter Lorre wastes no time in establishing an unsavory on-screen presence; his character, who is absurdly named Montresor Herringbone, is seen meandering down the avenue late one evening in a drunken stupor. Stumbling into his abode, he is greeted by cheerful but long-suffering wife Annabel (Joyce Jame-son), whose agreeable disposition is a humorous contrast to the dour demeanor displayed by Lorre. Anxious to continue his drunken revelry, Montresor berates both his wife and her beloved house cat while scouring the residence in search of Annabel's hidden nest egg. The exertion soon proves too much for the belligerent drunkard, who collapses from the effects of his favorite libation.

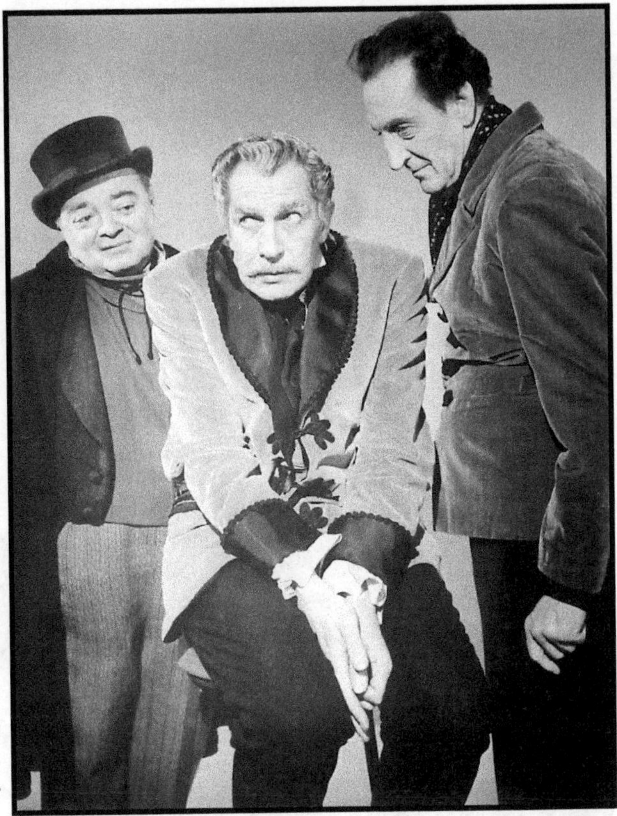

Lorre, Price and Basil Rathbone in a studio pose to promote *Tales of Terror*.

The next morning, Montresor regains consciousness and heads out on the town. To his surprise and delight, he observes a wine merchant's convention in progress, to which the assertive lout decides to pay a visit. In spite of Montresor's best efforts at making a spectacle of himself, all eyes are soon focused on a demonstration by Fortunato Lucresi (Vincent Price), the "foremost wine taster in the civilized world today." Perceiving a threat to his area of expertise, Montresor challenges the respected but foppish authority to a wine tasting duel. One by one, the opposing experts take turns correctly identifying the vintages of the various burgundies and merlots, with Fortunato's victories greeted by hearty applause and Montresor's successes met with deafening silence. The episode reaches a comic coda when Fortunato takes exception to his opponent's uncouth imbibing technique, an unsightly contrast to the master's highly stylized approach. "You do it your way and I do it my way," snorts Montresor to an incredulous and thoroughly mystified Fortunato.

Lorre's initial scenes convey a comedic talent seldom utilized in his straight film appearances. In his introductory vignette with Joyce Jameson, he is seen casually tossing

aside sundry household items in search of his wife's hidden cash stash while she tries in vain to save the miscellaneous bric-a-brac. The routine is played by Lorre with adroit timing, peppered with ad-libbed asides and insults that recall his days as a member of the German improvisational theater groups of the late 1920s. At the wine tasting soiree, Lorre exhibits all the social élan of a turd in a punchbowl, thirstily surveying the assorted vintages while the formally invited guests gape in disbelief. But it is in the one-on-one challenge with Vincent Price where Lorre's comic flair truly comes to the fore. Price's Fortunato scores the initial laughs; his wide-eyed, lip-pursing lampoon of

***Tales of Terror* grows dark when Montresor discovers Fortunato's interest in his wife.**

a wine connoisseur is memorable bit of parody. Just as important to the scene, however, are the reaction shots of Lorre's Montresor, whose irreverent comments and unassuming attitude abruptly pull the rug out from under his highly respected opponent. Horror and humor can be an awkward cinematic mix, but in this enjoyable episode Lorre and Price succeed in finding a balance that contributes to the quirky and comic mood of the segment.

After their night of drunken camaraderie, Fortunato accompanies Montresor on his unsteady walk back home. The wine maven displays a mastery of the social graces as he makes small talk with the buxom wife of his inebriated host. After Montresor passes out for the night, sparks begin to fly between Fortunato and the put-upon Annabel. Days later, Montresor is once again at the tavern, boasting that the missus now freely gives him the money to stay out until the morning hours. When the barkeep inquires when this change in his wife's attitude took place, Montresor mentally relives the night of the wine tasting episode and begins to suspect marital infidelity. In a drunken fury, he storms out into the night. After Montresor confronts Annabel and learns of her plans to start a new life with Fortunato, the seeds of revenge become firmly planted.

Montresor's scheme is set in motion when Fortunato accepts his invitation to a private dinner party. Putting on a pretense of conviviality, Montresor offers his guest a "special" glass of amontillado, which is offered with a toast for long life and good

The unsuspecting Fortunato is drugged by the cunning Montresor.

health. "Right now, I have a better chance than you have," hints Montresor under his breath. All too late, Fortunato realizes he has been drugged and slumps to the floor. He awakens to find himself chained in the cellar where Montresor has begun to wall up the doomed lovers. When the final brick is set in place, the triumphant Montresor resumes his quest for his wife's concealed bounty. "Eureka!" he cries, when a broken flower pot reveals the mother lode.

As the tone of this episode turns increasingly dark, Lorre's performance takes on additional shades of menace. The shift in the actor's voice and facial expression when he become aware of his wife's duplicity is subtle yet convincing, as is his demonstration of explosive rage when he smashes his empty glass against the bar. Later, these emotions simmer just below the surface while Montresor plays the role of cordial host with Fortunato, the plans for his rival's demise already well underway. While entombing Fortunato and Annabel, Lorre adopts a disarmingly carefree tone as he expounds on his captives' inescapable fate. "Haven't I convinced you of my sincerity yet? I am genuinely dedicated to your destruction," Montresor chuckles, delighted by the success of his vengeful retribution. Lorre's casualness while delivering such lines makes his Montresor Herringbone a memorable caricature of evil in a shockingly carefree guise.

Back at his favorite watering hole, Montresor is in a festive mood, buying round after round for his boozing acquaintances. As he offers up yet another toast, he carelessly lets slip a reference to his wife's disappearance. After too much wine and too much celebration, he returns home, where he collapses upon the bed. A wonderfully

Montresor is terrorized by his wife's black cat.

ghoulish dream sequence follows in which Montresor has visions of Fortunato and Annabel breaking free from their standing tomb, stealing his head and tossing it about like a volleyball. Disturbed from this restless slumber, he awakens to face frightful alcoholic hallucinations that vanish with the flick of his hand. Suddenly, Montresor is confronted with an image that won't go away—a pair of gendarmes, who have come to inquire about his missing wife's whereabouts.

Montresor's look of apprehension belies his protest of innocence. Undaunted by his claim that his wife fled with a lover, the police initiate a search of the residence. As they descend to the cellar, Montresor begins to imagine the phantom-like voices of Fortunato and Annabel, beckoning for the police to come find them. Oblivious to the illusory cries, the constables continue their search, eventually giving up when the trail grows cold. Relieved by this turn of events, Montresor suddenly grows overconfident. "Where would I have hidden them… In that wall?" he gloats, pounding upon the fresh brick and mortar. Suddenly, from inside the makeshift crypt comes an unearthly cry—the ghostly, sustained meow of Annabel's pet cat, whom Montresor unknowingly imprisoned along with the adulterous lovers. As the police tear down the freshly sealed edifice, Montresor adopts a look of fatal resignation, knowing that his feline nemesis has become his undoing. The story concludes with an obligatory tag line from Poe—"I had walled up the black monster within the tomb."

As the segment approaches its denouement, Lorre's performance shifts from comic caricature to a study in guilt-induced paranoia. First come the hallucinations—in typically improbable AIP fashion, an iguana, an oversized snake and a tarantula—which

A charming pair of villains. Price and Lorre enjoyed each other's sense of humor.

Lorre dismisses in laughably casual fashion. Next come the authorities, whom the actor tries to dissuade with awkward and almost incoherent banter. When the voices of his murder victims begin to taunt him (due, no doubt, to the combination of a nasty hangover and an overactive conscience), Lorre visibly sweats bullets, fearful that his mental tormentors will somehow be overheard by the dutiful detectives. Finally comes the moment of horror as the accursed cat emits its fateful, accusatory cry. "You can hear it too?" Lorre asks meekly, hoping against hope that this might be just one more mental delusion. (In a sly touch, the feline becomes a supernatural surrogate for the tortured souls of Annabel and Fortunato, who were both quite affectionate with the animal.) Our final glimpse of Lorre's Montresor leaves us with the impression of a broken man, whose sense of remorse is based less on his heinous act than on the fact that his crime has been discovered.

Tales of Terror's "Black Cat" episode is fondly remembered by most cinema mavens as the highlight of this enjoyable film. In contrast to the derivative introductory tale and the effective but grim closing piece, the film's midsection is an agreeable exercise in costume horror spiced with a refreshing dash of gallows humor. By their nature, anthology formats are difficult to pull off in the horror genre; the abrupt shifts in story line often do irrefutable harm to the carefully built layers of mood and suspense so

Lorre's comedic abilities helped make the "Black Cat" sequence a favorite of viewers.

essential to cinema horror. But with its sly, tongue-in-cheek approach, this sequence registers a memorable impression in spite of its abbreviated running time.

Lorre's colorful performance is among the best of an inconsistent lot. Vincent Price, who stars is the film's three episodes, is his usual enjoyable, scenery chewing self. Aging character star Basil Rathbone also scores as the icy, manipulative mesmerist in the movie's closing segment. But as usual with AIP, the lesser roles fall on the unsteady shoulders of relative newcomers. Maggie Pierce and Leona Gage, who appear in "Morella," are typical of the pleasant-looking but modestly talented ingenues who graced the studio's low-budget efforts. Joyce Jameson displays some reasonably effective comic flair as Lorre's bubbly blonde wife in "The Black Cat," although the role is too lightweight to leave any lasting impression. The most effective distaff performance was turned in by Debra Paget, then approaching the end of an up-and-down Hollywood career, who still had sufficient charisma to bring the heroine role of "Valdemar" to life. The other supporting parts are staffed by interchangeable young performers who look and sound far too American to convincingly portray 19th-century character types.

The film's limitations are kept fairly well hidden by Roger Corman's competent direction. Creative editing and the use of single frame blow-ups as transitional devices between scenes help camouflage an austere budget and a deceptively small number

Lorre with Joyce Jameson who offers a little cheesecake in this studio publicity shot.

of sets. Camera placement is unobtrusive but effective; wide angle shots during the celebrated wine tasting contest give the viewer a chance to enjoy Vincent Price's exaggerated mugging and Peter Lorre's amused reaction in one continuous image. Montresor's disturbing dream sequence is shot with distorted, wide angle lenses, making the characters look like escapees from an amusement park fun house while also disguising the mannequin head that stood in for Peter Lorre's detached noggin. Curious (almost surreal) images are also incorporated into the mix, a trick that would later be employed in the climactic sorcerer's battle of 1963's *The Raven*. In spite of the studio's notoriously tight ways with a dollar, the imagination that went into AIP's Poe cycle reinforces Corman's reputation as a solid and resourceful filmmaker who could deliver quality work on the thrift.

Richard Matheson's screenplay for the film retains the essence of Poe's stories while toning down some of their darker elements. In the original short story version of "The Black Cat," the narrator first maims, then kills, the titular feline during a drunken fury. In a later fit of rage, he murders his wife while attempting to attack a nearly identical looking house pet, disposing of her body behind the now familiar cellar wall. In "The Cask of Amontillado," Poe's narrator enacts a similar demise for friend and fellow wine aficionado Fortunato over some unspecified insult. By depicting Montresor as a victim of cuckoldry, Matheson interjects a measure of audience empathy for the wine-loving rogue. The intentional vagueness of the original tales, which worked well in print, is also eliminated, and the powerfully destructive effects of alcoholism (a reflection, no doubt, of the author's personal struggles) undergoes a shift in tone to reflect the episode's newly added comic slant.

Although the comic elements of "The Black Cat" segment are certainly enjoyable, this approach also leaves the film open to criticism. It seems almost regrettable to waste this first significant teaming of Peter Lorre and Vincent Price in such potentially frivolous fashion (the actors had previously shared screen billing in 1957's *The Story of Mankind* and 1959's *The Big Circus*). The casting of Price as Italian wine impresario Fortunato is difficult to take seriously, as is the notable age discrepancy between Lorre and his on-screen spouse. Another incredulous feature of the film, noted by several reviewers, is the fact that Lorre demonstrates considerably more interest in the bottle than in his amply endowed Ms. Jameson. Such obvious chicanery threatens to diminish the legitimacy of what could have been an effective straight horror tale down to the level of a television variety show skit. Fortunately, these deficiencies are more than offset by the unrestrained theatrical bravo with which Lorre and Price enact their roles. As an added bonus, how appropriate it was for Vincent Price, by now well established as AIP's quintessential Poe heavy, to be on the receiving end of the story's over-the-top skullduggery.

It is interesting to note the change in Peter Lorre's physical appearance over the years and how his look affected his screen persona. In the early 1930s, the actor's youthful, corpulent appearance made him an uncanny choice for the disagreeable characters portrayed in his early films. The actor's girth lessened noticeably in the following decade, and his leaner, sleepy-eyed appearance complimented the meek, manipulative stature of his classic World War II era performances. By the 1950s, the weight had returned accompanied by the effects of age, creating a pompous, semi-comic impression. Not surprisingly, his appearances during this period gravitated toward less menacing fare, where he was frequently overshadowed by performers with larger roles and greater box-office appeal. If nothing else, *Tales of Terror* provided Lorre a renewed opportunity to portray the type of role for which he was still well suited.

Critical acceptance of *Tales of Terror* upon original release appeared to be contingent upon the reaction of individual reviewers to the horror genre in general. *The Hollywood Reporter* described the film as "a class picture… superior to anything in its category in years." *Variety*'s film reviewer expressed some reservations, calling the film "a heavy dose, even for the thrill-prone teenage set," and adding that the "Black Cat" segment "is too long, but as a mad caper it has its moments." A derisive opinion, meanwhile, was expressed by *The New York Times*, which labeled the release as "dull, absurd and trashy," adding that only Basil Rathbone's performance could be taken seriously. At a time when horror films were commonly dismissed as juvenile-oriented rubbish, it was no surprise that the more "proper" film critics automatically uplifted their nose when reviewing AIP's latest cinema shockfest.

Modern film reviews, more partial to the venerable horror film tradition, are inclined to look back at *Tales of Terror*, and Lorre's performance, with a favorable eye. *The Overlook Film Encyclopedia's* review of horror films, edited by Phil Hardy, noted the episode's "sardonic humor" and singled out Lorre's "superb moments" (although, curiously, it also expressed a preference for the "perfection" of the warmed-over Morella tale). *VideoHound*, in its *Cult Flicks and Trash Pics* collection, observed that "Lorre, who is the real star of this segment, has a fine time ad-libbing his way through his role." Leonard Maltin's *Movie and Video Guide*, which gives the film three stars, also commented on Lorre's Montresor, labeling his performance a "standout." Looking back from the present decade, in which the theatrical flourishes of old-school horror have disappeared without a trace from the video screen, *Tales of Terror* is no less than a glad celebration of this fondly remembered lost art form.

Although the film was only a so-so performer at the box office, it did prove to be influential in a somewhat modest way. The anthology format championed by *Tales of Terror* soon became a popular trend among fright filmmakers of the 1960s. Italian giallo director Mario Bava utilized the multiple story arrangement in 1963's *Black Sabbath*, while diminutive Amicus Studios (a small-time competitor to England's Hammer Studios) employed the format extensively in an ongoing series of low-budget horror anthologies. The creative change of pace offered by the film also provided a much needed shot in the arm for AIP's flagging Poe series. After the studio exhausted the Gothic/comic approach with *The Raven* and *The Comedy of Terrors*, Corman and company refocused their energies and rebounded with the acknowledged classics of the Poe cycle—1964's *The Masque of the Red Death* and 1965's *The Tomb of Ligeia*.

Thanks to its fortuitous casting, *Tales of Terror* had another happy consequence—the return to the horror genre of Hollywood's most distinctive character performers. To film fans of the 1960s, the appearances of Peter Lorre, Basil Rathbone, Lon Chaney, Jr. and Boris Karloff in AIP's Gothic costumers brought back fond memories of the enjoyable B-movie shockers from Tinseltown's golden and silver ages. And after a decade- long spate of horror films with heavy science fiction overtones (often peopled by anonymous actors costumed in rubber suits and Ping-Pong eyeballs), the return of a human element to horror film villainy was long overdue. This welcome trend in movie casting did have one unfortunate side effect; one cannot help but cringe when observing the ultra cheap, cinematic dreck that lay ahead for performers like Rathbone and John Carradine. But for AIP, the dramatic flair contributed by Lorre and his fellow cinema veterans contributes immensely to the believable, tongue-in-cheek atmosphere for which the Poe series is remembered.

And what impact did *Tales of Terror* have on the career of Peter Lorre? For starters, it gave the actor a foot in the door in AIP's ongoing series of fantasy and horror films, for which he would make repeated appearances in the remaining years of his life. In terms of his cinematic legacy, this brought Lorre back full circle to the genre that first brought him international acclaim. By pairing Lorre with Vincent Price, AIP created a memorable tandem team that rivaled the effectiveness of the Lorre-Sydney Greenstreet appearances of two decades prior. And for movie fans of the 1960s, *Tales of Terror* provided a new opportunity to appreciate the skills of this talented and versatile performer. Though the actor might well have disdained being identified with "monster movies," he must have certainly appreciated the minor but noticeable career resurgence that this film helped spark.

Fans of serious horror might take issue with *Tales of Terror*'s flimsily sketched story lines and less than solemn approach. Even within the context of AIP's highly regarded Poe series, the film is seldom referred to as more than a footnote. But it did successfully capture a moment in time when the power of the performer was an integral component of the horror film. And for Peter Lorre, it opened up a new avenue that would provide a colorful and fitting finale to his enduring cinematic career. For this alone, the film deserves to be remembered.

CREDITS: Executive Producers: James H. Nicholson and Samuel Z. Arkoff; Producer/ Director: Roger Corman; Screenplay: Richard Matheson; Based on Stories by Edgar Allan Poe; Cinematography: Floyd Crosby; Production Design/Art Director: Daniel Haller; Set Decorator: Harry Reif; Music: Les Baxter; Editor: Anthony Carras; Wardrobe: Marjorie Corso; Make-up: Lou LaCava; Assistant Director: Jack Bohrer

CAST: "Morella": Vincent Price (Locke); Maggie Pierce (Lenora); Leona Gage (Morella); Edmond Cobb (Coachman); "The Black Cat": Vincent Price (Fortunato); Peter Lorre (Montresor Herringbone); Joyce Jameson (Annabel); Wally Campo (Bartender): Alan DeWit (Chairman); John Hackett (Policeman); "The Case of M. Valdemar": Vincent Price (Valdemar); Basil Rathbone (Carmichael); Debra Paget (Helene); David Frankham (Dr. Elliot James); Scotty Brown (Servant)

REFERENCES

Hardy, Phil: *The Overlook Film Encyclopedia—Horror*, The Overlook Press, Woodstock, New York, 1994

Katz, Ephraim: *The Film Encyclopedia*, HarperCollins Publishers, New York, New York, 1994

Maltin, Leonard: *Leonard Maltin's 1996 Movie & Video Guide*, Penguin Books, New York, New York, 1995

Naha, Ed: *The Films of Roger Corman: Brilliance on a Budget*, Arco Publishing, New York, New York, 1982

Schwartz, Carol: *VideoHound's Complete Guide to Cult Flicks and Trash Pics*, Visible Ink Press, Detroit, Michigan, 1996

Williams, Lucy Chase: *The Complete Films of Vincent Price*, Citadel Press, Secaucus, New Jersey, 1995

Wright, Bruce Lanier: *Nightwalkers: Gothic Horror Movies—The Modern Era*, Taylor Publishing Company, Dallas, Texas, 1995

Youngkin, Stephen, James Bigwood and James Cabana: *The Films of Peter Lorre*, Citadel Press, Secaucus, New Jersey, 1982

THE RAVEN 1963 by Bryan Senn

> Peter knew every line of the script perfectly, but loved to invent his own, and sometimes his ad-libs were so humorous Corman let them stay in.
>
> —Vincent Price

When director Roger Corman's Poe anthology *Tales of Terror* earned close to $1.5 million in 1962, Corman and screenwriter Richard Matheson decided (in Corman's words) "to transform Poe's classic poem *The Raven* into a lighter comedy-horror project and use those two again." Those two, of course, were Vincent Price and Peter Lorre.

> Teamed for a second time with Price in a Poe thriller is the master thespian Peter Lorre as Dr. Bedlo, another role similar to his much talked-about portrayal of the drunken Montresor in "The Black Cat" segment of *Tales of Terror*.
>
> —*The Raven* pressbook

Nearly two decades prior to *The Raven* (in a 1944 interview), Peter Lorre espoused:

> Much film acting isn't really acting, no matter how successful it may be at the box office. Often it's a trick of personality, a theatrical gag. Dogs have been box-office bonanzas.

While always thoroughly professional, Lorre began to rely more and more on his "tricks of personality" as his career wore on. And Lorre had no better vehicle in which to show off said personality than *The Raven*. In Roger Corman, Lorre also had the perfect director to showcase his particular brand of spontaneous humor, since Corman (in the words of co-star Boris Karloff) "expects an actor to get on with it himself." And that is exactly what Peter Lorre did—in spades. Lorre tosses a quip here and an aside there so frequently that amusing ad-libs come thicker than raven droppings—of which raven-toting co-star Jack Nicholson bitterly complained. "The raven we used shit endlessly over everybody and everything," recalled Nicholson (in Roger Corman's autobiography *How I Made a Hundred Movies in Hollywood and Never Lost a Dime*). "It just shit endlessly. My whole right shoulder was constantly covered with raven shit."

Peter Lorre as Dr. Bedlo, a pitiful excuse for a wizard.

> This was one instance where the actors and the director made a funny script into an even funnier picture. —Vincent Price

Although AIP publicity called *The Raven* "the most terrifying combination of Edgar Allen [sic] Poe story and cast ever assembled," and advertised it as a straight horror film ("The Supreme Adventure in Terror!"), it turned out anything *but* straight. *The Raven* was the fifth Poe movie directed by Corman and the fourth written by Richard Matheson, who was desperate for a change of pace. "*The Raven* was fun," recounted Matheson in John Brosnan's *The Horror People*.

> The AIP executives had found out that the middle portion in *Tales of Terror*, which had been done for laughs, was very successful, so they decided to do a whole funny picture. Anyway, I couldn't have done another serious one. It would have been more than I could stand. I had to do them for laughs by then.

Bedlo tries to lure Craven (Vincent Price) to the castle of Scarabus.

"Once upon a midnight dreary, while I pondered, weak and weary..." intones Vincent Price's mellifluous voice as *The Raven* opens with the actor reciting the first stanza of the famous Poe poem. (This brief recitation, and the fact that the protagonist is pining over the "lost Lenore" [his dead wife], is about all the film takes from Poe.) The story proper (set sometime during the Middle Ages) begins with Dr. Erasmus Craven (Vincent Price), sorcerer extraordinaire, lamenting the loss of his beloved wife Lenore two years earlier. "Gently there came a rapping" at Craven's window and in steps "a stately raven." Said raven turns out to be more than he appears, for the bird is actually another magician, the bumbling, wine-loving Dr. Bedlo (Peter Lorre). Bedlo was turned into the black bird by Dr. Scarabus (Boris Karloff), the powerful and ruthless head of the "Brotherhood of Magicians." After Craven effects a cure for Bedlo's feathery enchantment, Bedlo relates that he'd seen Craven's long-dead Lenore (Hazel Court) at Scarabus' home. Accompanied by Craven's daughter Estelle (Olive Sturgess) and Bedlo's son Rexford (Jack Nicholson), the two magicians journey to Castle Scarabus to investigate. There Craven glimpses his lost love—very much alive and in cahoots with Scarabus (for whose power and patronage she'd faked her own death and left the unambitious Craven). It soon transpires that Scarabus has lured Craven to his castle in order to torture from him the secret of his "hand manipulation" magic, with Dr. Bedlo as a deceiving accomplice in the elaborate plot. Fortunately, Bedlo has a change of heart (particularly after Scarabus rewards Bedlo's services by turning him into a raven

Craven's groundskeeper, Grimes (William Baskin), wonders who conked him on the head as Bedlo and Estelle (Olive Sturgess) look on.

yet again) and frees the captive Craven in time for the two master magicians to engage in a magical "duel to the death."

> It was the biggest-looking Poe film to date.
>
> —Roger Corman

"I have always felt that *The Raven*, for a three-week shoot, is one of the more accomplished films I directed," wrote Corman in his autobiography. "[Art director] Danny Haller again created lavish-looking, stylized sets that gave the film great-looking production value for the money." Indeed he did. From the creepy cobwebbed Craven crypt to the great hall of Scarabus Castle (with its towering pillars, overpowering stone staircase and blazing brazier centerpiece), Haller's sets create a grandiose, otherworldly atmosphere for this comedic medieval-style fairy tale. Corman and cinematographer Floyd Crosby shoot to best advantage, utilizing varying angles and lighting to generate a sense of grandeur and wonder perfectly suited to the larger-than-life characters and scenario.

> Roger gave me one direction on that picture: "Try to be as funny as Lorre, Karloff and Price." I loved those guys. I sat around with Peter all the time. I was mad about him.
>
> —Jack Nicholson

While Lorre's mad ad-libbing amused the cast and crew, Karloff was used to acting according to the script and was often nonplussed by Lorre's antics.

Undoubtedly, *The Raven*'s greatest asset is its cast—even beyond the three "Grand Masters of Horror" headliners. Though supporting players Olive Sturgess and Jack Nicholson seem lightweight and out-of-place amid the opulent surroundings (with the 26-year-old Nicholson's wooden demeanor and stilted delivery arguably making this his worst-ever performance), the beauteous Hazel Court is both desirable and despicable as the conniving, power-hungry, alluringly evil Lenore.

"I think *The Raven* was my favorite picture and the most fun because I was able to work with three such talented giants of horror films," recalled Court to interviewer Mark Miller.

> Peter Lorre and Vincent Price were having a sort of competition to see who had the best stories to tell, the same way they were vying on the screen for performing the best magical tricks.
>
> Boris Karloff was also in the film and he was a great charmer. So was Peter. In fact, Peter had great sex appeal. Many actresses who have been interviewed about him agree that when Peter talked to you, it was as though you were the only person in the world. He would laugh and seem to be interested in whatever it was you were saying. He was very intelligent and had a fine mind.

Grimes attacks Bedlo as Craven lies unconscious in the background.

> Peter, Boris and Vincent were wonderfully close friends, and then, of course, Jack Nicholson was also in the film. He was very amusing, but I never had an inkling that he would become what he is now. It's funny. I always think of Jack Nicholson as a little boy. In fact, when I look at him now, all I see is this charming little boy who popped around the set.

The undisputed star attraction of *The Raven*, however, is that "Triumvirate of Terror"—Vincent Price, Boris Karloff and Peter Lorre. Price is as charming as he's ever appeared on film, and he makes his self-effacing and kindly Dr. Craven a likable and engaging character. Karloff is insincerity personified, as he deceives with wickedly false smiles and empty flatteries while hatching his devious plots. And Lorre… well, Lorre is the comedic glue that binds it all together. His disarmingly garrulous and irascible demeanor both contrasts and complements Price and Karloff's flowery, Old World characters. Lorre's unpretentiousness takes all the starch out of the stuffiness around him, creating some wonderfully comedic moments. And he has all the best lines, most of them of his own devising.

Bedlo, Craven and Estelle are held prisoner by Scarabus.

> Peter loved to make jokes and ad-lib during the filming. He loved to invent; improvisation was part of his training in Germany.
>
> —Vincent Price

In an interview with Gregory J.M. Catsos (published in *Filmfax* magazine), Vincent Price recounted what it was like working with Peter Lorre:

> In one scene we had together in *The Raven*, I said, "Shall I ever see Lenore again?" And Peter said, "How the hell should I know? What am I—a fortune teller?" It was a marvelous ad-lib.

Indeed it was, and the first of many. Soon after, when the now half-man, half-bird Bedlo follows Craven into the dusty family crypt (to secure a lock of "dead man's hair" that will complete his transformation), Lorre observes, "Hard place to keep clean, huh?"—while daintily dusting at the casket with his feathers. Later, when Bedlo spies a rendering of Lenore in Craven's study, he asks, "What's the picture of that woman doing here?" "That woman, sir," answers an offended Craven, "was my wife." Lorre's face splits into a disarming grin as he snickers, "Left you, huh?" When Craven next leads Bedlo into the hall where Lenore's coffin resides like a shrine, Craven solemnly

Lorre engages in some wonderful comedy in *The Raven*.

states, "I keep her here." To this Lorre shoots back, "Where else?" Then, when Craven and his cohorts enter Scarabus' massive and imposing castle, Lorre sardonically quips, "Cozy little place, huh?"

Lorre engages in some wonderful physical comedy as well, taking a pratfall when Price steps on the back of his voluminous cloak (and deadpanning, "It's a little large isn't it?"), trying on an assortment of amusing hats and even using his cloak like a bullfighter's cape to fend off a (possessed) ax-wielding servant, acting like some rotund pixie-turned-matador.

Lorre seems unhappy with his raven costume in this posed shot.

> Peter kept everyone on their toes, myself included. He would just begin to improvise unexpectedly. Vincent was always willing to play along with it but Boris, who was very methodical in terms of his craft, was a bit befuddled. Amused, but befuddled...
>
> —Roger Corman

Midway through the film, when Bedlo challenges Scarabus to a duel of magic, the diminutive Bedlo begins by waving a magician's wand in front of his foe while intoning Latin incantations. Scarabus simply blows on the wand, causing it to go limp. Lorre looks at the flaccid wand and says, exasperated, "Oh you—you dirty old man." At this, Karloff makes a disgusted face—a face which probably reflected his feelings of annoyance at Lorre's frequent ad-libs, for the septuagenarian actor "wanted to stick to the script; he didn't like ad-libbing" (as reported by Vincent Price). Fortunately, Karloff held the minority opinion, and Lorre's ad-libs stayed.

"Peter ad-libbed his way through *The Raven*," wrote AIP head Sam Arkoff in his autobiography *Flying Through Hollywood by the Seat of My Pants*.

> It would have been a waste of time to attempt to restrain him, so after a while, we didn't even try. Lorre played the raven—a sorcerer whom Boris

This Gruesome Threesome aren't very terrifying as they share a laugh on the set.

> Karloff had partially transformed into a bird. And Peter sometimes found it hard to keep to the script while dressed like an oversized black bird with four-foot-long wings.
>
> [Peter was] a truly extemporaneous actor who could improvise beautifully. He didn't spend much time learning his lines but he knew his great strength was the vitality and humor and energy he brought to his scenes.
>
> —Roger Corman

While he took a light-hearted approach to this serio-comic take on Edgar Allan Poe, Lorre took the author and his works very seriously indeed. According to the October 8, 1962 edition of the *Hollywood Reporter*, "Lorre, Edgar Allan Poe fan and expert, called for a minute of silence yesterday on the Producers Studio set of *The Raven* in memory of the death of the great writer 113 years ago. Lorre then recalled briefly the genius of the author for his co-stars, Corman and the AIP production crew."

> He looked frightfully funny, like a chubby little black bird. Delighted the whole crew.
>
> —Boris Karloff

An impromptu marshmallow roast as the trio pose for this promotional shot.

"Of all the varied motion pictures with settings of every conceivable time and place for which I have designed costumes," wrote costume designer Marjorie Corso in an AIP publicity piece,

> *The Raven* presented me with my greatest challenge... My overall approach in *The Raven* was to create the costume to fit both the personality, physical makeup and role of the actors... Peter Lorre turned out to be my biggest problem, not only because of his height and weight but due to his role which calls for him to be half-man, half-raven. His costume had to match both his physical makeup and the grim aspect of the bird. My solution was to have Mr. Lorre resemble the bird as much as possible without appearing ridiculous. Naturally, black had to be the dominant color of everything he wore, from hat to huge wings and cloak. His hat turned out to be the key part of the raven cos-

> tume—its peaked front with its resemblance to the bird's beak does much to create the illusion of part man-part bird.

When in the guise of part man-part bird, Lorre had to wear huge four-foot wings. "It took three men over two weeks," claimed Corso, "to properly assemble over 10 pounds of [dyed coque] feathers (that's almost 50,000 feathers) so that they would look like huge raven's wings and could be used as hands." Corso even included a tail for Lorre, "which was put on at first as a joke. However, the result was so realistic and appropriate that we left it on."

> Should make more money in a week at one first-run house than Edgar Allan Poe made in his lifetime.
> —*The Hollywood Reporter*

Costing $350,000, *The Raven* reportedly earned over $1.4 million in rentals, making it a big financial success for AIP and inspiring them to continue in the horror-comedy vein with *The Comedy of Terrors* (whose much poorer box-office showing scotched AIP's plans as promptly as *The Raven* had spawned them).

The critics reacted positively to *The Raven* as well. *The Hollywood Reporter*'s James Powers was impressed: "Price, Lorre and Karloff perform singly and in tandem like what they are, three seasoned pros who can take a gentle burlesque and play it to the end of its value without stretching it past the entertainment point. They are performances, in their way, that are virtuoso."

Variety also felt it worthwhile: "Edgar Allan Poe might turn over in his grave at this nonsensical adaptation of his immortal poem, but audiences will find the spooky goings-on a cornpop of considerable comedic dimensions… Price makes his theatricalism pay off. Karloff plays it smooth. Lorre is almost cute."

Newsweek felt that, "Of all the horror pictures, *The Raven* flaps the wildest wings," while *Time* called it, "A sappy little parody of a horror picture cutely calculated to make the children scream with terror while their parents scream with glee."

Britain's *Kinematograph Weekly* concluded, "The high good humour with which this film takes the mickey out of Poe and itself cannot fail to make it a favorite support. Three of the film world's finest exponents of horror, Vincent Price, Peter Lorre, and Boris Karloff, get all the fun possible out of a funny idea."

> The HORROR BEGAN at MIDNIGHT!
> —ad line for *The Raven*

In addition to the usual "midnight screening" and "bravest boy and/or girl" contest (with the winner to sit alone in the theater watching *The Raven* after midnight), AIP came up with a few unusual tie-ins (including a *Raven* paperback and comic book) and seat-selling slants. "Offer free admission to see *The Raven* for anyone who brings a real raven to the theater," suggested the pressbook. No doubt *that* wouldn't have sat too well with the theater clean-up crew.

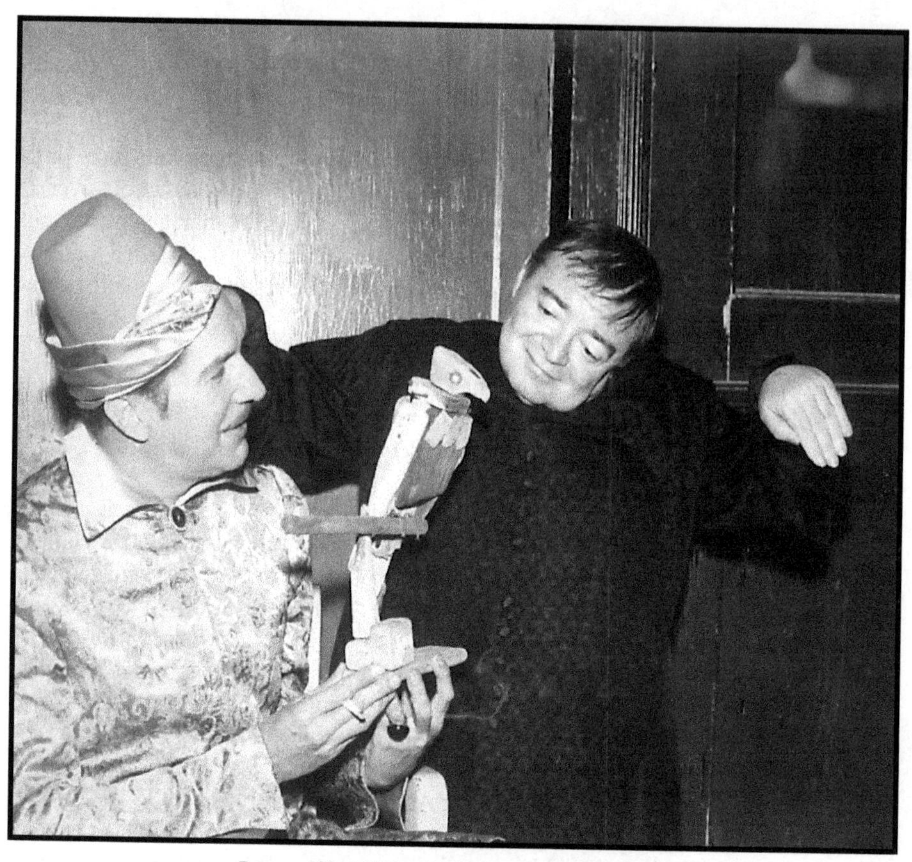

Lorre offers Price his best raven imitation.

> Because of typecasting, [Peter] was unhappy at the end of his career.
> —Vincent Price

In early 1963, Peter Lorre and Boris Karloff made a series of personal appearances at New York theaters showing *The Raven* (resulting in a first week's gross of a whopping $325,000 in the 80 New York houses showing the film). By his own admission, Lorre enjoyed these outings, remarking that he was enormously happy to be appearing before live audiences again. Privately, things were not so cheerful, for about this time Lorre separated from his third wife, Anna.

"Lorre was a likable fellow," wrote Arkoff, "but he was also a troubled, sensitive man. His marriage had disintegrated, he didn't see his daughter as much as he would have liked, he lived by himself in a modest apartment on Hollywood Boulevard and he didn't really enjoy doing the horror roles he was being offered."

In addition, Hazel Court recalled to interviewer Tom Weaver that:

> Peter Lorre was not well at all on that picture. I think his heart was bad—he perspired all the time,

and his eyes were always teary. But nothing would
hold him back, he was a wonderful pro.

Due to the success of *Tales of Terror* and *The Raven*, Peter Lorre was contracted by AIP to star in eight more of their films over the next four years. Sadly, he would only appear in two (*The Comedy of Terrors* and [in a brief cameo] *Muscle Beach Party*) before his death from a cerebral hemorrhage in 1964.

He was a very funny man.
—Vincent Price

During the shooting of *The Raven*, the late film historian William K. Everson visited the set and took his three-year-old daughter along with him. "One of the supporting players," recounted Everson in *Castle of Frankenstein* magazine, "in grotesque makeup as a decaying corpse, came lumbering out of the men's room. My daughter Bambi, then three years old, was much impressed. Used to King Kong, Dracula and the Frankenstein monster, and rather fond of them, she was quite excited at the prospect of seeing a real monster close up. 'Is that a *good* monster or a *bad* monster?' she asked. Looking around him to make sure that no-one was listening—although I'm sure this was done for effect, as he certainly never cared what he said or who heard him say it—Lorre informed her, "Oh it's a *bad* monster. There are *no* good monsters at American-International."

Fortunately, there were good *actors* at American-International, and Peter Lorre, ad-libs and all, was one.

CREDITS: Executive Producers: James H. Nicholson and Samuel Z. Arkoff; Producer-Director: Roger Corman; Screenplay: Richard Matheson (Suggested by the Poem by Edgar Allan Poe); Art Director: Daniel Haller; Photography: Floyd Crosby; Special Effects: Pat Dinga; Editor: Ronald Sinclair; Music: Les Baxter; Set Decorator: Harry Reif; Costumes: Marjorie Corso; Make-up: Ted Coodley; Raven Trainer: Moe Disesso; Music Coordinator: Al Simms; Sound: John Bury & Gene Corso; Hairstyles: Betty Pedretti; Production Supervisor: Bartlett A. Carre; Unit Manager: Robert Agnew; Assistant Director: Jack Bohrer; Pathe Color; Panavision; Distributed by American-International Pictures/Alta Vista Productions; 86 minutes

CAST: Vincent Price (Dr. Erasmus Craven), Peter Lorre (Dr. Adolphus Bedlo), Boris Karloff (Dr. Scarabus), Hazel Court (Lenore Craven), Jack Nicholson (Rexford Bedlo), Olive Sturgess (Estelle Craven), Connie Wallace (Maidservant), William Baskin (Grimes), Aaron Saxon (Gort), Jim Jr. (Raven)

THE COMEDY OF TERRORS
1964
by Bryan Senn

YOUR FAVORITE CREEPS TOGETHER AGAIN! —ad line

"Working with [Peter] never failed to fulfill the seventh and perhaps most sacred sense—the sense of fun." —Vincent Price delivering the eulogy at Peter Lorre's funeral, March 26, 1964

When producer-director Roger Corman and screenwriter Richard Matheson began injecting humor into their period horror films (first with the omnibus *Tales of Terror* and its comedic segment "The Black Cat," then with the full-length comedy of *The Raven*), American-International Pictures took notice—at least they did after seeing the healthy box-office receipts. After this, AIP decided to give its horror films "more production values and a comedy slant in keeping with current audience response" (as announced by *The Hollywood Reporter* in September 1963). To this end, the company procured term contracts or multipicture commitments from Vincent Price, Boris Karloff, Elsa Lanchester, Basil Rathbone and Peter Lorre, "all with the talent and stature to impart class and prestige to chill-and-thrill entertainment." (According to the *Reporter*, AIP planned to star Lorre and Lanchester as "lovers" in a series of such films [a rather odd concept to be sure, but one pregnant with all sorts of bizarre possibilities], starting with a production called *It's Alive*. Lorre's unexpected death in early 1964 put the kibosh on said plans.)

The Comedy of Terrors, the first of AIP's all-out horror-comedies, went into production on September 4, 1963 at Producers Studio under the working title *Graveside Story* (a moniker AIP later used for the film when it reissued *The Comedy of Terrors* in 1965 on a double bill with *The End of the World*—a re-titled *Panic in Year Zero!*). While the "comedy slant" was definitely there, AIP must have been saving the "more production values" for a future project, since *Comedy* carried an even smaller price tag than the Corman/Poe pictures that inspired it. The 15-day shooting schedule and tight budget (Director Jacques Tourneur even reused the graveyard set from *The Premature Burial*) meant that there was little time for such luxuries as retakes. In one scene, for instance, Waldo Trumbull (Vincent Price) and Felix Gillie (Peter Lorre) are creeping up a staircase and Trumbull steps on his underling's hand. At this, Lorre exclaims, "My foot!—uh—*your* foot, my *fingers*!" (Lorre's blunder—and amusing recovery—actually makes this otherwise mundane moment rather amusing.)

"The premise for *The Comedy of Terrors* was really very funny," explained star Vincent Price to interviewer Lawrence French.

Felix (Peter Lorre) and Waldo Trumbull (Vincent Price) search for a new customer.

> It shows you how simple comedy is. It's about a family of out-of-work undertakers. Now what do you do? You kill somebody! So you kill the richest man in town, who was Basil [Rathbone], and you have the most expensive funeral. That's all the plot was.

Undertaker's assistant Felix Gillie in *The Comedy of Terrors* was the last substantial film role Peter Lorre played before his death in early 1964 (the actor appeared in Jerry Lewis' *The Patsy* after this, but only in a cameo capacity). The vehicle was a fitting enough swan song—at least in terms of its title, since Lorre's career was based in large part on *Terror* performances (much to his dismay), even though he had a real affinity for *Comedy*. Sadly, like so many of his movie assignments, the part of the meek, bumbling mortician's helper served the actor poorly (and was a significant step down from his feisty, tippling sorcerer of the previous year's *The Raven*). While he managed to slip in a few of his trademark quips, the script (which gives the best lines to top-billed Vincent Price) and direction (which relies too heavily on slapstick humor) frequently wastes Lorre's talent and personality.

In a small New England town sometime before the turn of the century, underhanded undertaker Waldo Trumbull (Price) has hit on hard times after marrying into a thriving

Lorre as Trumbull's mild-mannered assistant Felix Gillie put his comedic talents to good use in *The Comedy of Terrors*.

mortuary business. Trumbull loathes his beautiful wife, Amaryllis (Joyce Jameson), doddering father-in-law (Boris Karloff) and even his mild-mannered, bumbling assistant, Felix Gillie (Lorre), a former burglar on the lam from the law. In fact, Trumbull seems to be fond of only two things—money and the bottle. When business is slow, Trumbull (with the aid of the reluctant Gillie) drums up new clients via murder. Even this doesn't do the trick, since the widow of his latest patron/victim skips town without paying. Drastic measures are needed, since Trumbull's boorish landlord, Mr. Black (Basil

Rathbone), is threatening eviction for non-payment of back rent. (Boris Karloff was originally cast in this larger role of Mr. Black, but the 75-year-old actor, suffering from arthritis, could not manage the physical action the part required, and the more robust Basil Rathbone switched roles with him.) Hence, Trumbull sets his sinister sights on Black himself. When they break into his house, Black (who loves to quote Shakespeare) obligingly drops dead of an apparent heart attack. The "corpse" revives (Black only suffers from catalepsy) in the mortuary basement, however, and (understandably) protests such treatment. After another cataleptic spell (and a whack on the head), Trumbull manages to keep Black in the coffin long enough to have him interred. But when Black awakens once more and is released from his crypt by a terrified night watchman (Joe E. Brown in an amusing cameo), the now-deranged, Shakespeare-spouting Black takes an ax to the house of Trumbull, resulting in a comical free-for-all that includes a sword fight, strangulation and even some mistakenly administered poison.

Studio portrait taken around the time of *The Comedy of Terrors*.

In 1963 Peter Lorre remarked, "I'm associated with horror movies, but I've only done one, *The Beast with Five Fingers*. I don't want to go down in history as a monster. I never played a frog that swallowed a city or something like that." He added that he disliked horrific films, particularly those that pandered "to the sadistic emotions of the audience by showing scenes of torture, whipping, etc." While his notion that he'd

Although ill during filming, Lorre still managed to bring some spark of life to Felix.

only made one horror movie (discounting such efforts as *Mad Love* [1935], *Invisible Agent* [1942] and *Tales of Terror* [1962]) can be put down to a certain rancor regarding the path his career took, Lorre's final genre entry was certainly much more focused on humor than horror (though not entirely successful at either).

Suspense and noir specialist Jacques Tourneur (*Cat People* [1942], *I Walked with a Zombie* [1943], *The Leopard Man* [1943], *Out of the Past* [1947], *Berlin Express* [1948], *Curse of the Demon* [1956], many others) seems an unlikely candidate to helm a farcical comedy, and the choice indeed turned out to be a rather unfortunate one. While Tourneur's direction is competent, and he generates some appropriately macabre mood at times (particularly in the graveyard sequences), his periodic injection of slapstick comedy and reliance on physical humor jars harshly with his penchant for atmosphere and leisurely build-ups. Richard Matheson claimed that AIP hired Tourneur only on his insistence. "I loved Jacques Tourneur's early movies," noted Matheson to *Filmfax*'s Matthew R. Bradley, "and thought he turned *The Comedy of Terrors* into a very amusing picture." The writer (who penned such classic genre films as *The Incredible Shrinking Man* [1957], *House of Usher* [1960], *The Pit and the Pendulum* [1961], *Burn Witch Burn* [1962], *Duel* [1971], *The Night Stalker* [1971], *The Legend of Hell House* [1973] and *Somewhere in Time* [1980]) numbers *The Comedy of Terrors* among his favorite produced screenplays. Not surprising, since whatever humor can be found in this *Comedy* is due more to Matheson's dialogue and what the actors do with it than to any directorial touches or pacing.

Tourneur's approach to comedy obviously ran to the hit-them-over-the-head school of thought, as he so frequently injects slapstick humor into the proceedings that one almost expects Lorre to come out with a few "nyuk, nyuk, nyuk"s before the night is through. (Fortunately, Matheson's genuinely witty dialogue deflects this trend and takes the comedy quotient to a more sophisticated level.) Tourneur uses speeded-up photography (complete with Silent era-style piano music) and a plethora of "zany" physical gags to hammer his point home that this is indeed a horror-COMEDY. He even has the *cat* (played by the legendary feline thespian Rhubarb) get in on the act by including a shot of Cleopatra (the cat) swallowing—complete with audible gulp on the soundtrack—when Trumbull makes one of his frequent poisoning threats. Time and again Tourneur returns to Rhubarb for a feline reaction in an attempt to wring a cheap laugh out of the moment. It all becomes a bit tiresome.

Actress Joyce Jameson was unimpressed with her *Comedy of Terrors* boss, recalling in *Cinefantastique* magazine: "[Tourneur] was very fierce and dogmatic about the way he wanted scenes played in comparison to Roger Corman [for whom Jameson worked in *Tales of Terror*], who let us do just about anything we wanted. We had established a wonderful rapport [with Corman]. We seemed to pick up on each other's ways of working. I think that had Roger Corman directed *Comedy of Terrors* it would have been faster-paced, lighter. It seemed like the heavy hand of Jacques Tourneur, along with the illness of Peter, gave the picture a feeling of heaviness. Even Vincent was over-acting, which he didn't do in *Tales of Terror*."

"Working on *Comedy of Terrors* was a lot of fun," enthused Richard Matheson in John Brosnan's *The Horror People*. "We had Boris Karloff, Peter Lorre, Basil Rathbone and Vincent Price. They were all very charming, marvelous people and it really was a delightful experience just talking with them on the set. They loved doing *Comedy of Terrors*. I remember the first luncheon we all went out to, and they were looking forward to doing the picture."

Lorre gives his typical devilish smile during *The Comedy of Terrors*.

Vincent Price agreed, commenting on his three fellow "horror stars": "They were all divine people, with great senses of humor. We used to sit around and say very seriously, 'How can we scare the little devils!' We'd say, 'Let's do this, let's do that, let's do the other thing.' We had a wonderful time."

Peter Lorre looks much older in *Comedy* than he did in *The Raven*, made only one year earlier, and the enthusiasm (and ad-libs) so prevalent in *The Raven* are far less evident here.

Richard Matheson remembers Lorre as being sweet and funny.

(The frequent and obvious use of a double [stunt veteran Harvey Parry] in a grotesque Lorre mask doesn't help matters.) Only once or twice does anything resembling Lorre's legendary ad-libs arise. One occurs when Trumbull agonizes over having to part with his one good casket (after having used this same coffin for 13 years) because Black is interred in a crypt rather than buried, thwarting the unctuous undertaker's modus operandi of burying the body while keeping the box. "I wonder what *idiot* ever thought of putting bodies in a crypt instead of in the ground where they belong," gripes Trumbull. At this, Lorre (sniffing a flower from a funeral wreath) quips, "Yeah, and they fertilize plants too." Here, an obviously amused Price (the flicker of a smile at the corner of his mouth) looks shocked and admonishes, "What a terrible thing to say; shut up!"

The only other glimmer of improvisation comes when Gillie and Amaryllis drunkenly celebrate the influx of money after Black's "death." With both of them literally under the table, Gillie professes his love for her, but the moralistic Amaryllis only answers sadly, "Forebear, Felix, forebear." Lorre's answer, "I don't know what that word means, but I can't take it any longer!" smacks of his spontaneous humor.

Vincent Price receives all the best dialogue (some of it quite clever), and he's obviously enjoying himself, infusing the erudite but black-hearted Trumbull with his trademark buttery charm and enthusiasm. Lorre, on the other hand, seldom becomes truly animated, though on one or two occasions his impish humor does manage to shine through. When Black first revives from his cataleptic trance, he points an accusing finger at Gillie and shouts, "You!" At this, a panicked Lorre squeaks "Not me!" and cowers comically. Later, Trumbull and Gillie sit atop the coffin from which Black is trying to escape, holding down the lid as it bounces with each push. Gillie comments, "Poor man, in his condition he certainly has a lot of energy," as he rides the coffin like a bucking bronco. Lorre's deadpan delivery makes the most of the line. But these are the exceptions rather than the rule, and, while he occasionally delivers his dialogue with a bit of his old flair, for the most part Lorre just seems tired.

"Lorre was so sweet and funny," remembered Matheson.

> The fact that he mangled all my dialogue and just came out with some approximation of what I had written—ordinarily that infuriates me, but with him, you just let it go. He would tell me how Sydney Greenstreet used to go absolutely ape over it, because he had stage training, and every line was exact. Even Price told me he would always do my lines word for word. That was the thing about American-International's pictures—although they weren't brilliantly done, they always did my dialogue word for word, except for Lorre. The others had to learn to adapt to his unexpected rejoinders.

AIP staff composer Les Baxter, who provided the musical score for *The Comedy of Terrors*, related to interviewer Tom Weaver:

> Peter Lorre was a wonderfully delightful person, and quite comic. They could have used his comic talent very much more than they did. He was used in horror films, I guess, because he looked a little strange, and had a strange way of pronouncing his speeches, but he had a very pixie sense of humor that went along with it. He was somewhat amusing in *The Raven*, although not as much as he could have been, and in *Comedy of Terrors* he was good.

Critical reaction to *The Comedy of Terrors* was (at best) mixed. *Variety* wrote, "As deliciously grotesque a gallery of histrionic rogues as could conceivably be assembled on one Hollywood sound stage was herded together for this project, making the result all the more disappointing." The *Los Angeles Times'* Philip K. Scheuer simply labeled the film "a monstrosity" in a review headed "Aging Actors Chew Scenery." Alton Cook of *The New York World-Telegram* complained that, "the story is one of the thinnest ever to find its way to a movie screen," and that it "...sends a bunch of horror and mystery

Price, Karloff, Rathbone and Lorre made beautiful music together.

actors off on a childish spree which may be giving them a lot of fun but does nothing for their audience." In the minority was John G. Houser of *The Los Angeles Herald Examiner*, who called it "one of the funniest satires ever made on 'horror' movies" and felt that "Boris Karloff, Peter Lorre, Vincent Price and Basil Rathbone… score in every reel." More common was the sentiment of *The New York Times*' Howard Thompson, who dismissed the film as "a musty, rusty bag of tricks rigged as a horror farce." Of Lorre, Thompson only noted that he "waddles through the picture like a stuffed owl."

Though it did make money, *The Comedy of Terrors* was less successful at the box office than *The Raven*, a result blamed on both the title ("there was a very definite antipathy toward combining Shakespeare and a murder story in a title," opined Price, "'comedy' and 'terror' didn't go together at that time") and the advertising's emphasis on humor. Consequently, AIP scrapped any plans for further horror-comedy installments.

In March 1964, three months after the release of *The Comedy of Terrors*, Peter Lorre remarked, "I am the last of the actors of my era. I am all alone, and it makes me sad." A few days later he was discovered by his housekeeper, dead from a stroke at the age of 59.

Vincent Price delivered the eulogy at Peter Lorre's funeral. In it, he termed Lorre a "facemaker." Explained Price:

> I used the expression because it was Peter's definition of actors. He was being facetious, of course, but he thought of actors as people who made faces for a living. And he had a face to make."

He did indeed, and the cinematic world is all the richer for it.

While Lorre's performance in *The Comedy of Terrors* was far from his best (with the same being said for the vehicle itself), it's still good to see the fast-failing actor surrounded one last time by his friends and fellow "bogey-men." And if nothing else, the film's title serves as a fitting epitaph for a facemaker who for over 30 years provided his audience with both chills and chuckles.

POST SCRIPT: A real-life Comedy of Terrors occurred six months after the film's release when, on June 24, 1964, Larry McLean (a 20-year-old, wheelchair-bound University of Oklahoma student) was arrested and charged with leading a secret cult that vandalized churches and planned to steal the body of their idol, Peter Lorre, in order to restore it to life. While this macabre plot was nipped in the bud, the actor's ashes were stolen three decades later and have yet to be recovered. Undoubtedly, Peter would have thought it all a deliciously macabre joke.

CREDITS: Director: Jacques Tourneur; Producers: James H. Nicholson and Samuel Z. Arkoff; Editor/Co-Producer: Anthony Carras; Associate Producer/Screenplay: Richard Matheson; Photography: Floyd Crosby; Music: Les Baxter; Music Coordinator: Al Simms; Production Designer and Art Director: Daniel Haller; Set Decorator: Harry Reif; Assistant Director: Robert Agnew; Special Effects: Pat Dinga; Sound: Don Rush; Costumes: Marjorie Corso; Make-up: Carlie Taylor; Hairdresser: Betty Pedretti; Production Manager: Joseph Wonder; Production Assistant: Jack Cash; Properties: Karl Brainard; Special Photographic Effects: Butler-Glouner; Released January 20, 1964 by American-International Pictures

CAST: Vincent Price (Waldo Trumbull), Peter Lorre (Felix Gillie), Boris Karloff (Amos Hinchley), Joyce Jameson (Amaryllis Trumbull), Beverly Hills (Mrs. Phipps), Basil Rathbone (John F. Black), Joe E. Brown (Cemetery Keeper), Rhubarb (Cleopatra the cat), Alan DeWitt, Buddy Mason (Mr. Phipps), Douglas Williams, Linda Rogers (Phipps' Maid), Luree Holmes [daughter of James H. Nicholson] (Black's Servant), Paul Barselow [unbilled] (Riggs), Harvey Parry [unbilled] (Stunt Double for Lorre)

MYSTERY IN THE AIR: PETER LORRE ON THE RADIO
by Gary D. Rhodes

Bela Lugosi, Boris Karloff, Vincent Price, Lon Chaney, Jr., Basil Rathbone, George Zucco, Lionel Atwill...all of the great horror and mystery film stars of the 1930s, 1940s and 1950s possessed voices heard over the radio waves of yesteryear. Movie theaters were a venue where—in a pre-television and -video era—audience members left with only fading memories and emotions; fan magazines offered only still photographs, and only rarely of those actors associated with horror. But radio was different. For years it was the forum through which horror film stars regularly crept into thousands of homes across the country. The sheer turn of the radio dial opened the door to terror, and behind that door—along with a host of others—stood Peter Lorre.

Like most stars of the 1930s, Lorre began his radio career by working on variety programs. Though horror programs were on the air in the 1930s (e.g., *The Witch's Tale*), they usually did not feature film personalities as guest stars. Indeed, many movie stars of all types during the Great Depression did not perform on radio at all, and when they did they often commanded exorbitant fees. In exchange, they were most commonly heard on variety shows that combined short skits—both comedic and dramatic—with commentary by the show's host and music by the show's orchestra.

For example, on May 7, 1936, Lorre debuted on U.S. radio with *The Fleishmann Hour*, which starred Rudy Vallee and His Connecticut Yankees. And on December 26, 1938, Lorre took time to guest star on Al Jolson's program to help promote his Mr. Moto film series. The following year, he appeared on the *Texaco Star Theatre* (October 4, 1939) with Fredric March.

Even into the 1940s, Lorre continued to headline on variety shows, including *Kay Kyser's Kollege of Musical Knowledge* (September 25, 1940) with Boris Karloff and Bela Lugosi; the horror trio were plugging their film with Kyser, *You'll Find Out*. Two years later, Lorre performed on *Radio's Readers Digest* (Jan. 31, 1943) in a sketch called "Education for Death." On March 4, 1945, it was the *Philco Radio Hall of Fame* with Paul Whiteman; other guests that same week included Beatrice Lillie, Jo Stafford, Bert Lahr and Artie Shaw. Lorre's skit consisted of an abbreviated version of Poe's "The Tell-Tale Heart." In 1946, Lorre was on Dinah Shore's program, and a year later (November 12, 1947) he guested on *Philco Radio Time* with Bing Crosby. He even appeared on *Spotlight Revue* in the late 1940s, the program featuring Spike Jones and his novelty band, the City Slickers.

To help in the war effort, Lorre also performed on numerous variety programs broadcast to troops stationed overseas. These usually co-starred him with various non-dramatic actors and musical talent. On *G.I. Journal*, for example, Lorre worked with Bing Crosby, Jo Stafford and Lynn Bari. On *Command Performance*, Lorre played in a skit with Sydney Greenstreet. And circa 1943-4, he guested on the *Stage Door Canteen* radio program. Generally speaking, stars were on wartime programs like these without salary or compensation of any kind; their time was donated out of kindness and gratitude for U.S. servicemen.

Lorre and wife Celia in their home in 1935.

As a costar of several dramatic films of note, Lorre also appeared on radio adaptations of those same movies. Most notably, he worked on *Lady Ester's Screen Guild Players* in *The Maltese Falcon*, heard over CBS on September 20, 1943. Bogart, Astor, Greenstreet and Lorre all reprised their famous film roles. Truman Bradley announced and Wilbur Hatch conducted the orchestra.

Comedy was another area in which Lorre excelled on the radio. Even more than Karloff and Lugosi, Lorre possessed a wonderful sense of timing for humor and jokes. Among other programs, he worked on *The Fred Allen Show* on January 3, 1943. "I'm just a lovable little guy trying to get a head!" he told the audience, which was of course followed by much laughter. On *Duffy's Tavern* with Ed "Archie" Gardner (October 19, 1943), Lorre joked around in a skit called " The Case of the Missing Salami." He asks Archie, "Please think of me as a sweet lovable man who makes certain people faint. A sort of a nonmusical Frank Sinatra." As usual in a comedic setting, his presence caused many laughs—most of which stemmed from his roots in mystery and horror.

During Fanny Brice's 1945 absence from her popular comedy program *Baby Snooks*, Lorre—along with other stars like Eddie Cantor, Robert Benchley and Sydney Greenstreet—came aboard to help. And toward the end of 1945, Lorre was one of several judges in the "I Can't Stand Jack Benny Because" contest, which featured $10,000 in Victory Bonds as prizes. Other officiates included Goodman Ace and Fred Allen. Winners were announced on Benny's show after the awards were determined. Lorre guested on Benny's program the following year (March 24, 1946) as well.

In the late 1940s, Lorre continued in a comedy vein on the *Abbott and Costello Show* in a skit called "At the Peter Lorre Sanitarium." The original date of broadcast is unknown at the present time, as the existing recording is from an Armed Forces Radio Services rebroadcast. The typical murder- and horror-related jokes arise. For example, Lorre claims: "I've had thousands of patients at my sanitarium and never had anyone complain. You know what that proves, don't you?" Costello's reply? "Yes, dead men tell no tales!" Later, Lorre himself told tales on the *Dean Martin and Jerry Lewis Show* (May 8, 1949).

1940 studio portrait

But Lorre's connection to serious horror plays on the radio represents his most memorable work in the medium, partially because he worked on the best horror programs in radio's history. For example, Lorre guested on *Inner Sanctum* numerous times in the early 1940s; his episodes were so popular that he once guested twice in a single month (December 13 and December 27, 1942).

Lorre also took the lead role in an early episode of *Suspense*, "Till Death Do Us Part" on December 15, 1942. The "Man in Black"—the host of the program—introduced him as "one of the screen's past masters of suspense" whose character had "something terrible on his mind. Was it perhaps... *murder?*" His popularity spawned further *Suspense* episodes with Lorre as the lead player, including "The Devil's Saint" on January 19, 1943, "Moment of Darkness" on April 20, 1943 and "Back For Christmas" on December 23, 1943.

Work on less renowned horror shows came as well. For example, Lorre appeared on *Creeps By Night* in 1944. The atmospheric show had begun as a showcase for Boris Karloff. But Karloff bowed out after only a handful of episodes, with his replacement being a host named "Dr. X." It was during the latter's tenure that Lorre performed on a single episode.

It was also Lorre's connection to the offbeat, myserious and unusual that caused commercial interest in the creation of his own program. One attempt—perhaps the first—at a Lorre radio show came in 1944 with *Journey into Fear*. Its writer/director was Norman Winters; the show was packaged by Dell Peters. It's unclear whether any episodes ever hit the airwaves at all. *Variety* mentioned the program as being available in June 1944; it seemingly wasn't heard from again.

Unlike *Journey into Fear*, the next idea for a Lorre show—this one entitled *Mystery Playhouse*—did become realized. *Mystery Playhouse* rebroadcast episodes of *Inner Sanctum*, *The Whistler* and others with new opening credits and introductions by

Lorre. These were aired in 1944 over the Armed Forces Radio Service, heard by troops overseas. Lorre introduced at least 55 shows in this anthology, including "Those Who Walk in Darkness" with Boris Karloff and "The Mote Farm Murder" with Charles Laughton. Most interesting perhaps is *Mystery Playhouse* #5, a rebroadcast of "Death is a Joker" starring Lorre from *Inner Sanctum*. Lorre introduced Lorre on the rebroadcast.

But far more interesting than rebroadcasts of old shows was 1947's *Mystery in the Air*, Lorre's greatest achievement on radio. It was *his* show, starring him in a series of literary adaptations. This was not a simple guest spot on a variety show, nor was it a hosting job with only moments of time to talk at the beginning and end of a program. Each week of *Mystery in the Air* was a showcase for Lorre, a tour-de-force for his dramatic talent.

Lorre at work on *Mystery in the Air*.

An earlier incarnation of *Mystery in the Air* had been heard on NBC during the summer of 1945. Stephen Courtleigh, Joan Vitez and Ed Jerome starred in the Camel Cigarettes–sponsored series that lasted from July 5-September 27 of that year. Apparently no shows from that run exist, but it seems that the leads played recurring characters—a distinctly different formula than the 1947 incarnation of the series would employ.

For the version starring Peter Lorre, Don Bernard produced, Cal Kul directed and Camel Cigarettes sponsored. Henry Morgan—who later changed his name to Harry Morgan and starred in TV programs like *M*A*S*H*—acted on the first episode, but generally hosted the show. Michael Ray announced the commercials, and Paul Baron conducted the music. *Mystery in the Air* was a 13-week summer replacement for Abbott and Costello's radio show, being heard at 10 p.m. Eastern on Thursday nights over NBC. It was broadcast live in front of a live audience.

The show began with an eerie theme played by strings and punctuated by the orchestra's horn section, and then a few brief lines of dialogue from the week's radio play as a hook. Next was Henry Morgan's introduction: "Each week at this hour, Peter Lorre brings us the excitement of the great stories of the strange and unusual...of dark and compelling masterpieces culled from the four corners of world literature." Sometimes Morgan prefaced mention of Lorre's name with the title "Mr.," which prompted *Variety* (July 9, 1947) to proclaim that Lorre was "distinguished in his way, but doesn't need to be Mistered by the producers."

Each episode also featured Camel commercials at the beginning and end, as well as a disconcerting commercial break in the middle. The "first act" would end with applause, with the program switching gears to a Camel promo and then on to the story's conclusion. "Experience is the best teacher. More people are smoking Camels than ever before," the sponsor proudly proclaimed. *Variety* noted the trio of commercials, claiming them to be "too much. Reynolds ought to be able to forego the middle one."

Also during *Mystery in the Air* episodes, commercials sugggested to listeners, "Let your *T-zone* decide. That's *T* for taste and *T* for throat, your proving ground for any cigarette." Even more interesting, some commercials mentioned the heartwarming information that "More doctors smoke Camels than any other cigarrette," as well as names of the individual veterans' hospitals to which free packs were sent. In retrospect, the tobacco commercials are probably more frightening than anything in the narratives themselves.

The premiere show of July 3, 1947 featured Lorre in Poe's "The Tell-Tale Heart." According to *Variety* (July 9, 1947), the "yarn was artfully adapted, with Lorre carrying almost the entire telling. Sound effects effectively heightened the tenseness, which, incidentally, Lorre eased as the stanza signed off with a comment on the classic chillers to come." Though the premiere episode does not exist, *Variety* claimed that Lorre ended by inviting listeners to hear the future "chillers," then jokingly asked "or would you rather have a hotfoot?"

While Lorre worked at his own microphone, the secondary players spoke into a separate mike. Usually by the end of the program, Lorre would be soaking in sweat, exhausted from the intensity he exerted during the broadcast. One of his co-stars even remembered Lorre once accidentally throwing the pages of his script into the air as a result of his intense hand movements and gestures. Rapid response on the soundstage placed the script back into his hands, but only after he ad-libbed his way through a portion of the show.

Though 13 episodes were broadcast, only eight exist. Those surviving shows are chronicled in the following sections:

"The Marvellous Barastro" (August 7, 1947). Co-stars included Jane Morgan. Lorre essays the title role, a hypnotist and magician named Barastro. The radio play was adapted from a story by Ben Hecht.

While performing in Russia, Barastro meets a young blind woman named Anna. He foresees that he will bring trouble to her life, but marries her anyway. During their travels, a fellow magician named Ricoh begins to spend a great deal of time with the married couple. Though he frightens Anna, his flattery of Barastro helps keep him near their house.

But one day Barastro returns home to find Ricoh and Anna alone. Ricoh has fooled Barastro's wife into believing that he is himself Barastro. His voice mimics Barastro's with precision. After a fight, Ricoh escapes and Anna is left confused and scared. Later, Ricoh again visits Anna. When Barastro interrupts them again, the shock proves too much for Anna, who dies soon thereafter.

Barastro eventually catches up to Ricoh, planning to kill him. Before moving ahead with his plan, however, Barastro informs an attorney that he will murder his foe. The widower confronts his enemy on a train, and only one man survives. The attorney visits the survivor in a hospital. Allegedly he is Barastro, but bandages hide his face. The voice sounds like Barastro's, but is it? Which of the two men is behind the gauze remains unknown to the attorney or the audience.

Though an unexplained pause briefly interrupts the show just before the end of Act One, "The Marvellous Barastro" overall is a wonderful adaptation which includes a fascinating inclusion of the audience into the story. By the end of the story, the point-of-view is that of the attorney. Rather than speaking to another character or recording notes in his journal, he speaks directly to the "ladies and gentlemen" of the listening audience at home.

"The Lodger" (August 14, 1947). Co-stars included Agnes Moorehead as Mrs. Bunting. Lorre takes the title role, a lodger named Mr. Sleuth. The story was adapted from Marie Belloc Lowndes' novel.

"Everything wicked and sinful should be purged from the earth," Sleuth, a religious fanatic, tells the Bunting family with whom he lodges. Using the basic plot of the famed novel, this adaptation features an effective Agnes Moorehead performance. It is her character who realizes that Sleuth is the "Avenger," a Jack the Ripper–style murderer whose exploits had been haunting the streets of London and filling the newspapers.

Sleuth apparently believes he will take seven lives for the Lord, and after the sixth he begins to concentrate on the Buntings' daughter. "Rejoice with me in your heart, for the moment is at hand," he instructs her as he prepares her for the stabbing. But the Buntings interrupt the murder, with the daughter rescued and the knife penetrating Sleuth's body instead. "The Vengeance is fulfilled," he claims, happy to be the seventh life taken for God's greater glory.

The novel had twice been adapted to the screen prior to this radio show, and audiences familiar with the tale would have found this version to be lacking in the mood possessed by the films and the book. Lorre's portrayal is quite subtle and very eerie, certainly one of his best on radio. But overall the show is mired by its brevity, which doesn't allow time for much suspense to be built.

"The Horla" (August 21, 1947). Co-stars included Ben Wright and Lureen Tuttle, an able actress who also worked at times with Bela Lugosi and Boris Karloff on the radio. This week *Mystery in the Air* featured an adaptation of Guy de Maupassant's famous ghost story. The commercial on this episode features a Camel endorsement by champion polo player Cecil Smith, though it seems unlikely a large number of listeners would have been that acquainted with him.

The story features Lorre as a man living in England in 1889 who begins to have problems sleeping, becoming encumbered with "feelings of oppression." After a bad dream, he realizes the water carafe on a table by his bed is empty—and yet he has had nothing to drink.

Believing an invisible being is living in his home, he flees to Paris. But the change of scenery doesn't help. The more time that passes, the more he realizes the invisible being—the "Horla"—is taking over his own soul. He even tries to lock the Horla in his home, burning it to the ground.

Lorre's unmistakable voice was perfect for radio.

As with most episodes, the story ends unhappily for Lorre's character, who decides to destroy himself in order to destroy the Horla. After working up to a high level of intensity, Lorre ended the show with a very campy conclusion, shouting: "Let me go, yes I know I'm Peter Lorre, I know it's a story, I know it's by de Maupassant yes, I know it's Thursday and we are on the air, but it's the Horla!"

The show is certainly among the most interesting survivors of the run, with Lorre's performance—despite his rather kitschy ending—a very subtle one. The adaptation is a rather eerie one, featuring even some religious implications. "The rule of man is over, and He has come," Lorre's character says, speaking not of God but of the Horla.

"Beyond Good and Evil" (August 28, 1947). Lorre's co-stars included Russell Thorson. "I can kill," Lorre's character Phillip Gentry tells listeners at the beginning of this adaptation of Ben Hecht's story. "I have the mind and the will and the hands."

After escaping from prison, Gentry comes into contact with Reverend Pierce, who is on his way to assume a new position at a church. After murdering the good reverend, Gentry assumes his identity. The only person to realize Gentry is a *fakir* is the retiring reverend at the church; unfortunately, he can't unmask Gentry due to a stroke which has left him without the ability to speak or write. If anything, Gentry delights in taunting the reverend, believing himself safe in his identity.

In the meantime, a bank teller confides in Gentry about some of his personal worries; one burden includes information about a day that his bank has $200,000 in cash and only one worker, the teller. Gentry tells a criminal colleague, who is to shoot the teller and take the cash. But shortly before the robbery, Gentry apparently undergoes a religious conversion, taking the teller's place and the bullet meant for him.

Interesting in this episode is the opportunity to hear Lorre speak part of a religious sermon, which he does with a great deal of sincerity.

"The Mask of Medusa" (September 4, 1947). Russell Thorson co-stars with Lorre in this adaptation of Nelson Vaughn's short story. "No one suspects we are still alive!" Lorre's character Arisztid exclaims to listeners.

The story chronicles a wax museum in which all statues are of known criminals. Their incredibly lifelike appearances are due to the fact that all are alive and all are actually the criminals they purport to be. Rather than being dipped in wax à la *Mystery of the Wax Museum* (1932), the criminals have seen the head of Medusa, which freezes them permanently. But the "statues" learn to communicate by ESP, and eventually develop movement. "We are moving," Arisztid thinks to himself with excitement and intensity. "The Walking Dead!" Given that the audience has heard more of the criminals' torturous state as wax figures than of their own crimes, much sympathy is evoked for their plight.

Radio provides the perfect medium for this tale, which is so reliant on Lorre's character thinking both to himself and others. Volume itself proves an interesting tool to aurally indicate the nature of ESP-transmitted thought; at first Arisztid hears his colleagues only faintly, but over time and with greater concentration he hears the fellow wax statues with more clarity. The episode ends with a plea for listeners to buy U.S. Savings Bonds, as well as a commercial for the *Grand Ole Opry*.

"The Queen of Spades" (September 11, 1947). Co-stars in this adaptation of the Alexander Pushkin story included Luis Van Rooten and Ben Wright. Peter Lorre stars as Herrmann, a character who has a keen interest in gambling though he doesn't gamble himself. "He has the profile of Napoleon and the soul of Mephistopheles," one character says of Herrmann.

One of Herrmann's friends mentions a relative, a Countess who discovered a winning combination of cards that cannot lose. However, the "Muscovite Venus," as she is called, will not tell anyone the secret. Herrmann attempts to become close to one of her servants, eventually sneaking into the Countess' room in an effort to learn the card secret. When she refuses to tell him, Herrmann kills her. But she later appears to him

Peter Lorre during a NBC radio program. (Photofest)

as a spirit, revealing the winning cards—3, 7, and Ace. But they bring only bad luck for Herrmann.

The episode does not feature one of Lorre's better performances. For example, a scene in which he attends the Countess' funeral and then faints aurally illustrates the manner in which Lorre's intensity could easily drift into overstatement.

"The Black Cat" (September 18, 1947). For this episode, Lorre's co-stars were Luis Van Rooten and Joseph Kearns. NBC News interrupted the show's opening due to a hurricane off the Gulf of Mexico, which was expected to strike Louisiana.

Poe's short story inspired an intriguing interpretation with Lorre explaining in a Freudian reference that "there was nothing in my childhood to forecast" what he would do later in life. A framing device begins the story, with Lorre telling listeners that "I have to tell you the facts, because tomorrow I die."

In his and his wife's home existed "quite a collection of birds, goldfish, rabbits, dogs, and a cat." The cat's name was Pluto, whom he loved once; after battles with "intemperance," however, Lorre's character grows to hate the "hideous beast." Their house burns soon, with the black cat dead.

Soon a new cat, one as "black as Pluto," appears and is the new addition to their pet collection. After Lorre's character in a rage walls his wife up alive in the basement, visiting police hear the cat's cry. They charge him with murder. "May heaven deliver me from the archfiend," he pleas, adding another dimension to the cat's name, Pluto.

Lorre later played much the same part for "The Black Cat" episode in the film *Tales of Terror* (1962). Given that he played the film version more for comedy, this radio adaptation acts as an interesting dramatic counterpoint.

"Crime and Punishment" (September 25, 1947). Co-stars included Luis Van Rooten and Joseph Kearns in this very abridged version of Fyodor Dostoyevsky's novel. Just as Lorre had played character Raskolnikov in the 1935 Columbia Studios film, he essays the same role for *Mystery in the Air*.

The same problems faced by the earlier film starring Lorre are even more overwhelming in this radio adaptation. Raskolnikov's academic rise and financial fall, his theft and subsequent descent into guilt—these aspects of the narrative occur so rapidly in this radio adaptation that almost no semblance of the novel's mood is preserved. Though Lorre's portrayal is itself credible, it offers no distinctive growth or departure from his work in the 1935 film *Crime and Punishment*. As a result of these problems, this is probably the weakest episode of the surviving shows.

"Crime and Punishment" ends with a mention that it was the last in the *Mystery in the Air* series, which would be replaced the following week with the *Bob Hawks' Quiz Show*. "They tell me Mr. Hawks doesn't murder anyone; he just quizzes them," Lorre said. "Well, to each his own."

Several years after *Mystery in the Air*, Lorre hosted yet another radio show, one called *Nightmare*. The opening dialogue on each program proclaimed: "Out of the dark of night, from the shadows of the senses, comes this—the fantasy of fear." Beginning in October 1953, *Nightmare* was 30 minutes in length, transcribed in Hollywood and aired over the Mutual Broadcasting System. Lorre made an effective and—according to the show itself— an "exciting guide to terror"; he also starred in the dramatizations. His functions on *Mystery Playhouse* and *Mystery in the Air* had merged.

From the start, the *Nightmare* was doomed because of Mutual's overall failed network option plan. Initial reviews of the program were strong, with *The Billboard* (Nov. 21, 1953) calling one of Lorre's performances on it a "tour-de-force." Though the trade publication said its "eerie sort of stream-of-consciousness" merited "continuation," but it was not to be. Radio listeners woke up to no more Lorre after only 12 *Nightmares*.

But nightmares can still be had from Peter Lorre. Fortunately for more modern ears, a large number of Lorre's radio shows still exist, some sold by underground radio show dealers and others offered by more legitimate companies on record and cassette. A number of Lorre radio shows are now even available on compact disc. And, at least according to some theories about the nature of radio waves, somewhere, somehow—perhaps even in the dark, vast reaches of the galaxy—Lorre's mystery is still "in the air."

AN ANIMATED PETER LORRE
by John Stell

Before they created characters (Bugs Bunny, Daffy Duck, etc.) that would become famous in their own right, the animators of Warner Bros. had much fun with the stars of Hollywood's golden age. If you look at a short from the 1930s or early 1940s, chances are you'll see likenesses of Cary Grant, Katherine Hepburn, Clark Cable, the Marx Brothers, or Mae West. Edward G. Robinson was especially a favorite. When Peter Lorre's likeness finally appeared, it was a sure sign that Lorre had made it, because seldom did the animators attach a name tag to the person you were seeing. In other words, they counted on audiences recognizing the people because they were stars. And Lorre was a star.

Surprisingly, the classic horror stars (Karloff, Lugosi) made but a few appearances in Warner Bros.' early 'toons. In *Porky's Road Race* (1937), the popular pig races against Borax Karloff, a combination Karloff/Frankenstein's monster. 1938's *Have You Got Any Castles?* features likenesses of the Monster, Mr. Hyde, Fu Manchu, and the Phantom of the Opera doing "sissy" dances in one of several cartoons that featured classic literary characters come to life. Despite the musicals, however, these same animators had proved adept at making atmospheric "thrillers," such as in *The Case of the Stuttering Pig*, a 1937 short, "shot" in black and white, that parodies *The Cat and the Canary* (1927) by having the inheritors threatened by a shadowy figure. In truth, the studio's animation department produced mostly musical 'toons and the occasional mystery parody during the 1930s.

Thus Warner Bros.' first full-length ode to Lorre came with an homage to the detective character Lorre portrayed in eight features for Twentieth Century-Fox from 1937–1939; namely, Mr. Moto. In 1939's *Porky's Movie Mystery* ("Any resemblance this picture has to the original story from which it was stolen is purely accidental.") the sleuthing swine plays Mr. Motto, complete with oversized glasses, accent, and comb-over. Mr. Motto is called in from vacation to solve the mystery of the accidents plaguing a movie studio. The police interrogate Frankenstein's monster ("Start talking, small fry!"), who bites his own fingernails off typewriter style, while Walter Windshield announces the Phantom is still on the prowl. At first it appears the villain is the Invisible Man ("They star me in one picture, then drop me!"). But after Mr. Motto applies some anti-invisibility solution, the true culprit is revealed to be… Hugh Herbert ("Hoo-hoo-hoo!") Aside from the obvious character reference, however, *Porky's Movie Mystery* dispenses with any other Lorre references.

Hollywood Steps Out

It was, instead, 1941's *Hollywood Steps Out* where Lorre, the same year he appeared in Warner's *The Maltese Falcon*, gets the full caricature treatment. Featuring a gala of famous pusses (Cary

Grant, Jimmy Stewart, Judy Garland, Clark Gable, Harpo Marx, Oliver Hardy, to name but a few) Lorre can be seen eyeing the naked dancing girl whose only cover would appear to be the giant bubble she uses. "I haven't seen such a beautiful bubble since I was child," Lorre says from his table. The image is perfect: short stature, wide eyes, and a slightly nasal voice. It is also worth noting that Lorre's co-star from *You'll Find Out* (1940), Kay Kyser, instructs his "students" to ogle the dancing beauty ("Baby!"). Frankenstein's monster does a little dance, while the Invisible Man uses binoculars to observe the action. The short features so many images (one of whom seems to be Boris Karloff) that Lorre is gone before you know it.

A familiar-looking mad doctor in *Hair-Raising Hare.*

But in 1946, Lorre found his way into two classic Warners 'toons, each of which pitted him against the studio's most popular non-human creation: Bugs Bunny. One of the all-time great (animated) parodies of horror movies, *Hair-Raising Hare* finds Bugs being watched by an evil scientist, a sinister likeness of Lorre. (We know he's an evil scientist because of the flashing neon sign posted on his castle.) "Patience, little one," the doc tells his anxious monster. "Your dinner will soon be here: a nice, tender little rabbit." Lorre lures the rabbit to his castle via a mechanical beauty, and, as Bugs arrives, Lorre locks the door ("You don't need to lock that door, Mac. I don't wanna leave!") But Bugs' kiss destroys the robotic rabbit ("That's the trouble with some dames: Kiss 'em and they fly apart."). "I have another little friend who'd like to eat, uh, meet you," the doc tells him. But the roar behind the bolted door sends Bugs running. ("Well…Good-bye! And don't think it hasn't been a little slice of heaven, 'cause it hasn't.") The orange, furry monster chases Bugs around the castle, ultimately being scared by the fact that the audience is watching *him*. Bugs is about to leave when another mechanical female shows up. ("So? She's mechanical!")

While Lorre wasn't playing mad scientists anymore by 1946, his image here is perfect. Clad in the quintessential white lab coat, and featuring his sleepy-eyed look and sinister voice, the Lorre character blends right in with his horrific surroundings: mad scientist lab, castle complete with dark passages, hidden peepholes, and, of course, a ferocious beast. Lorre grins throughout his entire appearance, which is about half of the

Bugs is taken for a ride by Hugo in *Racketeer Rabbit.*

seven-minute running time. For the most part, Bugs is genuinely frightened, finally gaining his confidence by simply chatting with the monster ("I'll bet you monsters lead *interesting* lives."). Bugs even refers to the orange ogre, at various points, as Frankenstein and Dracula. Ironically, classic horror was on its last legs in 1946, despite Lorre's appearance in Warners' *The Beast With Five Fingers* that year. But *Hair-Raising Hare* presents a perfect homage to Lorre and the genre overall, considering that, like the Frankenstein creation, even monsters get scared and cry.

Bugs and Lorre, however, would meet again that very same year. In *Racketeer Rabbit*, the homeless hare escapes the rain by hiding out in a deserted home. (The ominous music and creaking front door cause Bugs to comment, "Sounds like *Inner Sanctum*.") But Rocky (an Edward G. Robinson look-alike) and Hugo (a Peter Lorre clone) arrive on the scene, shooting it out with the police. Hugo is so slight in stature, however, that he must brace himself with a piece of timber nailed to the floor lest his machine gun cause him to "dance" around the house. "Well, we got rid 'a those mugs!" Rocky states proudly. "They make me laugh. Uh-hah," Hugo responds, revealing only two vampire-like teeth. As Rocky starts splitting the take ("Two for you, one, two for me...") Bugs gets in on the act, while Hugo watches in dismay. Rocky catches on ("Rocky's too smart for ya, see!") and Hugo takes Bugs for "a ride." We never see Hugo again, nor do we find out what Bugs did to him! Bugs returns and tricks Rocky into thinking he's tough guy Mugsy. "It's curtains for you, Rocky. Curtains!" Mugsy says, just before giving Rocky some curtains. ("Oh, they're adorable!" Rocky responds.) Later Bugs fools Rocky into believing that the police have arrived. But Bugs' attempts to "hide" Rocky almost cause the gangster's death. Rocky flees the scene, preferring prison to that "screwy rabbit."

Hair-Raising Hare took advantage of Lorre's horror image.

Whereas *Hair-Raising Hare* took advantage of Lorre's horror image, *Racketeer Rabbit* "casts" Lorre in a sinister henchman role à la *The Maltese Falcon*, or *Arsenic and Old Lace*. Again, he is only in half the picture as Bugs gets rid of him early on. But the laughs are generated by having fun with Lorre's persona: his simple, quick laugh when the cops are smoked, and the fact that he's so short he can't control his own machine gun. Again, Lorre is so unique that the audience instantly recognizes his likeness, which is always the intent of the animators in such parodies.

By the 1950s, however, such targets as old-fashioned horror films and gangster pictures had worn out their box-office welcome. Furthermore, the Warner Bros. creations were such stars themselves that the characters were being paired with each other, e.g., Bugs and Daffy, or Tweety and Sylvester. Still, the occasional Lorre animated caricature can be spotted. For instance, in a first season episode of *Scooby-Doo, Where Are You?* entitled, "That's Snow Ghost," two jewel thieves named Mr. Greenway and Mr. Leech are fashioned after Sydney Greenstreet and Lorre, their partnership recalling *The Maltese Falcon*. And while, as opposed to the Warners cartoons, *Scooby-Doo* was a cartoon designed specifically for children, adults could still get a kick out of the passing reference.

An animated Lorre and Greenstreet meet Scooby-Doo in "That's Snow Ghost."

Despite his varied roles, Peter Lorre is mostly thought of as a villain. But he was a villain with his own unique image, an image that animators have always had fun with thanks to that very same uniqueness. Clearly this is some of the best evidence of the extent to which Lorre had endeared himself to the movie-going public. To see him was to know him. Not only was Lorre a great actor, he was also a star.

TELEVISION CREDITS

77 Sunset Strip "5," ABC, 1963
Alfred Hitchcock Presents "The Diplomatic Corpse," CBS
Alfred Hitchcock Presents "The Man from the South," CBS, 1960
All Star Review, NBC, 1951
Best of Broadway "Arsenic and Old Lace," CBS, 1955
Best of the Post "The Baron Loved his Wife," SYN, 1960
Checkmate "The Human Touch" CBS, 1961
Climax! "A Promise to Murder," 1955
Climax! "A Taste for Crime," CBS, 1957
Climax! "Casino Royale," CBS, 1954
Climax! "The Fifth Wheel," CBS, 1956
Climax! "The Man Who Lost His Head," CBS, 1956
Encore Theatre "Queen's Bracelet," NBC, 1956
Five Fingers "Thin Ice," NBC, 1959
Kraft Suspense Theatre "The End of the World, Baby," NBC, 1963
Lux Video Theatre "Taste," CBS, 1952
Mrs. G Goes to College "First Test," CBS, 1961
Mrs. G Goes to College "The Trouble with Crayton," CBS, 1961
Playhouse 90 "Sizeman and Son," CBS, 1956
Playhouse 90 "The Last Tycoon," CBS, 1957
Producers Showcase "Reunion in Vienna," NBC, 1955
Rawhide "Incident of the Slavemaster," CBS, 1960
Route 66 "Lizard's Leg and Owlet's Wing," CBS, 1962
Schlitz Playhouse of Stars "The Pipe," CBS, 1954
Studio 57 "The Finishers," 1955
Studio 57 "Young Couples Only," 1955
Suspense "The Tortured Hand," CBS, 1952
Texaco Star Theatre, NBC, 1949
The 20th Century-Fox Hour "Operation Cicero," CBS, 1956
The Arrow Show, NBC, 1949
The du Pont Show "Diamond Fever," NBC, 1963
The Jack Benny Program, CBS, 1963
The Red Skelton Show "Appleby the Weatherman," CBS, 1959
The Red Skelton Show "The Honeymooners," CBS, 1955
The Red Skelton Show, CBS 1957
The Red Skelton Show, CBS 1960
The Star and the Story "The Blue Landscape," 1955
The Tennessee Ernie Ford Show, ABC, 1963
The Tonight Show Starring Johnny Carson, NBC, 1963
The Tonight Show, NBC, 1962
U.S. Steel Hour "The Vanishing Point," ABC, 1953
Wagon Train "The Alexander Portlass Story," NBC, 1960
You Bet Your Life, NBC

FILMOGRAPHY

20,000 Leagues Under the Sea, 1954
A Shot at Dawn, 1934
All Through the Night, 1942
Around the World in 80 Days, 1956
Arsenic and Old Lace, 1944
Background to Danger, 1943
Beat the Devil, 1953
Black Angel, 1946
Casablanca, 1942
Casbah, 1948
Confidential Agent, 1945
Congo Crossing, 1956
Crime and Punishment, 1935
Double Confession, 1950
F.P. 1 Doesn't Answer 1933
Five Weeks in a Balloon, 1962
From Top to Bottom, 1933
Hell Ship Mutiny, 1957
Hollywood Canteen, 1944
Hotel Berlin, 1945
I Was an Adventuress, 1940
I'll Give a Million, 1938
In This Our Life, 1942
Invisible Agent, 1942
Invisible Opponent, 1933
Island of Doomed Men, 1940
Lancer Spy, 1937
M, 1931
Mad Love, 1935
Mr. District Attorney, 1941
Mr. Moto on Danger Island, 1939
Mr. Moto Takes a Chance, 1938
Mr. Moto Takes a Vacation, 1939
Mr. Moto's Gamble, 1938
Mr. Moto's Last Warning, 1939
Muscle Beach Party, 1964
My Favorite Brunette, 1947
Mysterious Mr. Moto, 1938
Nancy Steele is Missing, 1937
Passage to Marseille, 1944
Quicksand, 1950
Rope of Sand, 1949
Scent of Mystery, 1960
Secret Agent, 1936
Silk Stockings, 1957
Strange Cargo, 1940
Stranger on the Third Floor, 1940
Tales of Terror, 1962
Thank You, Mr. Moto, 1937
The Beast with Five Fingers, 1946
The Big Circus, 1959
The Bombardment of Monte Carlo, 1931
The Boogie Man Will Get You, 1942
The Buster Keaton Story, 1957
The Chase, 1946
The Comedy of Terrors, 1964
The Conspirators, 1944
The Constant Nymph, 1943
The Crack-Up, 1937
The Cross of Lorraine, 1943
The Face Behind the Mask, 1941
The Jazzband Five, 1932
The Lost One, 1951
The Maltese Falcon, 1941
The Man Who Knew Too Much, 1935
The Mask of Dimitrios, 1944
The Patsy, 1964
The Raven, 1963
The Sad Sack, 1957
The Story of Mankind, 1957
The Trunks of Mr. O.F., 1932
The Verdict, 1946
The White Demon, 1932
They Met in Bombay, 1941
Think Fast, Mr. Moto, 1937
Three Strangers, 1946
Voyage to the Bottom of the Sea, 1954
What Women Dream, 1933
You'll Find Out, 1940

Peter Lorre probably guest-starred on numerous television programs during the 1950s and early 1960s that are not documented. The Filmography does not include foreign titles.

INDEX

AUTHORS

Anthony Ambrogio has written horror fiction novels including *Nuns Blood* and has contributed to *Midnight Marquee* magazine and edited Midnight Marquee Actors Series: Peter Cushing.

Mark Clark has contributed to *Midnight Marquee Actors Series Vincent Price* and has authored *Smirk, Sneer and Scream: Great Acting in Horror Cinema.*

Cindy Ruth Collins has contributed to *Midnight Marquee* magazine and books. She is married to fellow writer Brian Smith and lives in Falls Church, VA with her wonderful husband and their two adorable cats.

Bruce Dettman is a San Francisco-based writer whose film-related articles have appeared in *Filmfax, The Monster Times* and *Fangoria.* He is co-author of *The Horror Factory* and contributed to *Midnight Marquee Actors Series Vincent Price.*

Dennis Fischer is the author of *Horror Film Directors* (McFarland) and contributes to *Midnight Marquee, Filmfax* and *Cinefantastique.*

Joe Guilfoyle is a long-time classic cinema fan who has contributed to *Midnight Marquee* magazine. Unfortunately, Joe passed away in 2004.

David J. Hogan is the author of *Who's Who of the Horrors and Other Fantasy Films, Dark Romance: Sexuality in the Horror Film* and *Movie Guide to Drama Video Tapes and Discs.*

Steven Kronenberg has contributed to several Midnight Marquee volumes.

Jonathan Malcolm Lampley is a frequent contributor to *Midnight Marquee* as well as *Midnight Marquee Actors Series Vincent Price.*

Scott Allen Nollen is the author of *Robert Louis Stevenson: Life, Literature and the Silver Screen* and *Sir Arthur Conan Doyle at the Cinema* as well as *Boris Karloff: A Gentleman's Life* and *Boris Karloff: A Critical Account of His Screen, Stage, Radio, Television and Recording Work.*

Michael H. Price is co-author with George E. Turner of the Midnight Marquee *Forgotten Horror* series as well as Spawn of Skull Island.

Gary D. Rhodes is the author of *Bela Lugosi* (McFarland) and had contributed the *Classic Images, The Big Reel, Filmfax* and *Cult Movies.* He is also a documentary filmmaker who produced a film about Bela Lugosi.

Bryan Senn is the co-author of *Fantastic Cinema Subject Guide* and author of *Golden Horrors* and *Drums of Terror: Voodoo in the Cinema.*

David H. Smith has contributed to several Midnight Marquee Press books, including *Cinematic Hauntings*, *Son of Guilty Pleasures of the Horror Film* and *We Belong Dead: Frankenstein on Film*, as well as to the Actors Series editions on Bela Lugosi, Vincent Price, Boris Karloff and Lon Chaney, Jr. He is a frequent contributor to *Midnight Marquee* magazine, and has been featured in *Bare Bones*, *Fantastyka* and *Santo Street* magazines, as well as the book *Sci-Fi Invasions*. He would like to thank Bill Crider for his biographical and literary research assistance on *Strange Cargo* and Special thanks to Ensign Kimberly Watson of the Navy Office of Information for technical assistance on *Voyage to the Bottom of the Sea*.

Don G. Smith is the author of *Lon Chaney, Jr.* and *The Cinema of Edgar Allan Poe*. He has also contributed to the *Midnight Marquee Actors Series* on Bela Lugosi, Boris Karloff, Lon Chaney, Jr. and Vincent Price.

John Stell is the author of *Psychos, Sickos and Sequels: Horror Films of the 1980s*. He also contributed to the *Midnight Marquee Actors Series* on Bela Lugosi, Boris Karloff, Lon Chaney, Jr. and Vincent Price.

Gary J. Svehla has contributed to *Midnight Marquee Actors Series* on Bela Lugosi, Boris Karloff, Lon Chaney, Jr. and Vincent Price. Gary has edited his magazine Midnight Marquee since the age of 13. It is now in its 41st year of publication.He is also a high school teacher at North County High School located in Anne Arundel, Maryland.

Susan Svehla is the co-author, along with Gary Svehla, of *It's Christmas Time at the Movies* and contributed to Lon Chaney, Jr. and Vincent Price. She chaired FANEX for 18 years and is currently working on a graphic novel as well as a FANEX film project.

Jeff Thompson has contributed to several film magazines including *Midnight Marquee*.

Steven Thornton is a contributor to *Midnight Marquee* magazine as well as *Bitches, Bimbos and Virgins* and *MM Actors Series: Peter Cushing* from Midnight Marquee Press

Alan Warren has contributed to *Film Comment, The Armchair Detective* and *Isaac Asimov's Science Fiction Magazine* among others. He is author of *Roald Dahl* and *This is a Thriller*.

At Midnight Marquee We Know Movies!

Ingram Content Group UK Ltd.
Milton Keynes UK
UKHW021810100423
419936UK00010B/490